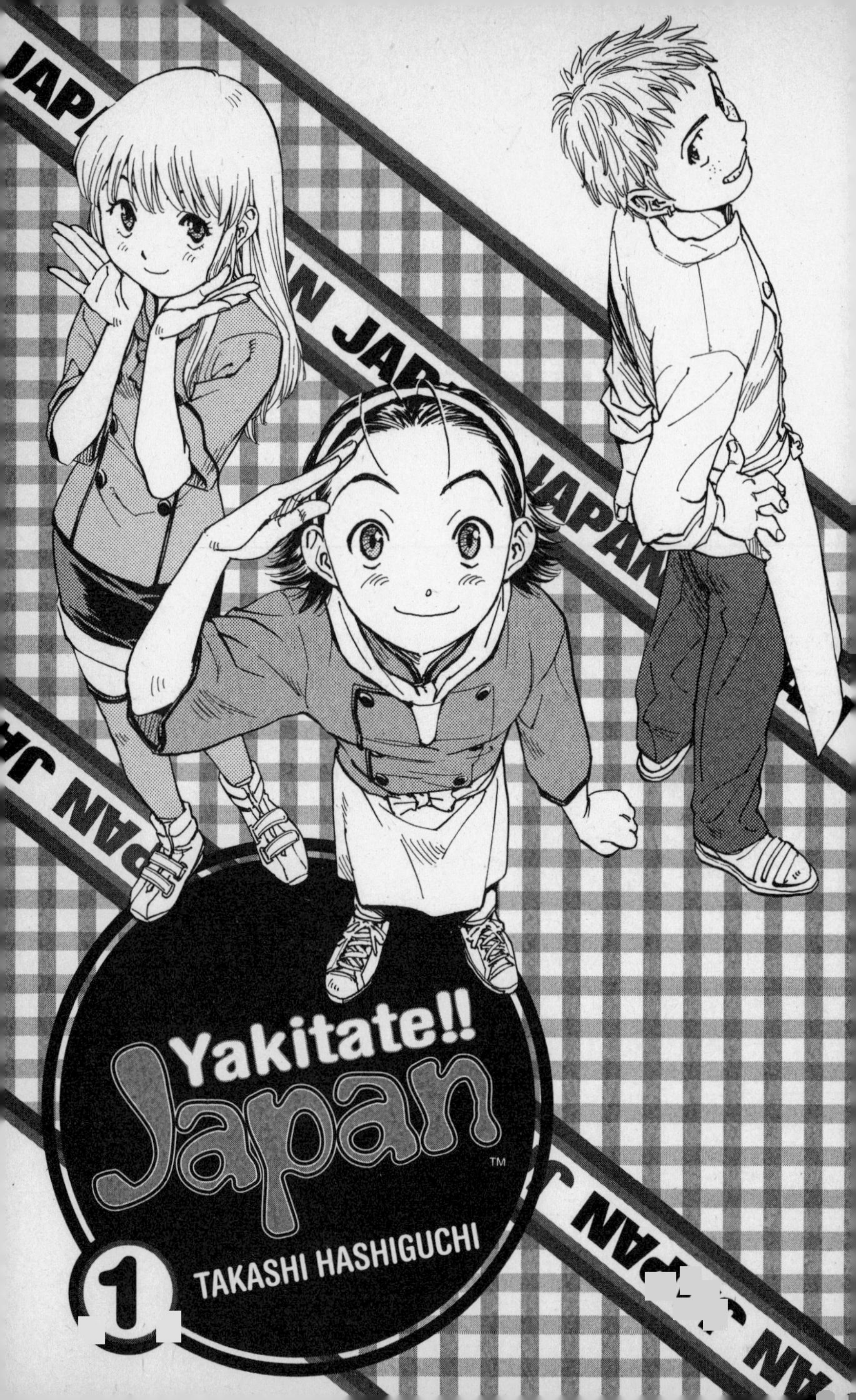
Yakitate!!
Japan™
1
TAKASHI HASHIGUCHI

YAKITATE!! JAPAN
1
VIZ Media Edition

CONTENTS

Research Assistance: Aruru Sugamo,
Andersen Aoyama, Shikishima-sei Pan (Pasco).

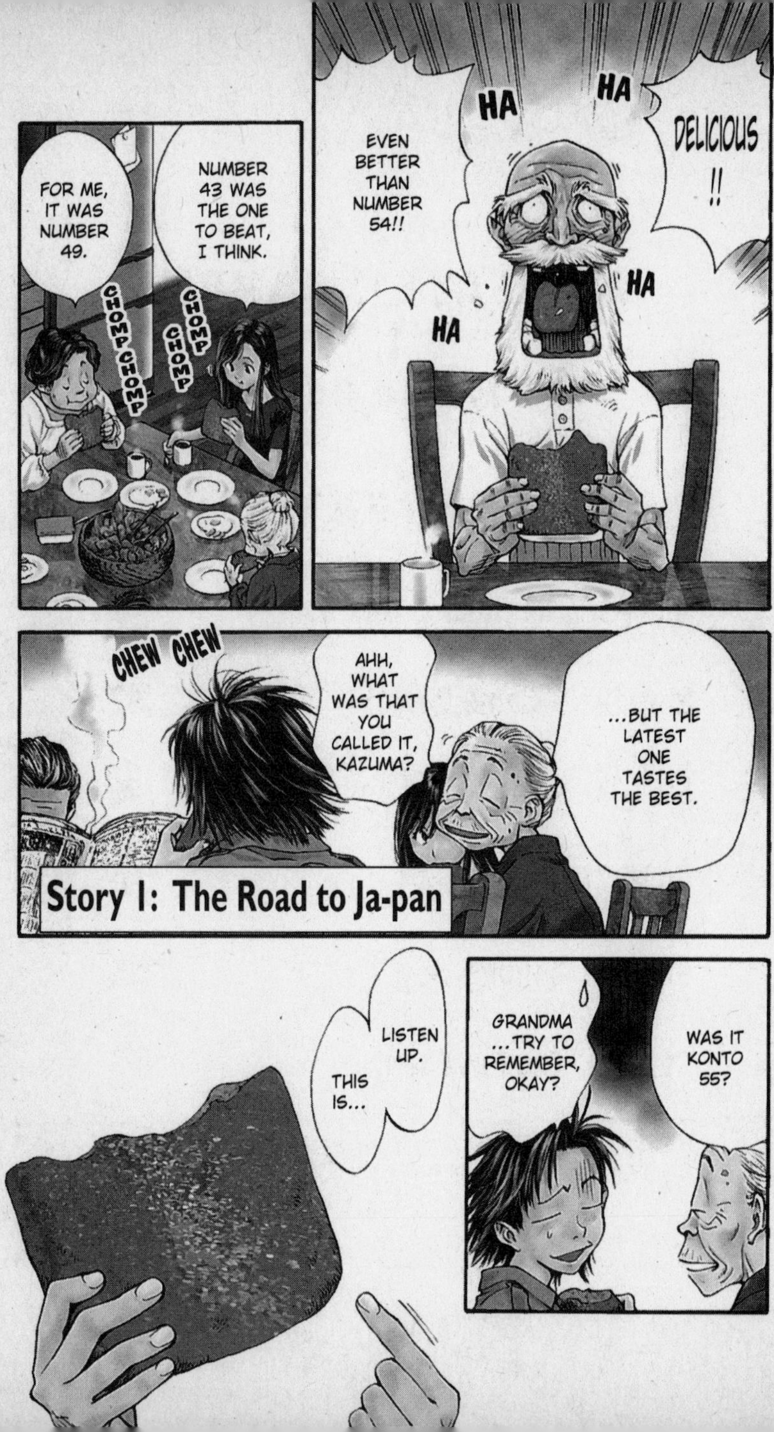
HA
DELICIOUS!!
HA
EVEN BETTER THAN NUMBER 54!!
HA
HA
NUMBER 43 WAS THE ONE TO BEAT, I THINK.
FOR ME, IT WAS NUMBER 49.
CHOMP CHOMP
CHOMP CHOMP
...BUT THE LATEST ONE TASTES THE BEST.
AHH, WHAT WAS THAT YOU CALLED IT, KAZUMA?
CHEW CHEW
Story 1: The Road to Ja-pan
WAS IT KONTO 55?
GRANDMA ...TRY TO REMEMBER, OKAY?
LISTEN UP.
THIS IS...

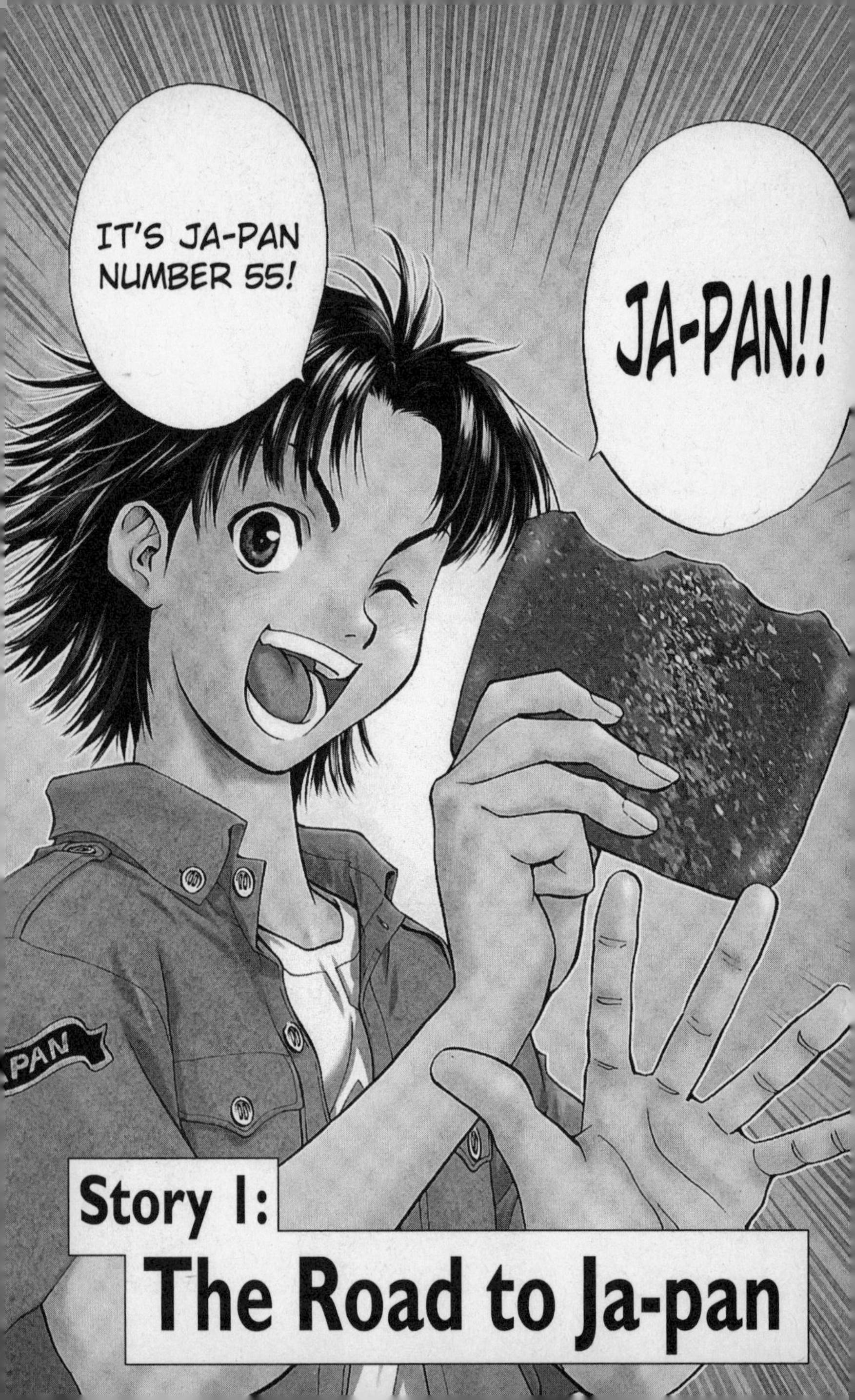
JA-PAN!!
IT'S JA-PAN NUMBER 55!
PAN

Story 1: The Road to Ja-pan

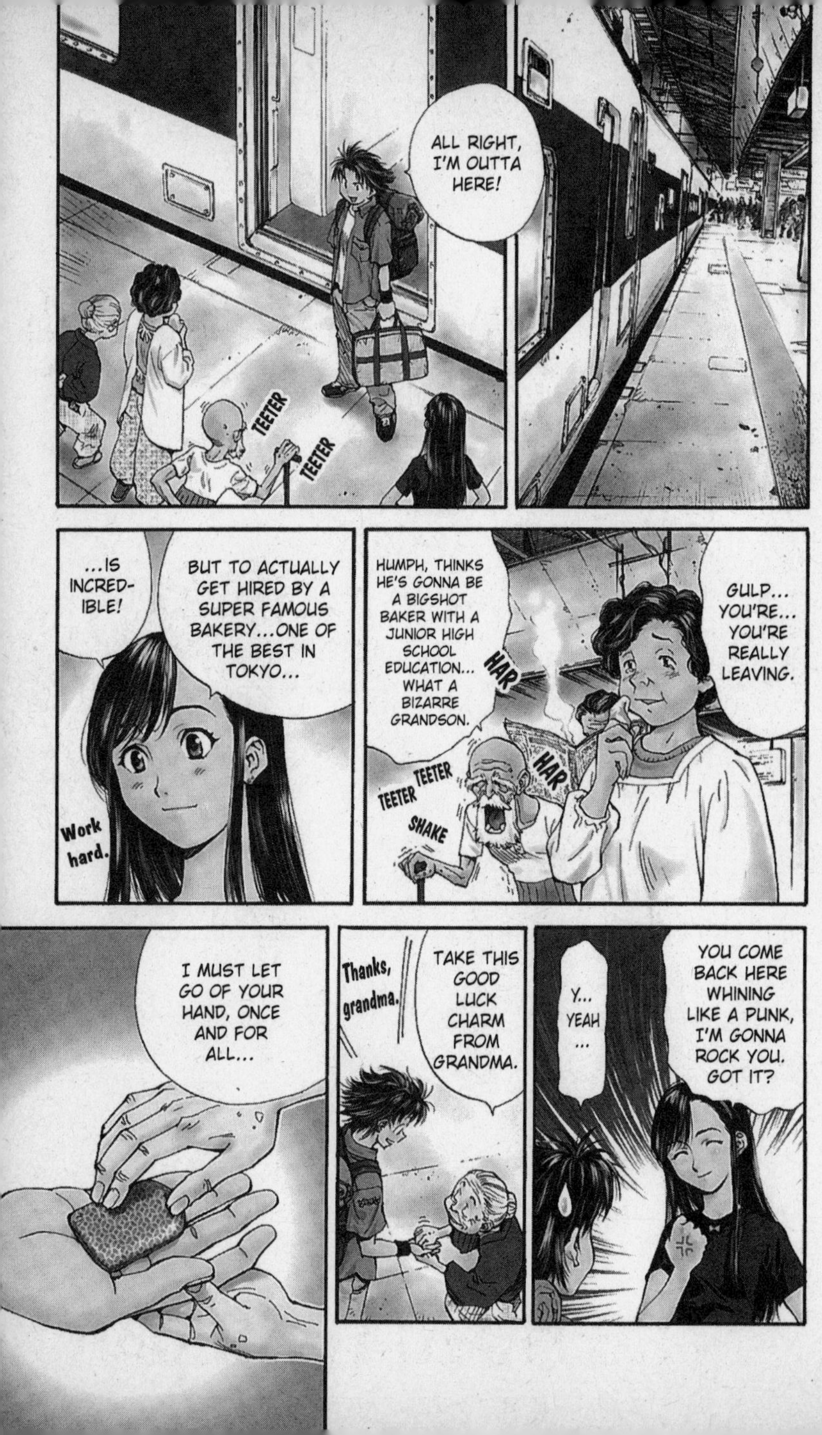
ALL RIGHT, I'M OUTTA HERE!
TEETER
TEETER
GULP... YOU'RE... YOU'RE REALLY LEAVING.
HUMPH, THINKS HE'S GONNA BE A BIGSHOT BAKER WITH A JUNIOR HIGH SCHOOL EDUCATION... WHAT A BIZARRE GRANDSON.
HAR
HAR
TEETER
TEETER
SHAKE
BUT TO ACTUALLY GET HIRED BY A SUPER FAMOUS BAKERY...ONE OF THE BEST IN TOKYO...
...IS INCREDIBLE!
Work hard.
YOU COME BACK HERE WHINING LIKE A PUNK, I'M GONNA ROCK YOU. GOT IT?
Y... YEAH...
TAKE THIS GOOD LUCK CHARM FROM GRANDMA.
Thanks, grandma.
I MUST LET GO OF YOUR HAND, ONCE AND FOR ALL...

Yakitate!! Japan

TAKASHI
HASHIGUCHI

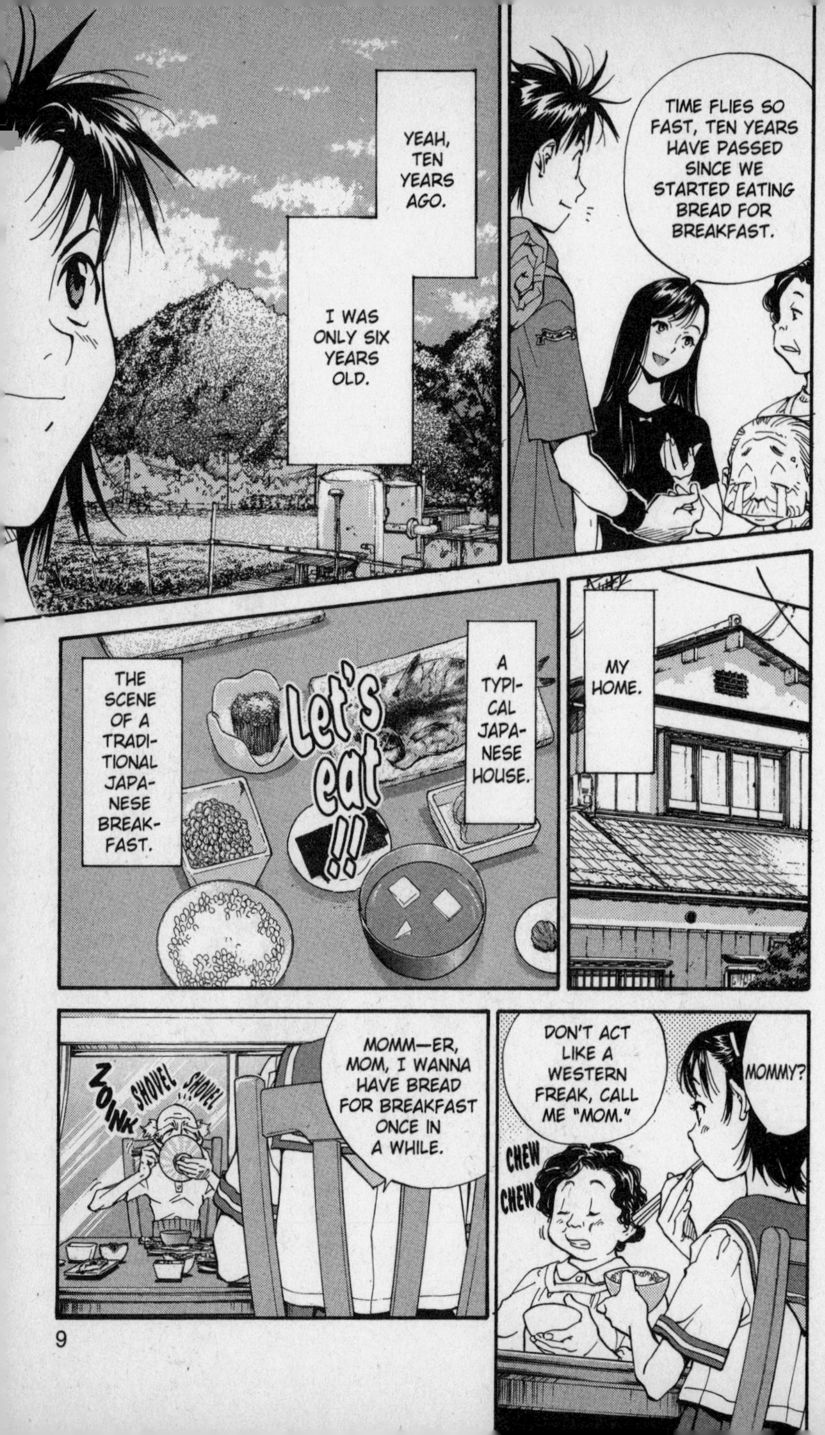
TIME FLIES SO FAST, TEN YEARS HAVE PASSED SINCE WE STARTED EATING BREAD FOR BREAKFAST.
YEAH, TEN YEARS AGO.
I WAS ONLY SIX YEARS OLD.
MY HOME.
A TYPICAL JAPANESE HOUSE.
THE SCENE OF A TRADITIONAL JAPANESE BREAKFAST.
Let's eat!!
MOMMY?
DON'T ACT LIKE A WESTERN FREAK, CALL ME "MOM."
CHEW CHEW
MOMM—ER, MOM, I WANNA HAVE BREAD FOR BREAKFAST ONCE IN A WHILE.
SHOVEL SHOVEL
ZOINK

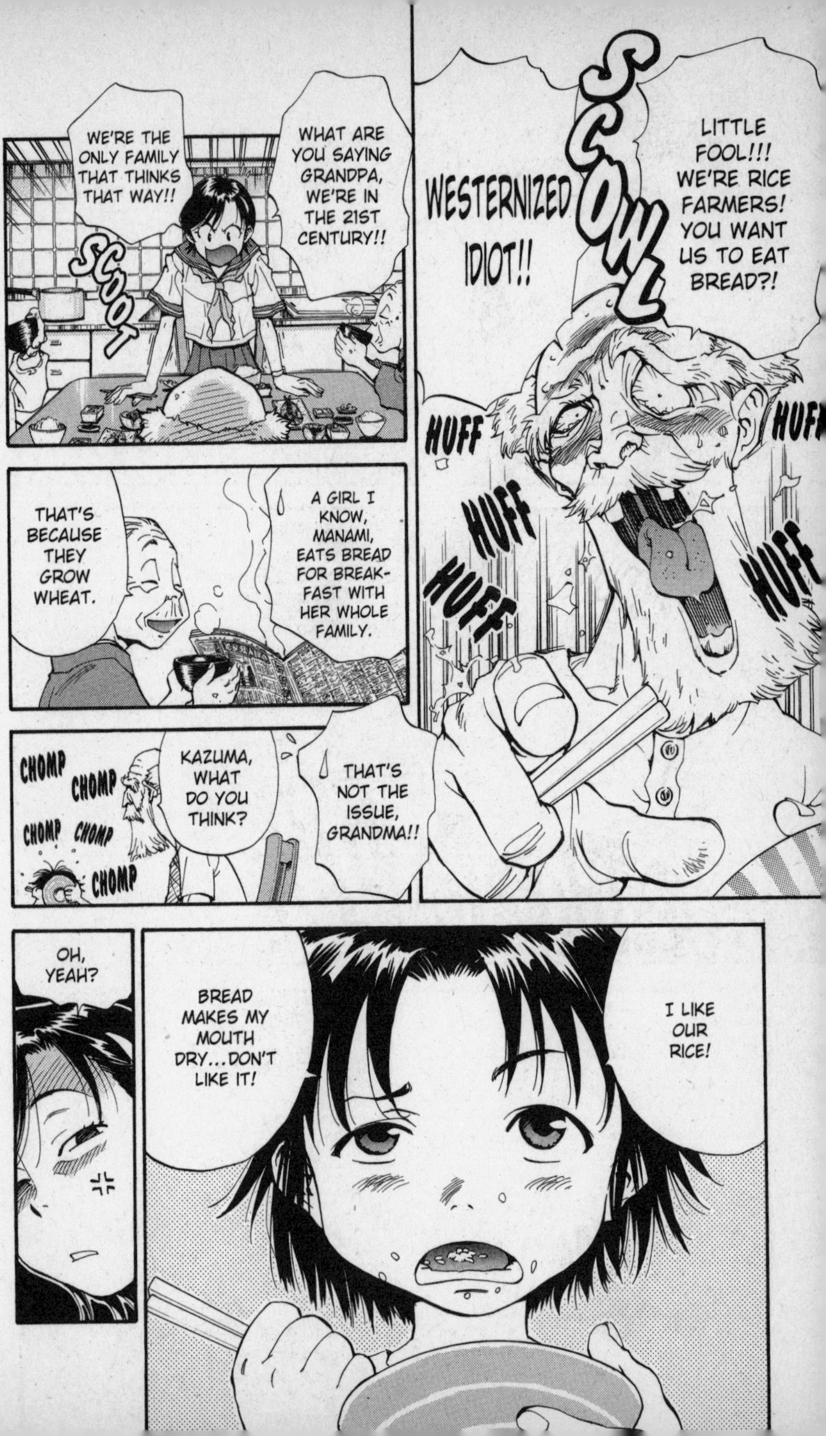
SCOWL
LITTLE FOOL!!! WE'RE RICE FARMERS! YOU WANT US TO EAT BREAD?!
WESTERNIZED IDIOT!!
HUFF
HUFF
HUFF
HUFF
HUFF
WHAT ARE YOU SAYING GRANDPA, WE'RE IN THE 21ST CENTURY!!
WE'RE THE ONLY FAMILY THAT THINKS THAT WAY!!
SCOOT
A GIRL I KNOW, MANAMI, EATS BREAD FOR BREAK-FAST WITH HER WHOLE FAMILY.
THAT'S BECAUSE THEY GROW WHEAT.
THAT'S NOT THE ISSUE, GRANDMA!!
KAZUMA, WHAT DO YOU THINK?
CHOMP
CHOMP
CHOMP
CHOMP
CHOMP
I LIKE OUR RICE!
BREAD MAKES MY MOUTH DRY...DON'T LIKE IT!
OH, YEAH?

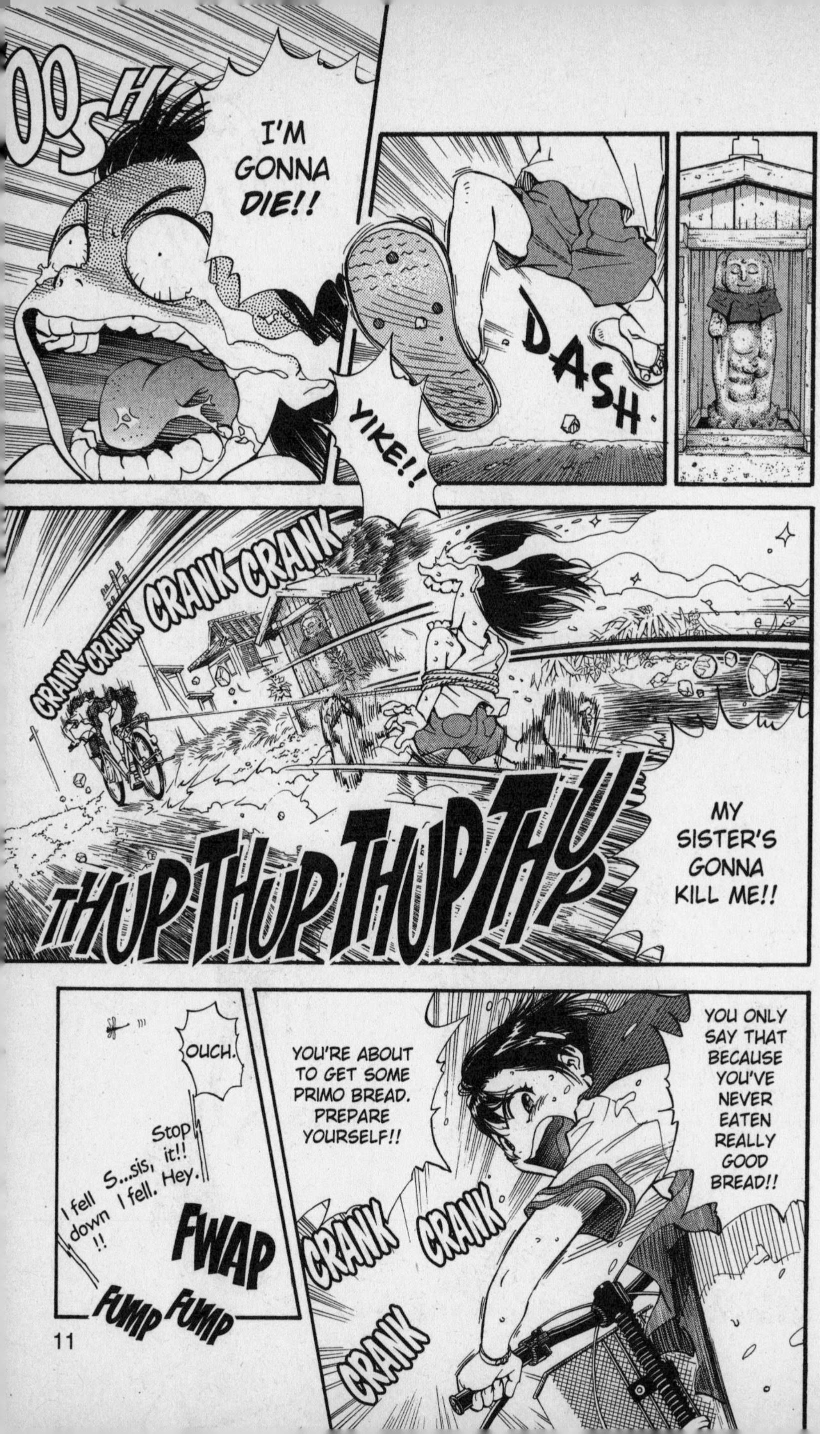
DASH
YIKE!!
OOSH
I'M GONNA DIE!!
MY SISTER'S GONNA KILL ME!!
THUP THUP THUP THUP
CRANK CRANK CRANK CRANK
YOU ONLY SAY THAT BECAUSE YOU'VE NEVER EATEN REALLY GOOD BREAD!!
YOU'RE ABOUT TO GET SOME PRIMO BREAD. PREPARE YOURSELF!!
CRANK CRANK
CRANK
OUCH.
Stop it!!
S...sis, I fell. Hey.
I fell down!!
FWAP
FUMP FUMP

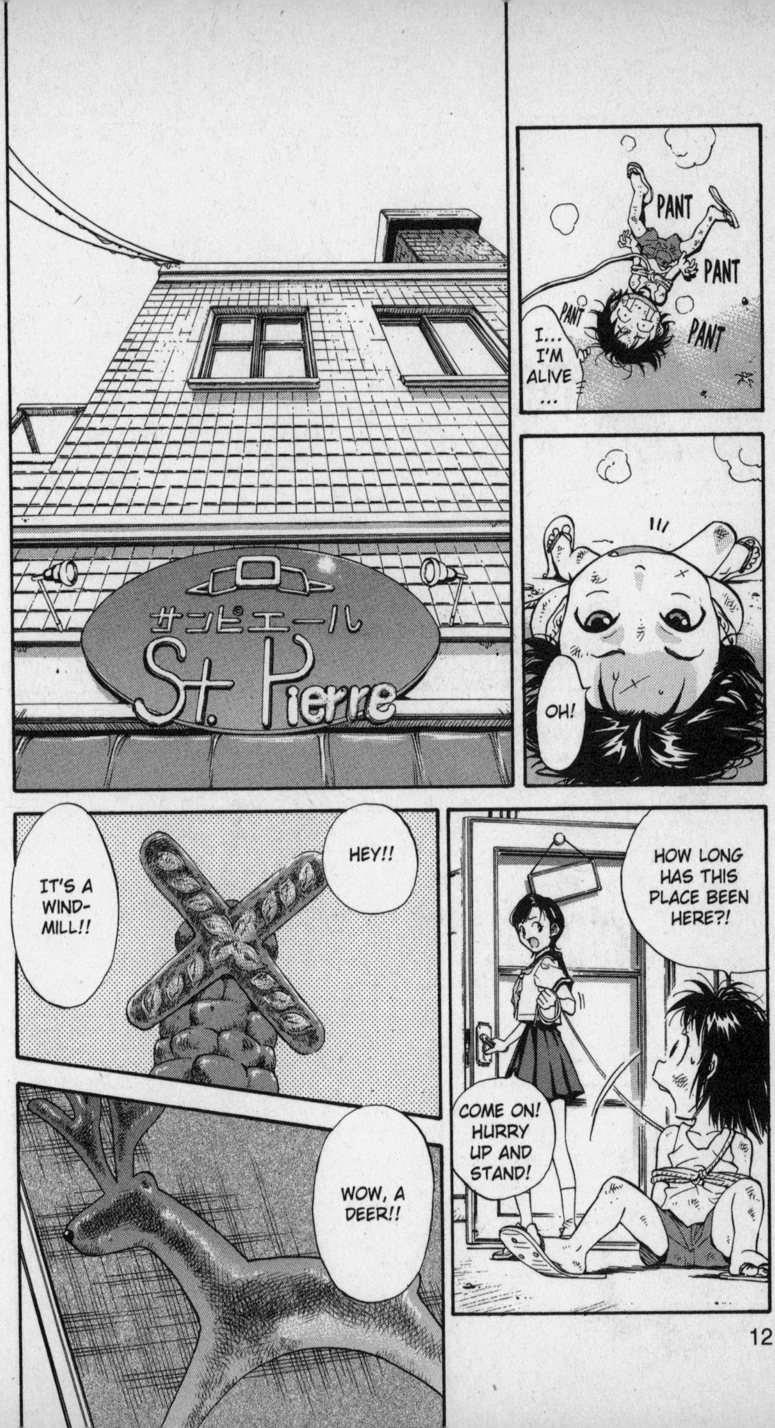
PANT
PANT
PANT
PANT
I... I'M ALIVE...
OH!
サンピエール
St. Pierre
HOW LONG HAS THIS PLACE BEEN HERE?!
COME ON! HURRY UP AND STAND!
HEY!!
IT'S A WIND-MILL!!
WOW, A DEER!!

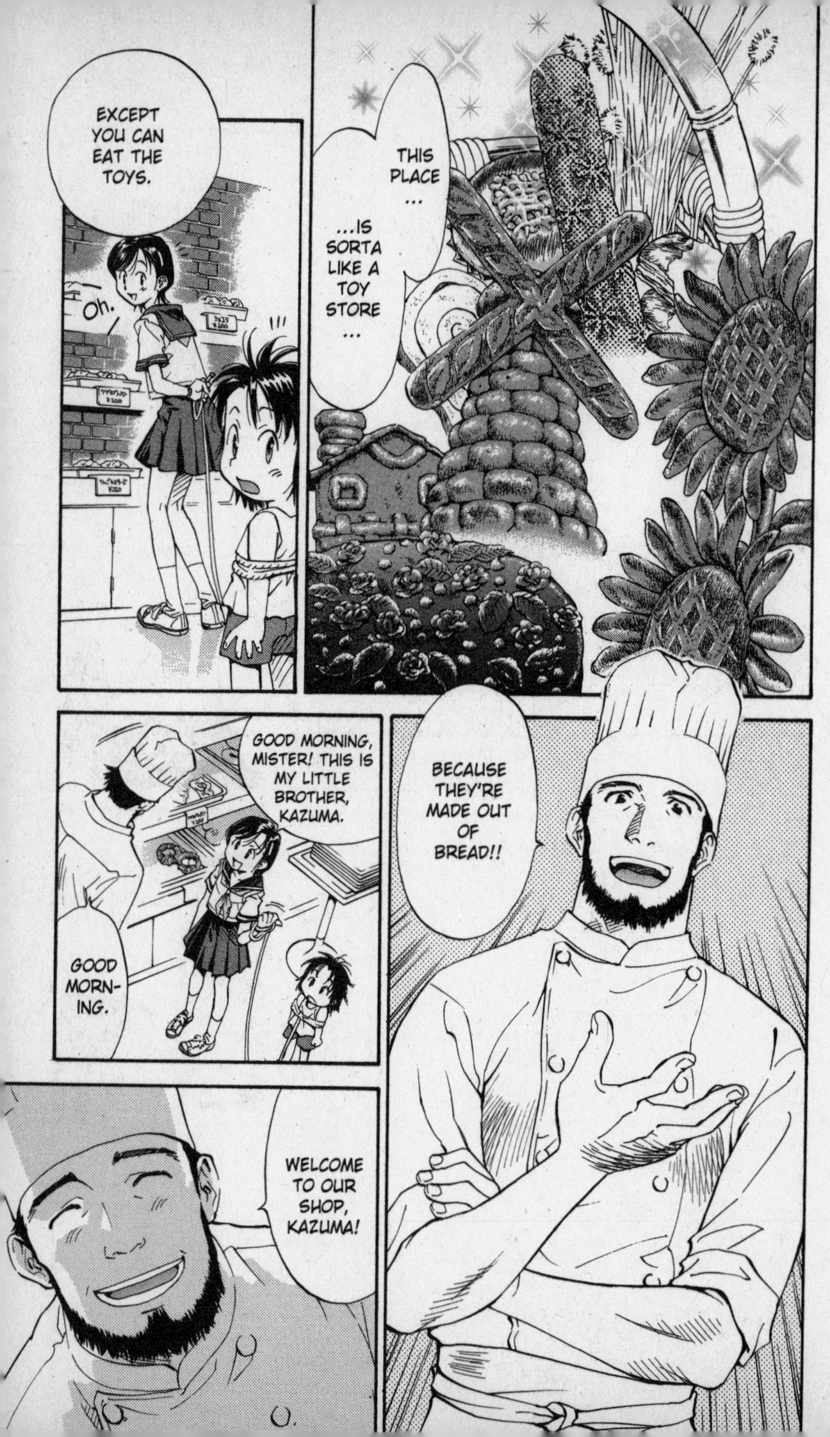
THIS PLACE ...
...IS SORTA LIKE A TOY STORE ...
EXCEPT YOU CAN EAT THE TOYS.
Oh.
!!!
BECAUSE THEY'RE MADE OUT OF BREAD!!
GOOD MORNING, MISTER! THIS IS MY LITTLE BROTHER, KAZUMA.
GOOD MORNING.
WELCOME TO OUR SHOP, KAZUMA!

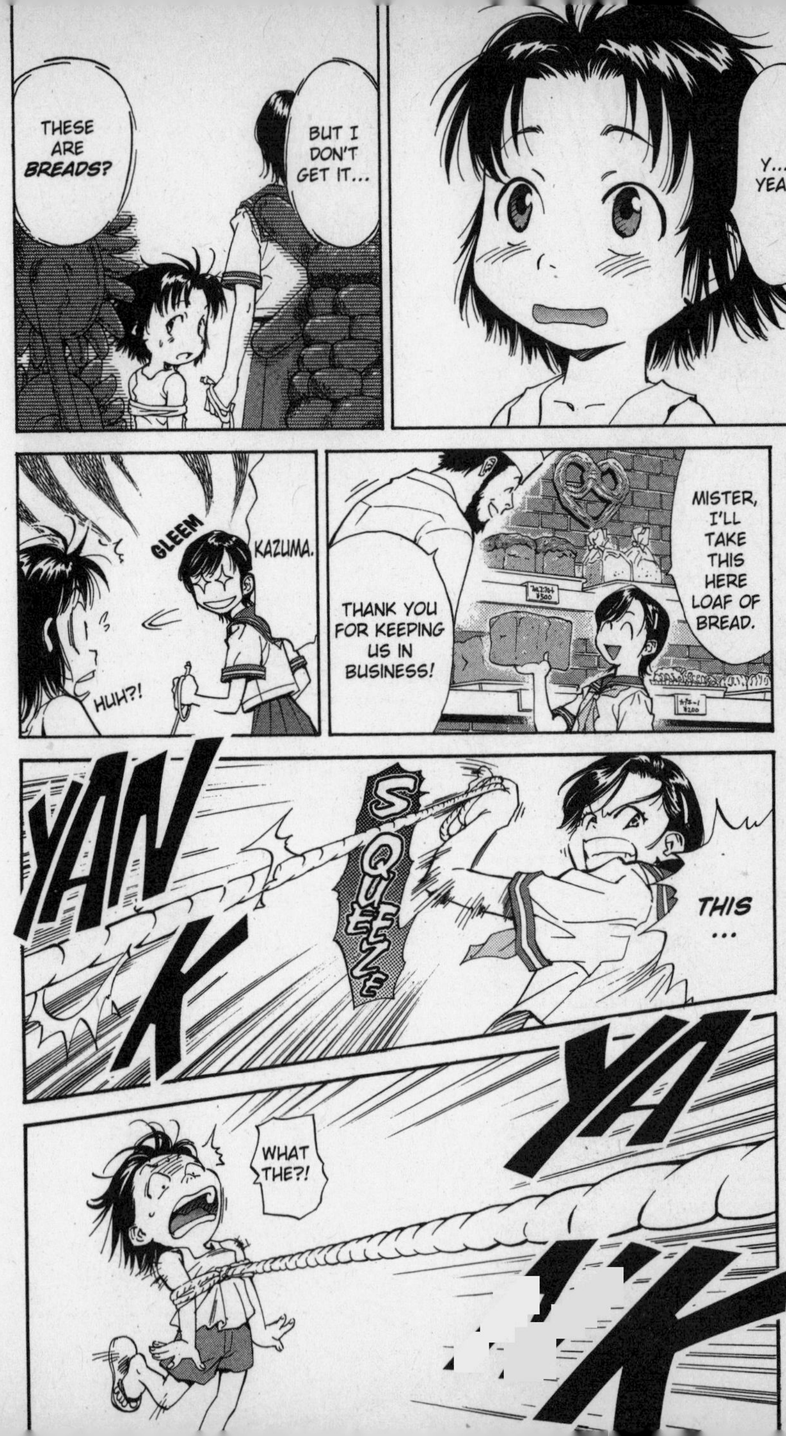
Y... YEAH.
BUT I DON'T GET IT...
THESE ARE *BREADS?*
MISTER, I'LL TAKE THIS HERE LOAF OF BREAD.
THANK YOU FOR KEEPING US IN BUSINESS!
KAZUMA.
GLEEM
HUH?!
THIS...
SQUEEZE
YANK
YA
K
WHAT THE?!

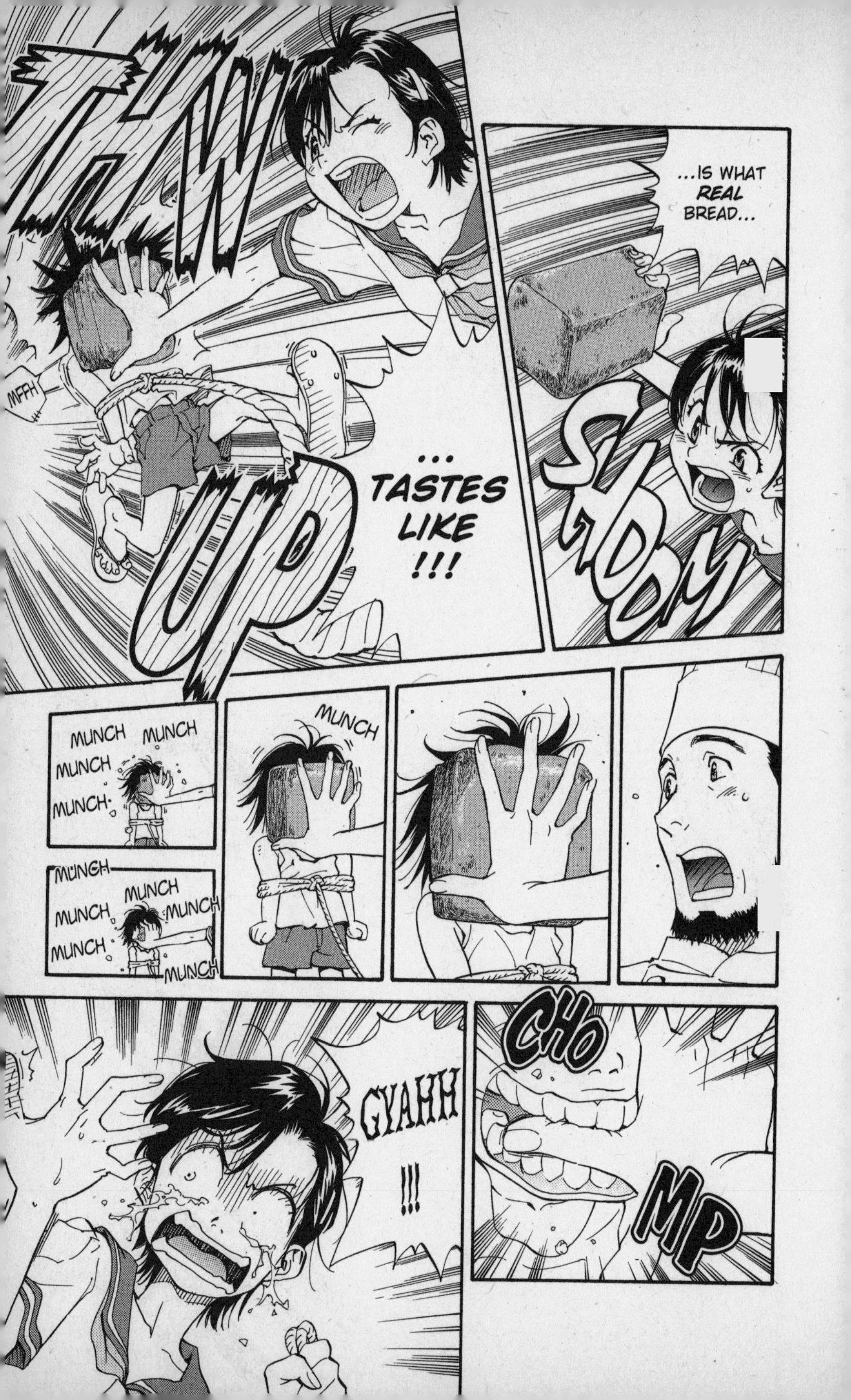
...IS WHAT REAL BREAD...
SHOOM
THW
UP
...TASTES LIKE !!!
MFFH
MUNCH
MUNCH
MUNCH MUNCH
MUNCH
MUNCH
MUNCH
MUNCH
MUNCH MUNCH
MUNCH
MUNCH
MUNCH
CHO
MP
GYAHH
!!!

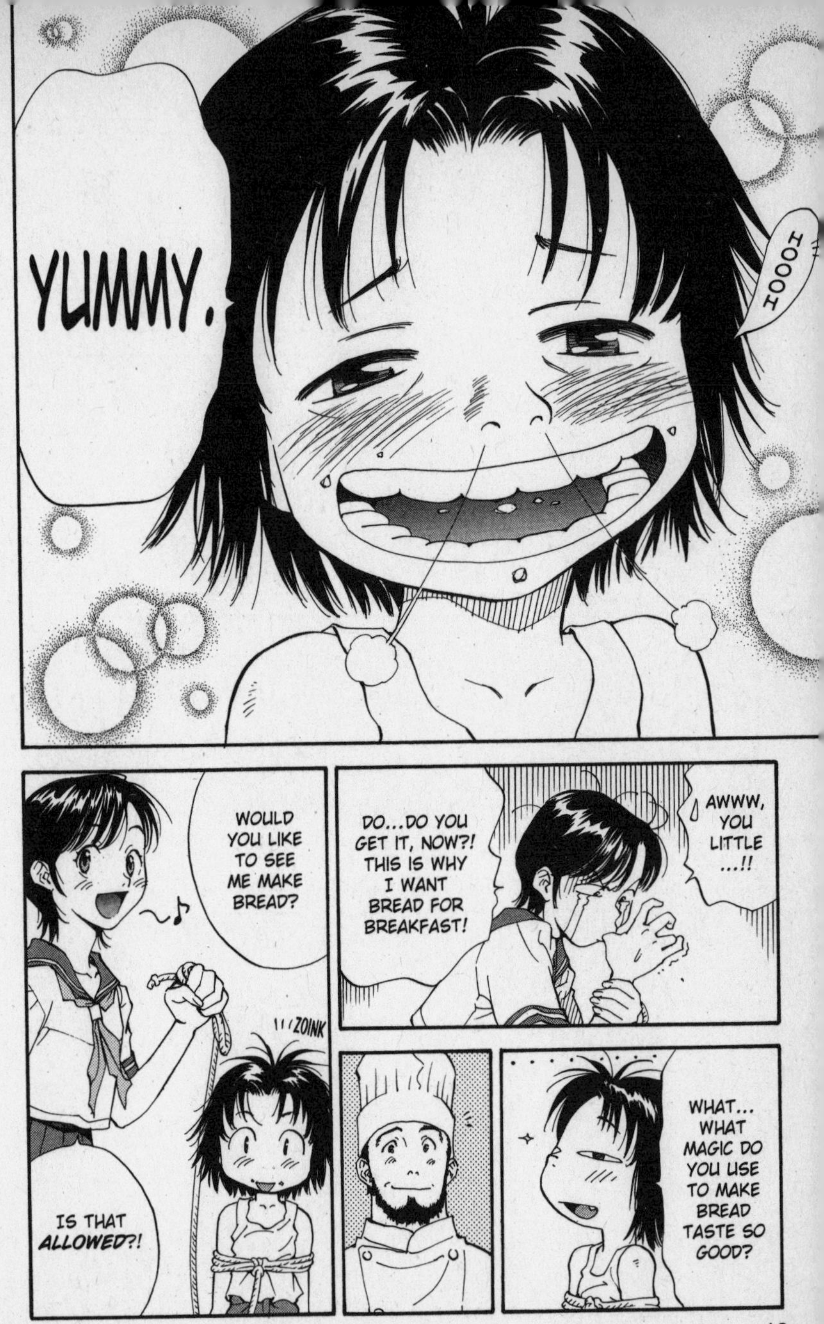
HOOOH
YUMMY.
AWWW, YOU LITTLE ...!!
DO...DO YOU GET IT, NOW?! THIS IS WHY I WANT BREAD FOR BREAKFAST!
WHAT... WHAT MAGIC DO YOU USE TO MAKE BREAD TASTE SO GOOD?
WOULD YOU LIKE TO SEE ME MAKE BREAD?
~♪
!!!ZOINK
IS THAT ALLOWED?!

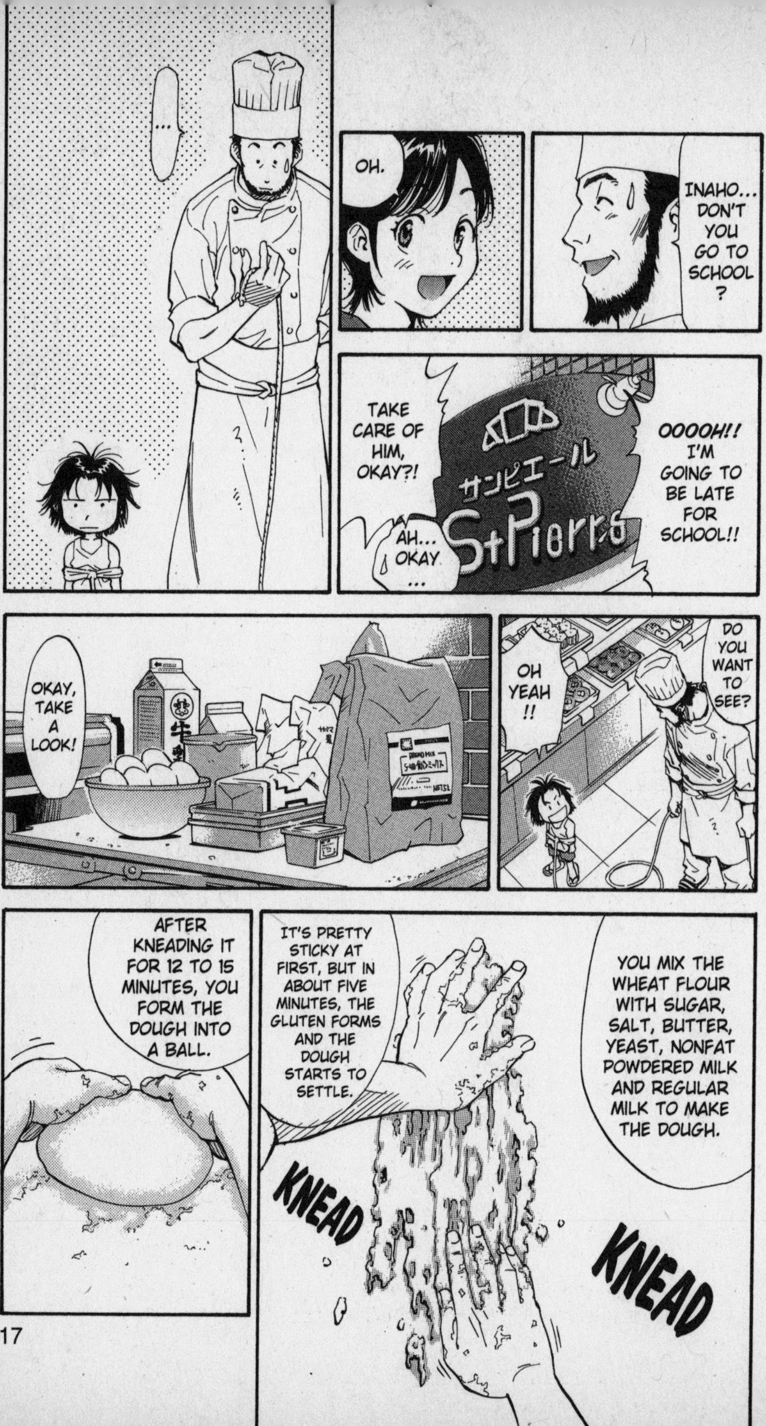
INAHO... DON'T YOU GO TO SCHOOL?
OH.
OOOOH!! I'M GOING TO BE LATE FOR SCHOOL!!
サンピエール
St Pierre
TAKE CARE OF HIM, OKAY?!
AH... OKAY...
...
DO YOU WANT TO SEE?
OH YEAH!!
OKAY, TAKE A LOOK!
YOU MIX THE WHEAT FLOUR WITH SUGAR, SALT, BUTTER, YEAST, NONFAT POWDERED MILK AND REGULAR MILK TO MAKE THE DOUGH.
IT'S PRETTY STICKY AT FIRST, BUT IN ABOUT FIVE MINUTES, THE GLUTEN FORMS AND THE DOUGH STARTS TO SETTLE.
KNEAD
KNEAD
AFTER KNEADING IT FOR 12 TO 15 MINUTES, YOU FORM THE DOUGH INTO A BALL.

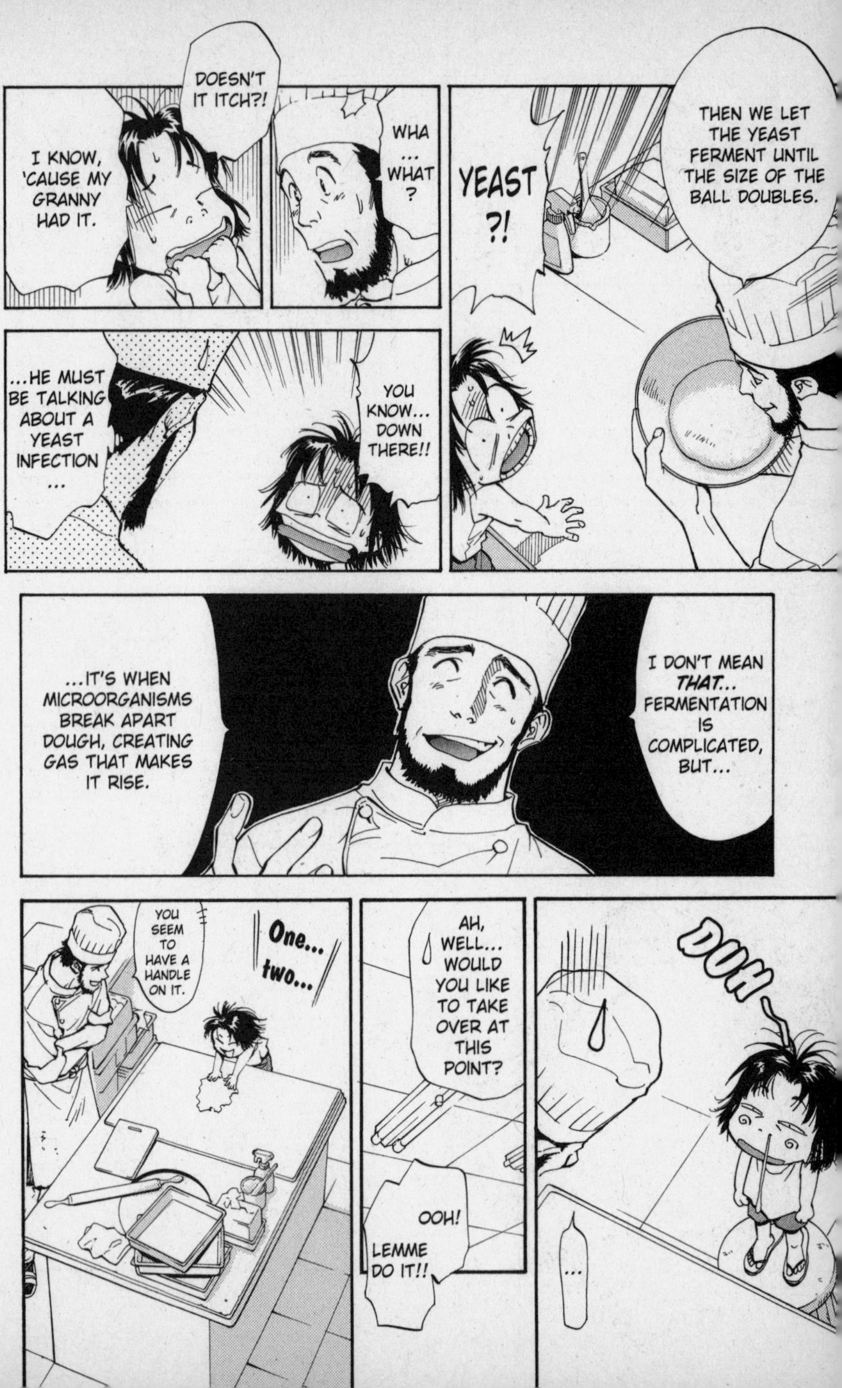
THEN WE LET THE YEAST FERMENT UNTIL THE SIZE OF THE BALL DOUBLES.
YEAST ?!
DOESN'T IT ITCH?!
WHA ... WHAT ?
I KNOW, 'CAUSE MY GRANNY HAD IT.
YOU KNOW... DOWN THERE!!
...HE MUST BE TALKING ABOUT A YEAST INFECTION ...
I DON'T MEAN *THAT*... FERMENTATION IS COMPLICATED, BUT...
...IT'S WHEN MICROORGANISMS BREAK APART DOUGH, CREATING GAS THAT MAKES IT RISE.
DUH—
...
AH, WELL... WOULD YOU LIKE TO TAKE OVER AT THIS POINT?
OOH!
LEMME DO IT!!
One... two...
YOU SEEM TO HAVE A HANDLE ON IT.

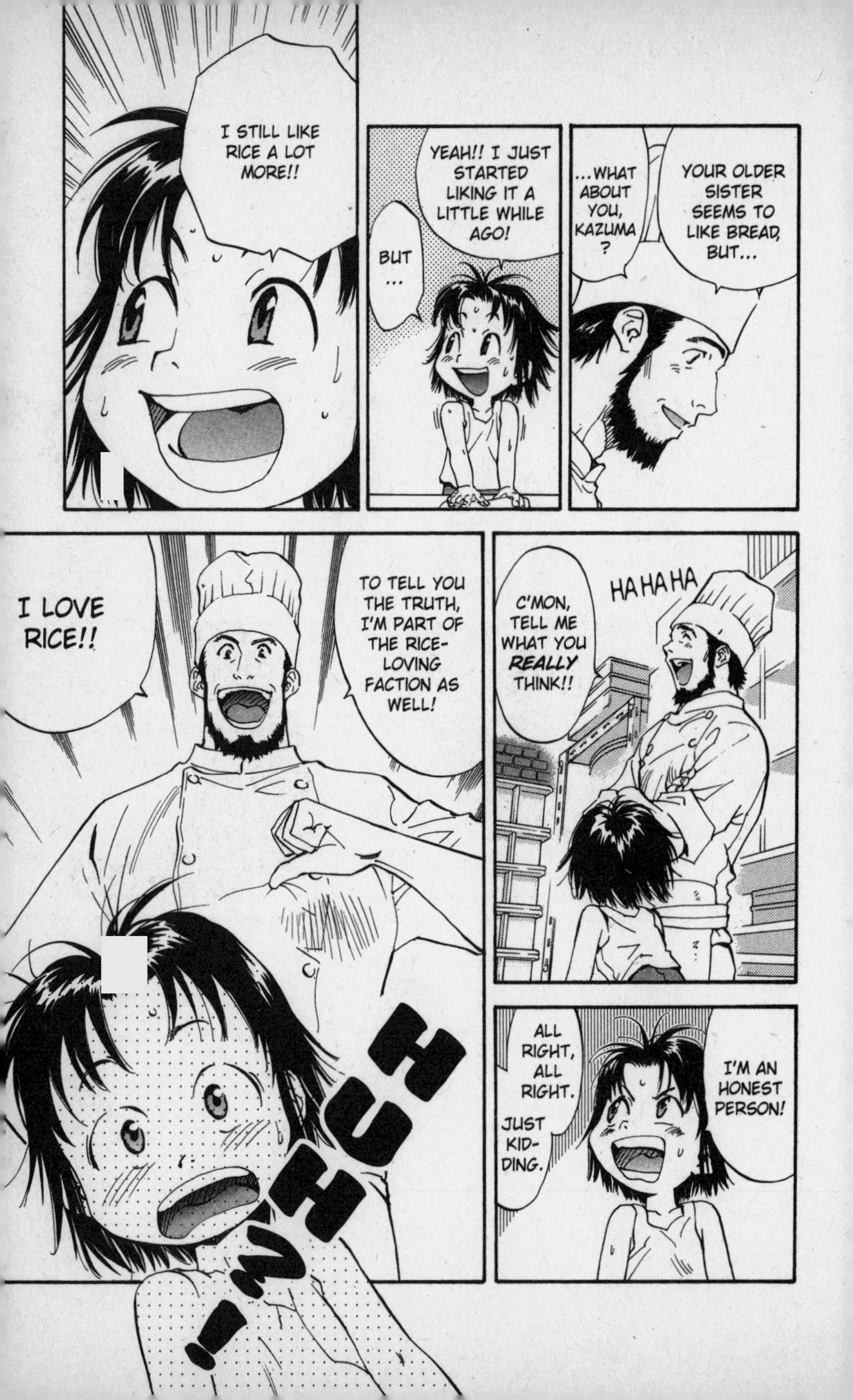
YOUR OLDER SISTER SEEMS TO LIKE BREAD, BUT...
...WHAT ABOUT YOU, KAZUMA?
YEAH!! I JUST STARTED LIKING IT A LITTLE WHILE AGO!
BUT...
I STILL LIKE RICE A LOT MORE!!
HAHAHA
C'MON, TELL ME WHAT YOU ***REALLY*** THINK!!
I'M AN HONEST PERSON!
ALL RIGHT, ALL RIGHT.
JUST KIDDING.
TO TELL YOU THE TRUTH, I'M PART OF THE RICE-LOVING FACTION AS WELL!
I LOVE RICE!!
HUH?!

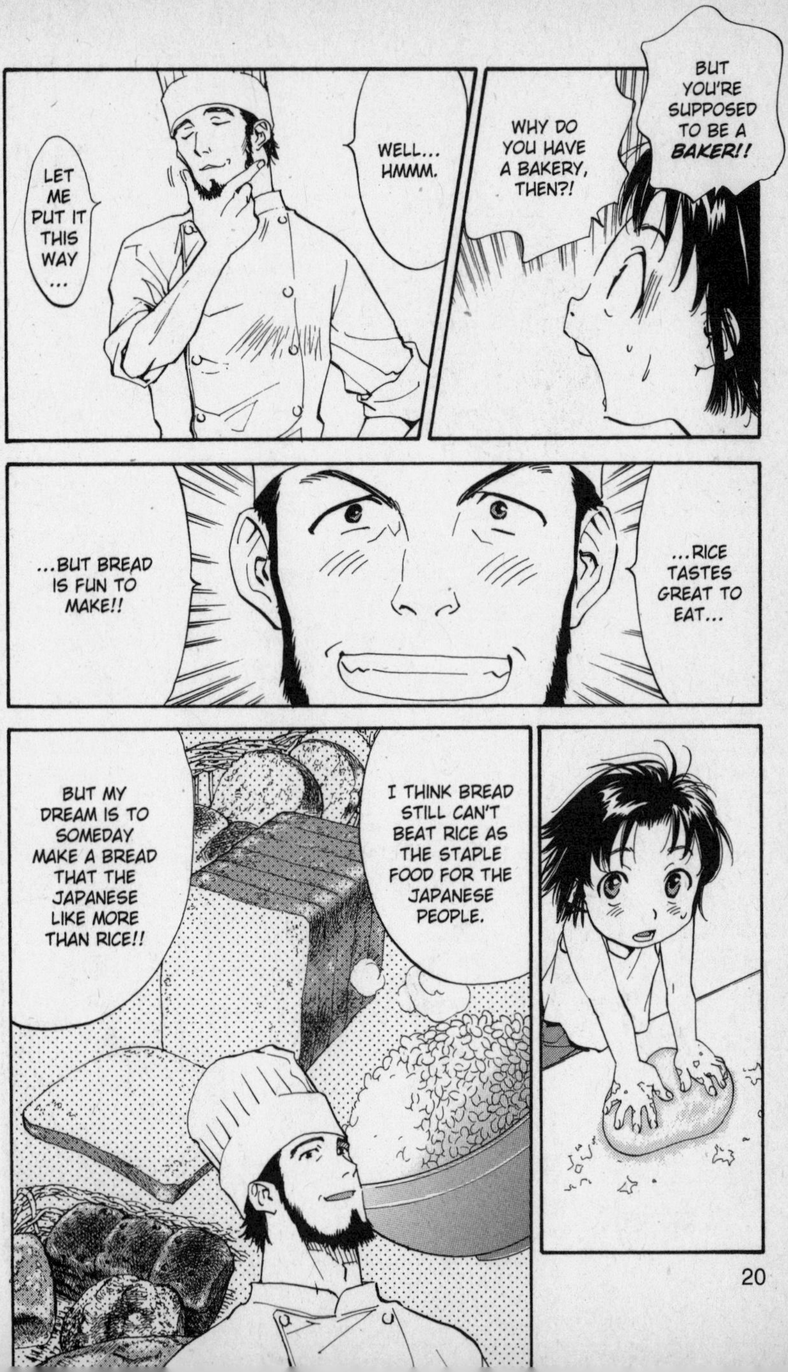
BUT YOU'RE SUPPOSED TO BE A ***BAKER!!***
WHY DO YOU HAVE A BAKERY, THEN?!
WELL... HMMM.
LET ME PUT IT THIS WAY...
...RICE TASTES GREAT TO EAT...
...BUT BREAD IS FUN TO MAKE!!
I THINK BREAD STILL CAN'T BEAT RICE AS THE STAPLE FOOD FOR THE JAPANESE PEOPLE.
BUT MY DREAM IS TO SOMEDAY MAKE A BREAD THAT THE JAPANESE LIKE MORE THAN RICE!!

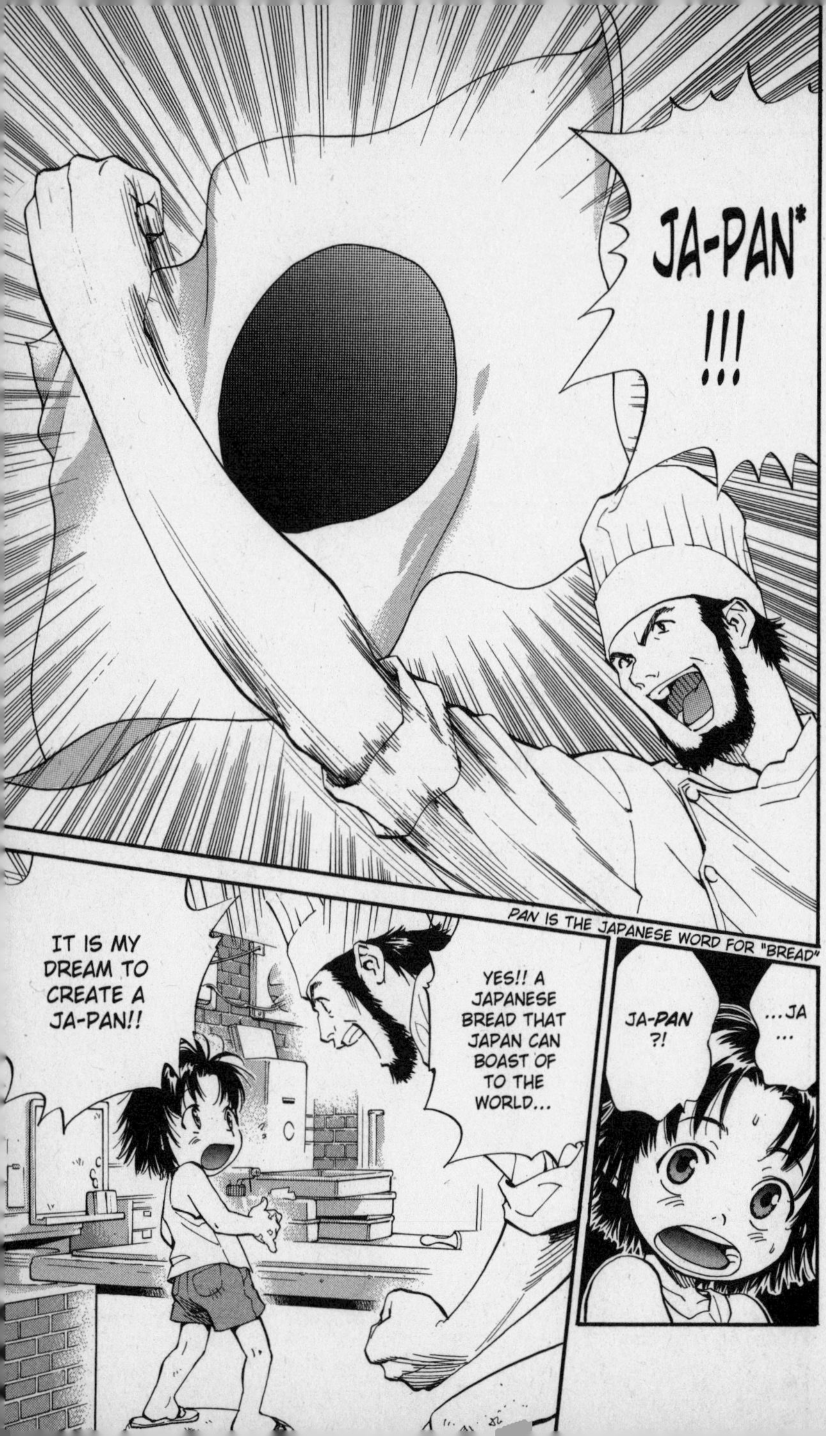
JA-PAN* !!!
PAN IS THE JAPANESE WORD FOR "BREAD"
...JA ...
JA-PAN ?!
YES!! A JAPANESE BREAD THAT JAPAN CAN BOAST OF TO THE WORLD...
IT IS MY DREAM TO CREATE A JA-PAN!!

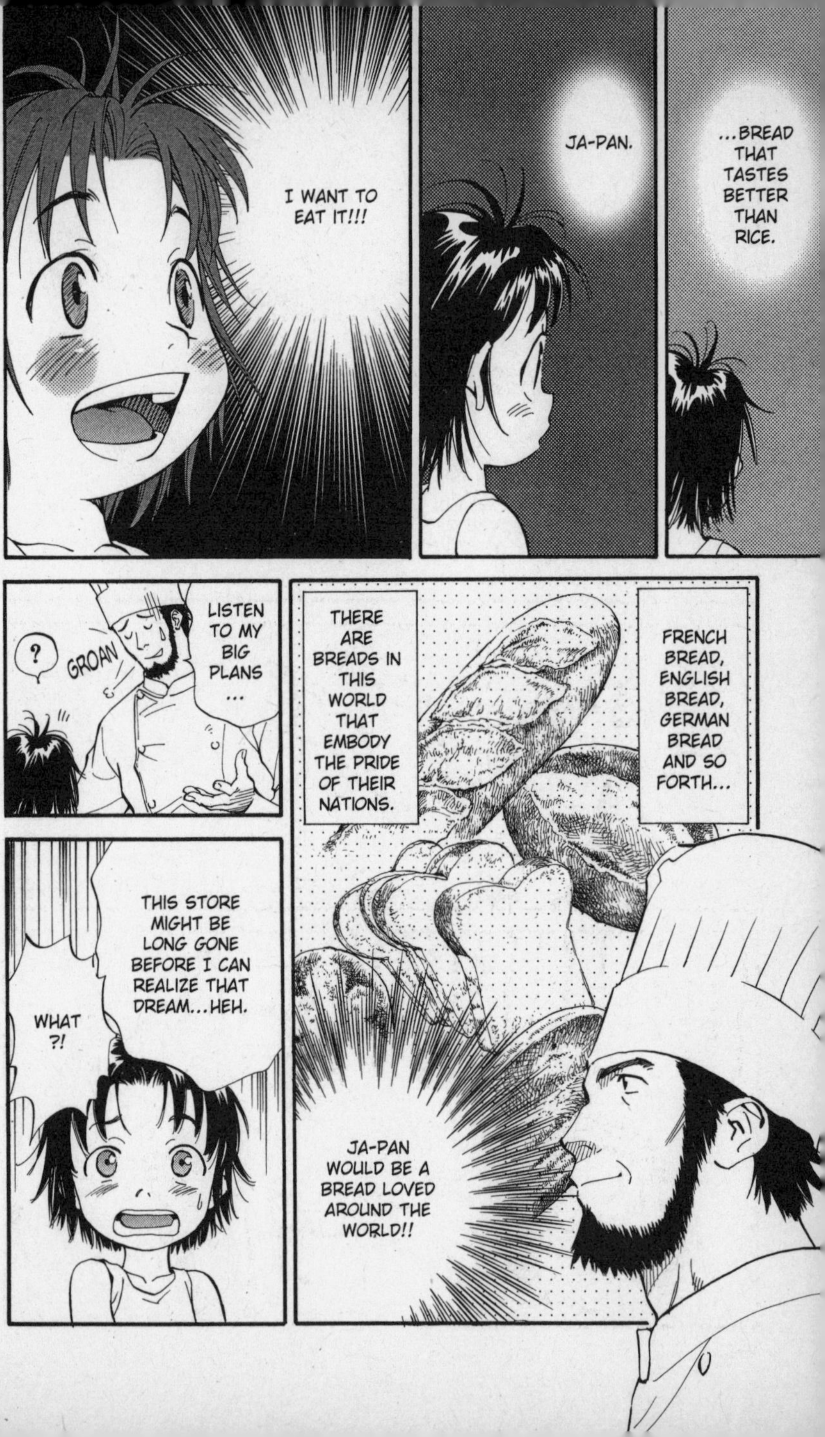
...BREAD THAT TASTES BETTER THAN RICE.
JA-PAN.
I WANT TO EAT IT!!!
FRENCH BREAD, ENGLISH BREAD, GERMAN BREAD AND SO FORTH...
THERE ARE BREADS IN THIS WORLD THAT EMBODY THE PRIDE OF THEIR NATIONS.
JA-PAN WOULD BE A BREAD LOVED AROUND THE WORLD!!
LISTEN TO MY BIG PLANS ...
GROAN
?
THIS STORE MIGHT BE LONG GONE BEFORE I CAN REALIZE THAT DREAM...HEH.
WHAT ?!

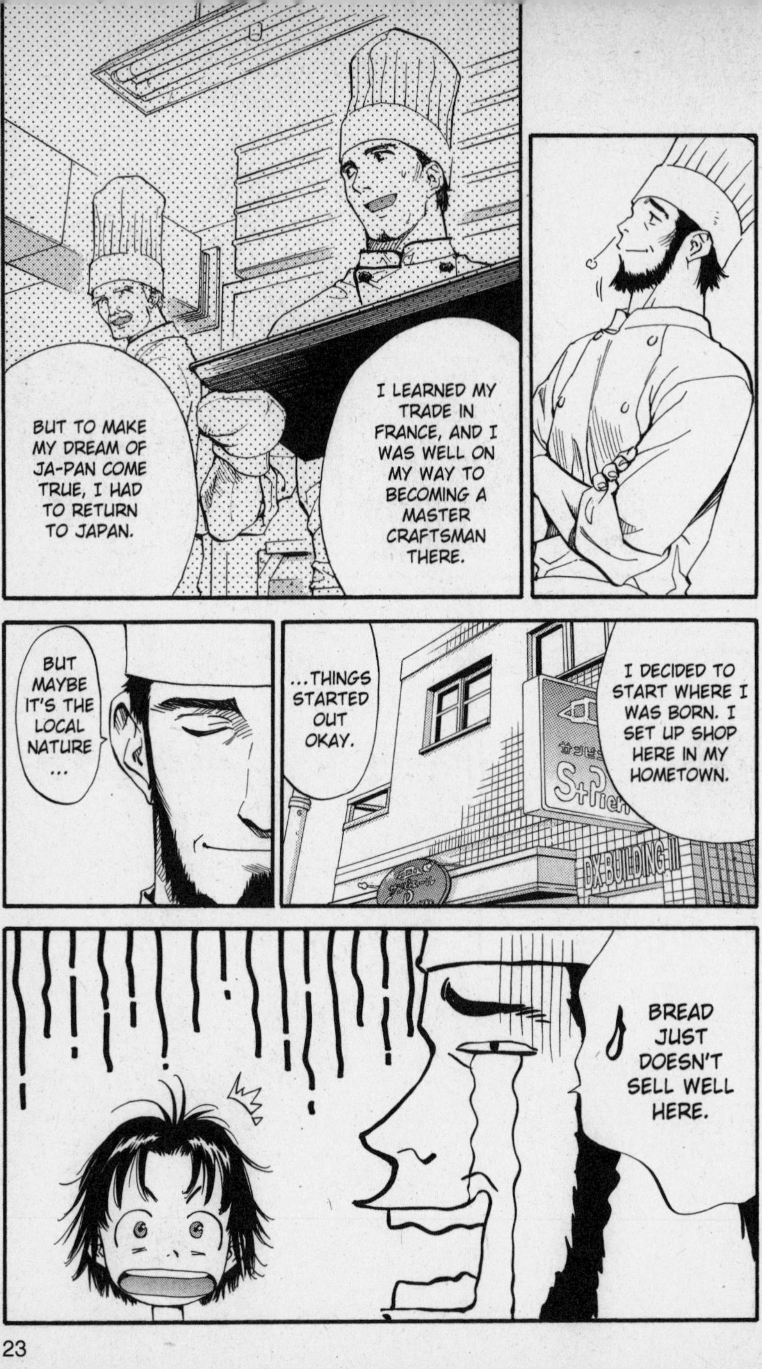
I LEARNED MY TRADE IN FRANCE, AND I WAS WELL ON MY WAY TO BECOMING A MASTER CRAFTSMAN THERE.
BUT TO MAKE MY DREAM OF JA-PAN COME TRUE, I HAD TO RETURN TO JAPAN.
I DECIDED TO START WHERE I WAS BORN. I SET UP SHOP HERE IN MY HOMETOWN.
DX-BUILDING II
...THINGS STARTED OUT OKAY.
BUT MAYBE IT'S THE LOCAL NATURE ...
BREAD JUST DOESN'T SELL WELL HERE.

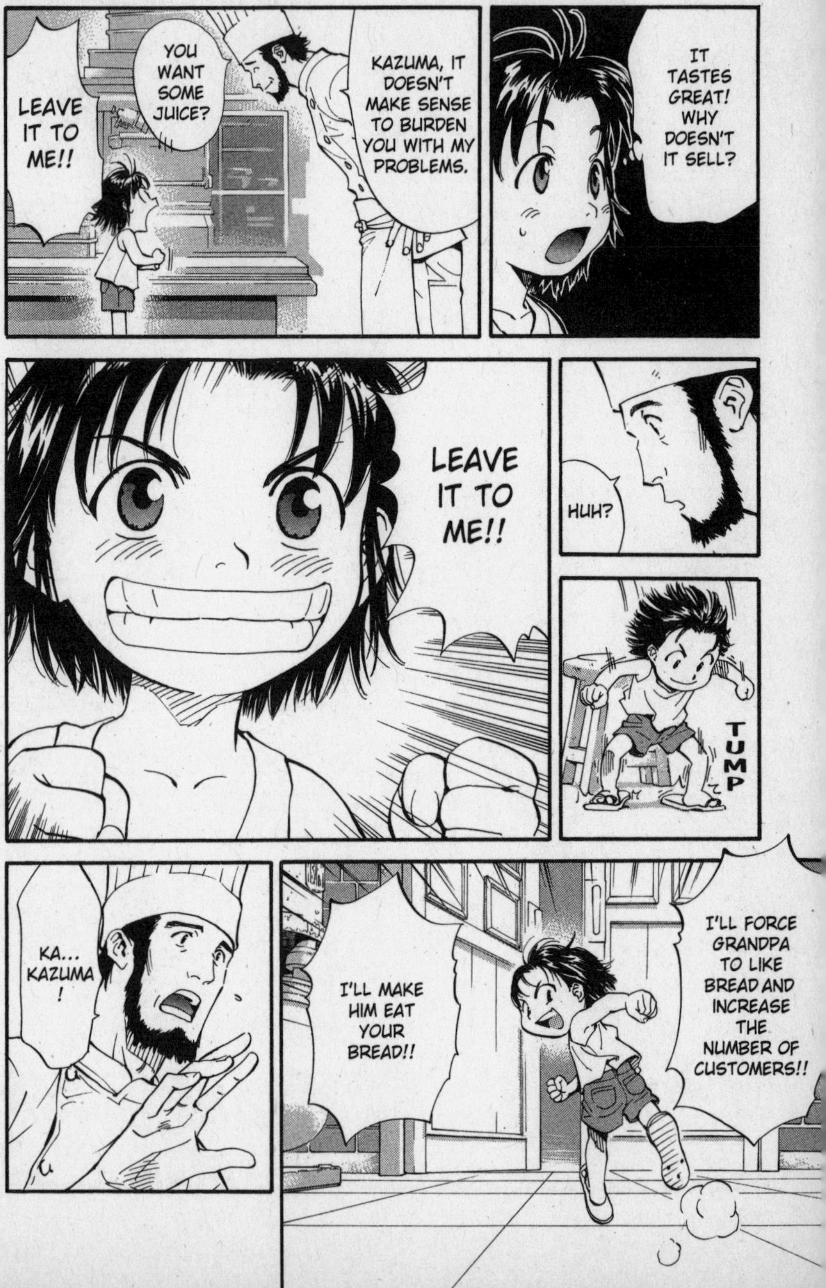
IT TASTES GREAT! WHY DOESN'T IT SELL?
KAZUMA, IT DOESN'T MAKE SENSE TO BURDEN YOU WITH MY PROBLEMS.
YOU WANT SOME JUICE?
LEAVE IT TO ME!!
HUH?
TUMP
LEAVE IT TO ME!!
I'LL FORCE GRANDPA TO LIKE BREAD AND INCREASE THE NUMBER OF CUSTOMERS!!
I'LL MAKE HIM EAT YOUR BREAD!!
KA... KAZUMA!

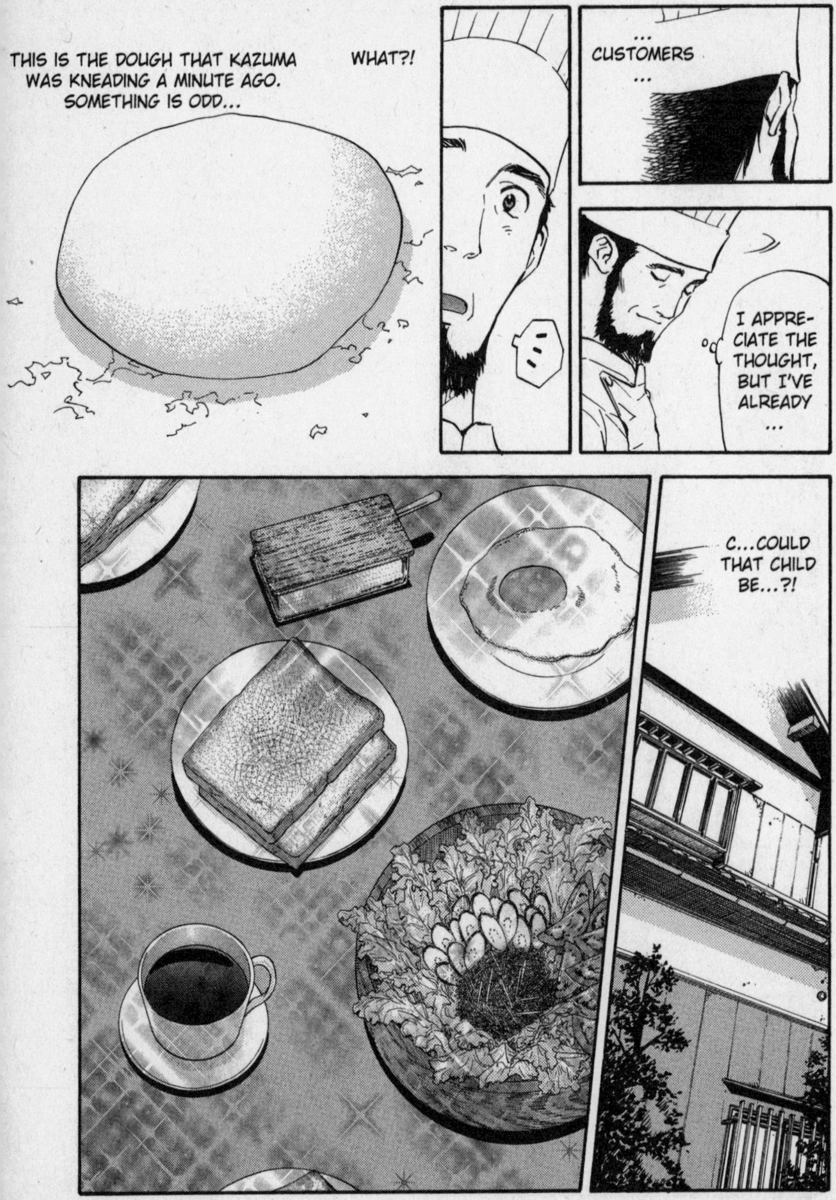
... CUSTOMERS ...
I APPRE-CIATE THE THOUGHT, BUT I'VE ALREADY ...
WHAT?!
THIS IS THE DOUGH THAT KAZUMA WAS KNEADING A MINUTE AGO. SOMETHING IS ODD...
C...COULD THAT CHILD BE...?!

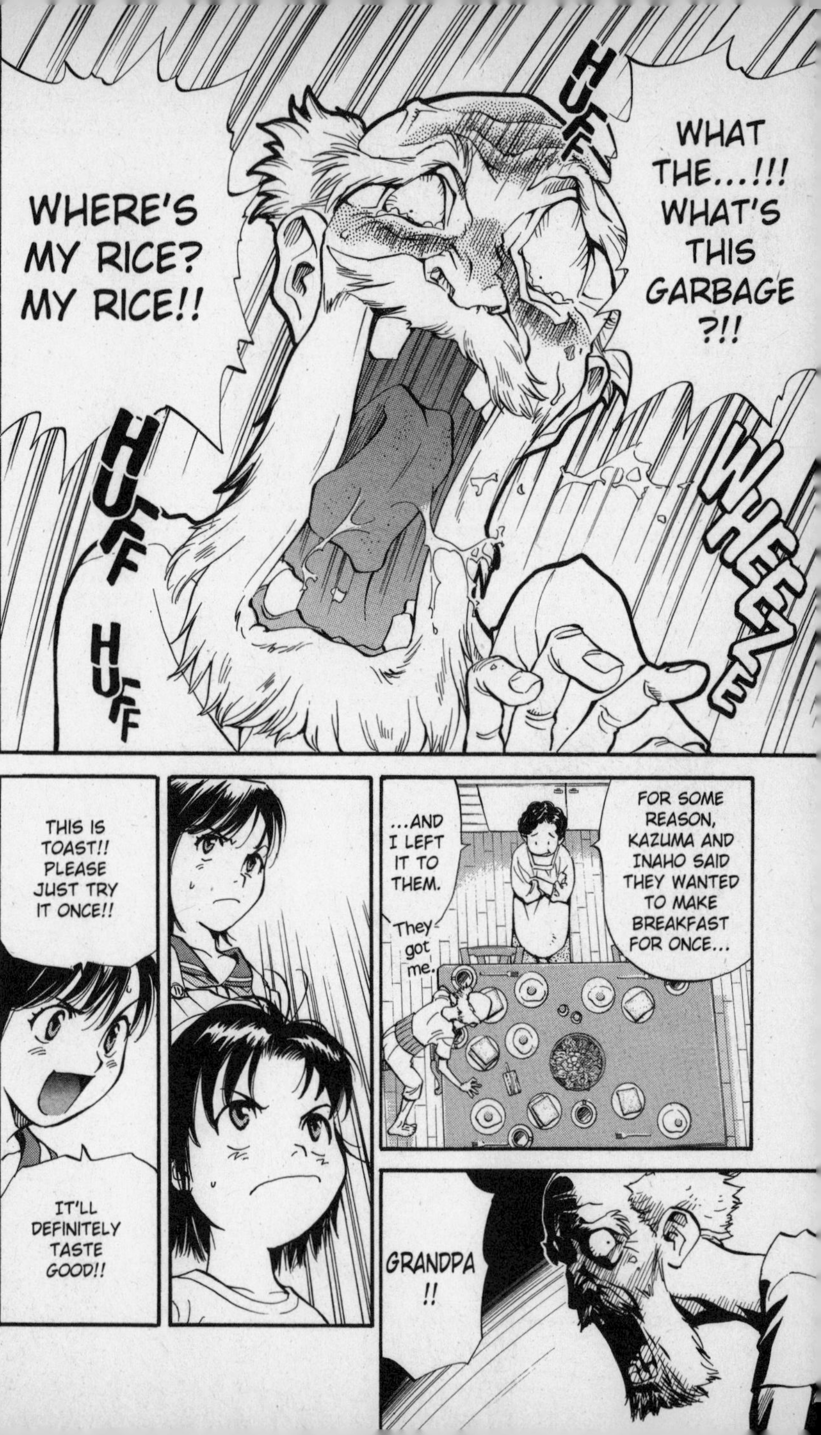
HUFF
WHAT THE...!!! WHAT'S THIS GARBAGE?!!
WHERE'S MY RICE? MY RICE!!
WHEEZE
HUFF
HUFF
HUFF
FOR SOME REASON, KAZUMA AND INAHO SAID THEY WANTED TO MAKE BREAKFAST FOR ONCE...
...AND I LEFT IT TO THEM.
They got me.
GRANDPA!!
THIS IS TOAST!! PLEASE JUST TRY IT ONCE!!
IT'LL DEFINITELY TASTE GOOD!!

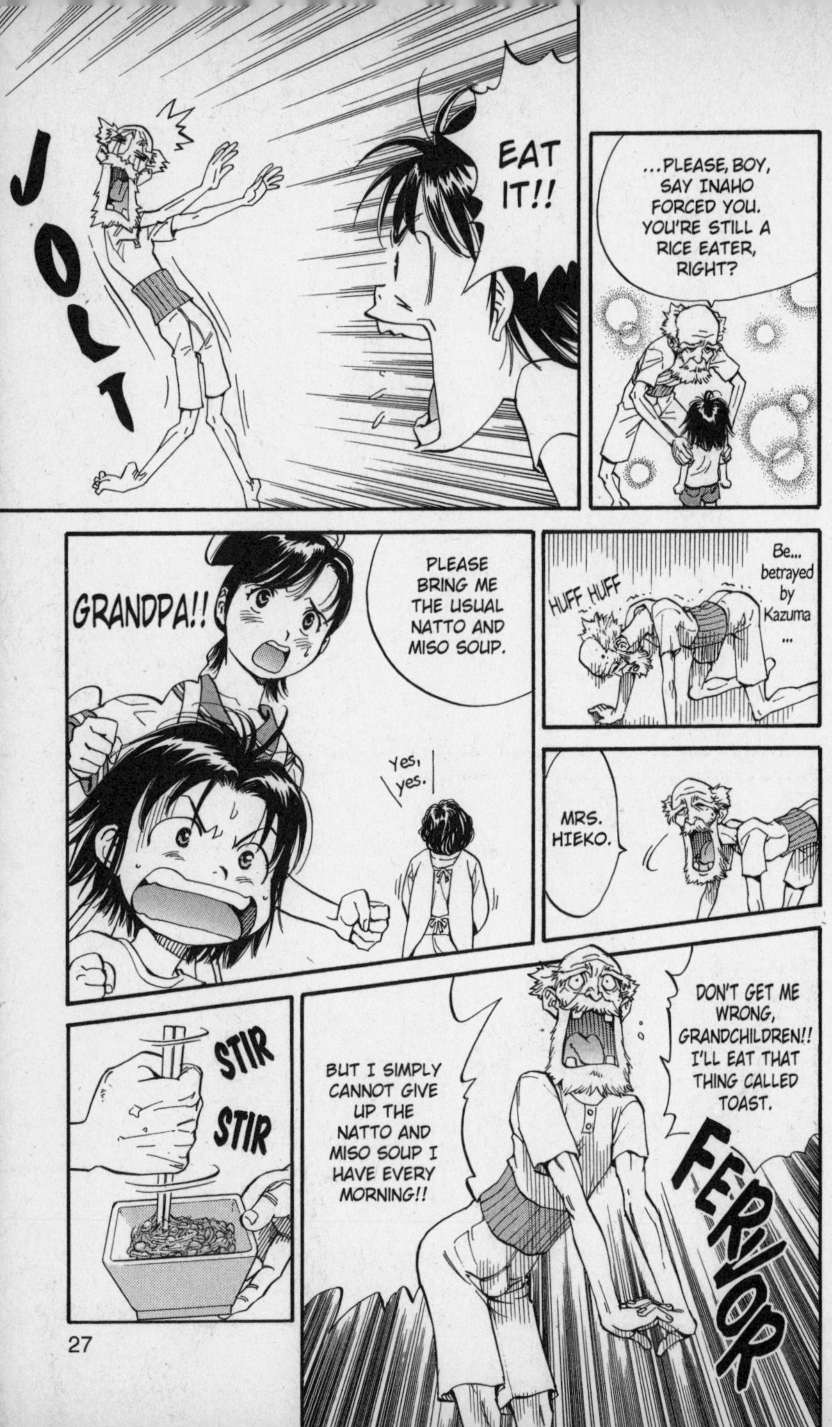
...PLEASE, BOY, SAY INAHO FORCED YOU. YOU'RE STILL A RICE EATER, RIGHT?
EAT IT!!
JOLT
Be... betrayed by Kazuma ...
HUFF HUFF
MRS. HIEKO.
PLEASE BRING ME THE USUAL NATTO AND MISO SOUP.
GRANDPA!!
Yes, yes.
DON'T GET ME WRONG, GRANDCHILDREN!! I'LL EAT THAT THING CALLED TOAST.
BUT I SIMPLY CANNOT GIVE UP THE NATTO AND MISO SOUP I HAVE EVERY MORNING!!
FERVOR
STIR
STIR

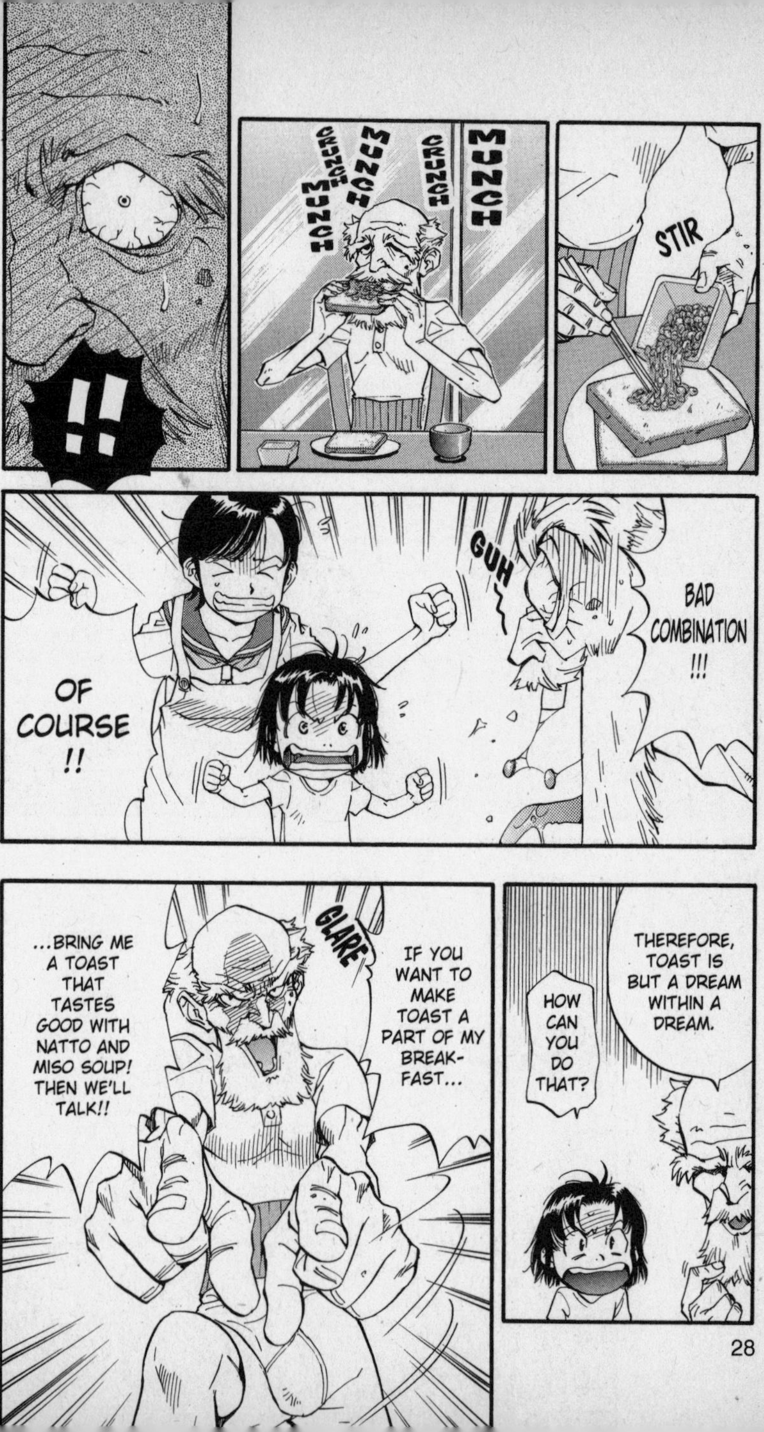
STIR
MUNCH
CRUNCH
MUNCH
CRUNCH
MUNCH
!!
BAD COMBINATION !!!
GUH
OF COURSE !!
THEREFORE, TOAST IS BUT A DREAM WITHIN A DREAM.
HOW CAN YOU DO THAT?
IF YOU WANT TO MAKE TOAST A PART OF MY BREAK-FAST...
GLARE
...BRING ME A TOAST THAT TASTES GOOD WITH NATTO AND MISO SOUP! THEN WE'LL TALK!!

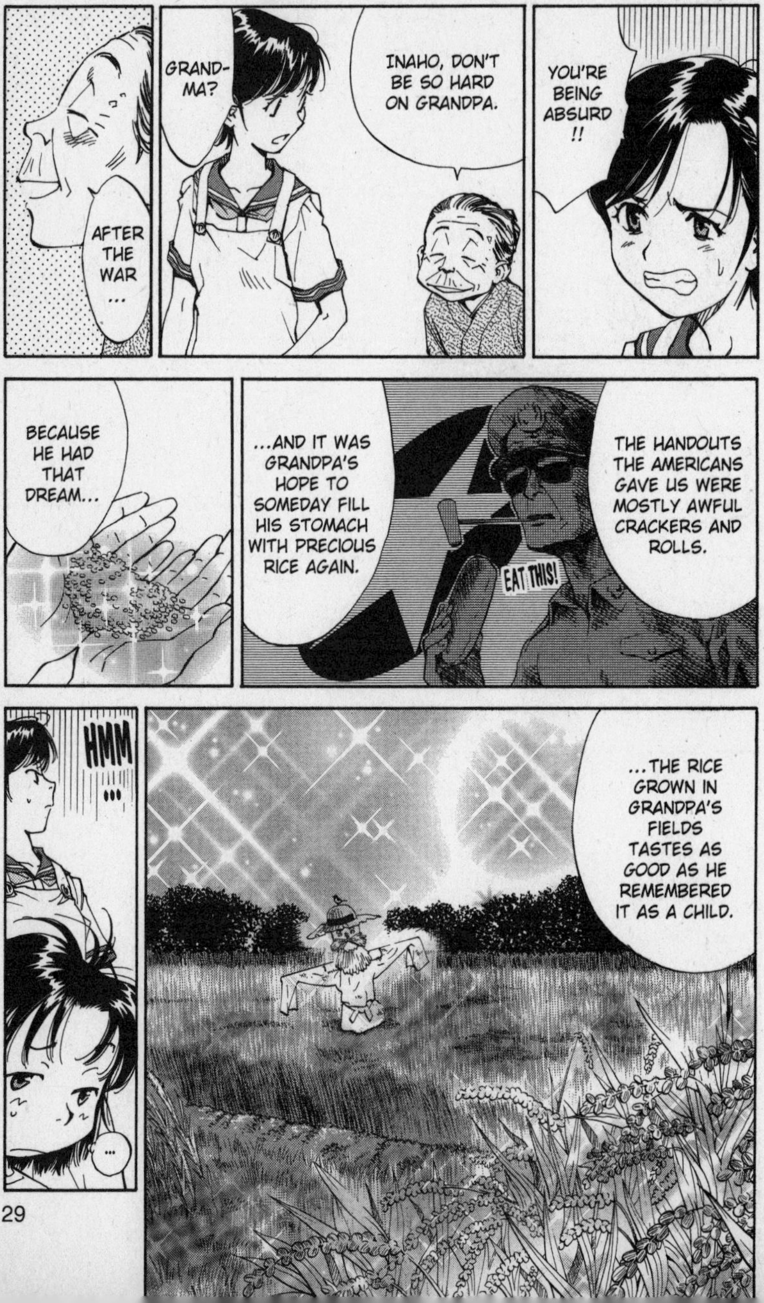
YOU'RE BEING ABSURD !!
INAHO, DON'T BE SO HARD ON GRANDPA.
GRAND-MA?
AFTER THE WAR ...
THE HANDOUTS THE AMERICANS GAVE US WERE MOSTLY AWFUL CRACKERS AND ROLLS.
EAT THIS!
...AND IT WAS GRANDPA'S HOPE TO SOMEDAY FILL HIS STOMACH WITH PRECIOUS RICE AGAIN.
BECAUSE HE HAD THAT DREAM...
...THE RICE GROWN IN GRANDPA'S FIELDS TASTES AS GOOD AS HE REMEMBERED IT AS A CHILD.
HMM ...
...

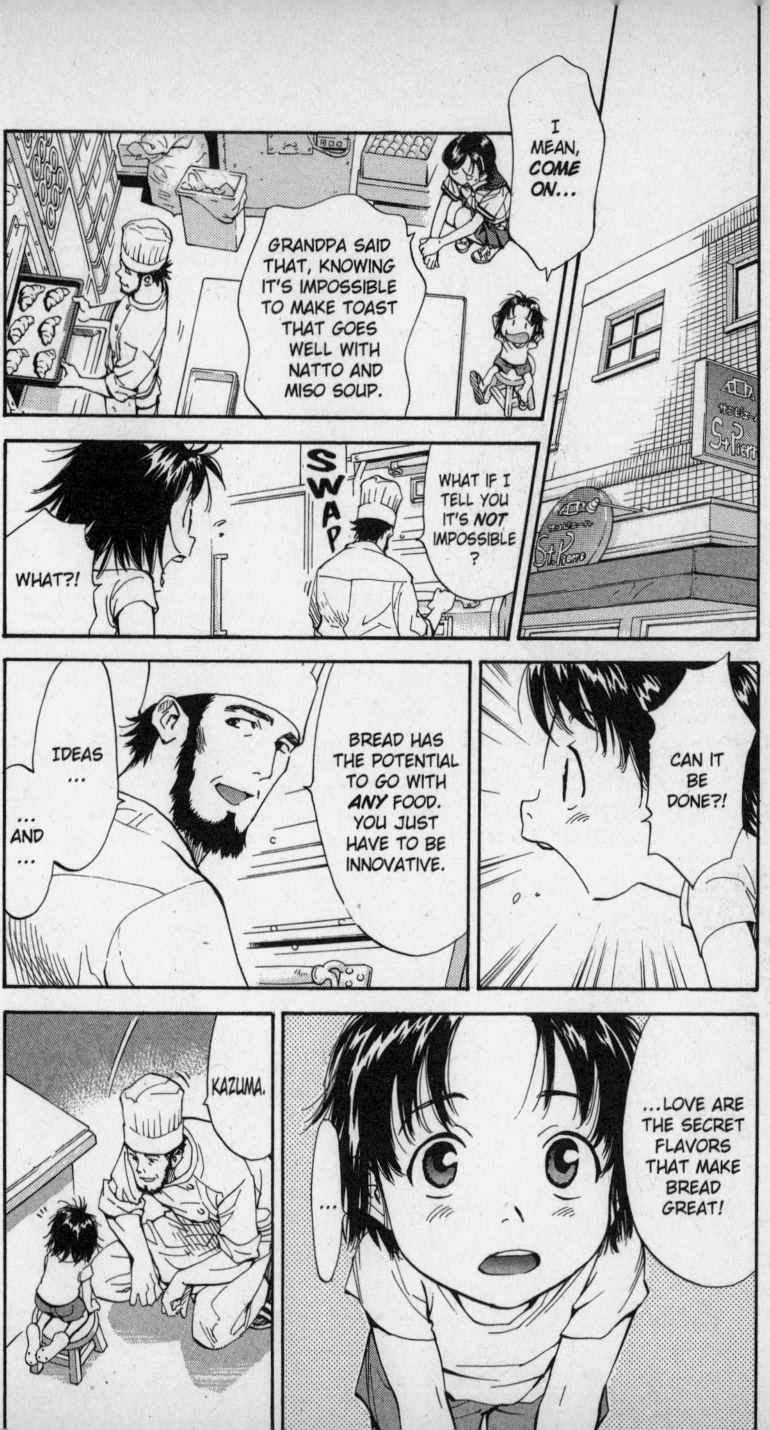
I MEAN, COME ON...
GRANDPA SAID THAT, KNOWING IT'S IMPOSSIBLE TO MAKE TOAST THAT GOES WELL WITH NATTO AND MISO SOUP.
WHAT IF I TELL YOU IT'S NOT IMPOSSIBLE?
SWAP
WHAT?!
CAN IT BE DONE?!
BREAD HAS THE POTENTIAL TO GO WITH ANY FOOD. YOU JUST HAVE TO BE INNOVATIVE.
IDEAS...
...AND...
...LOVE ARE THE SECRET FLAVORS THAT MAKE BREAD GREAT!
...
KAZUMA.

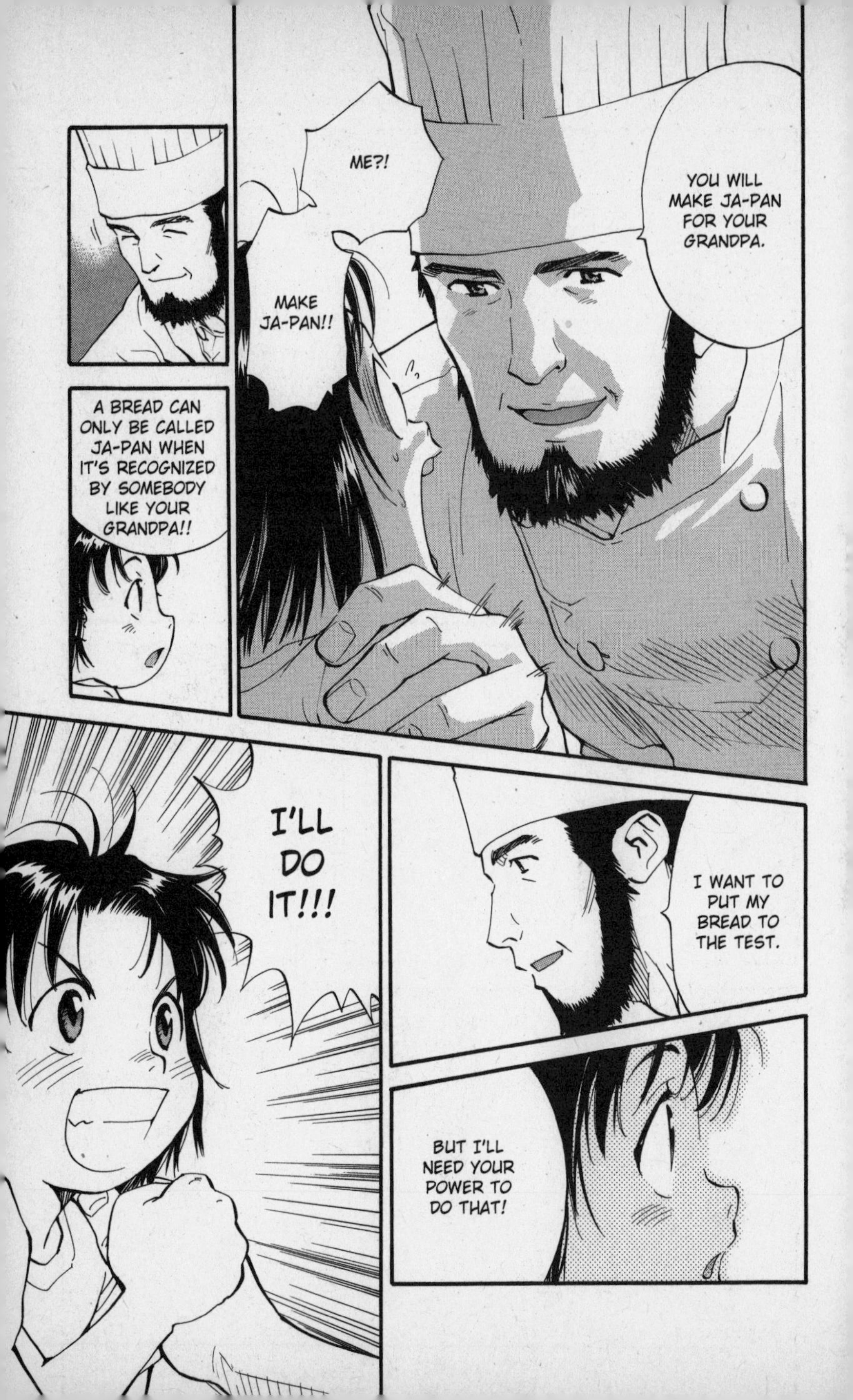
YOU WILL MAKE JA-PAN FOR YOUR GRANDPA.
ME?!
MAKE JA-PAN!!
A BREAD CAN ONLY BE CALLED JA-PAN WHEN IT'S RECOGNIZED BY SOMEBODY LIKE YOUR GRANDPA!!
I WANT TO PUT MY BREAD TO THE TEST.
BUT I'LL NEED YOUR POWER TO DO THAT!
I'LL DO IT!!!

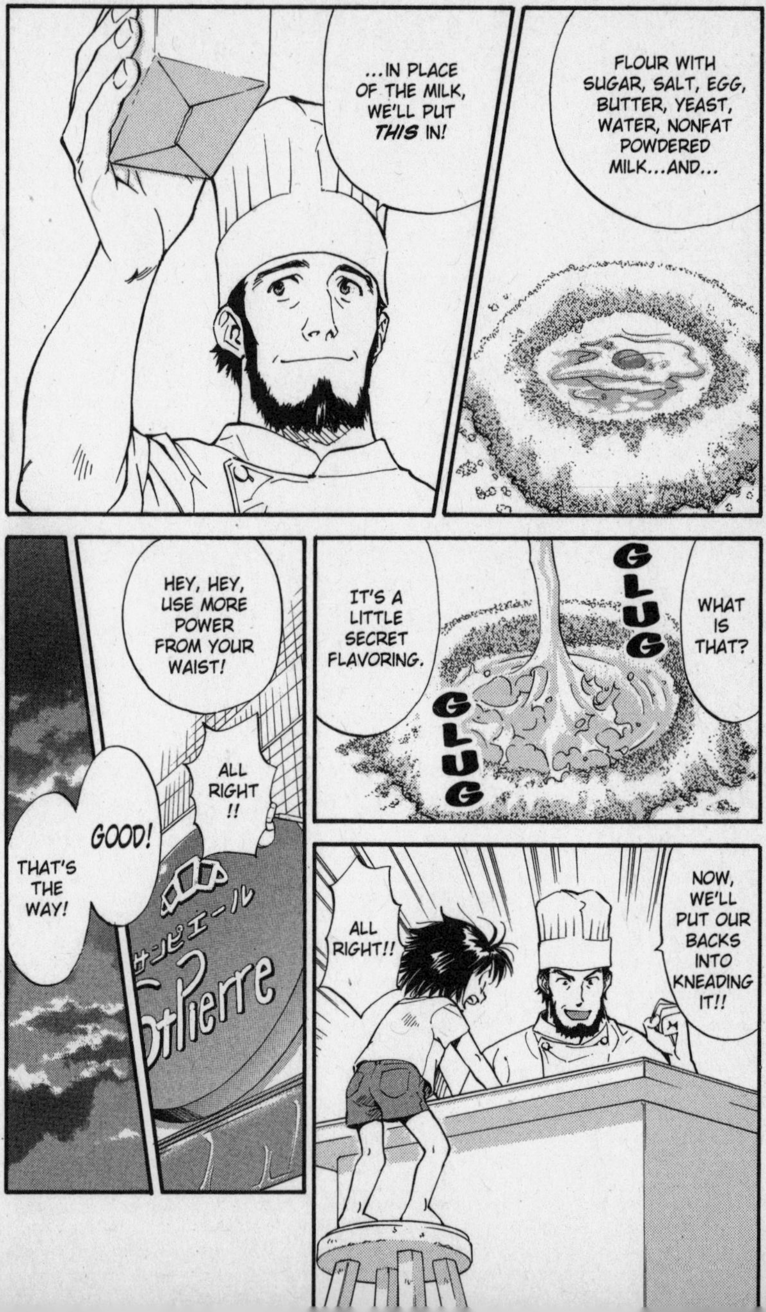
FLOUR WITH SUGAR, SALT, EGG, BUTTER, YEAST, WATER, NONFAT POWDERED MILK...AND...
...IN PLACE OF THE MILK, WE'LL PUT *THIS* IN!
WHAT IS THAT?
GLUG GLUG
IT'S A LITTLE SECRET FLAVORING.
GLUG GLUG
NOW, WE'LL PUT OUR BACKS INTO KNEADING IT!!
ALL RIGHT!!
HEY, HEY, USE MORE POWER FROM YOUR WAIST!
ALL RIGHT !!
GOOD!
THAT'S THE WAY!
サンピエール

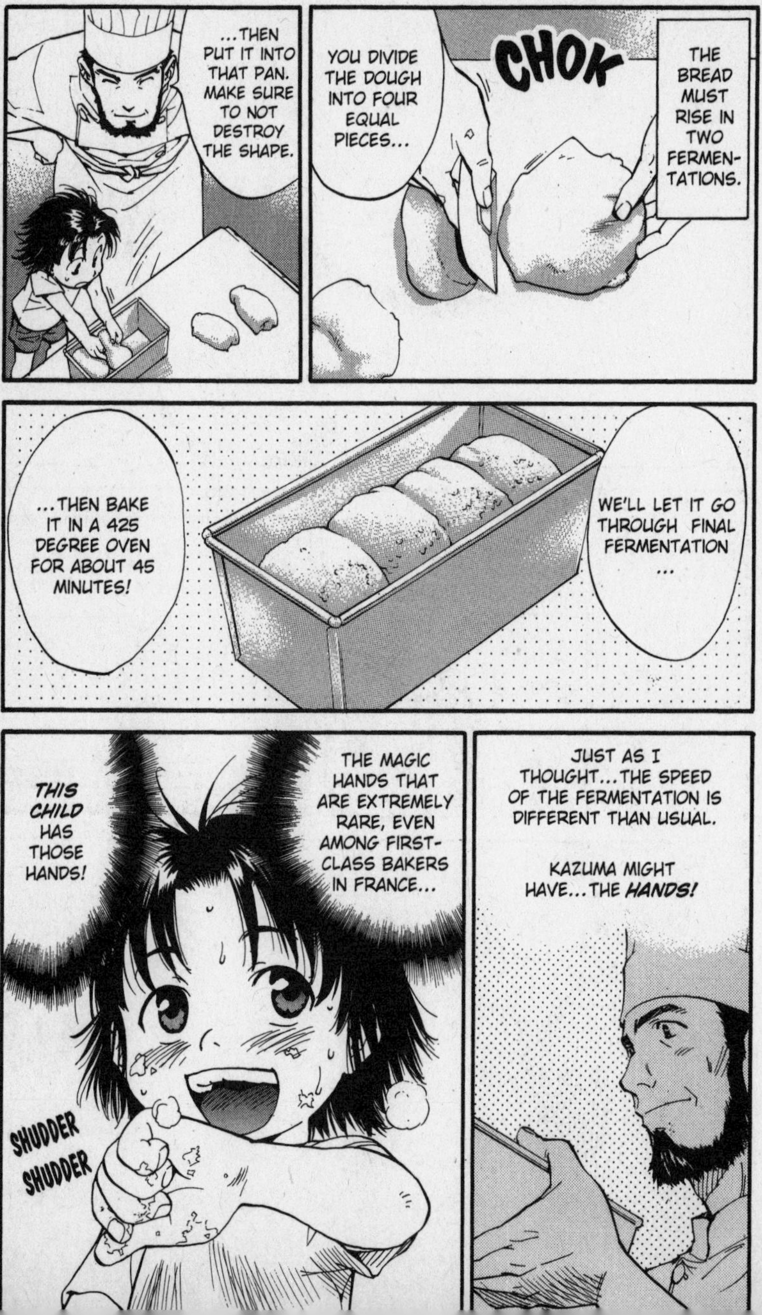
THE BREAD MUST RISE IN TWO FERMENTATIONS.
CHOK
YOU DIVIDE THE DOUGH INTO FOUR EQUAL PIECES...
...THEN PUT IT INTO THAT PAN. MAKE SURE TO NOT DESTROY THE SHAPE.
WE'LL LET IT GO THROUGH FINAL FERMENTATION ...
...THEN BAKE IT IN A 425 DEGREE OVEN FOR ABOUT 45 MINUTES!
JUST AS I THOUGHT...THE SPEED OF THE FERMENTATION IS DIFFERENT THAN USUAL.
KAZUMA MIGHT HAVE...THE *HANDS!*
THE MAGIC HANDS THAT ARE EXTREMELY RARE, EVEN AMONG FIRST-CLASS BAKERS IN FRANCE...
THIS CHILD HAS THOSE HANDS!
SHUDDER SHUDDER

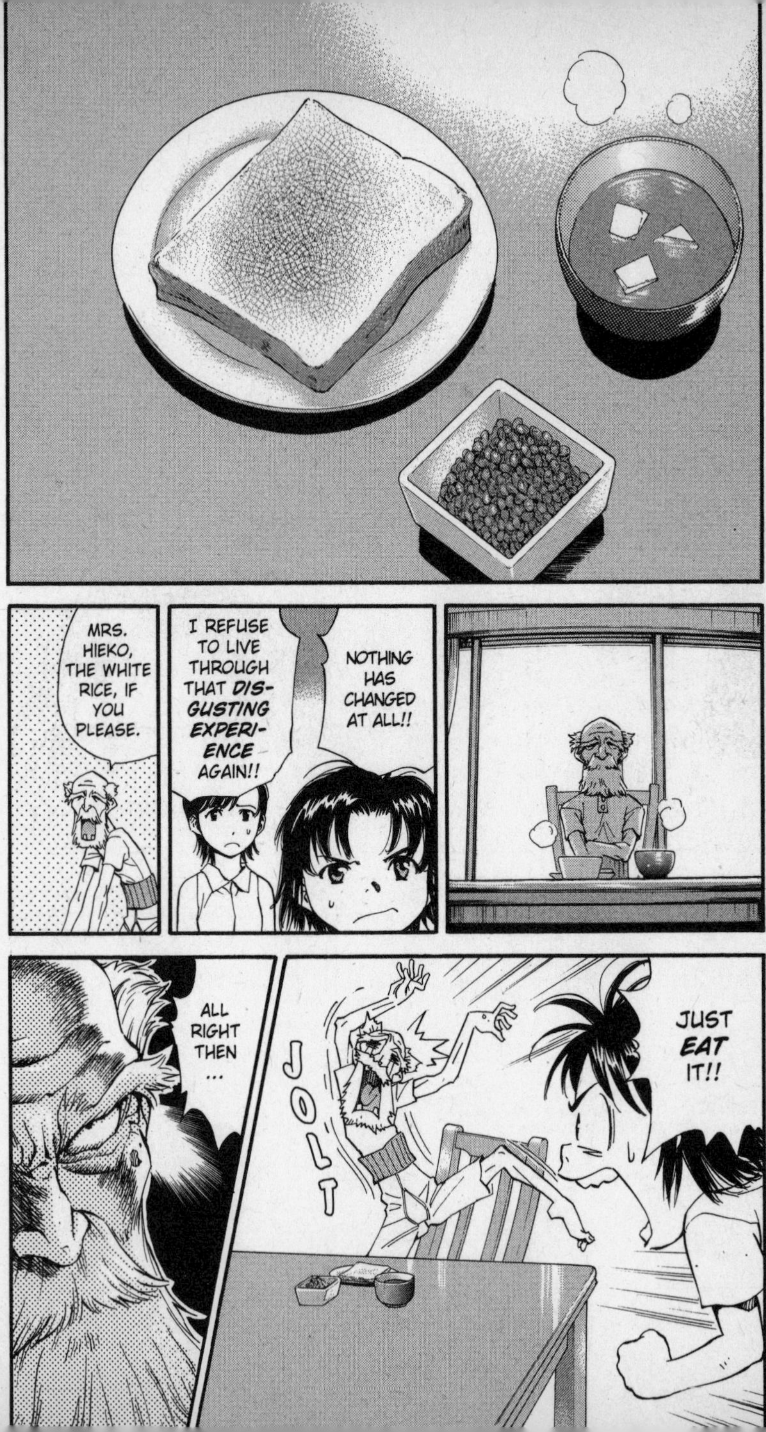
NOTHING HAS CHANGED AT ALL!!
I REFUSE TO LIVE THROUGH THAT *DISGUSTING EXPERIENCE* AGAIN!!
MRS. HIEKO, THE WHITE RICE, IF YOU PLEASE.
JUST *EAT* IT!!
JOLT
ALL RIGHT THEN ...

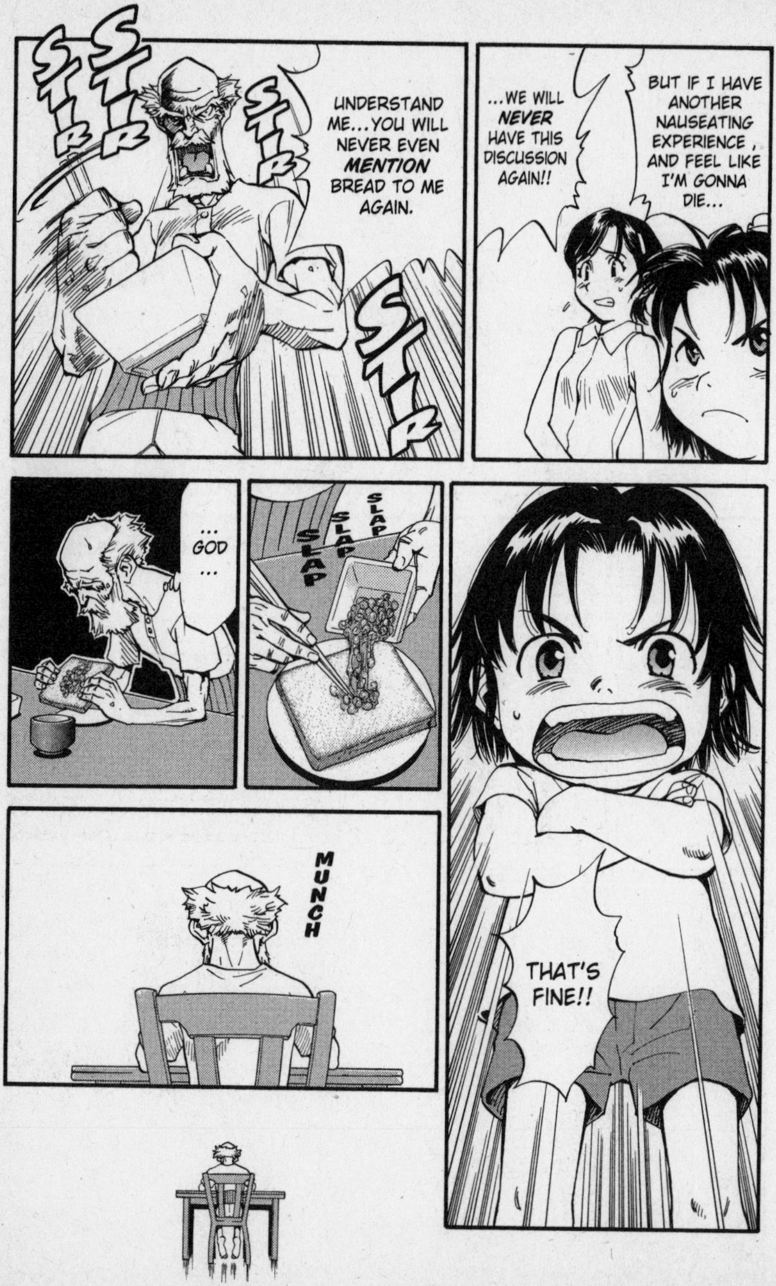
BUT IF I HAVE ANOTHER NAUSEATING EXPERIENCE , AND FEEL LIKE I'M GONNA DIE...
...WE WILL NEVER HAVE THIS DISCUSSION AGAIN!!
UNDERSTAND ME...YOU WILL NEVER EVEN MENTION BREAD TO ME AGAIN.
STIR
STIR
STIR
STIR
STIR
THAT'S FINE!!
SLAP
SLAP
SLAP
... GOD ...
MUNCH

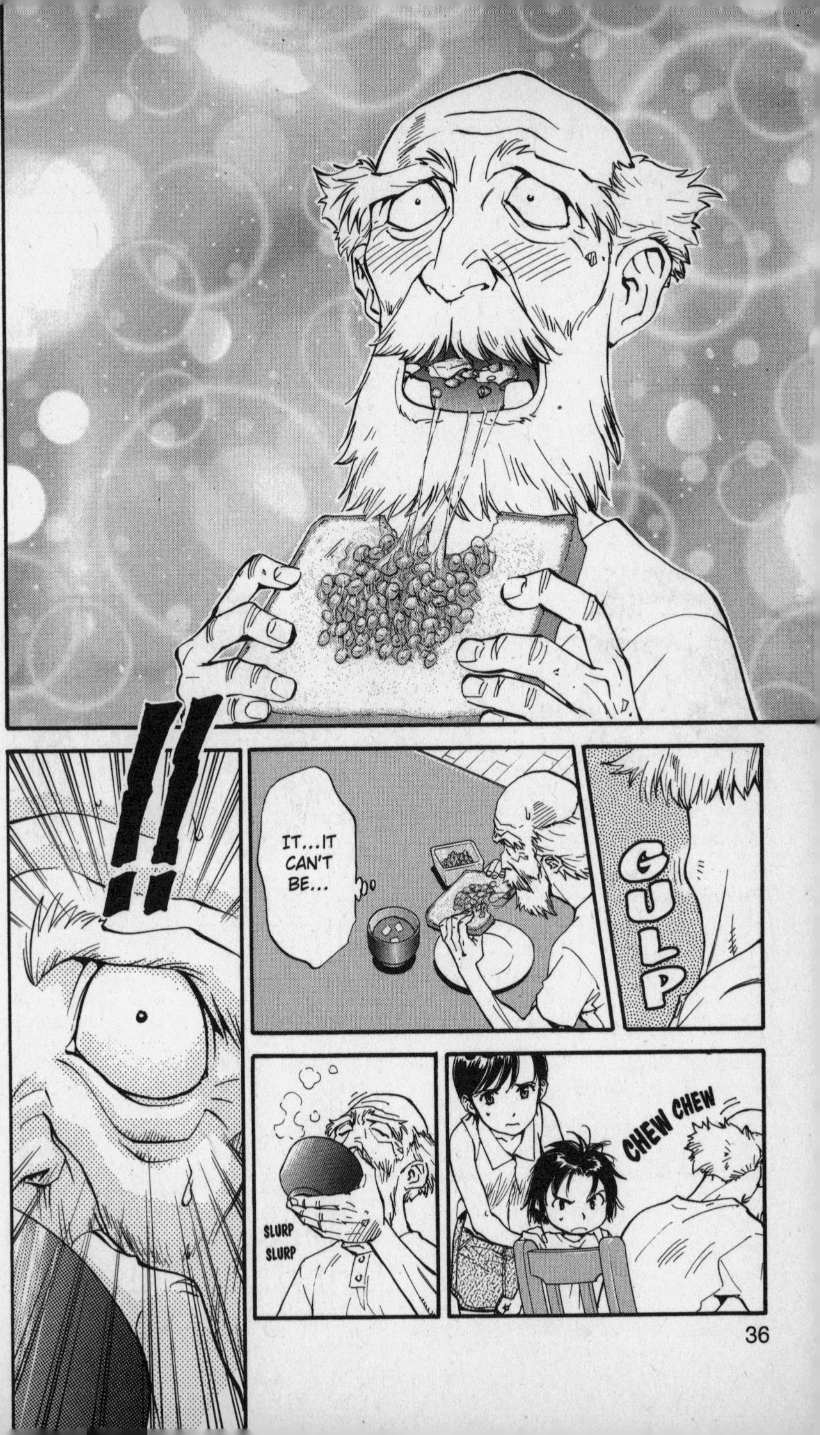
GULP
IT...IT CAN'T BE...
CHEW CHEW
SLURP SLURP
!!

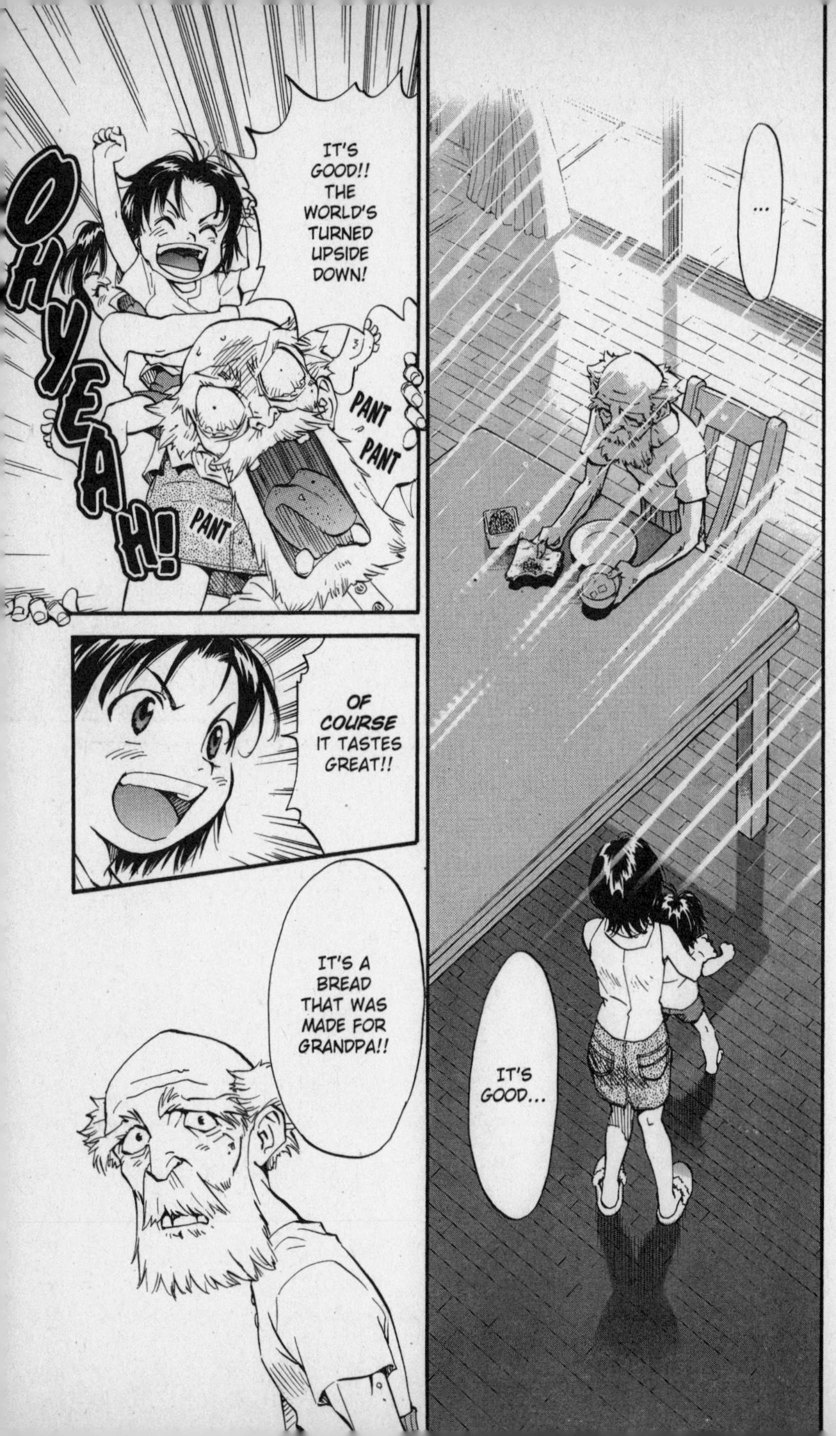
...
IT'S GOOD...
IT'S GOOD!! THE WORLD'S TURNED UPSIDE DOWN!
OHYEAAH!
PANT PANT
PANT
OF COURSE IT TASTES GREAT!!
IT'S A BREAD THAT WAS MADE FOR GRANDPA!!

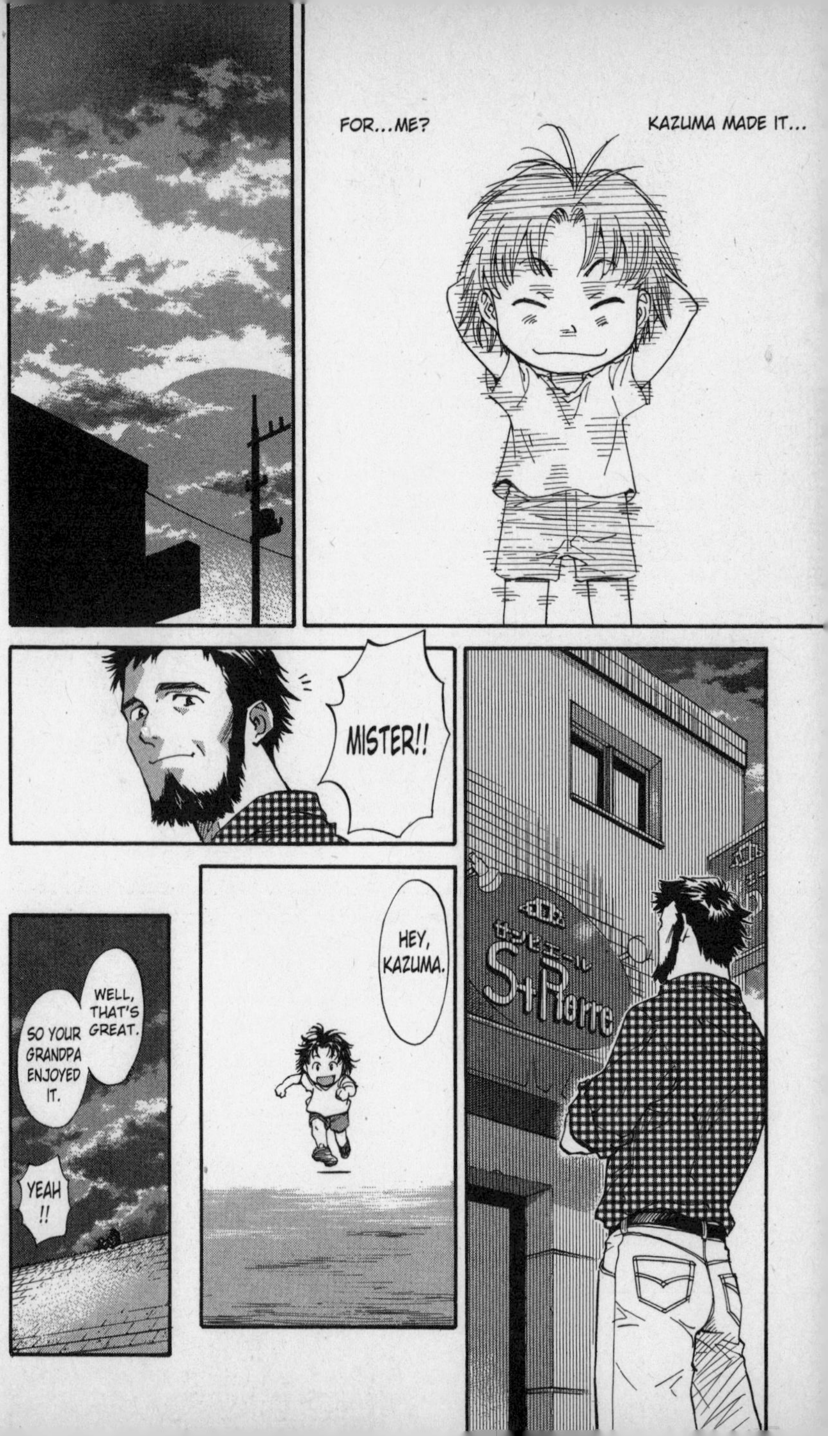
KAZUMA MADE IT...
FOR...ME?
サンピエール
St Pierre
MISTER!!
HEY, KAZUMA.
WELL, THAT'S GREAT.
SO YOUR GRANDPA ENJOYED IT.
YEAH!!

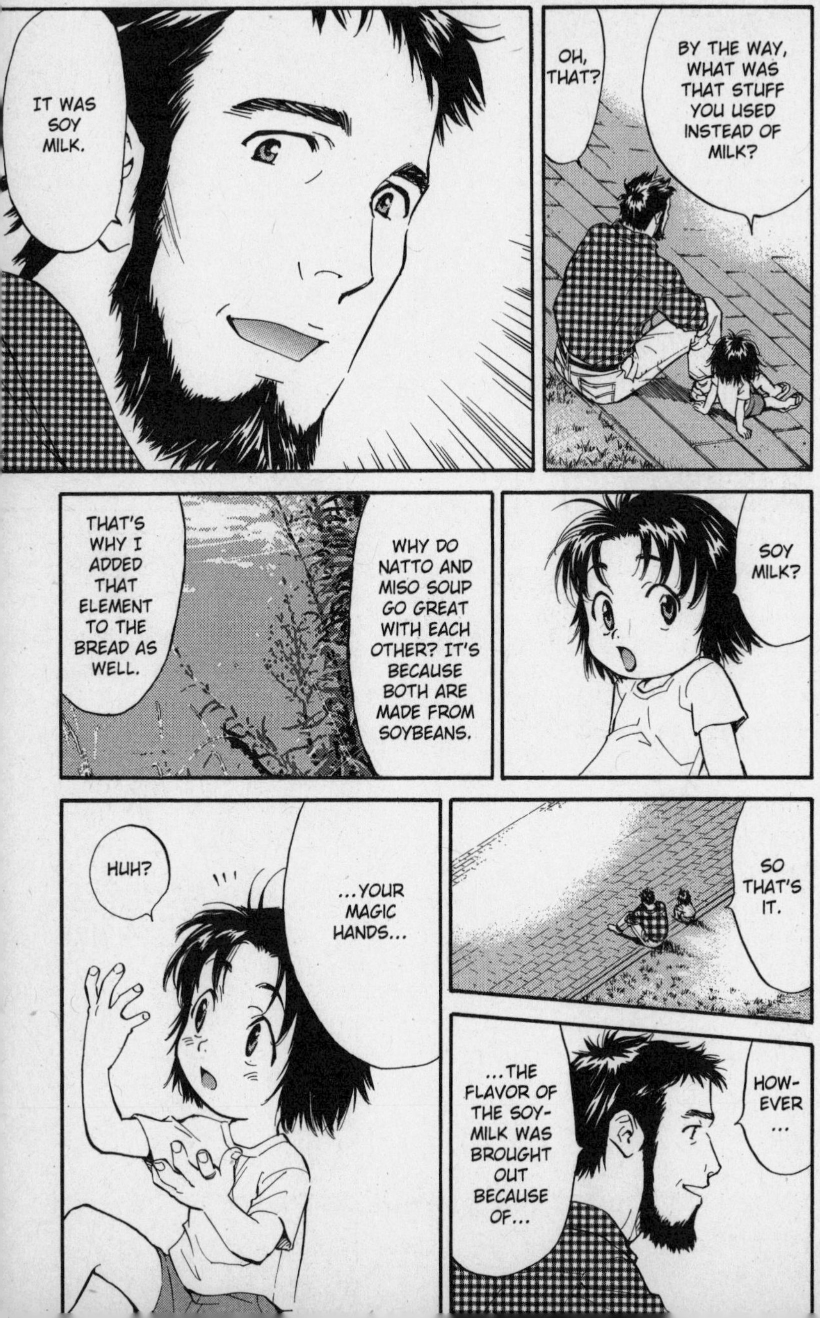
BY THE WAY, WHAT WAS THAT STUFF YOU USED INSTEAD OF MILK?
OH, THAT?
IT WAS SOY MILK.
SOY MILK?
WHY DO NATTO AND MISO SOUP GO GREAT WITH EACH OTHER? IT'S BECAUSE BOTH ARE MADE FROM SOYBEANS.
THAT'S WHY I ADDED THAT ELEMENT TO THE BREAD AS WELL.
SO THAT'S IT.
HOW-EVER...
...THE FLAVOR OF THE SOY-MILK WAS BROUGHT OUT BECAUSE OF...
...YOUR MAGIC HANDS...
HUH?

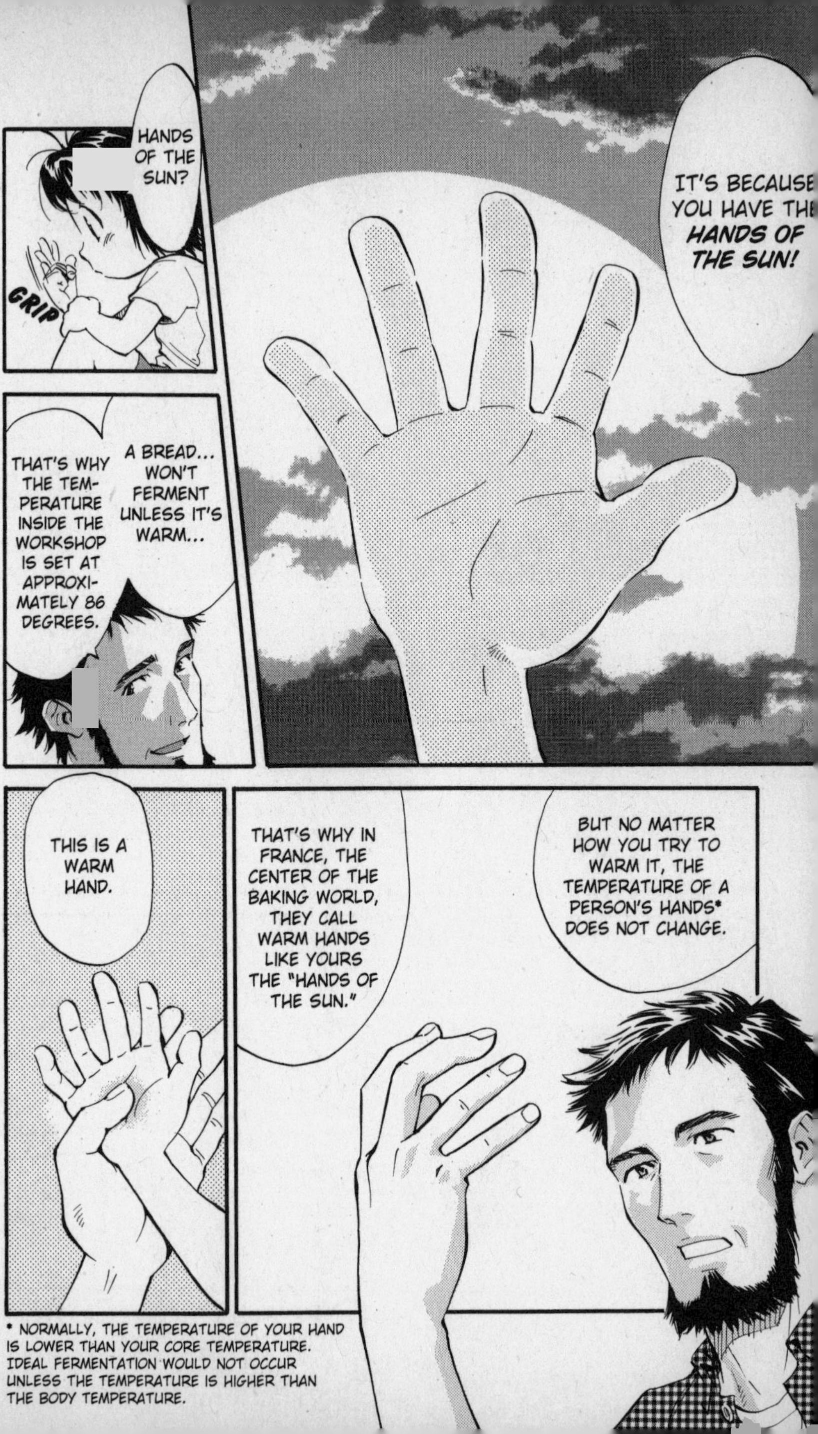
IT'S BECAUSE YOU HAVE THE *HANDS OF THE SUN!*
HANDS OF THE SUN?
GRIP
A BREAD... WON'T FERMENT UNLESS IT'S WARM...
THAT'S WHY THE TEM-PERATURE INSIDE THE WORKSHOP IS SET AT APPROXI-MATELY 86 DEGREES.
BUT NO MATTER HOW YOU TRY TO WARM IT, THE TEMPERATURE OF A PERSON'S HANDS* DOES NOT CHANGE.
THAT'S WHY IN FRANCE, THE CENTER OF THE BAKING WORLD, THEY CALL WARM HANDS LIKE YOURS THE "HANDS OF THE SUN."
THIS IS A WARM HAND.

* NORMALLY, THE TEMPERATURE OF YOUR HAND IS LOWER THAN YOUR CORE TEMPERATURE. IDEAL FERMENTATION WOULD NOT OCCUR UNLESS THE TEMPERATURE IS HIGHER THAN THE BODY TEMPERATURE.

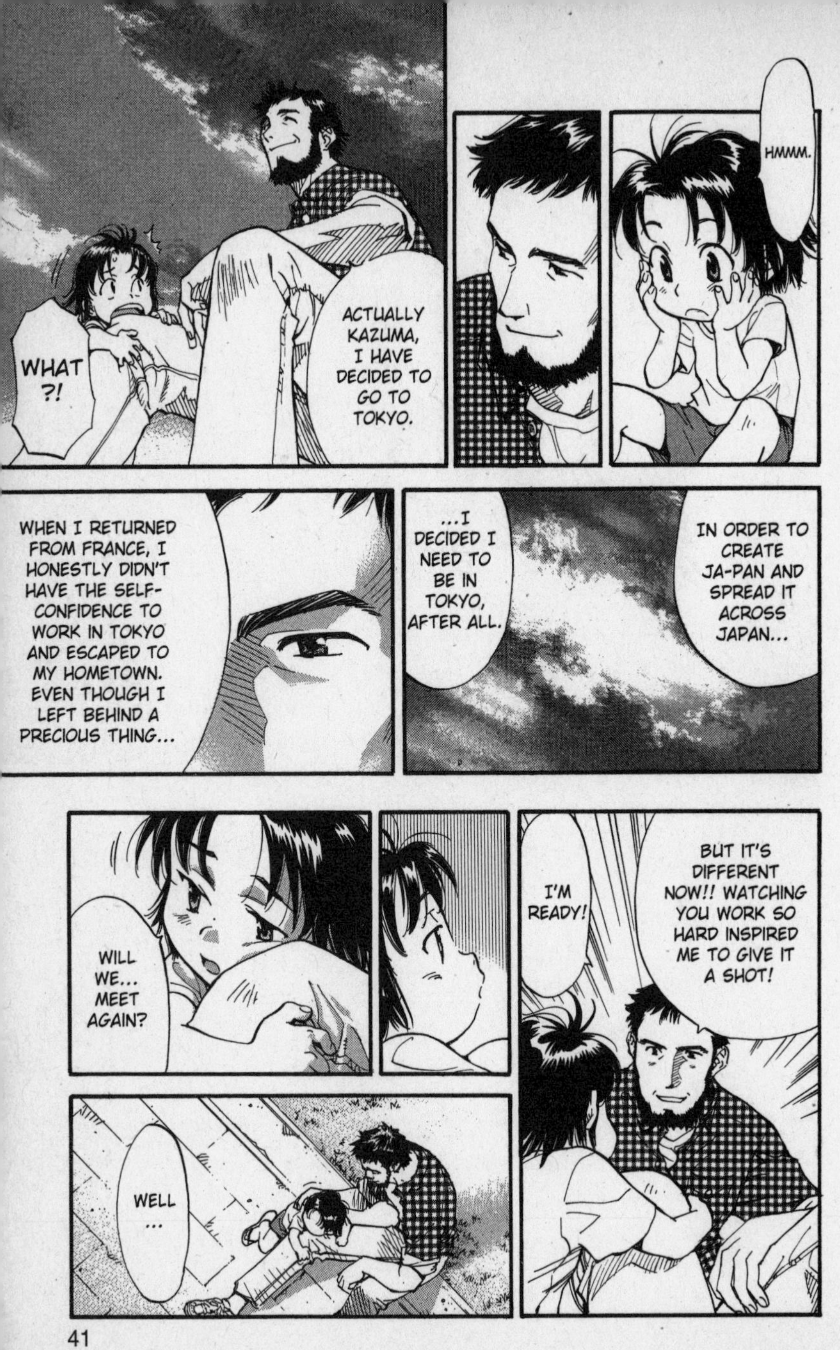
HMMM.
ACTUALLY KAZUMA, I HAVE DECIDED TO GO TO TOKYO.
WHAT ?!
IN ORDER TO CREATE JA-PAN AND SPREAD IT ACROSS JAPAN...
...I DECIDED I NEED TO BE IN TOKYO, AFTER ALL.
WHEN I RETURNED FROM FRANCE, I HONESTLY DIDN'T HAVE THE SELF-CONFIDENCE TO WORK IN TOKYO AND ESCAPED TO MY HOMETOWN. EVEN THOUGH I LEFT BEHIND A PRECIOUS THING...
BUT IT'S DIFFERENT NOW!! WATCHING YOU WORK SO HARD INSPIRED ME TO GIVE IT A SHOT!
I'M READY!
WILL WE... MEET AGAIN?
WELL ...

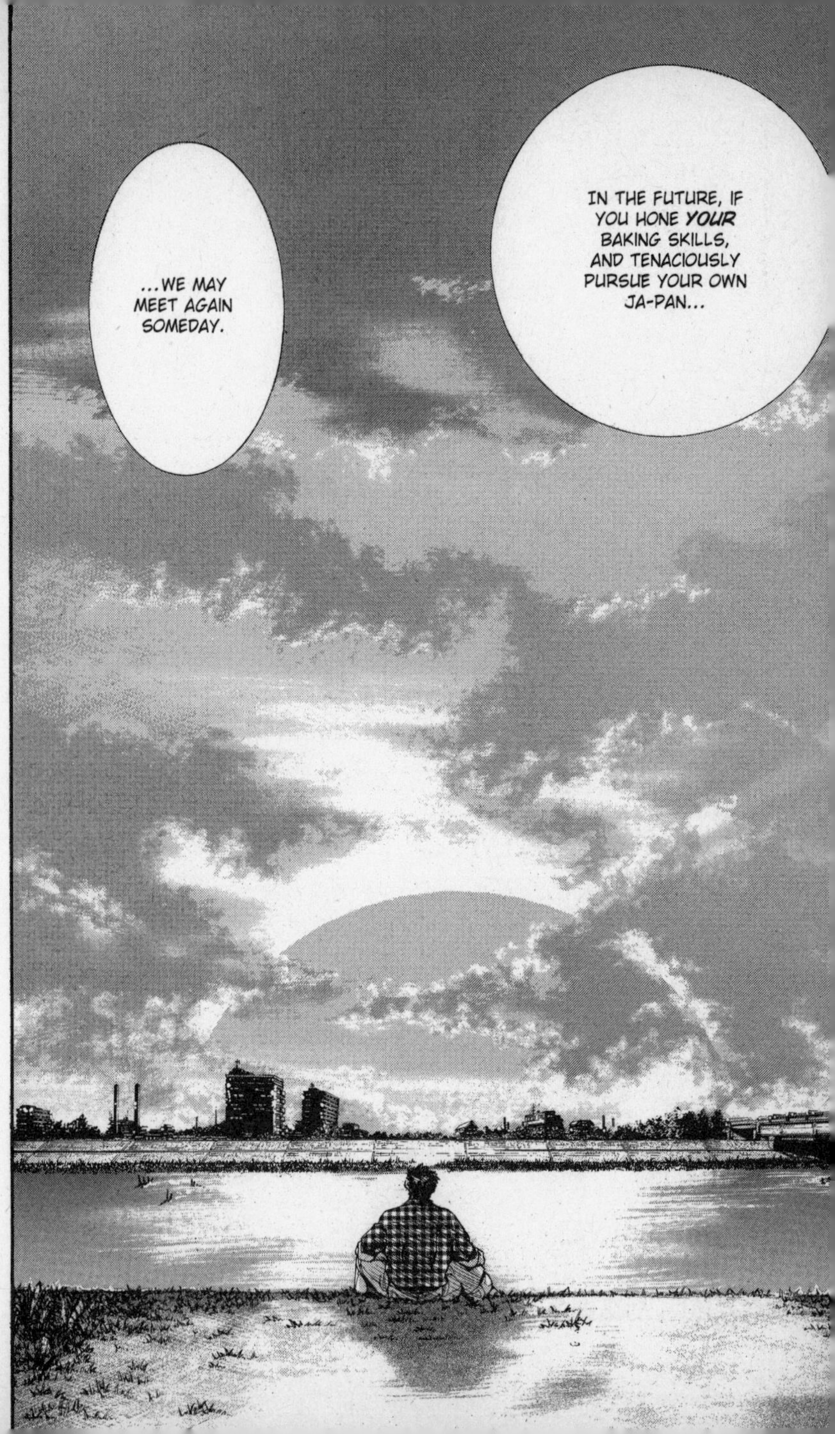
IN THE FUTURE, IF YOU HONE *YOUR* BAKING SKILLS, AND TENACIOUSLY PURSUE YOUR OWN JA-PAN...
...WE MAY MEET AGAIN SOMEDAY.

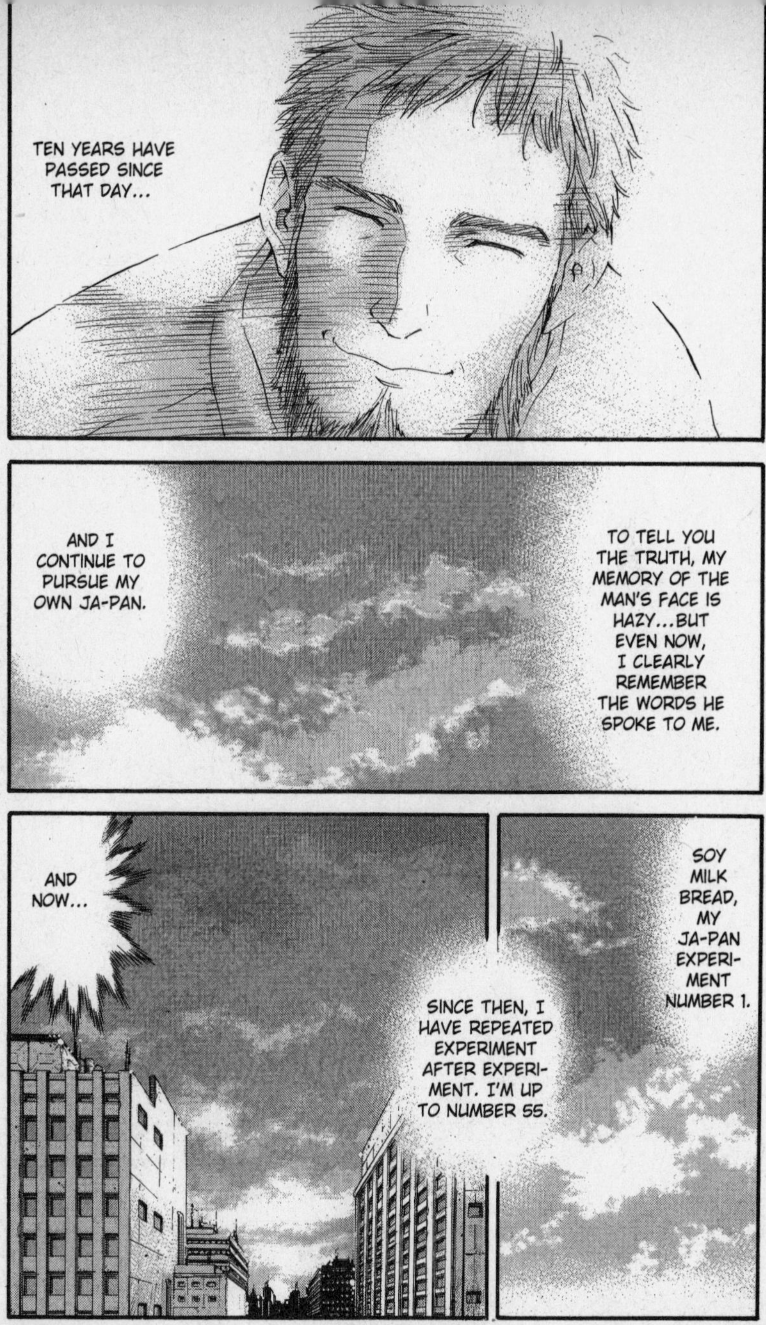
TEN YEARS HAVE PASSED SINCE THAT DAY...
TO TELL YOU THE TRUTH, MY MEMORY OF THE MAN'S FACE IS HAZY...BUT EVEN NOW, I CLEARLY REMEMBER THE WORDS HE SPOKE TO ME.
AND I CONTINUE TO PURSUE MY OWN JA-PAN.
SOY MILK BREAD, MY JA-PAN EXPERIMENT NUMBER 1.
SINCE THEN, I HAVE REPEATED EXPERIMENT AFTER EXPERIMENT. I'M UP TO NUMBER 55.
AND NOW...

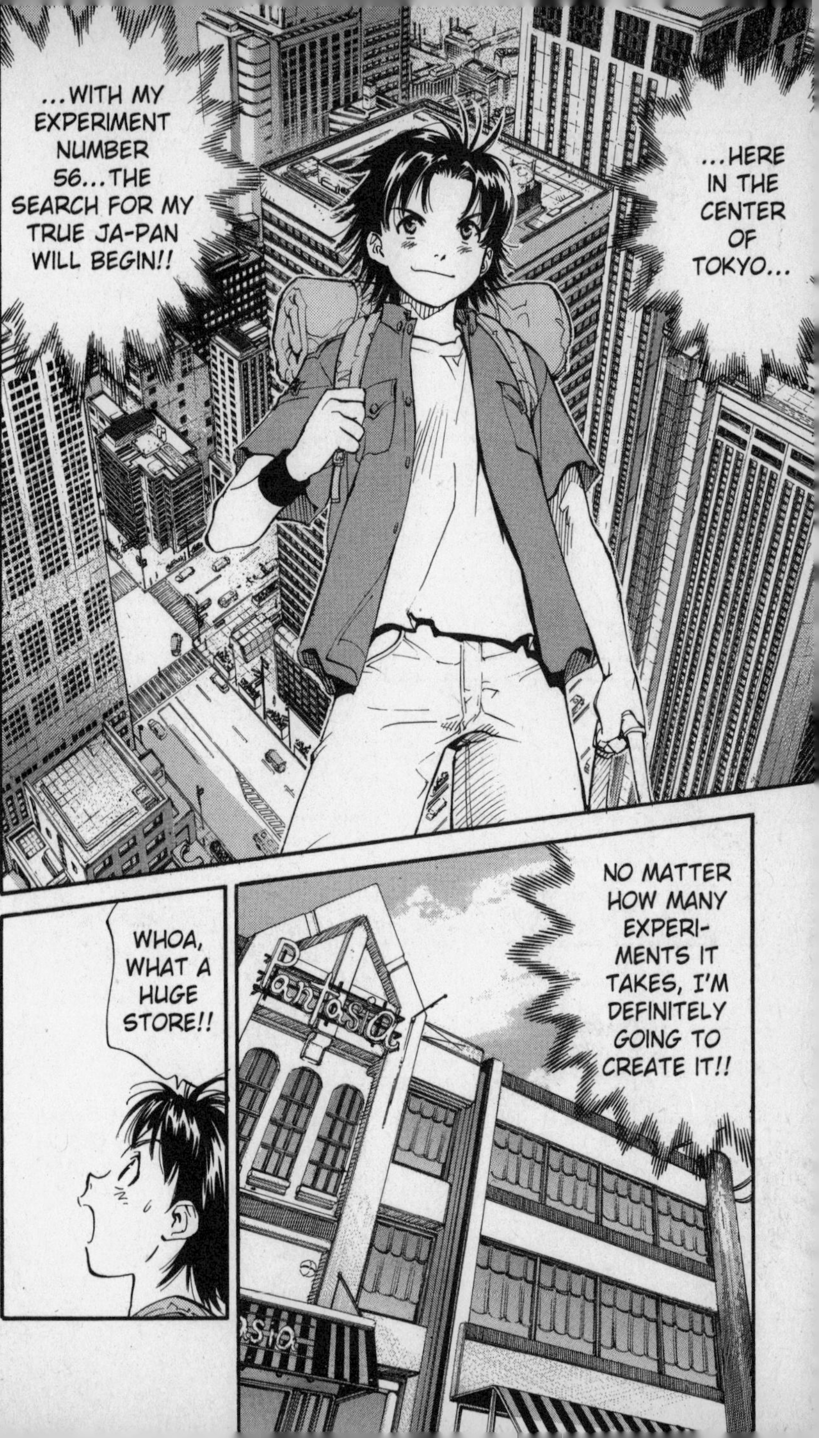
...HERE IN THE CENTER OF TOKYO...
...WITH MY EXPERIMENT NUMBER 56...THE SEARCH FOR MY TRUE JA-PAN WILL BEGIN!!
NO MATTER HOW MANY EXPERIMENTS IT TAKES, I'M DEFINITELY GOING TO CREATE IT!!
Pantasia
WHOA, WHAT A HUGE STORE!!

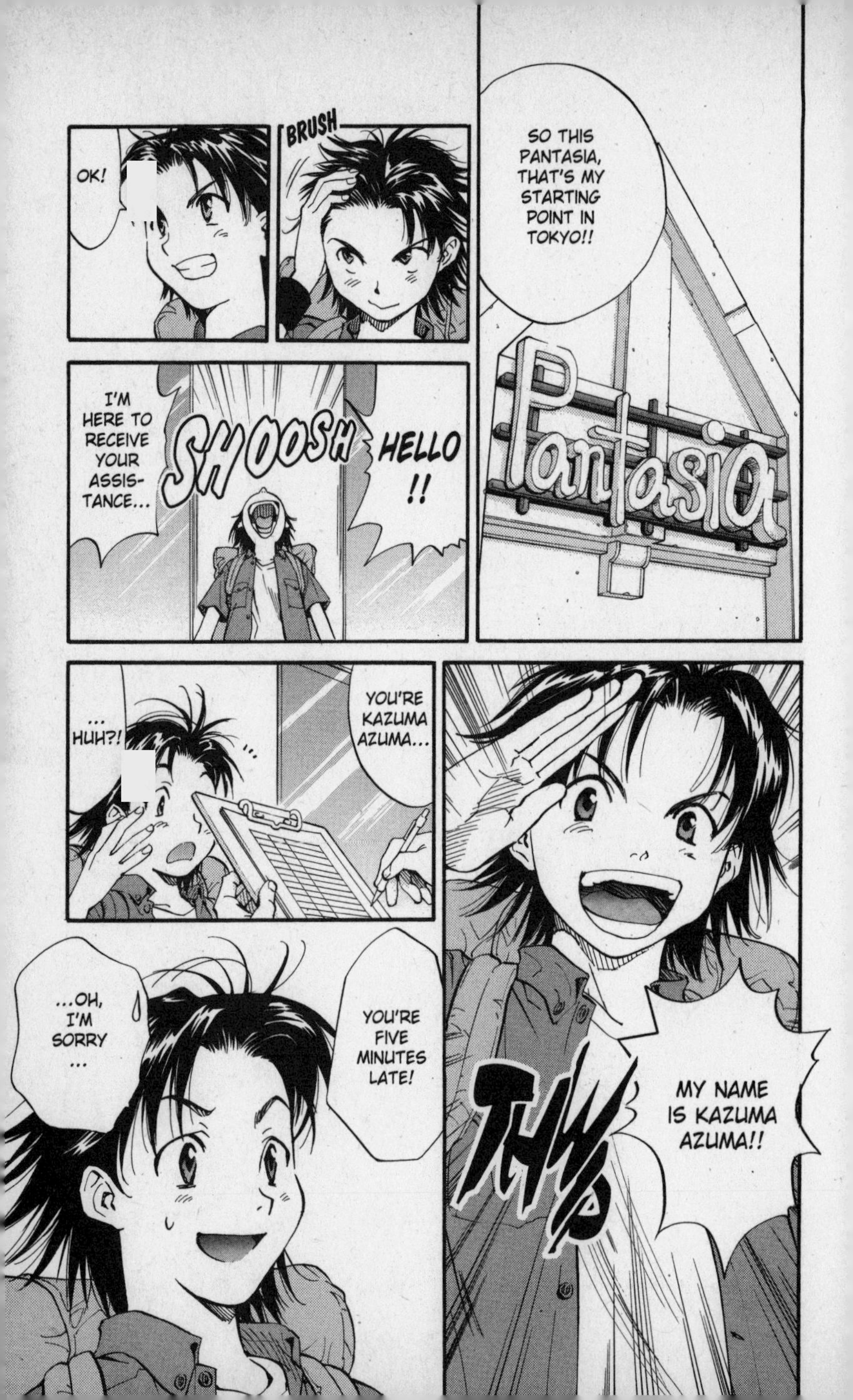
SO THIS PANTASIA, THAT'S MY STARTING POINT IN TOKYO!!
Pantasia
BRUSH
OK!
HELLO !!
SHOOSH
I'M HERE TO RECEIVE YOUR ASSIS-TANCE...
MY NAME IS KAZUMA AZUMA!!
YOU'RE KAZUMA AZUMA...
... HUH?!
YOU'RE FIVE MINUTES LATE!
...OH, I'M SORRY ...

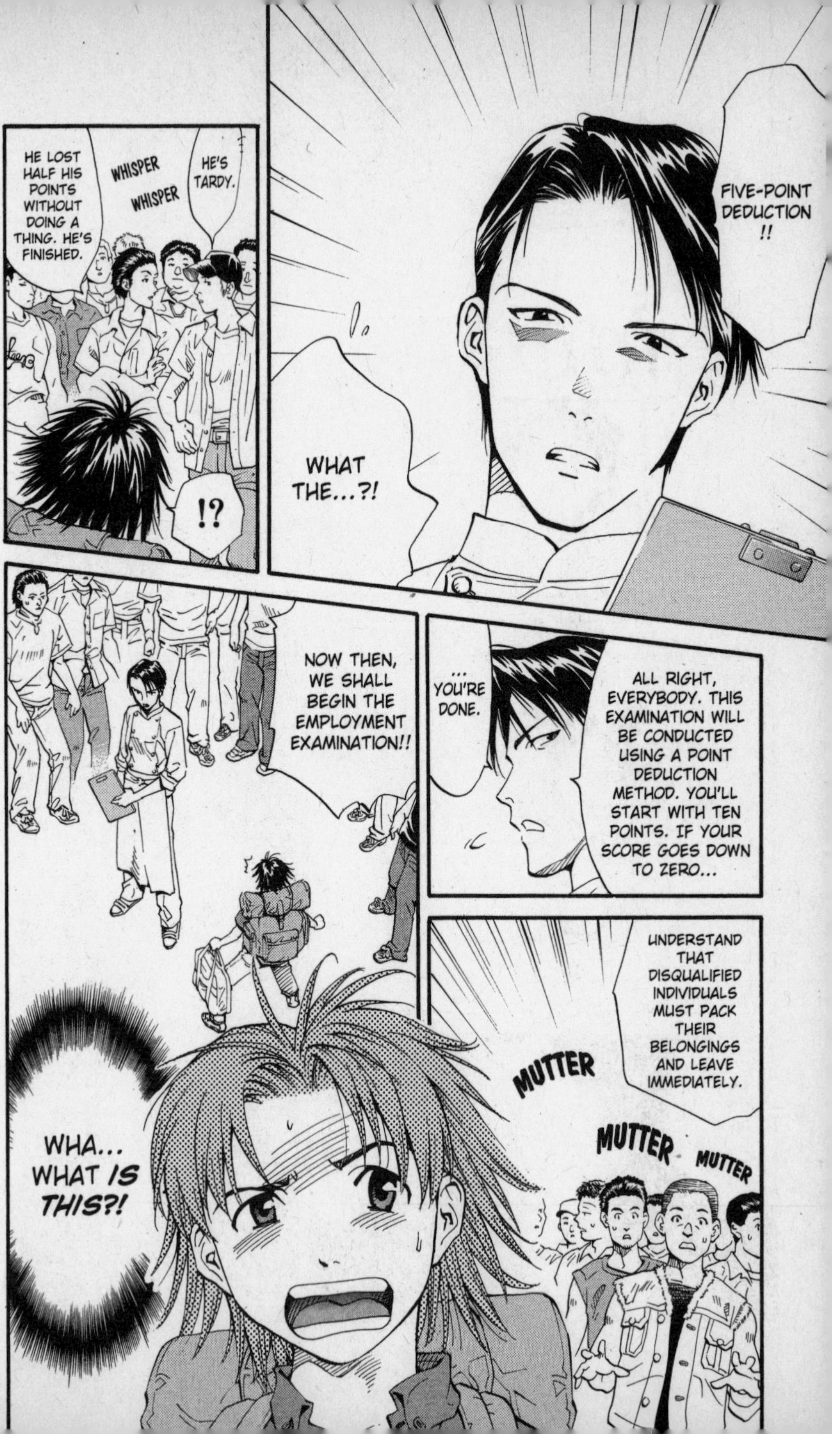
FIVE-POINT DEDUCTION !!
WHAT THE...?!
HE'S TARDY.
WHISPER
WHISPER
HE LOST HALF HIS POINTS WITHOUT DOING A THING. HE'S FINISHED.
!?
ALL RIGHT, EVERYBODY. THIS EXAMINATION WILL BE CONDUCTED USING A POINT DEDUCTION METHOD. YOU'LL START WITH TEN POINTS. IF YOUR SCORE GOES DOWN TO ZERO...
... YOU'RE DONE.
UNDERSTAND THAT DISQUALIFIED INDIVIDUALS MUST PACK THEIR BELONGINGS AND LEAVE IMMEDIATELY.
MUTTER
MUTTER
MUTTER
NOW THEN, WE SHALL BEGIN THE EMPLOYMENT EXAMINATION!!
WHA... WHAT *IS* *THIS*?!

Story 2: It Came Down!

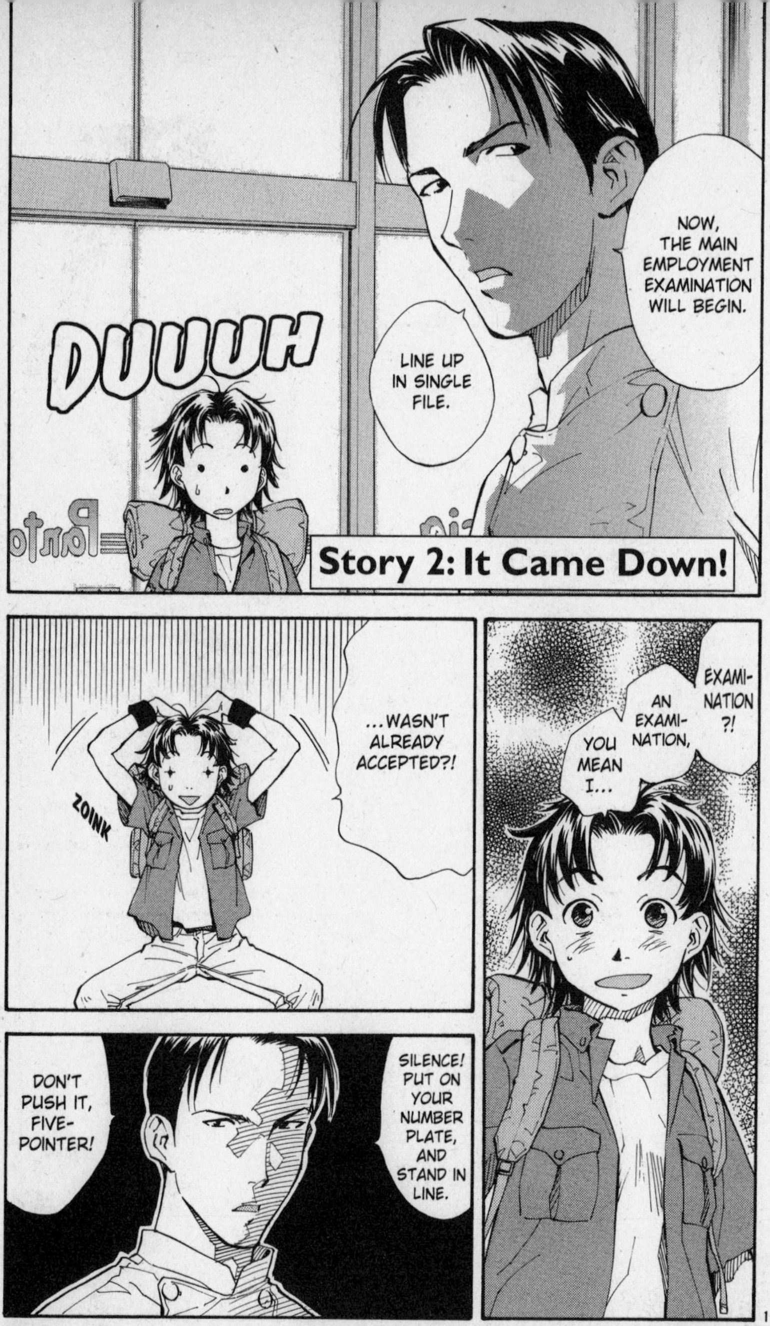
NOW, THE MAIN EMPLOYMENT EXAMINATION WILL BEGIN.
LINE UP IN SINGLE FILE.
DUUUH
EXAMI-NATION?!
AN EXAMI-NATION,
YOU MEAN I...
...WASN'T ALREADY ACCEPTED?!
ZOINK
SILENCE! PUT ON YOUR NUMBER PLATE, AND STAND IN LINE.
DON'T PUSH IT, FIVE-POINTER!

Story 2: It Came Down!

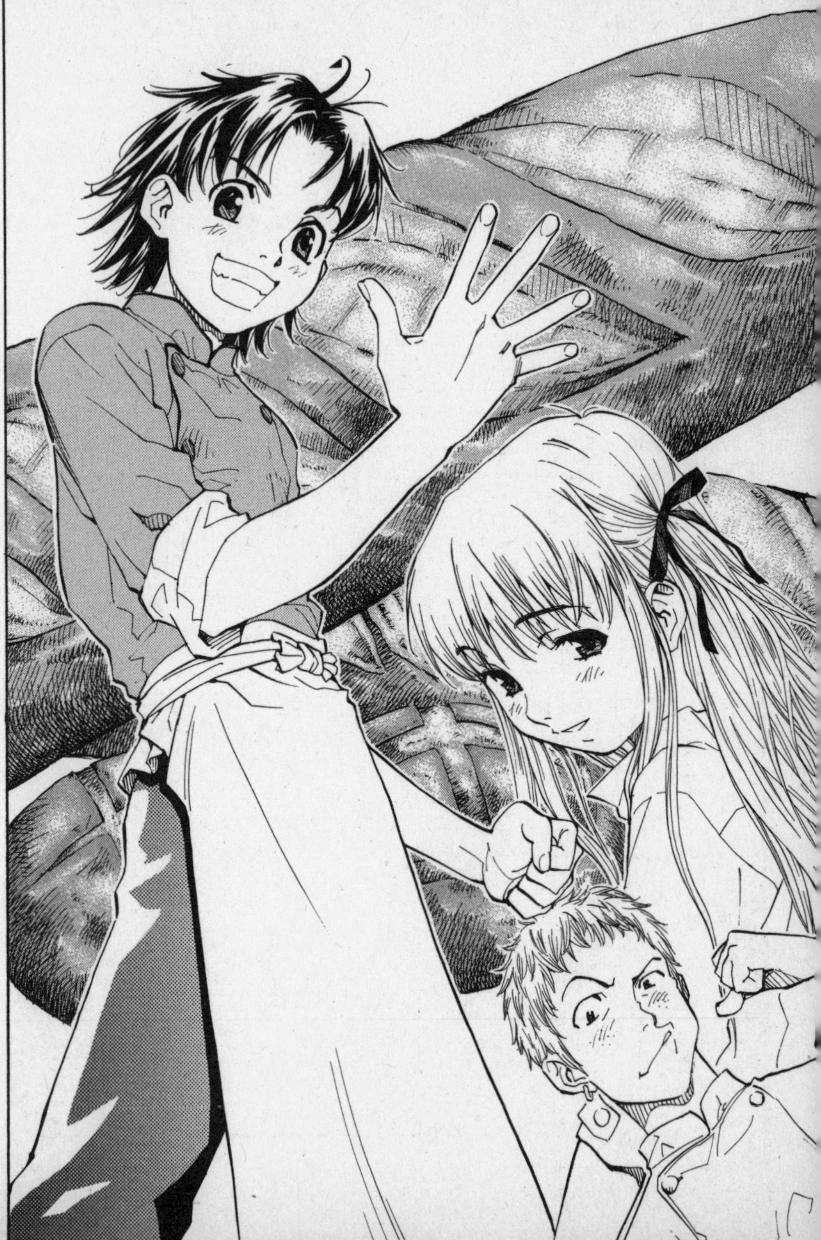

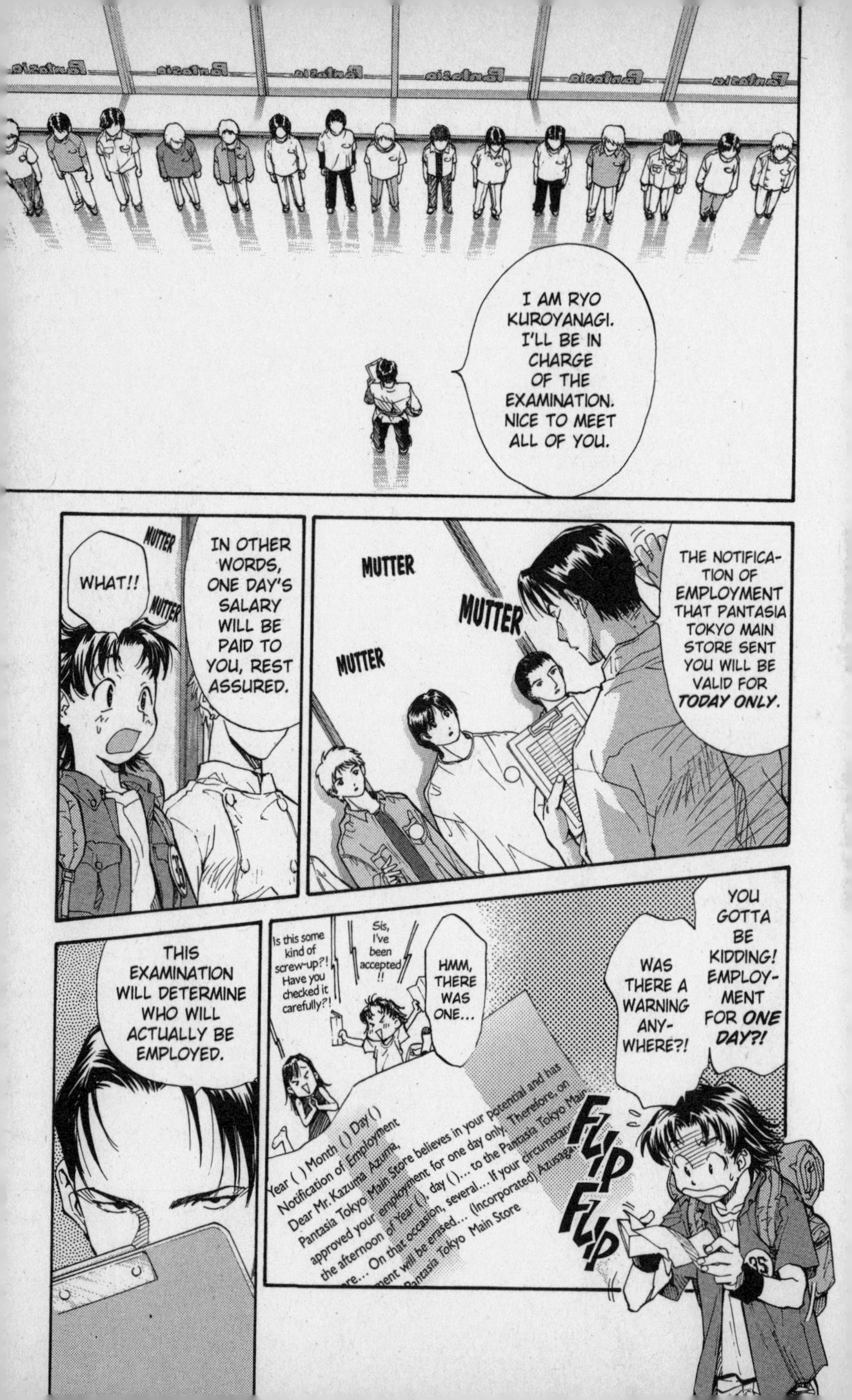
I AM RYO KUROYANAGI. I'LL BE IN CHARGE OF THE EXAMINATION. NICE TO MEET ALL OF YOU.
MUTTER
MUTTER
MUTTER
THE NOTIFICATION OF EMPLOYMENT THAT PANTASIA TOKYO MAIN STORE SENT YOU WILL BE VALID FOR TODAY ONLY.
IN OTHER WORDS, ONE DAY'S SALARY WILL BE PAID TO YOU, REST ASSURED.
MUTTER
MUTTER
WHAT!!
YOU GOTTA BE KIDDING! EMPLOYMENT FOR ONE DAY?!
WAS THERE A WARNING ANYWHERE?!
FLIP FLIP
HMM, THERE WAS ONE...
Sis, I've been accepted!!
Is this some kind of screw-up?! Have you checked it carefully?!
Year ( ) Month ( ) Day ( )
Notification of Employment
Dear Mr. Kazuma Azuma,
Pantasia Tokyo Main Store believes in your potential and has approved your employment for one day only. Therefore, on the afternoon of Year ( ), day ( )... to the Pantasia Tokyo Main
On that occasion, several... If your circumstan
ment will be erased... (Incorporated) Azusaga
Pantasia Tokyo Main Store
THIS EXAMINATION WILL DETERMINE WHO WILL ACTUALLY BE EMPLOYED.

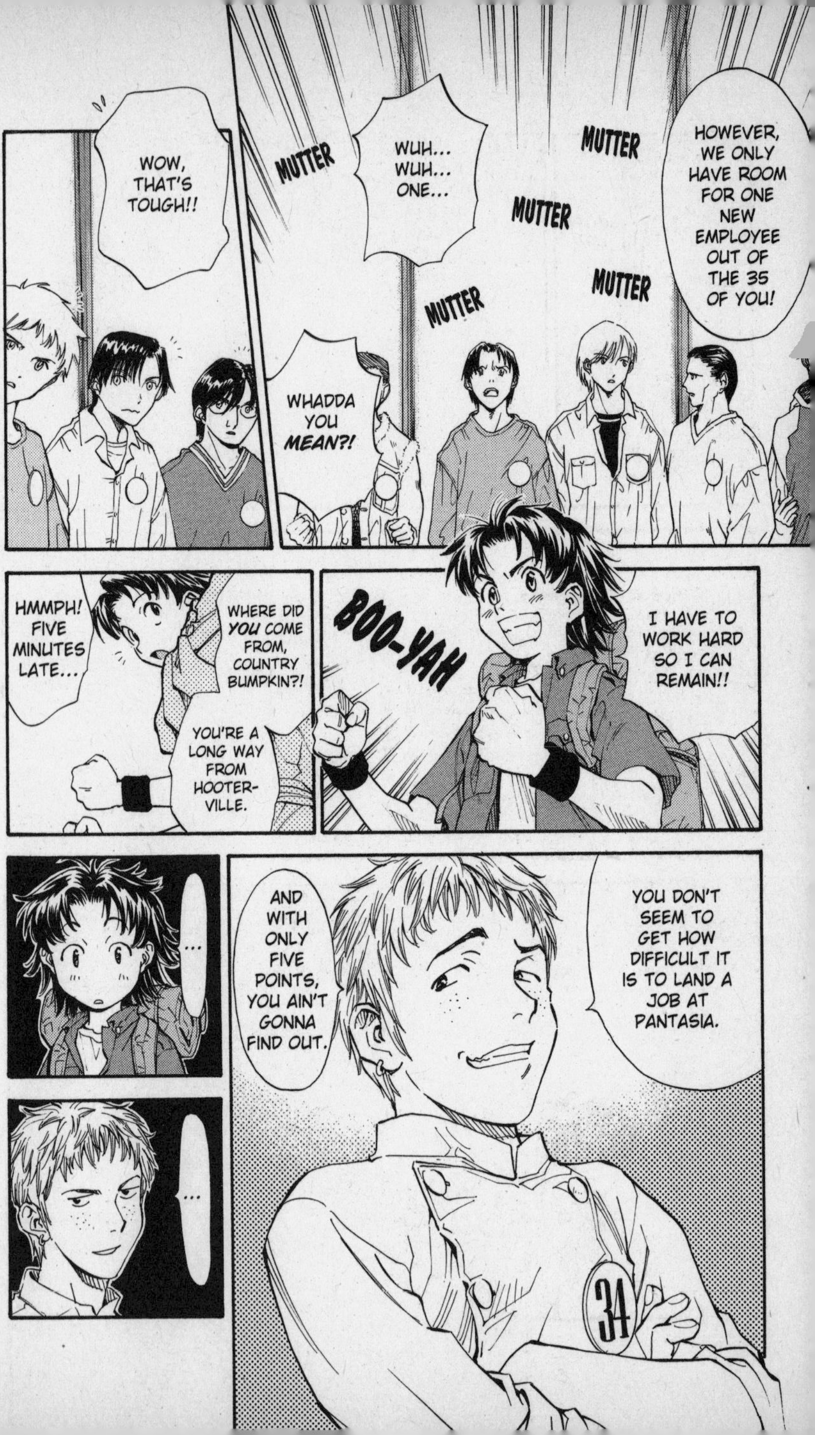
HOWEVER, WE ONLY HAVE ROOM FOR ONE NEW EMPLOYEE OUT OF THE 35 OF YOU!
MUTTER
MUTTER
MUTTER
WUH... WUH... ONE...
MUTTER
MUTTER
WHADDA YOU *MEAN?!*
WOW, THAT'S TOUGH!!
I HAVE TO WORK HARD SO I CAN REMAIN!!
BOO-YAH
WHERE DID *YOU* COME FROM, COUNTRY BUMPKIN?!
HMMPH! FIVE MINUTES LATE...
YOU'RE A LONG WAY FROM HOOTER-VILLE.
YOU DON'T SEEM TO GET HOW DIFFICULT IT IS TO LAND A JOB AT PANTASIA.
AND WITH ONLY FIVE POINTS, YOU AIN'T GONNA FIND OUT.
34
...
...

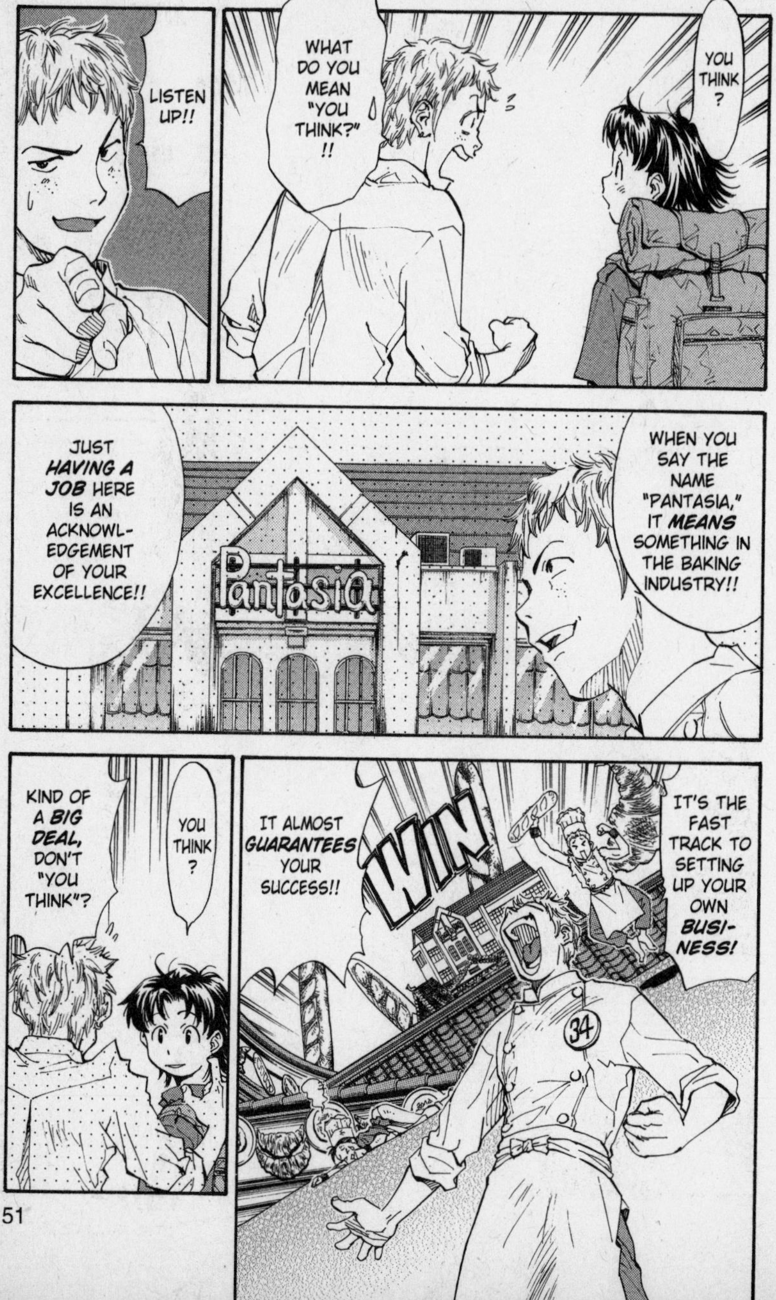
YOU THINK?
WHAT DO YOU MEAN "YOU THINK?"!!
LISTEN UP!!
WHEN YOU SAY THE NAME "PANTASIA," IT **MEANS** SOMETHING IN THE BAKING INDUSTRY!!
JUST **HAVING A JOB** HERE IS AN ACKNOWLEDGEMENT OF YOUR EXCELLENCE!!
Pantasia
IT'S THE FAST TRACK TO SETTING UP YOUR OWN **BUSINESS!**
WIN
IT ALMOST **GUARANTEES** YOUR SUCCESS!!
34
YOU THINK?
KIND OF A **BIG DEAL,** DON'T "YOU THINK"?

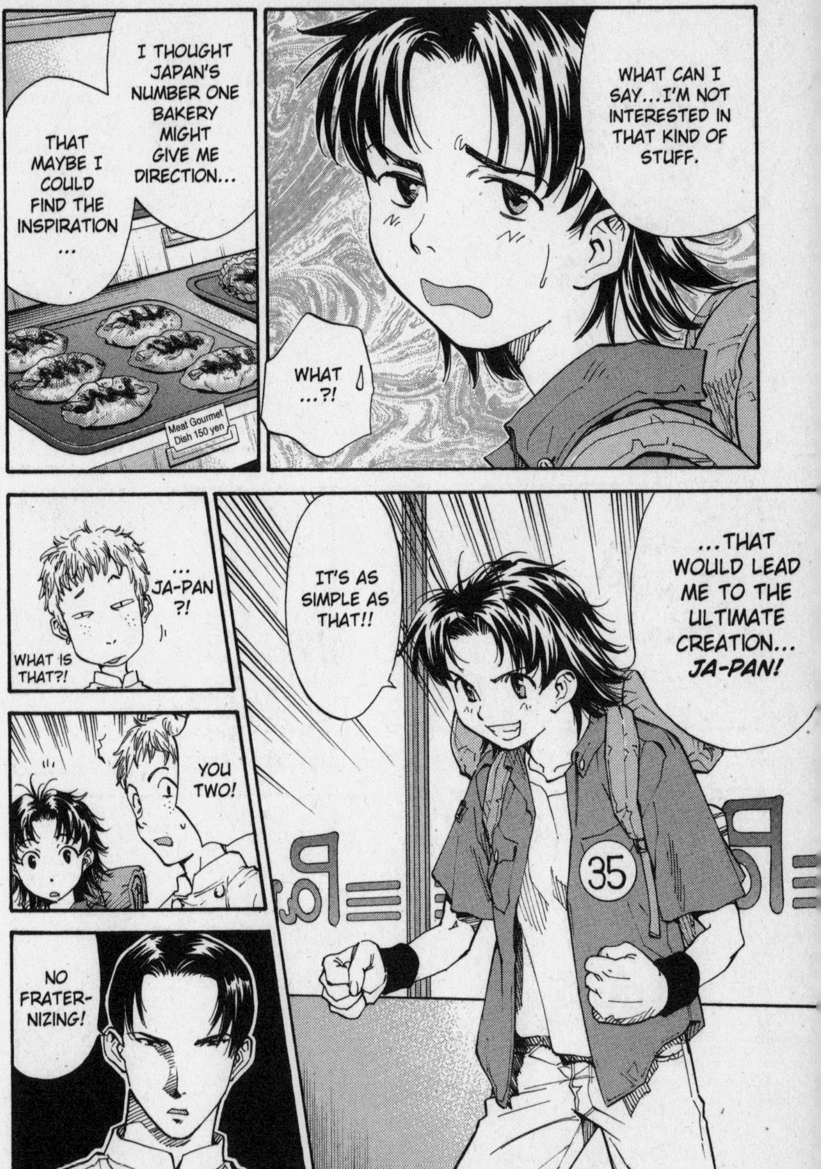
WHAT CAN I SAY...I'M NOT INTERESTED IN THAT KIND OF STUFF.
WHAT ...?!
I THOUGHT JAPAN'S NUMBER ONE BAKERY MIGHT GIVE ME DIRECTION...
THAT MAYBE I COULD FIND THE INSPIRATION ...
Meat Gourmet Dish 150 yen
...THAT WOULD LEAD ME TO THE ULTIMATE CREATION... *JA-PAN!*
IT'S AS SIMPLE AS THAT!!
35
... JA-PAN ?!
WHAT IS THAT?!
YOU TWO!
NO FRATER-NIZING!

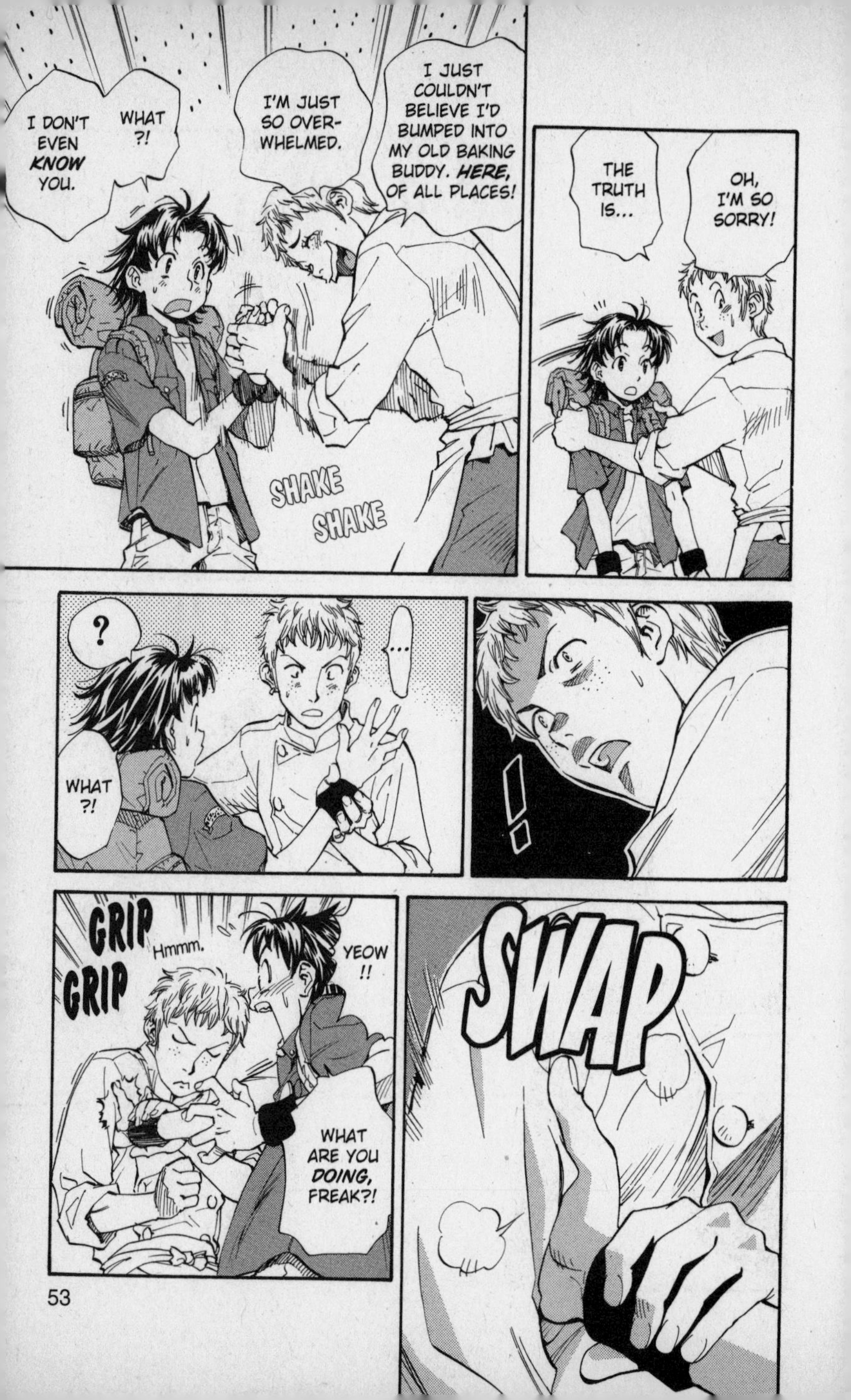
OH, I'M SO SORRY!
THE TRUTH IS...
I JUST COULDN'T BELIEVE I'D BUMPED INTO MY OLD BAKING BUDDY. *HERE*, OF ALL PLACES!
I'M JUST SO OVER-WHELMED.
WHAT?!
I DON'T EVEN *KNOW* YOU.
SHAKE SHAKE
!
...
?
WHAT?!
SWAP
YEOW!!
Hmmm.
GRIP GRIP
WHAT ARE YOU *DOING*, FREAK?!

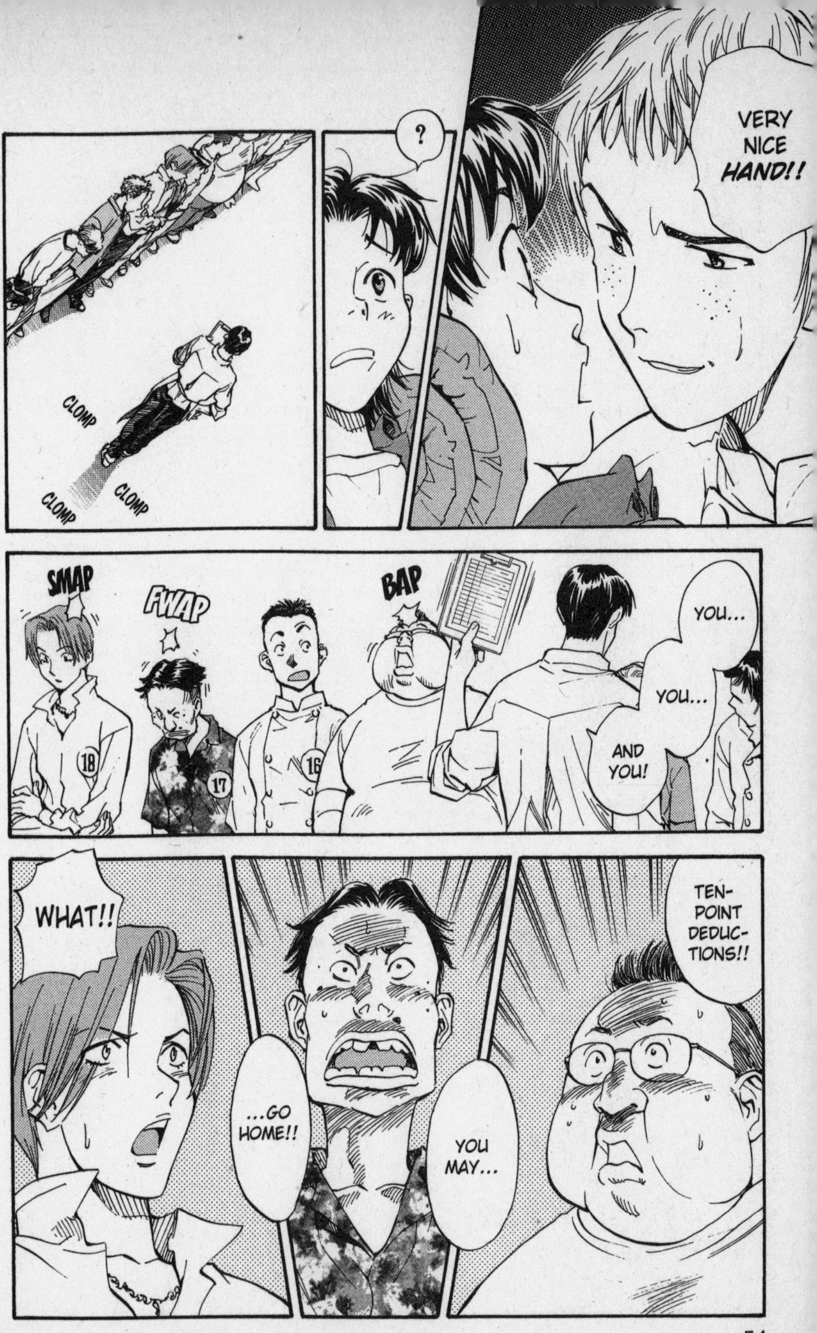
VERY NICE HAND!!
?
CLOMP
CLOMP
CLOMP
YOU...
YOU...
AND YOU!
BAP
FWAP
SMAP
TEN-POINT DEDUC-TIONS!!
YOU MAY...
...GO HOME!!
WHAT!!

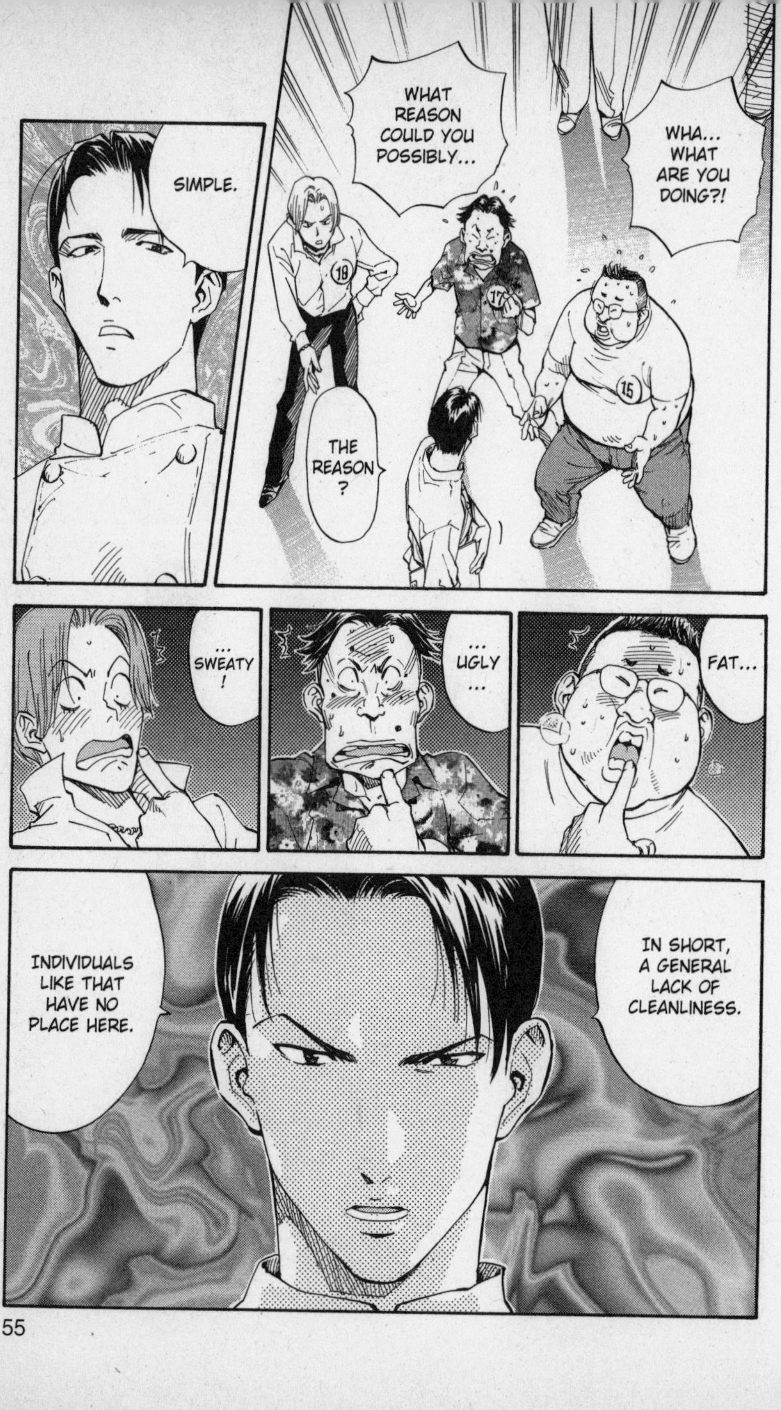
WHA... WHAT ARE YOU DOING?!
WHAT REASON COULD YOU POSSIBLY...
THE REASON?
SIMPLE.
FAT...
... UGLY ...
... SWEATY!
IN SHORT, A GENERAL LACK OF CLEANLINESS.
INDIVIDUALS LIKE THAT HAVE NO PLACE HERE.

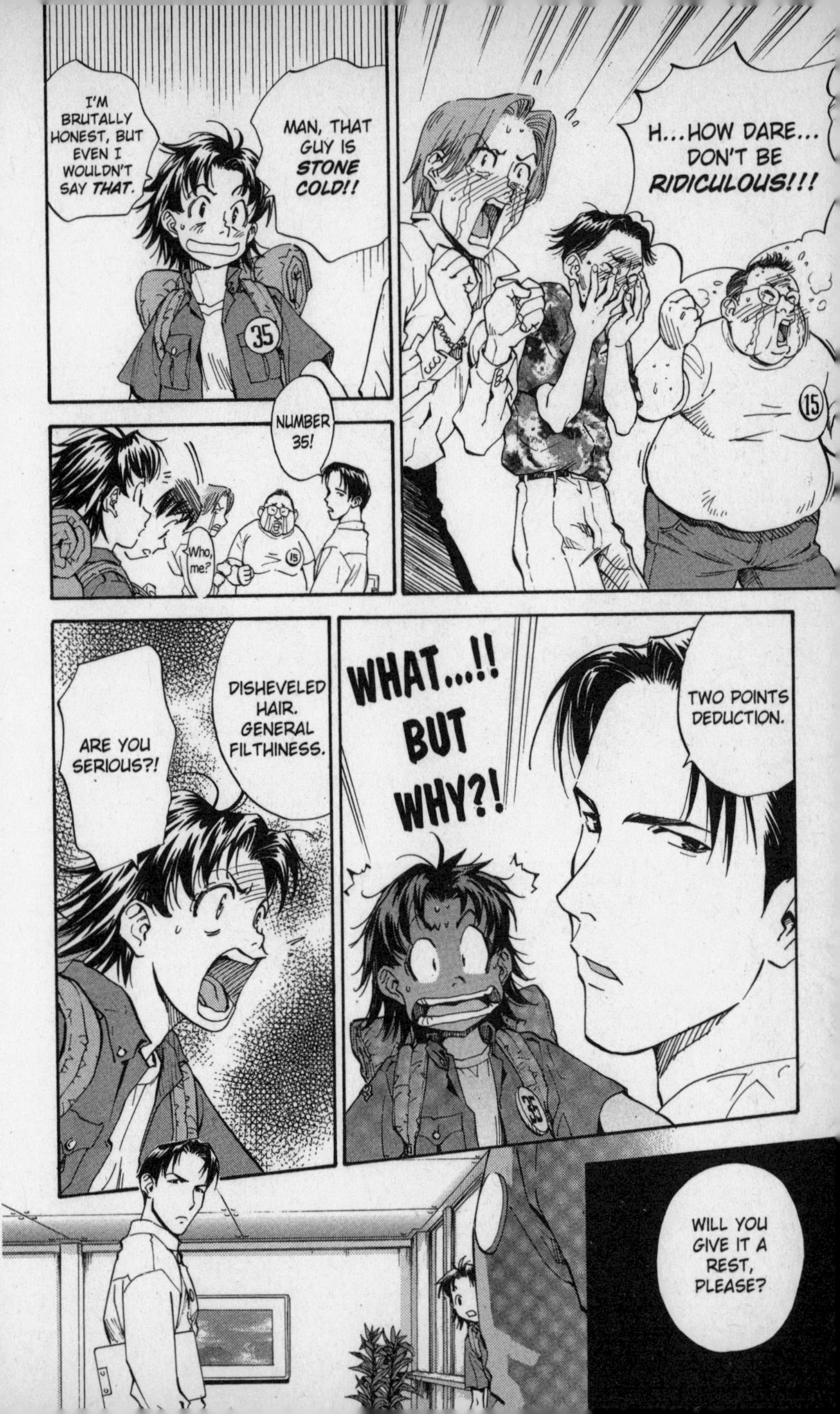
H...HOW DARE... DON'T BE RIDICULOUS!!!
MAN, THAT GUY IS STONE COLD!!
I'M BRUTALLY HONEST, BUT EVEN I WOULDN'T SAY THAT.
NUMBER 35!
Who, me?
TWO POINTS DEDUCTION.
WHAT...!! BUT WHY?!
DISHEVELED HAIR. GENERAL FILTHINESS.
ARE YOU SERIOUS?!
WILL YOU GIVE IT A REST, PLEASE?

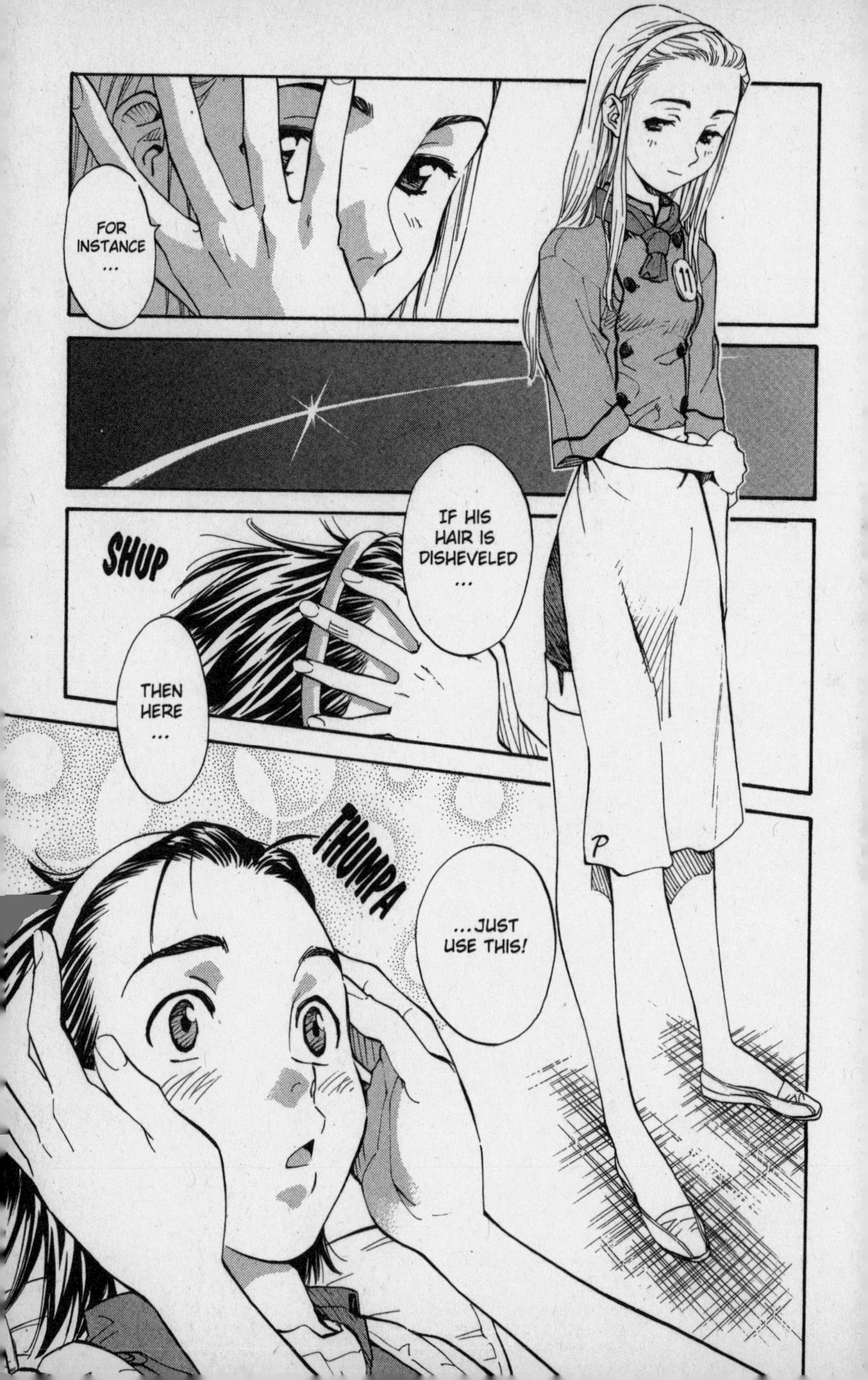
FOR INSTANCE ...
IF HIS HAIR IS DISHEVELED ...
THEN HERE ...
SHUP
...JUST USE THIS!
THUMPA

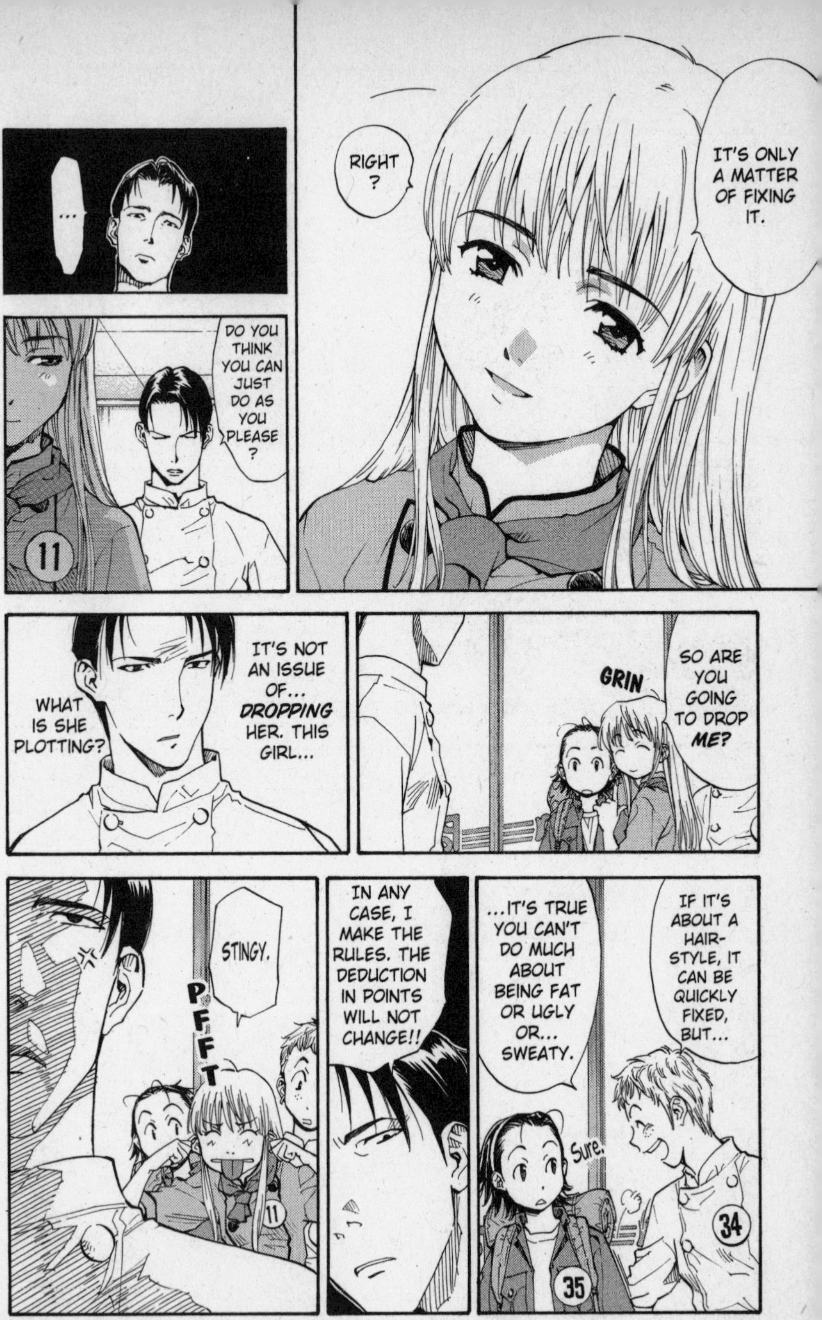
IT'S ONLY A MATTER OF FIXING IT.
RIGHT?
...
DO YOU THINK YOU CAN JUST DO AS YOU PLEASE?
GRIN
SO ARE YOU GOING TO DROP *ME?*
IT'S NOT AN ISSUE OF... *DROPPING* HER. THIS GIRL...
WHAT IS SHE PLOTTING?
IF IT'S ABOUT A HAIR-STYLE, IT CAN BE QUICKLY FIXED, BUT...
...IT'S TRUE YOU CAN'T DO MUCH ABOUT BEING FAT OR UGLY OR... SWEATY.
Sure.
IN ANY CASE, I MAKE THE RULES. THE DEDUCTION IN POINTS WILL NOT CHANGE!!
STINGY.
PFFT

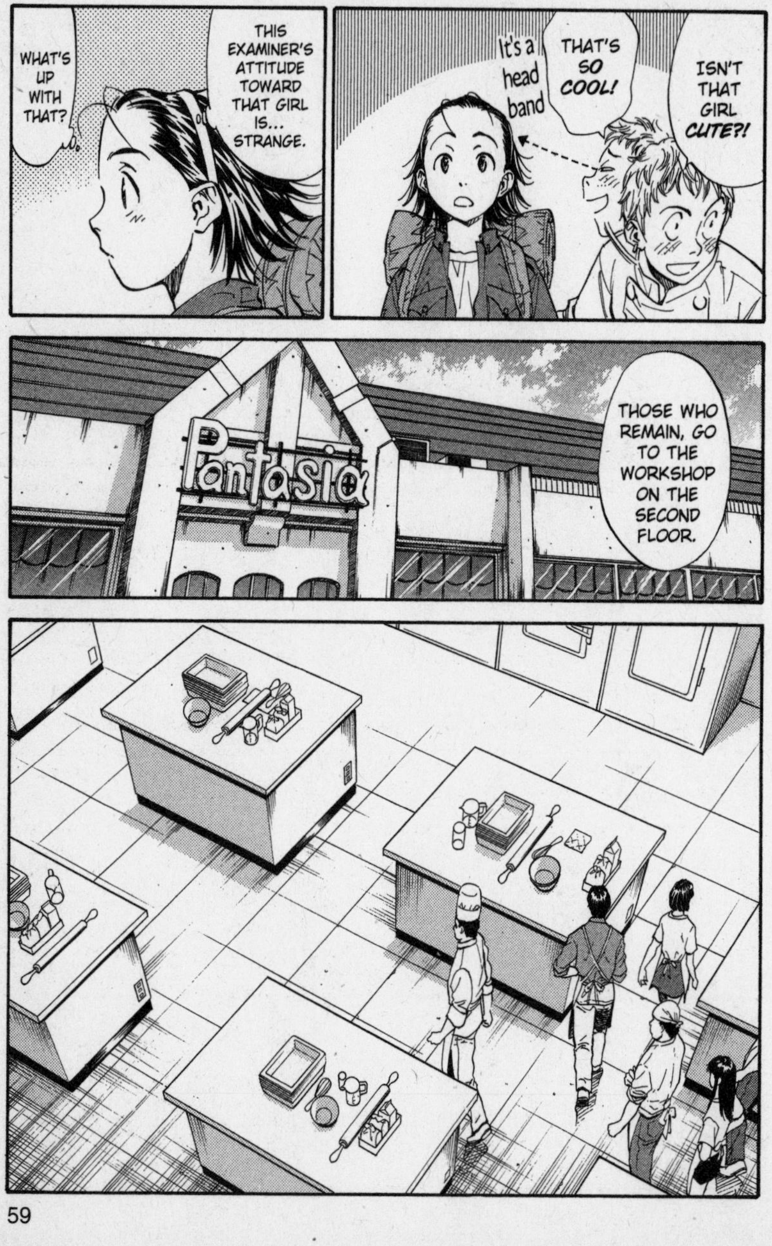
ISN'T THAT GIRL CUTE?!
THAT'S SO COOL!
It's a head band
THIS EXAMINER'S ATTITUDE TOWARD THAT GIRL IS... STRANGE.
WHAT'S UP WITH THAT?
Pantasia
THOSE WHO REMAIN, GO TO THE WORKSHOP ON THE SECOND FLOOR.

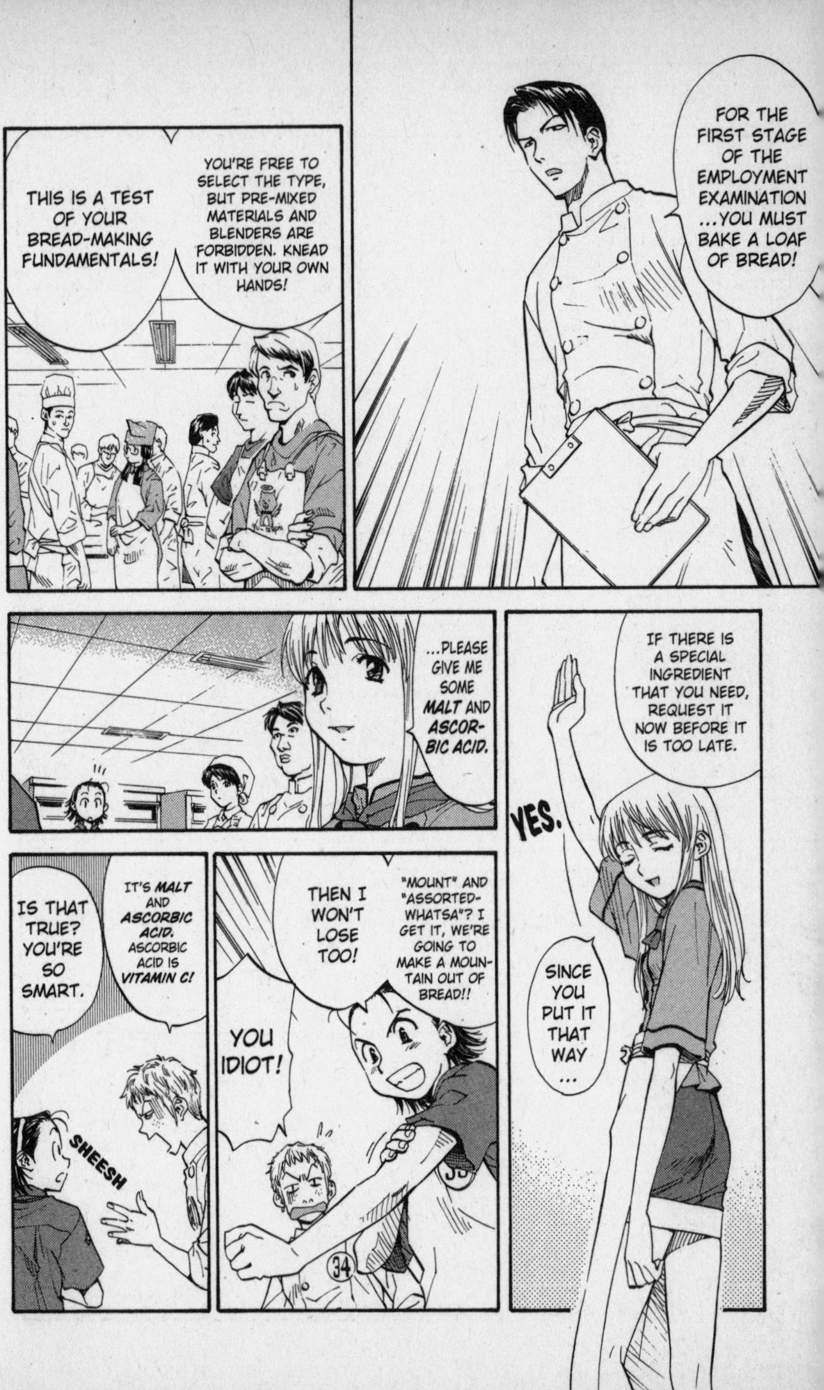
FOR THE FIRST STAGE OF THE EMPLOYMENT EXAMINATION ...YOU MUST BAKE A LOAF OF BREAD!
YOU'RE FREE TO SELECT THE TYPE, BUT PRE-MIXED MATERIALS AND BLENDERS ARE FORBIDDEN. KNEAD IT WITH YOUR OWN HANDS!
THIS IS A TEST OF YOUR BREAD-MAKING FUNDAMENTALS!
IF THERE IS A SPECIAL INGREDIENT THAT YOU NEED, REQUEST IT NOW BEFORE IT IS TOO LATE.
YES.
SINCE YOU PUT IT THAT WAY ...
...PLEASE GIVE ME SOME MALT AND ASCORBIC ACID.
"MOUNT" AND "ASSORTED-WHATSA"? I GET IT, WE'RE GOING TO MAKE A MOUNTAIN OUT OF BREAD!!
THEN I WON'T LOSE TOO!
YOU IDIOT!
34
IT'S MALT AND ASCORBIC ACID. ASCORBIC ACID IS VITAMIN C!
IS THAT TRUE? YOU'RE SO SMART.
SHEESH

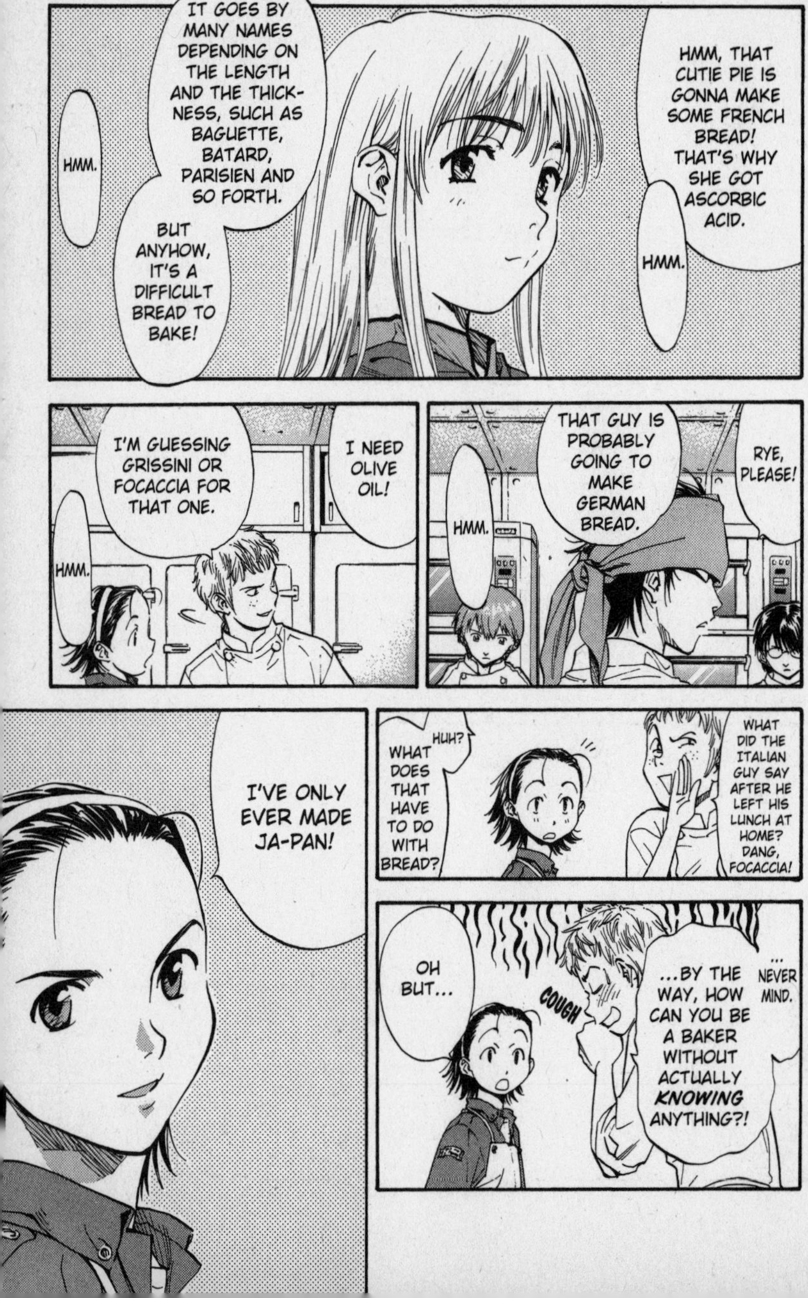
HMM, THAT CUTIE PIE IS GONNA MAKE SOME FRENCH BREAD! THAT'S WHY SHE GOT ASCORBIC ACID.
HMM.
IT GOES BY MANY NAMES DEPENDING ON THE LENGTH AND THE THICK-NESS, SUCH AS BAGUETTE, BATARD, PARISIEN AND SO FORTH.
HMM.
BUT ANYHOW, IT'S A DIFFICULT BREAD TO BAKE!
RYE, PLEASE!
THAT GUY IS PROBABLY GOING TO MAKE GERMAN BREAD.
HMM.
I NEED OLIVE OIL!
I'M GUESSING GRISSINI OR FOCACCIA FOR THAT ONE.
HMM.
WHAT DID THE ITALIAN GUY SAY AFTER HE LEFT HIS LUNCH AT HOME? DANG, FOCACCIA!
HUH?
WHAT DOES THAT HAVE TO DO WITH BREAD?
...NEVER MIND.
...BY THE WAY, HOW CAN YOU BE A BAKER WITHOUT ACTUALLY ***KNOWING*** ANYTHING?!
COUGH
OH BUT...
I'VE ONLY EVER MADE JA-PAN!

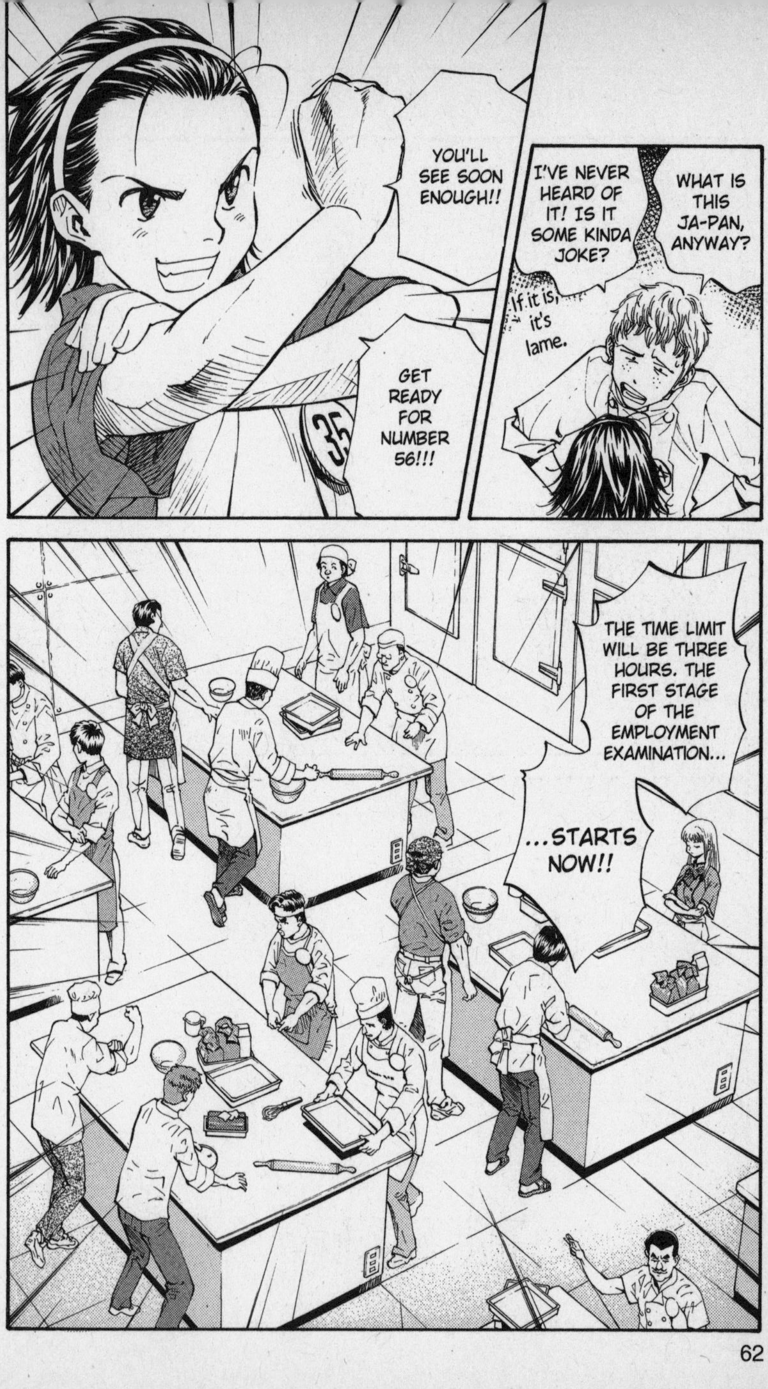
WHAT IS THIS JA-PAN, ANYWAY?
I'VE NEVER HEARD OF IT! IS IT SOME KINDA JOKE?
If it is, it's lame.
YOU'LL SEE SOON ENOUGH!!
GET READY FOR NUMBER 56!!!
35
THE TIME LIMIT WILL BE THREE HOURS. THE FIRST STAGE OF THE EMPLOYMENT EXAMINATION...
...STARTS NOW!!

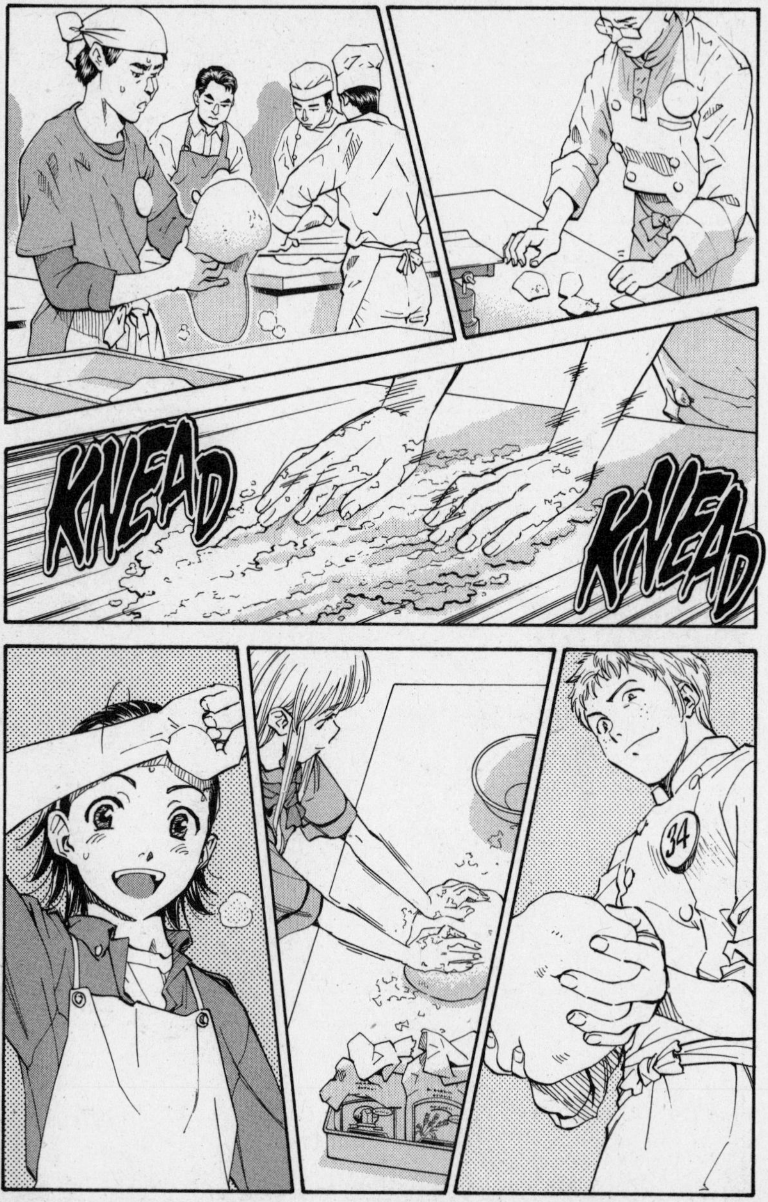
KNEAD
KNEAD
34

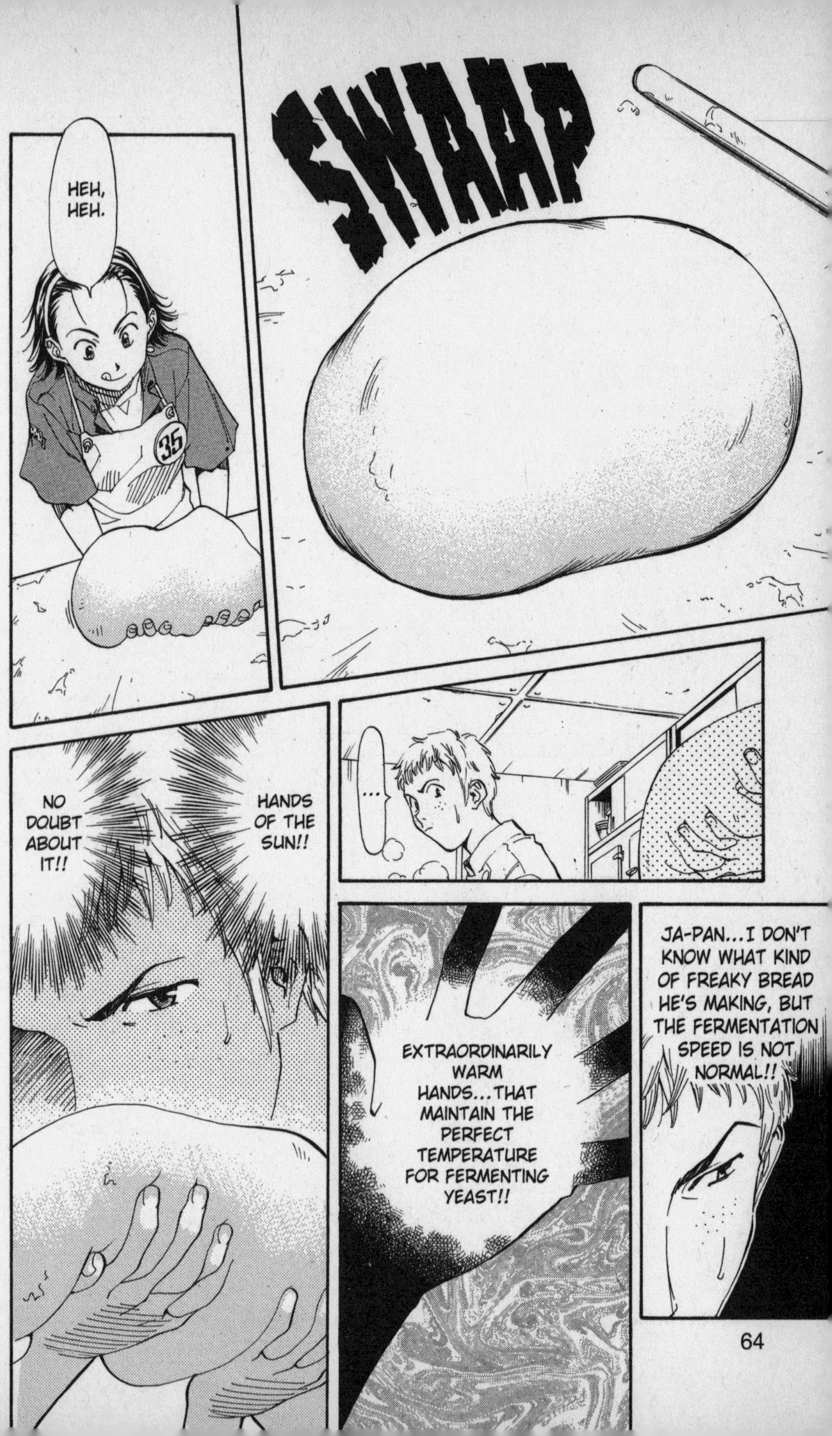
SWAAP
HEH, HEH.
...
JA-PAN...I DON'T KNOW WHAT KIND OF FREAKY BREAD HE'S MAKING, BUT THE FERMENTATION SPEED IS NOT NORMAL!!
EXTRAORDINARILY WARM HANDS...THAT MAINTAIN THE PERFECT TEMPERATURE FOR FERMENTING YEAST!!
HANDS OF THE SUN!!
NO DOUBT ABOUT IT!!

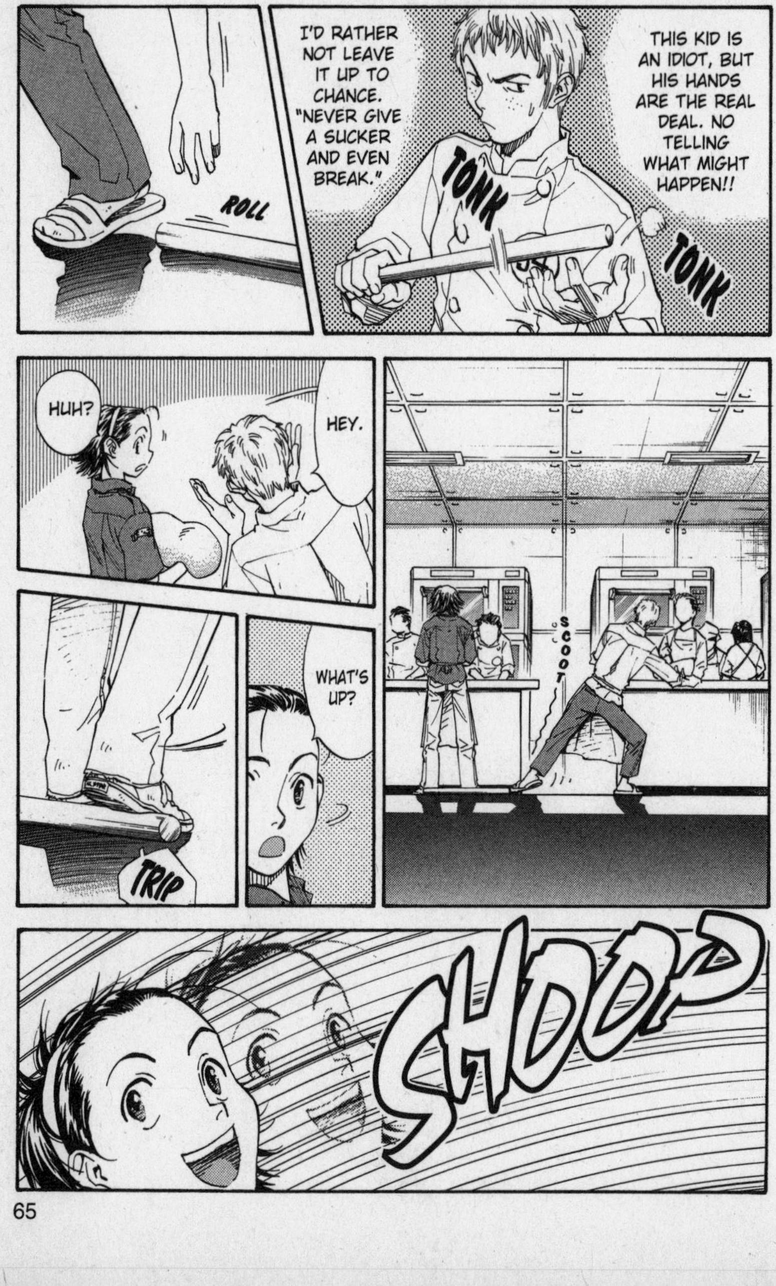
THIS KID IS AN IDIOT, BUT HIS HANDS ARE THE REAL DEAL. NO TELLING WHAT MIGHT HAPPEN!!
I'D RATHER NOT LEAVE IT UP TO CHANCE. "NEVER GIVE A SUCKER AND EVEN BREAK."
TONK
TONK
ROLL
SCOOT
HEY.
HUH?
WHAT'S UP?
TRIP
SHOOP

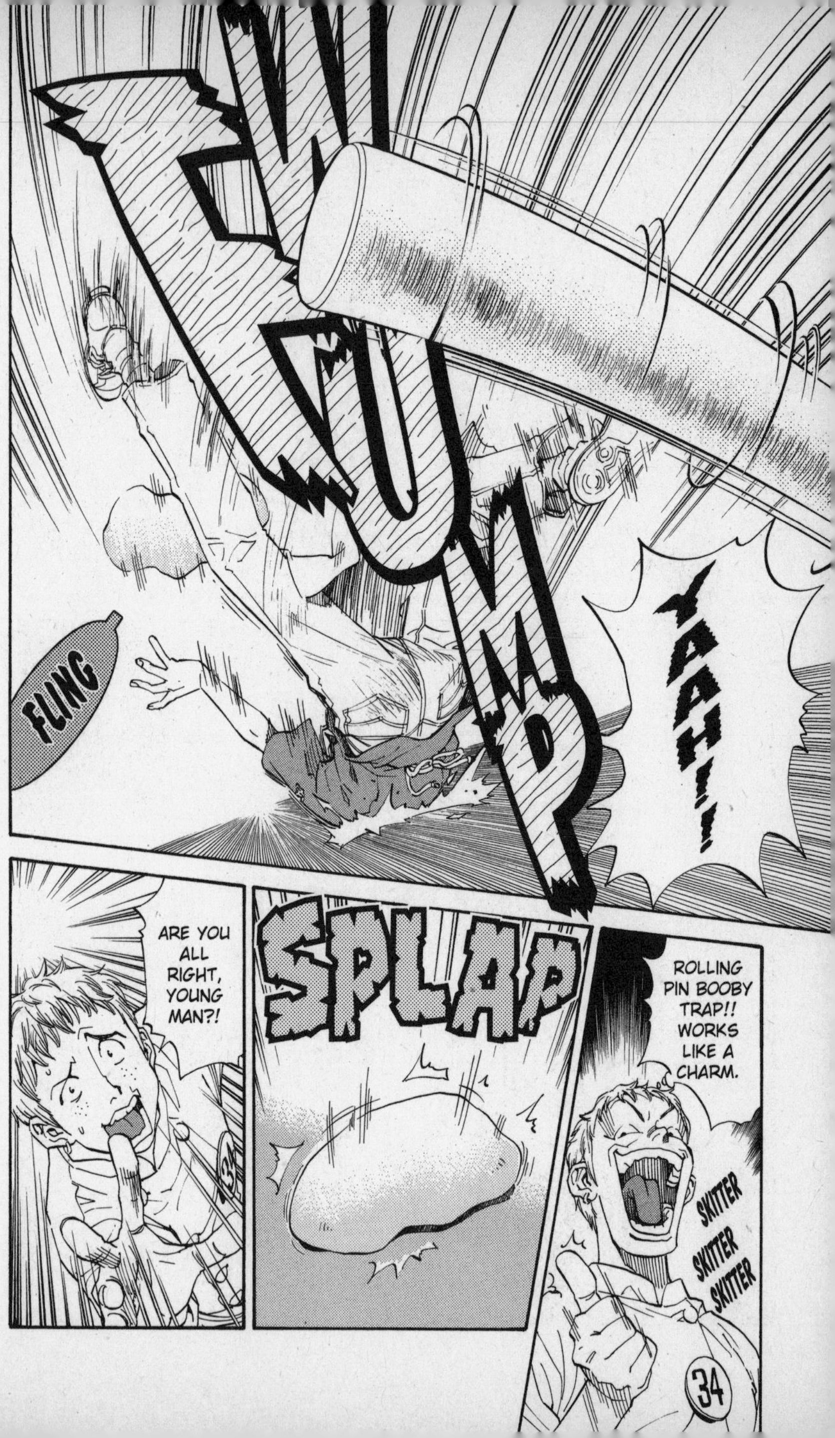
YAAH!!!
FLING
ROLLING PIN BOOBY TRAP!! WORKS LIKE A CHARM.
SKITTER SKITTER SKITTER
SPLAP
ARE YOU ALL RIGHT, YOUNG MAN?!

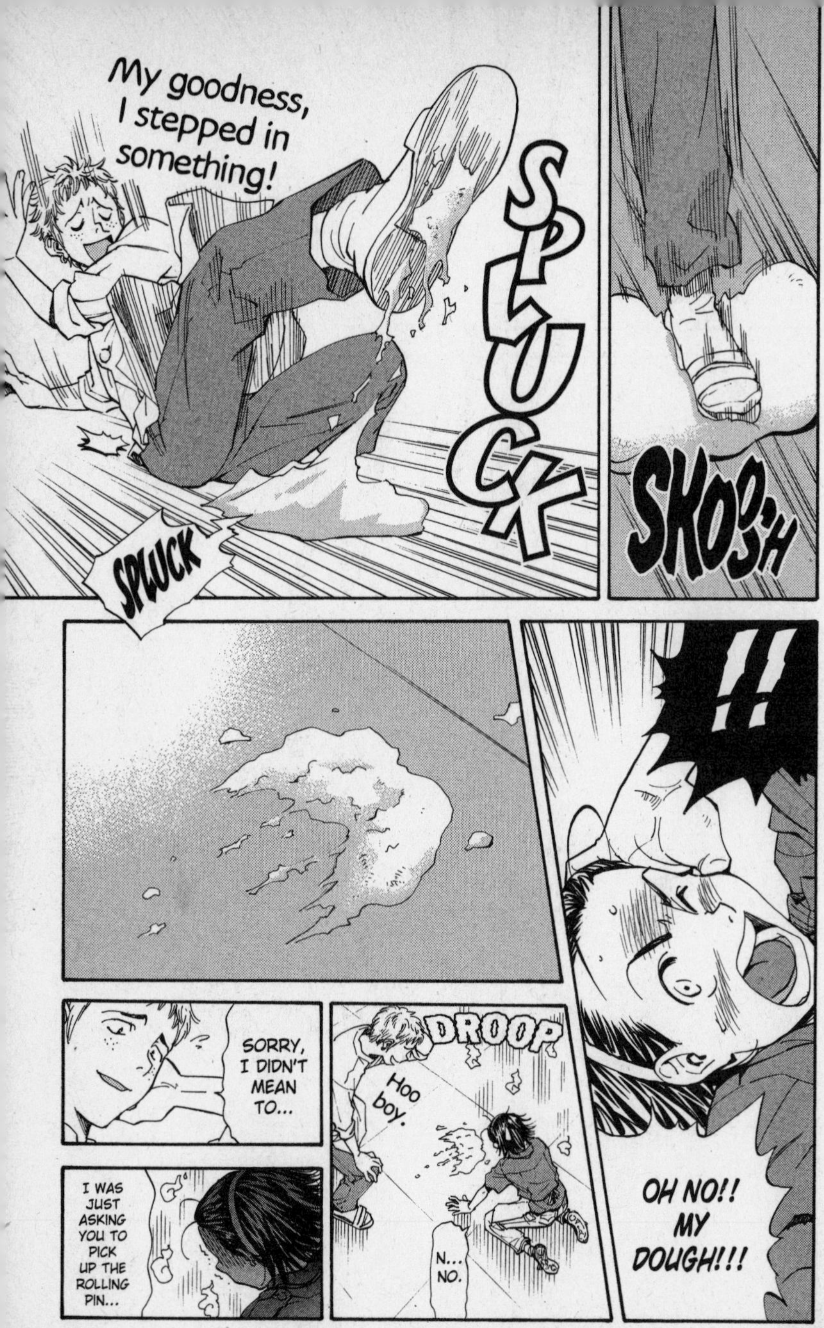

SHOOSH
My goodness, I stepped in something!
SPLUCK
SPLUCK
!!
OH NO!! MY DOUGH!!!
DROOP
Hoo boy.
N... NO.
SORRY, I DIDN'T MEAN TO...
I WAS JUST ASKING YOU TO PICK UP THE ROLLING PIN...

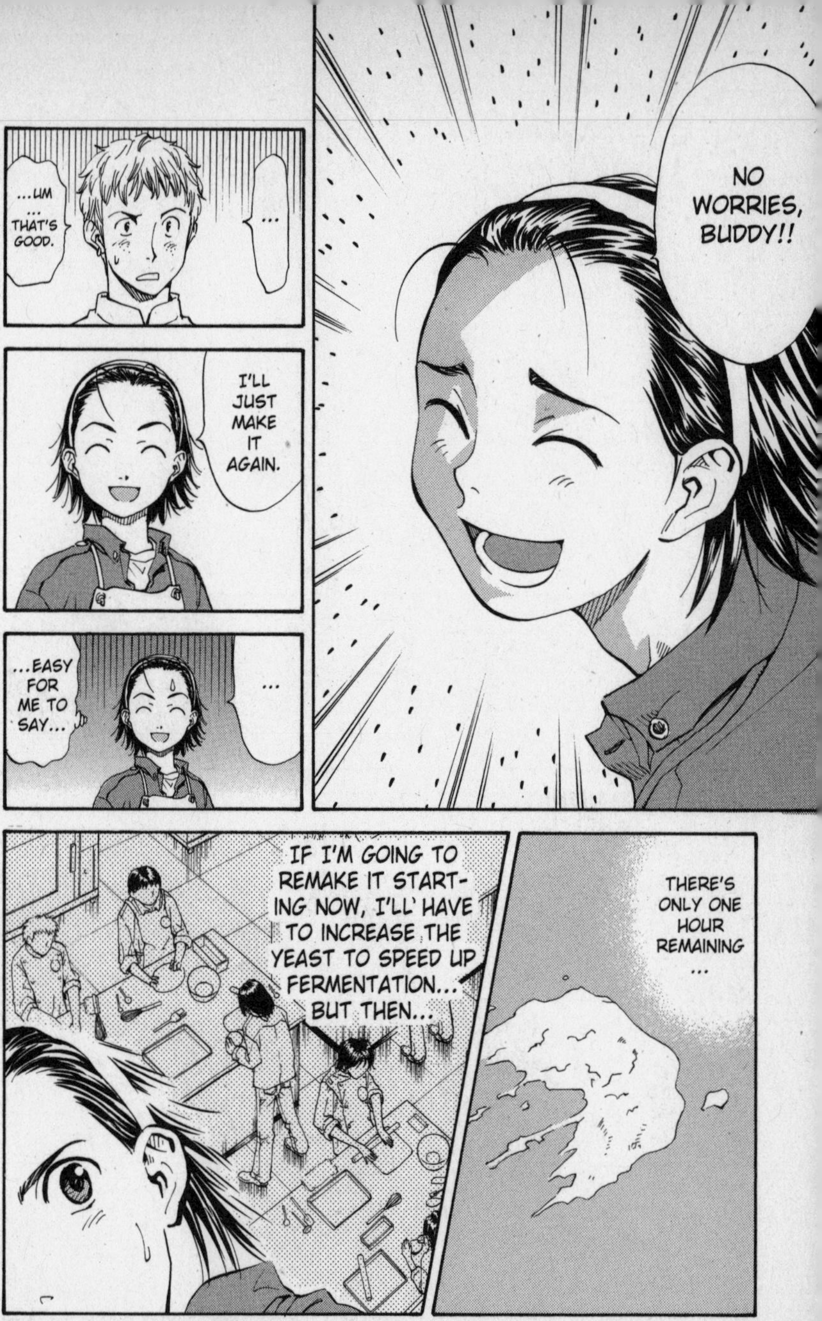
NO WORRIES, BUDDY!!
...
...UM ... THAT'S GOOD.
I'LL JUST MAKE IT AGAIN.
...
...EASY FOR ME TO SAY...
THERE'S ONLY ONE HOUR REMAINING ...
IF I'M GOING TO REMAKE IT STARTING NOW, I'LL HAVE TO INCREASE THE YEAST TO SPEED UP FERMENTATION... BUT THEN...

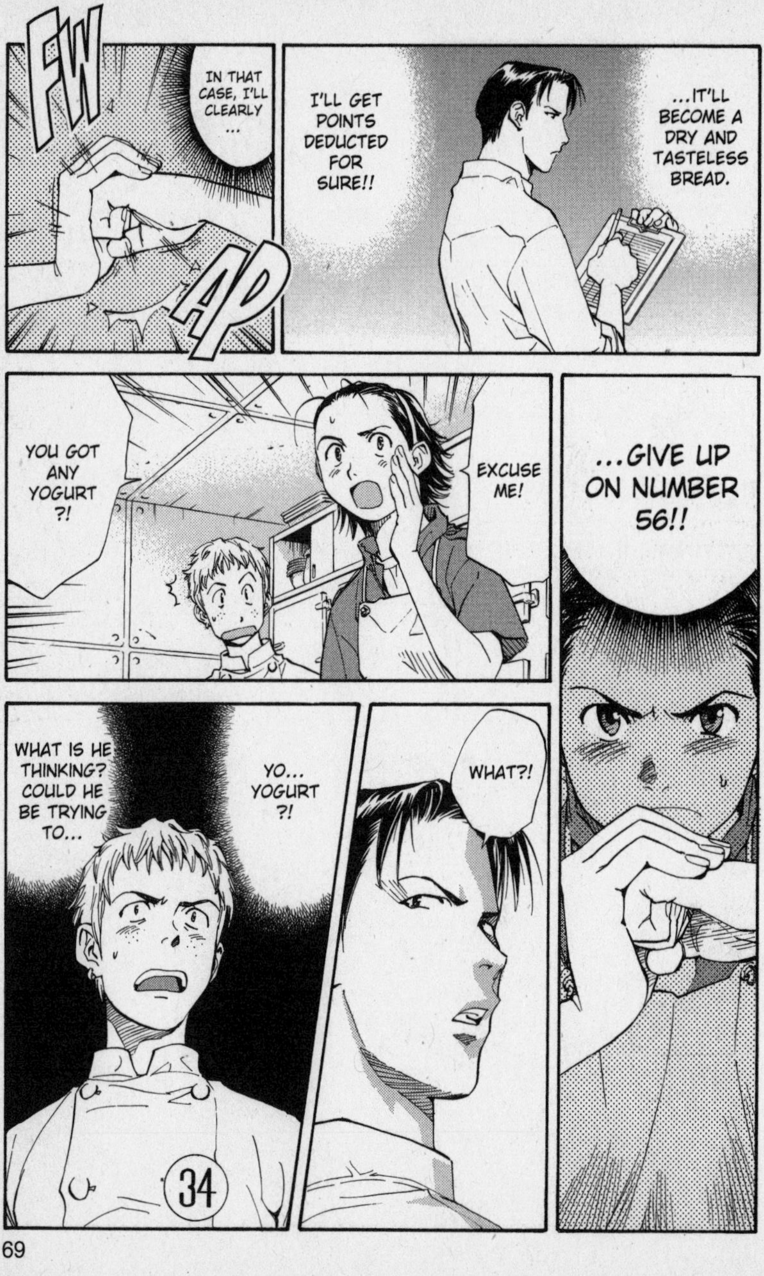
...IT'LL BECOME A DRY AND TASTELESS BREAD.
I'LL GET POINTS DEDUCTED FOR SURE!!
IN THAT CASE, I'LL CLEARLY ...
FWAP
...GIVE UP ON NUMBER 56!!
EXCUSE ME!
YOU GOT ANY YOGURT ?!
WHAT?!
YO... YOGURT ?!
WHAT IS HE THINKING? COULD HE BE TRYING TO...
34

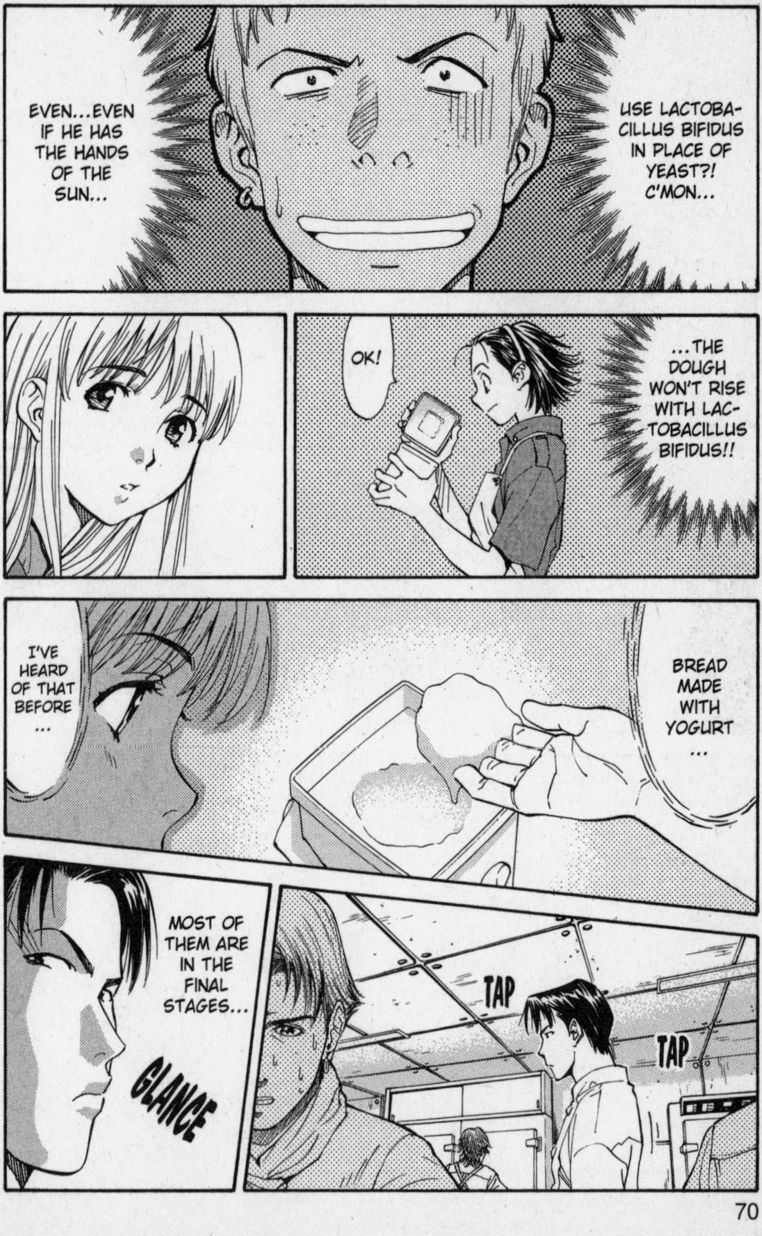
USE LACTOBACILLUS BIFIDUS IN PLACE OF YEAST?! C'MON...
EVEN...EVEN IF HE HAS THE HANDS OF THE SUN...
...THE DOUGH WON'T RISE WITH LACTOBACILLUS BIFIDUS!!
OK!
BREAD MADE WITH YOGURT...
I'VE HEARD OF THAT BEFORE...
TAP
TAP
MOST OF THEM ARE IN THE FINAL STAGES...
GLANCE

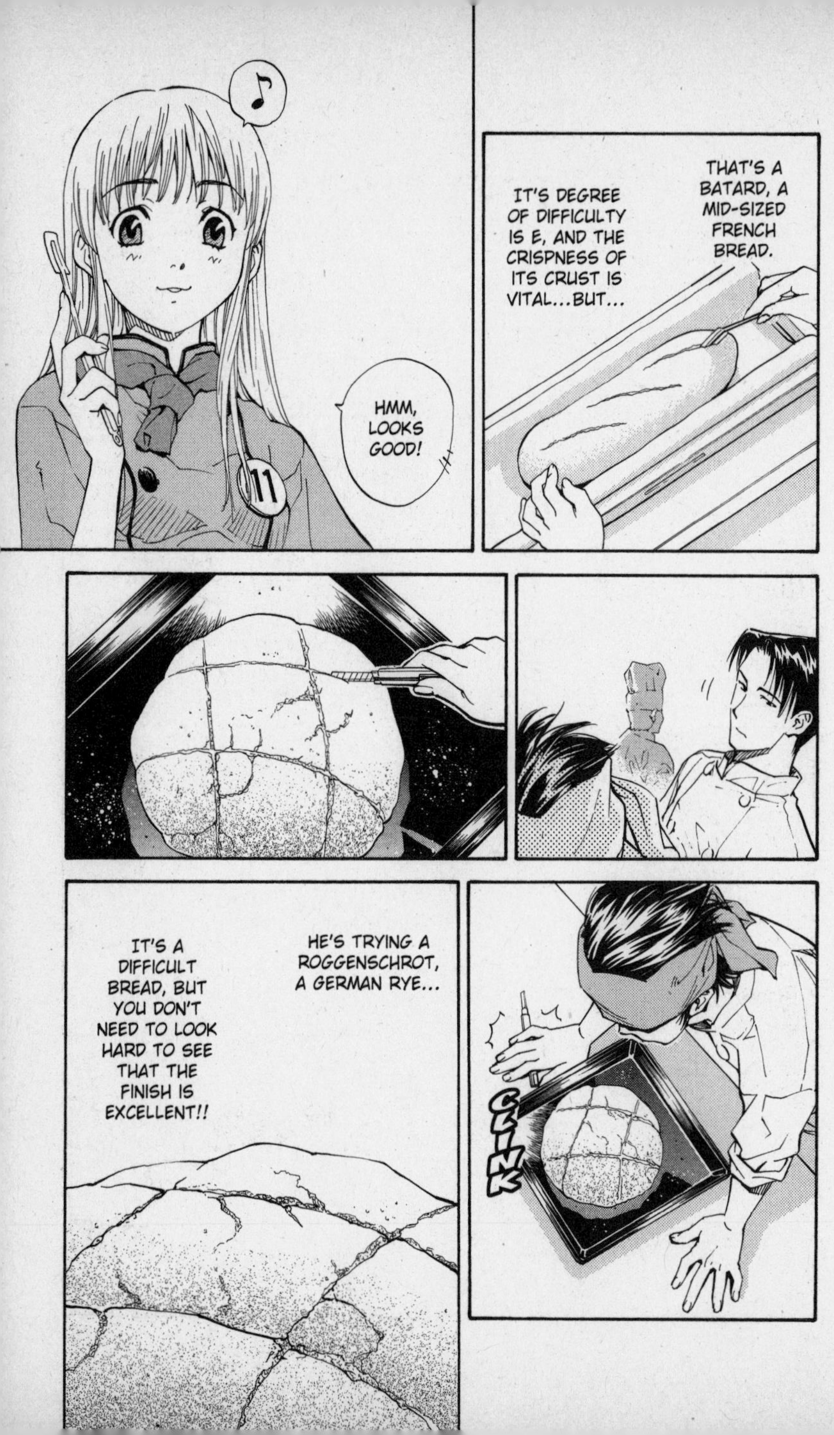
THAT'S A BATARD, A MID-SIZED FRENCH BREAD.
IT'S DEGREE OF DIFFICULTY IS E, AND THE CRISPNESS OF ITS CRUST IS VITAL...BUT...
♪
HMM, LOOKS GOOD!
CLINK
HE'S TRYING A ROGGENSCHROT, A GERMAN RYE...
IT'S A DIFFICULT BREAD, BUT YOU DON'T NEED TO LOOK HARD TO SEE THAT THE FINISH IS EXCELLENT!!

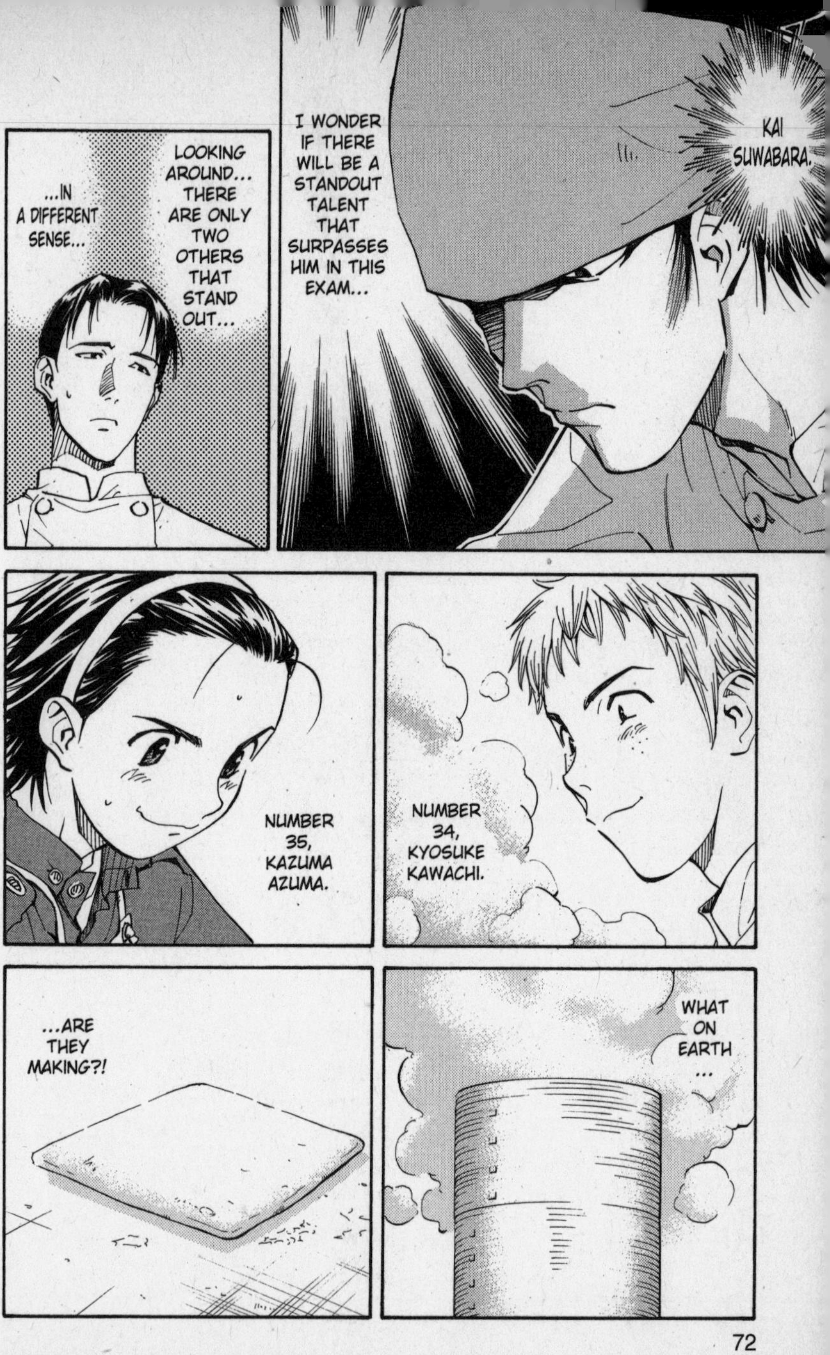
KAI SUWABARA.
I WONDER IF THERE WILL BE A STANDOUT TALENT THAT SURPASSES HIM IN THIS EXAM...
LOOKING AROUND... THERE ARE ONLY TWO OTHERS THAT STAND OUT...
...IN A DIFFERENT SENSE...
NUMBER 34, KYOSUKE KAWACHI.
NUMBER 35, KAZUMA AZUMA.
WHAT ON EARTH ...
...ARE THEY MAKING?!

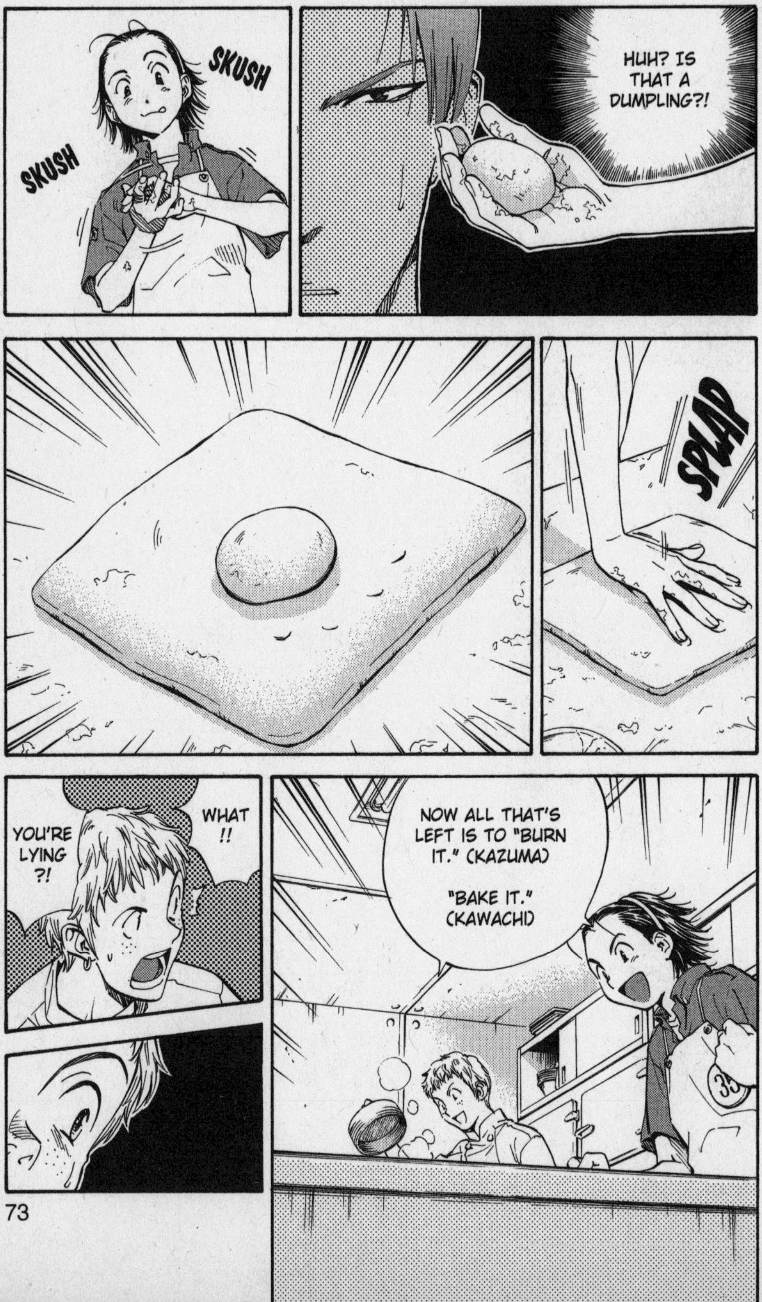
HUH? IS THAT A DUMPLING?!
SKUSH
SKUSH
SPLAP
NOW ALL THAT'S LEFT IS TO "BURN IT." (KAZUMA)
"BAKE IT." (KAWACHI)
WHAT !!
YOU'RE LYING ?!

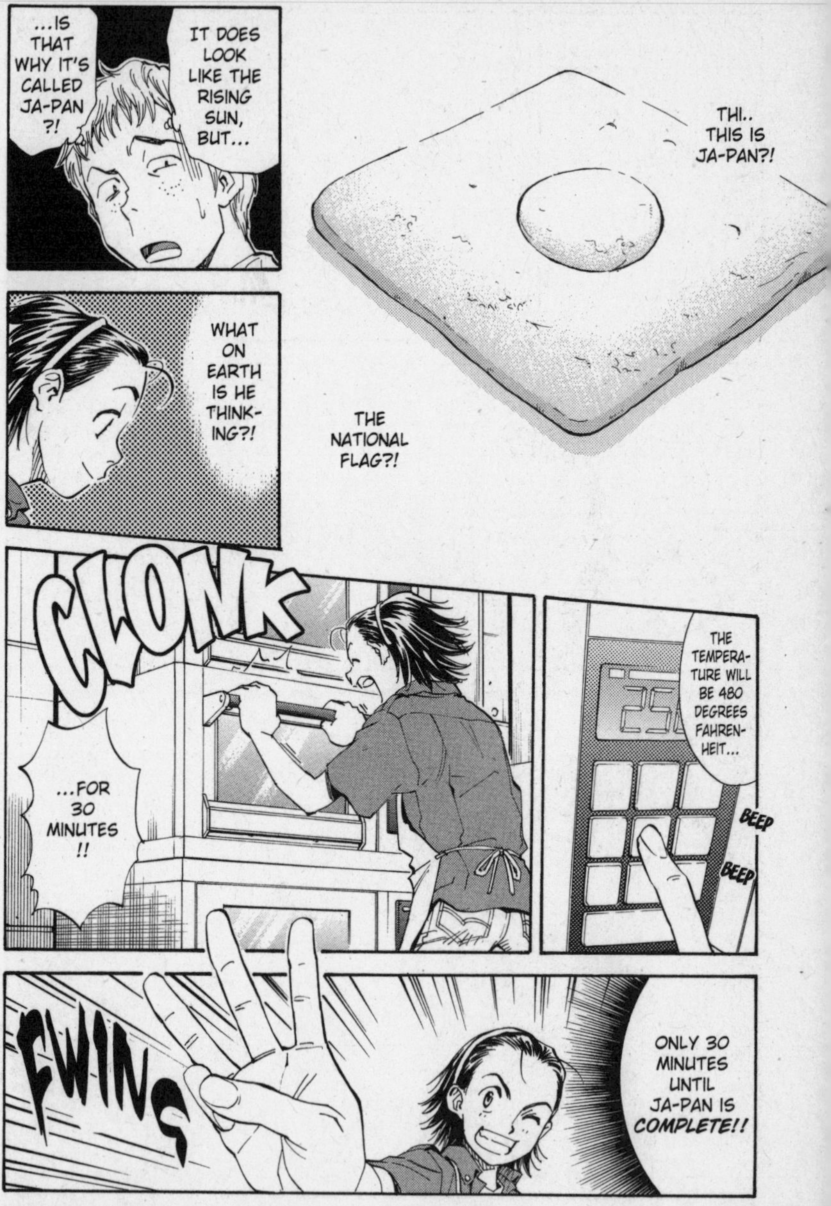
THI.. THIS IS JA-PAN?!
THE NATIONAL FLAG?!
IT DOES LOOK LIKE THE RISING SUN, BUT...
...IS THAT WHY IT'S CALLED JA-PAN?!
WHAT ON EARTH IS HE THINKING?!
THE TEMPERATURE WILL BE 480 DEGREES FAHRENHEIT...
BEEP
BEEP
CLONK
...FOR 30 MINUTES!!
ONLY 30 MINUTES UNTIL JA-PAN IS COMPLETE!!
FWING

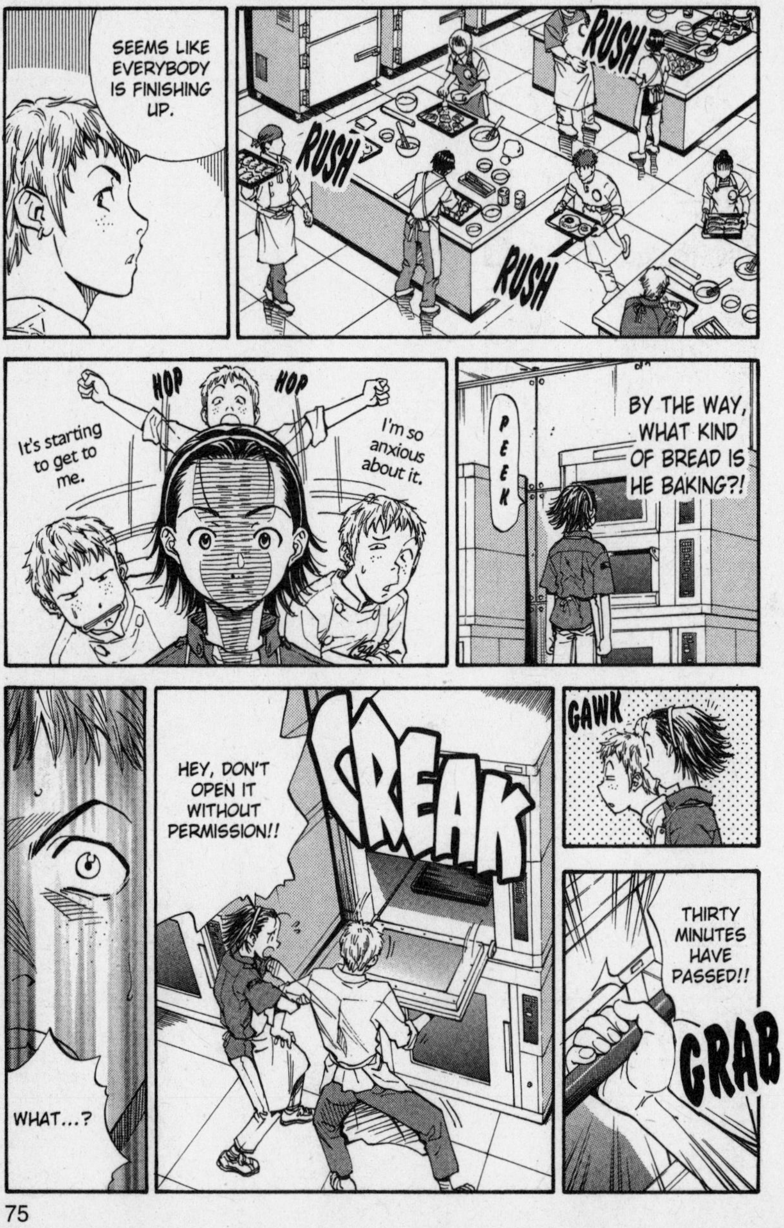
RUSH
RUSH
RUSH
SEEMS LIKE EVERYBODY IS FINISHING UP.
BY THE WAY, WHAT KIND OF BREAD IS HE BAKING?!
PEEK
HOP
HOP
I'm so anxious about it.
It's starting to get to me.
GAWK
THIRTY MINUTES HAVE PASSED!!
GRAB
CREAK
HEY, DON'T OPEN IT WITHOUT PERMISSION!!
WHAT...?

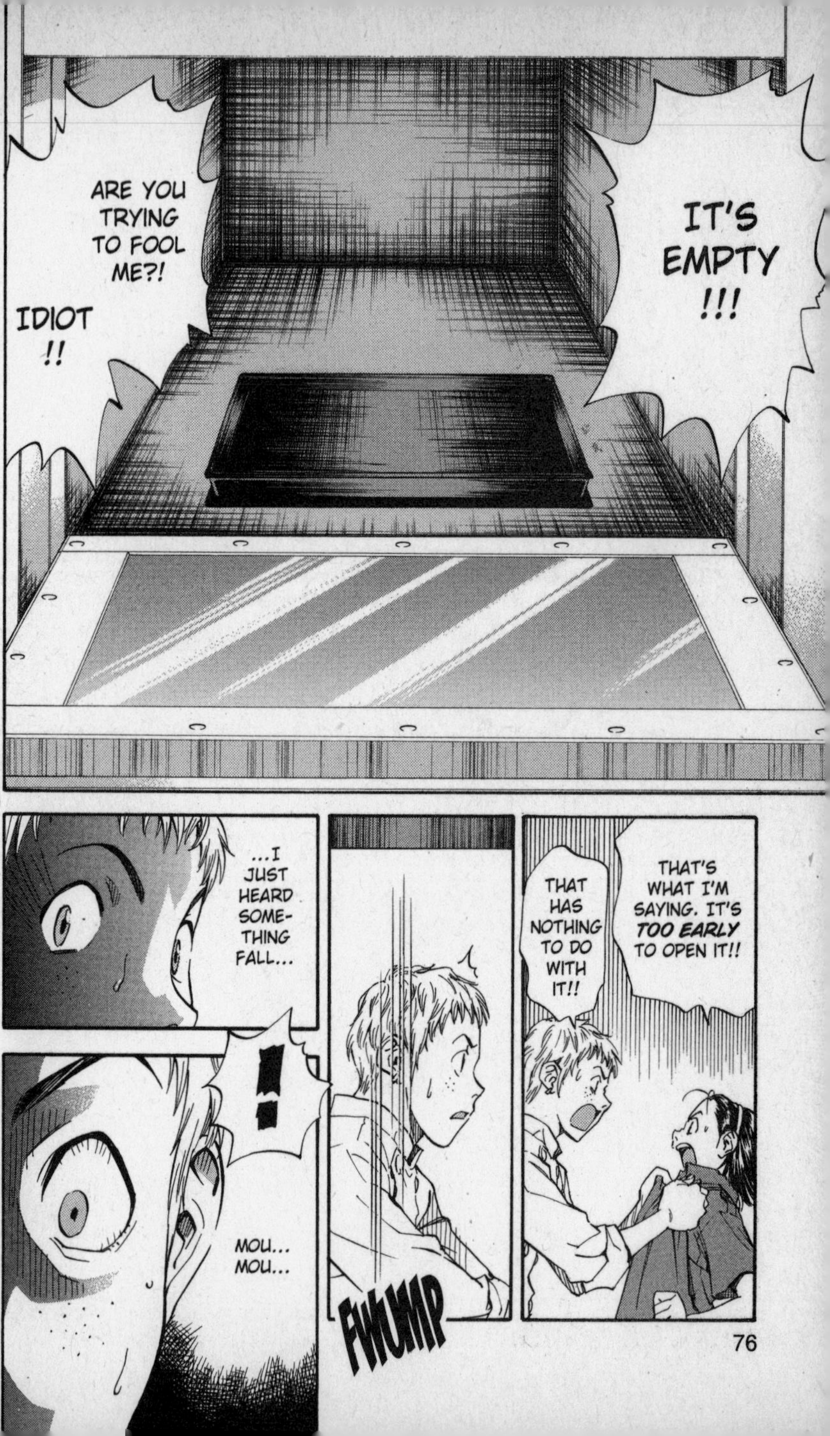
IT'S EMPTY !!!
ARE YOU TRYING TO FOOL ME?!
IDIOT !!
THAT'S WHAT I'M SAYING. IT'S *TOO EARLY* TO OPEN IT!!
THAT HAS NOTHING TO DO WITH IT!!
FWUMP
...I JUST HEARD SOME-THING FALL...
!
MOU... MOU...

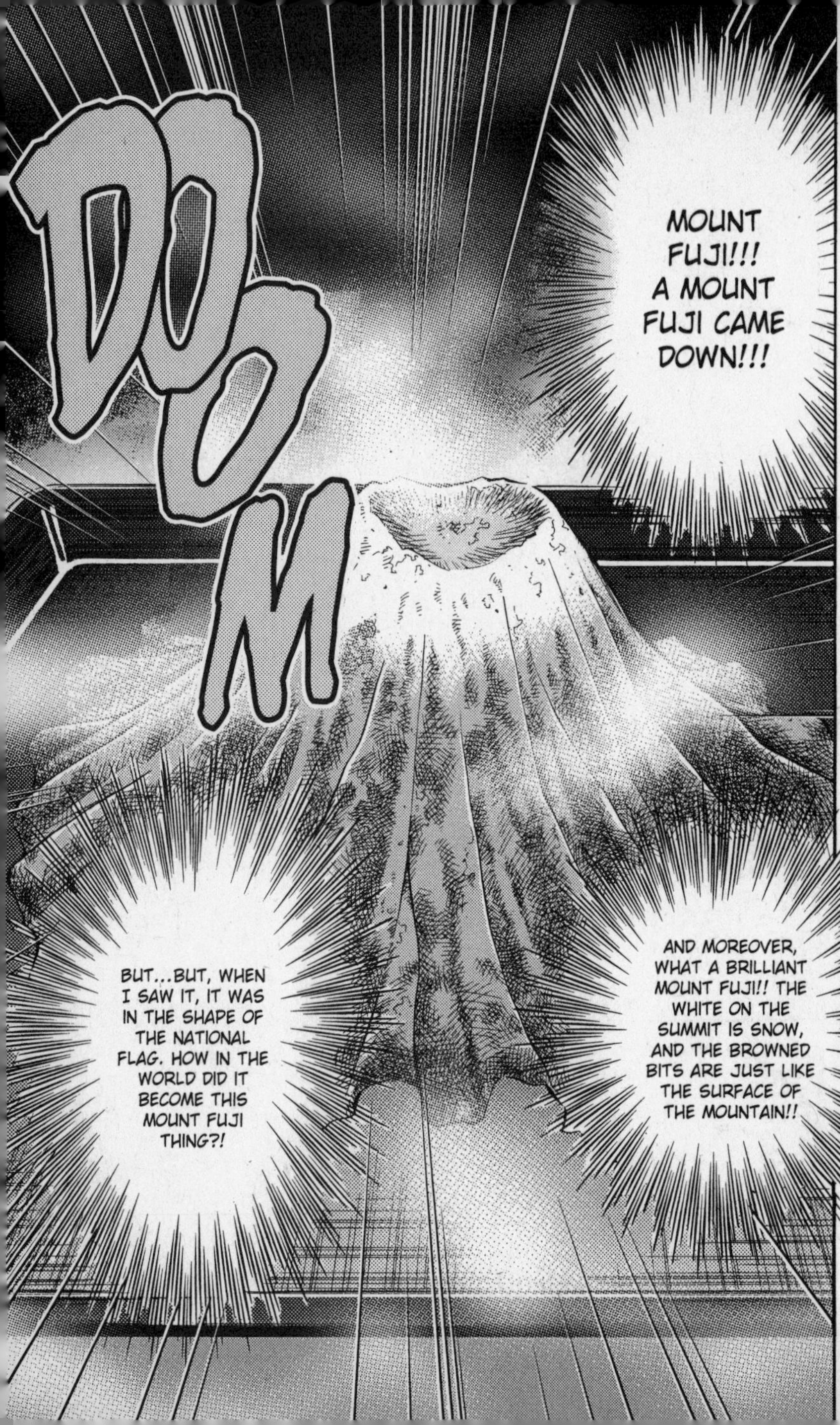
DOOM
MOUNT FUJI!!! A MOUNT FUJI CAME DOWN!!!
AND MOREOVER, WHAT A BRILLIANT MOUNT FUJI!! THE WHITE ON THE SUMMIT IS SNOW, AND THE BROWNED BITS ARE JUST LIKE THE SURFACE OF THE MOUNTAIN!!
BUT...BUT, WHEN I SAW IT, IT WAS IN THE SHAPE OF THE NATIONAL FLAG. HOW IN THE WORLD DID IT BECOME THIS MOUNT FUJI THING?!

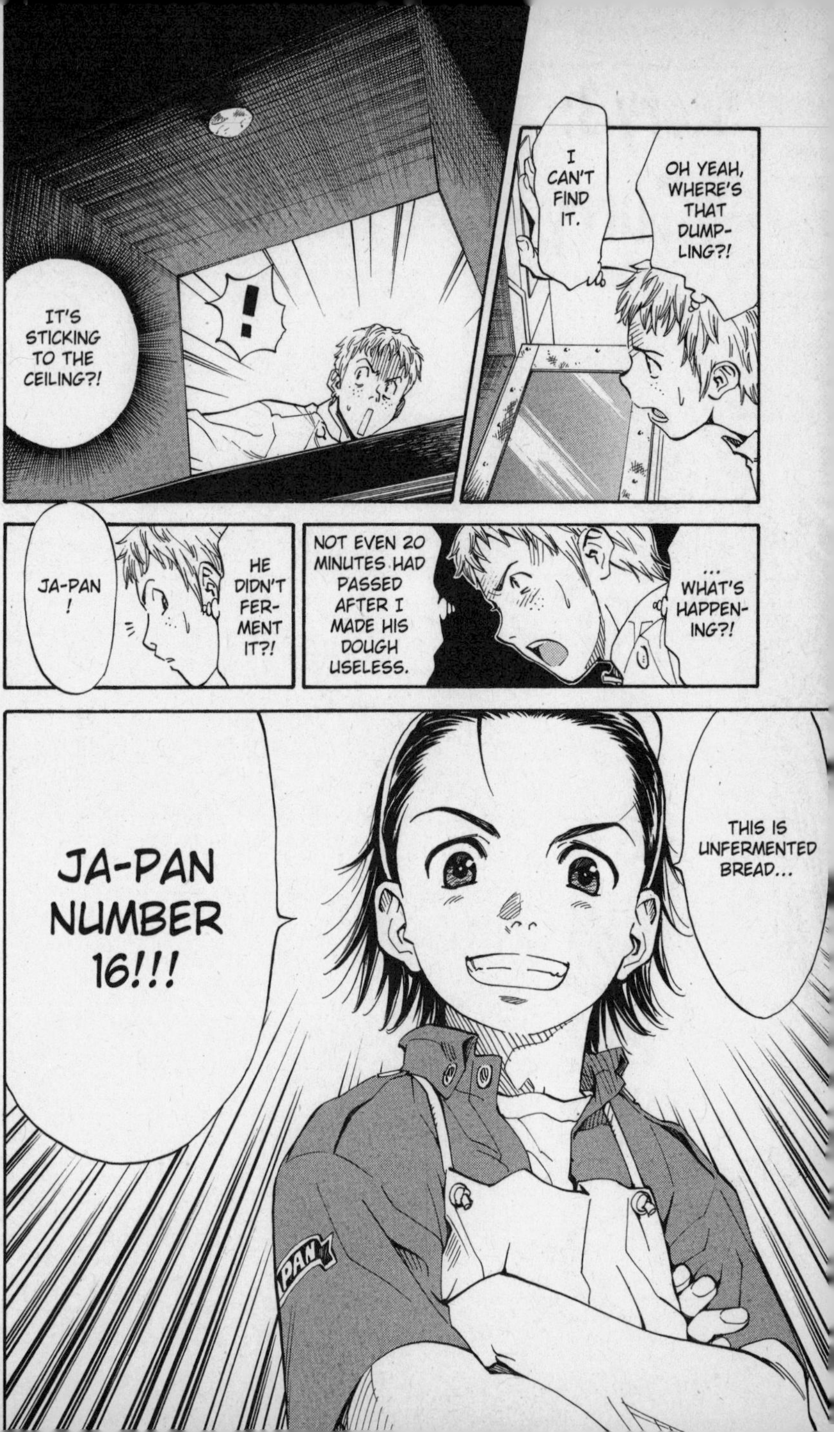
OH YEAH, WHERE'S THAT DUMP-LING?!
I CAN'T FIND IT.
!
IT'S STICKING TO THE CEILING?!
...WHAT'S HAPPEN-ING?!
NOT EVEN 20 MINUTES HAD PASSED AFTER I MADE HIS DOUGH USELESS.
HE DIDN'T FER-MENT IT?!
JA-PAN!
THIS IS UNFERMENTED BREAD...
JA-PAN NUMBER 16!!!
PAN

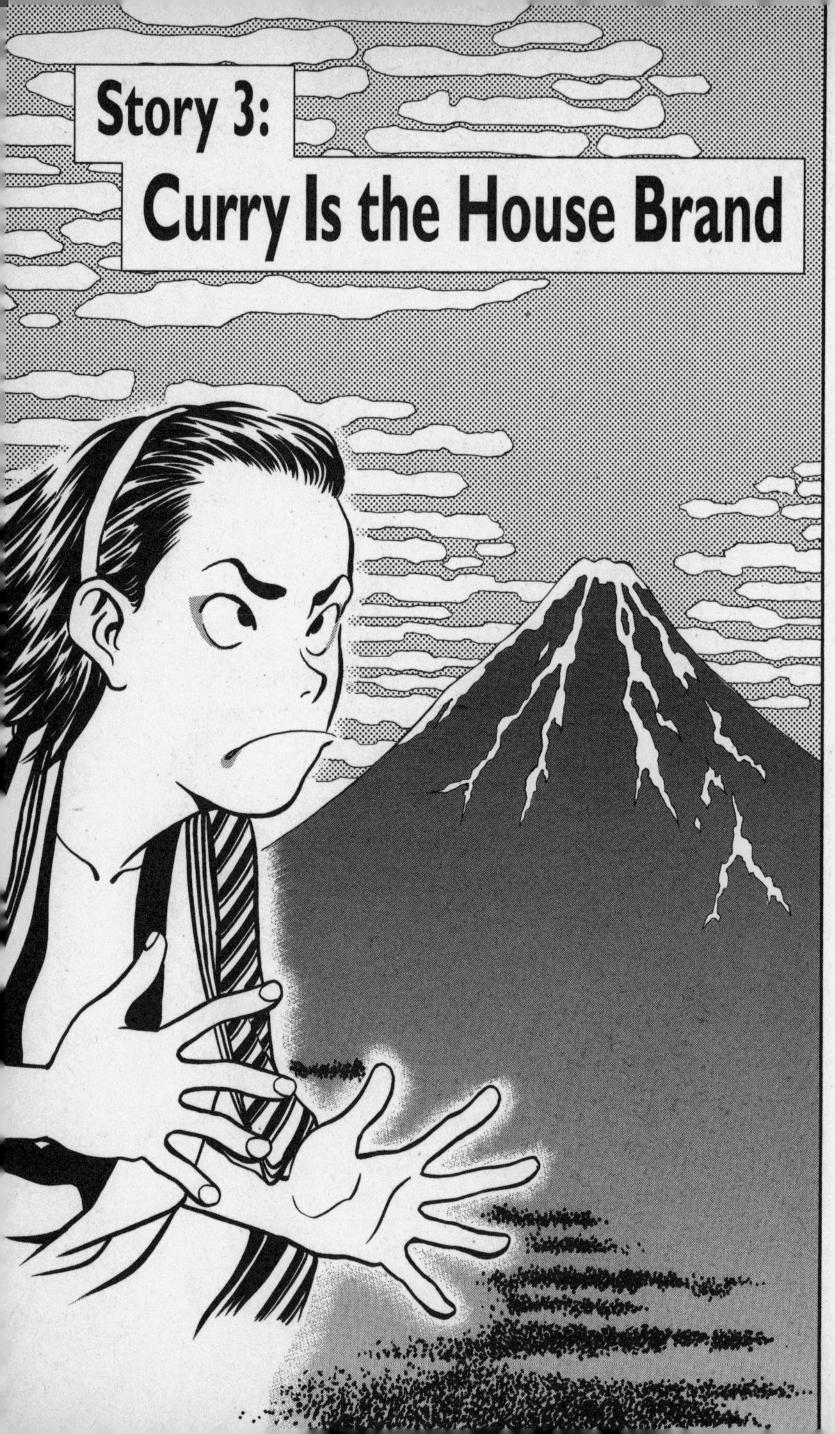
Story 3:
Curry Is the House Brand

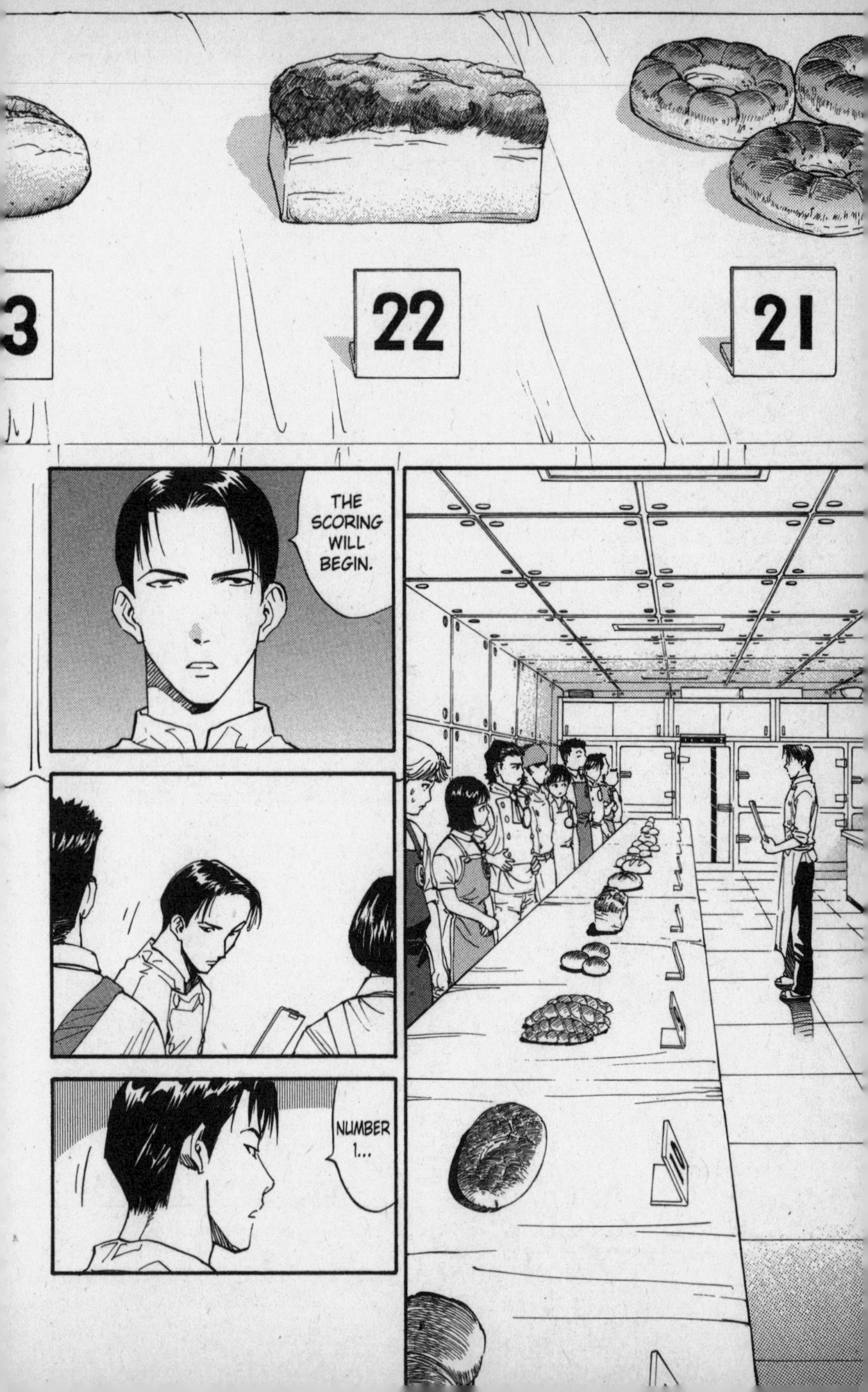
3
22
21
THE SCORING WILL BEGIN.
NUMBER 1...

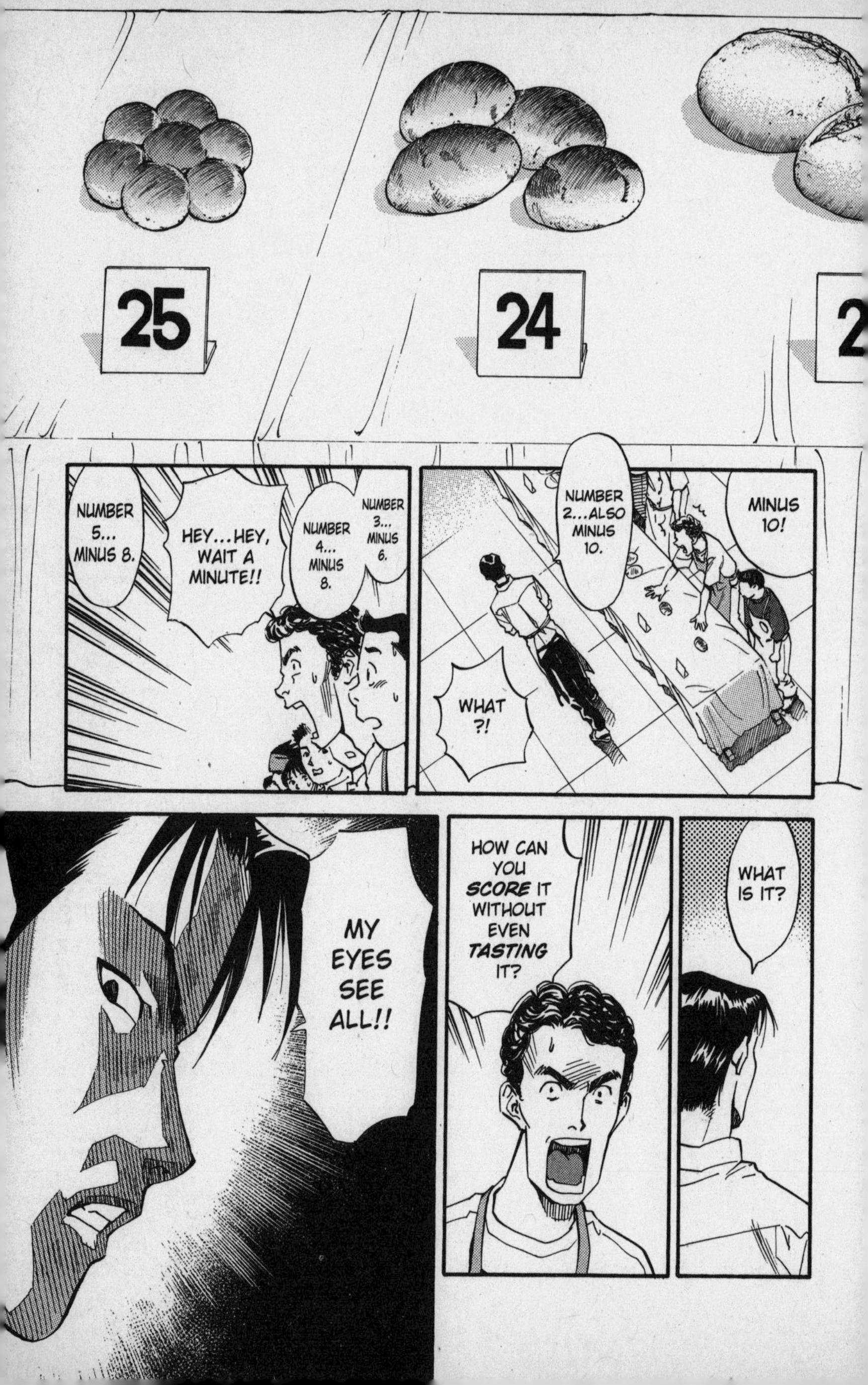
2
24
25
MINUS 10!
NUMBER 2...ALSO MINUS 10.
WHAT ?!
NUMBER 3... MINUS 6.
NUMBER 4... MINUS 8.
HEY...HEY, WAIT A MINUTE!!
NUMBER 5... MINUS 8.
WHAT IS IT?
HOW CAN YOU *SCORE* IT WITHOUT EVEN *TASTING* IT?
MY EYES SEE ALL!!

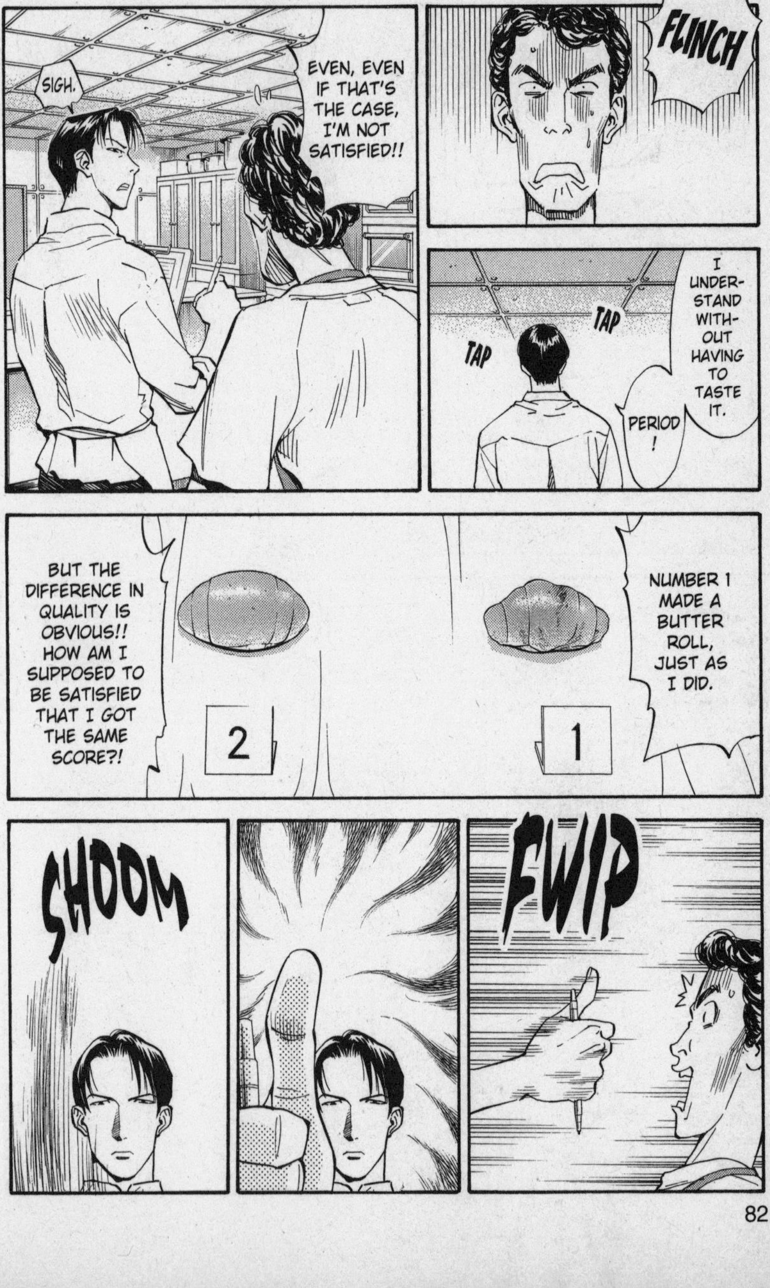
FLINCH
I UNDERSTAND WITHOUT HAVING TO TASTE IT.
TAP
TAP
PERIOD!
EVEN, EVEN IF THAT'S THE CASE, I'M NOT SATISFIED!!
SIGH.
NUMBER 1 MADE A BUTTER ROLL, JUST AS I DID.
1
2
BUT THE DIFFERENCE IN QUALITY IS OBVIOUS!! HOW AM I SUPPOSED TO BE SATISFIED THAT I GOT THE SAME SCORE?!
FWIP
SHOOM

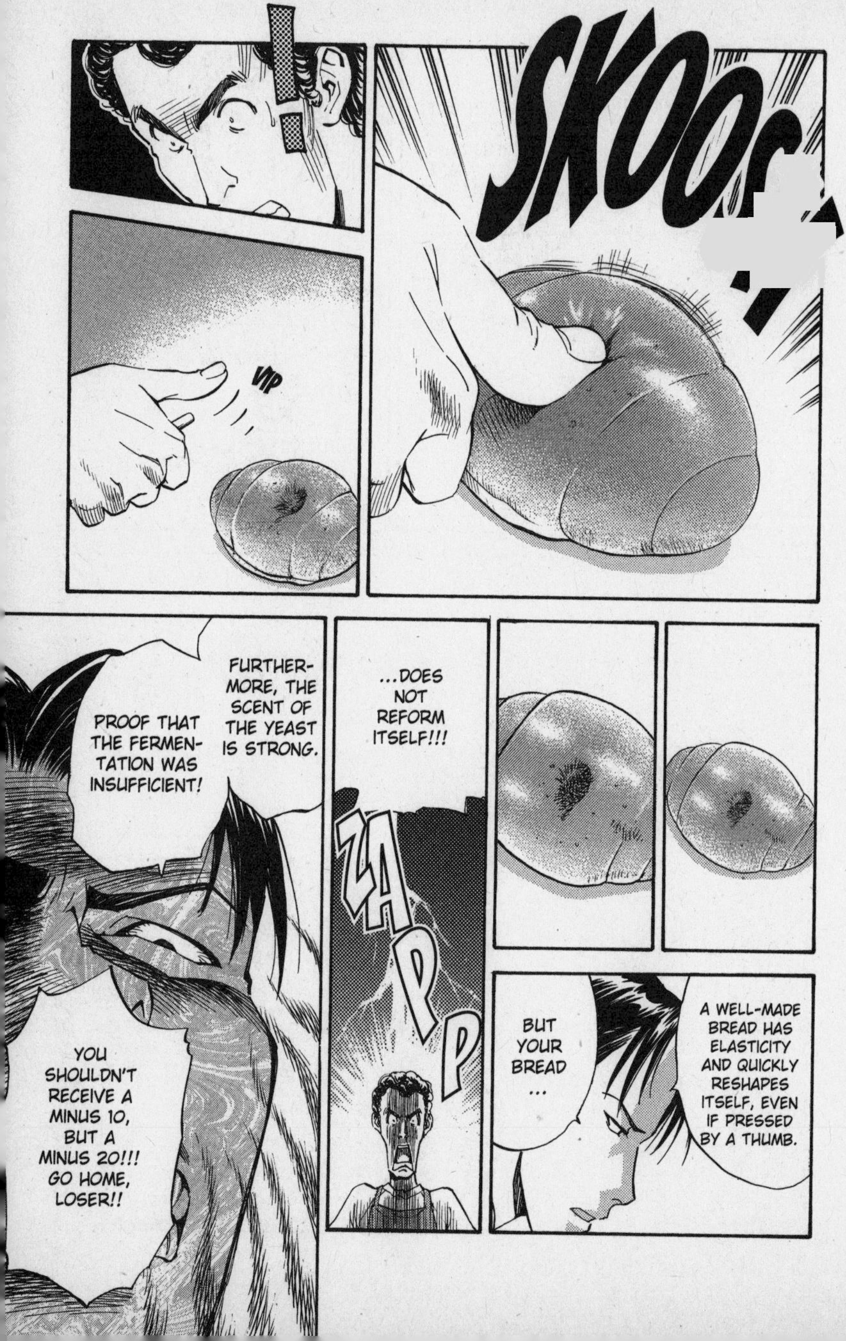
SKOOS
!!
VIP
A WELL-MADE BREAD HAS ELASTICITY AND QUICKLY RESHAPES ITSELF, EVEN IF PRESSED BY A THUMB.
BUT YOUR BREAD ...
...DOES NOT REFORM ITSELF!!!
ZAPP
FURTHER-MORE, THE SCENT OF THE YEAST IS STRONG.
PROOF THAT THE FERMEN-TATION WAS INSUFFICIENT!
YOU SHOULDN'T RECEIVE A MINUS 10, BUT A MINUS 20!!! GO HOME, LOSER!!

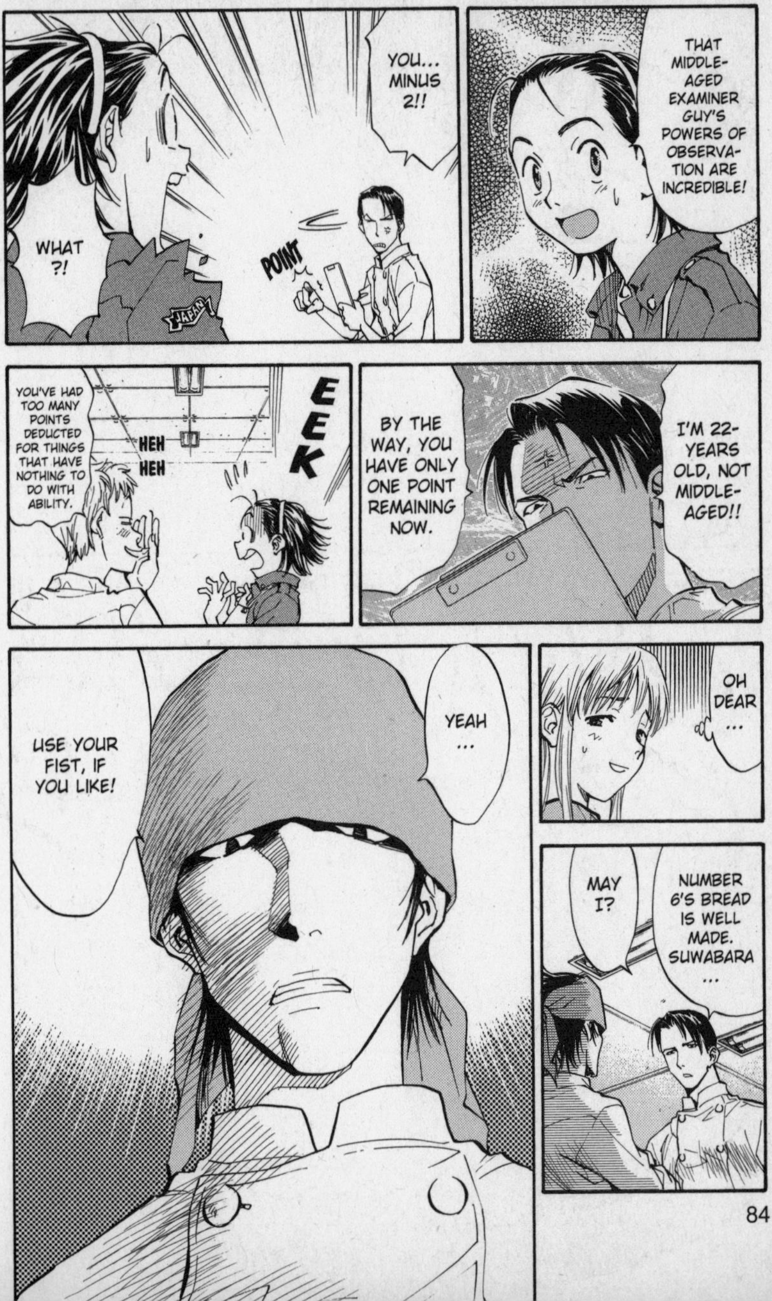
THAT MIDDLE-AGED EXAMINER GUY'S POWERS OF OBSERVATION ARE INCREDIBLE!
YOU... MINUS 2!!
POINT
WHAT ?!
I'M 22-YEARS OLD, NOT MIDDLE-AGED!!
BY THE WAY, YOU HAVE ONLY ONE POINT REMAINING NOW.
EEK
HEH HEH
YOU'VE HAD TOO MANY POINTS DEDUCTED FOR THINGS THAT HAVE NOTHING TO DO WITH ABILITY.
OH DEAR ...
NUMBER 6'S BREAD IS WELL MADE. SUWABARA ...
MAY I?
YEAH ...
USE YOUR FIST, IF YOU LIKE!

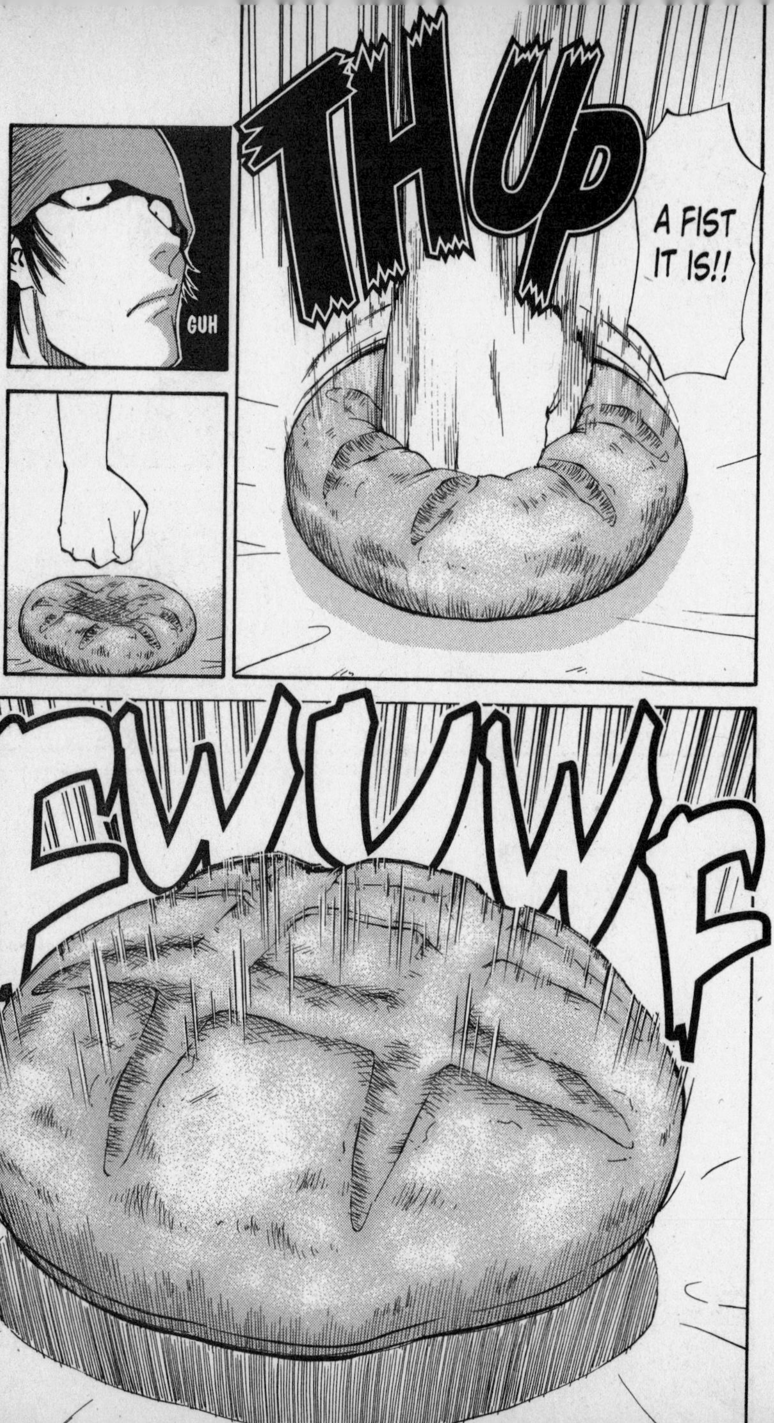
THUP
A FIST IT IS!!
GUH
FWUMF

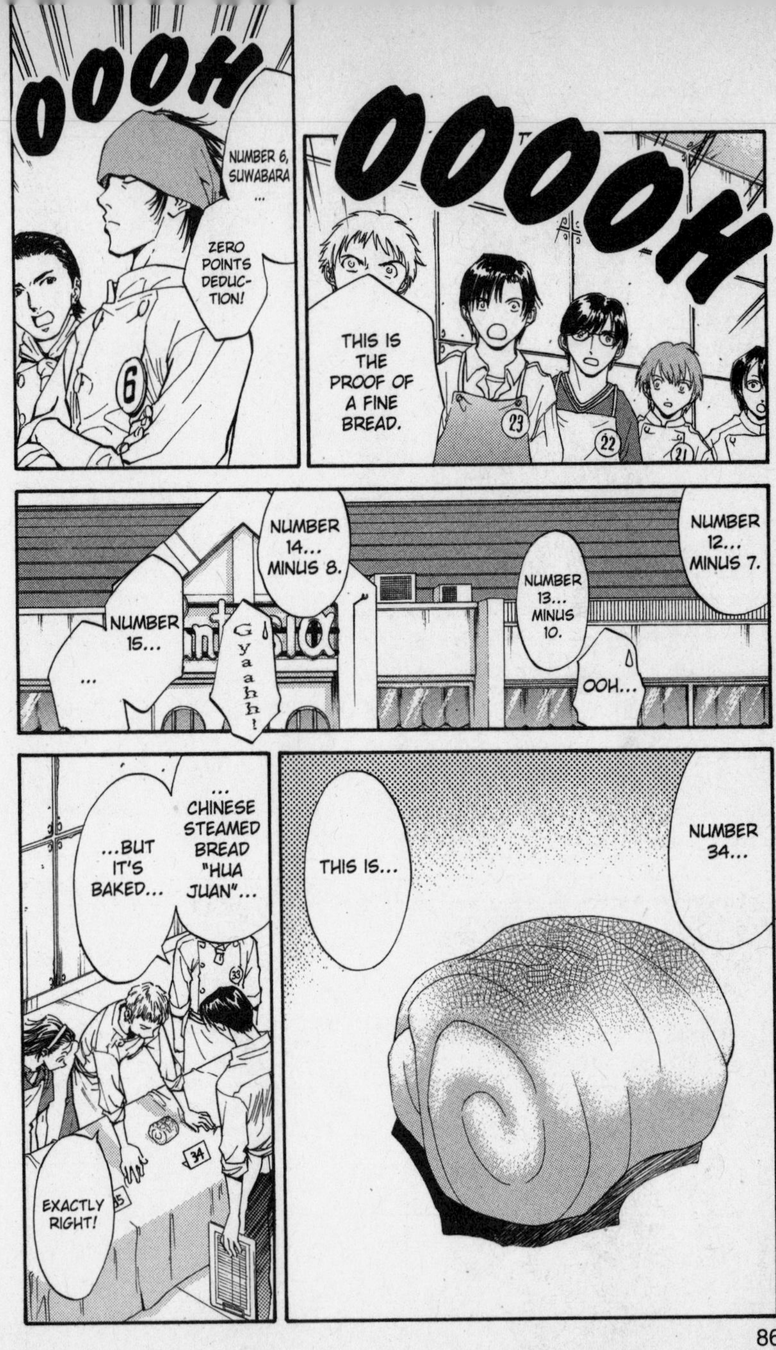
OOOOH
THIS IS THE PROOF OF A FINE BREAD.
NUMBER 6, SUWABARA ...
OOOH
ZERO POINTS DEDUCTION!
NUMBER 12... MINUS 7.
NUMBER 13... MINUS 10.
OOH...
NUMBER 14... MINUS 8.
Gyaahh!
NUMBER 15... ...
NUMBER 34...
THIS IS...
... CHINESE STEAMED BREAD "HUA JUAN"...
...BUT IT'S BAKED...
EXACTLY RIGHT!

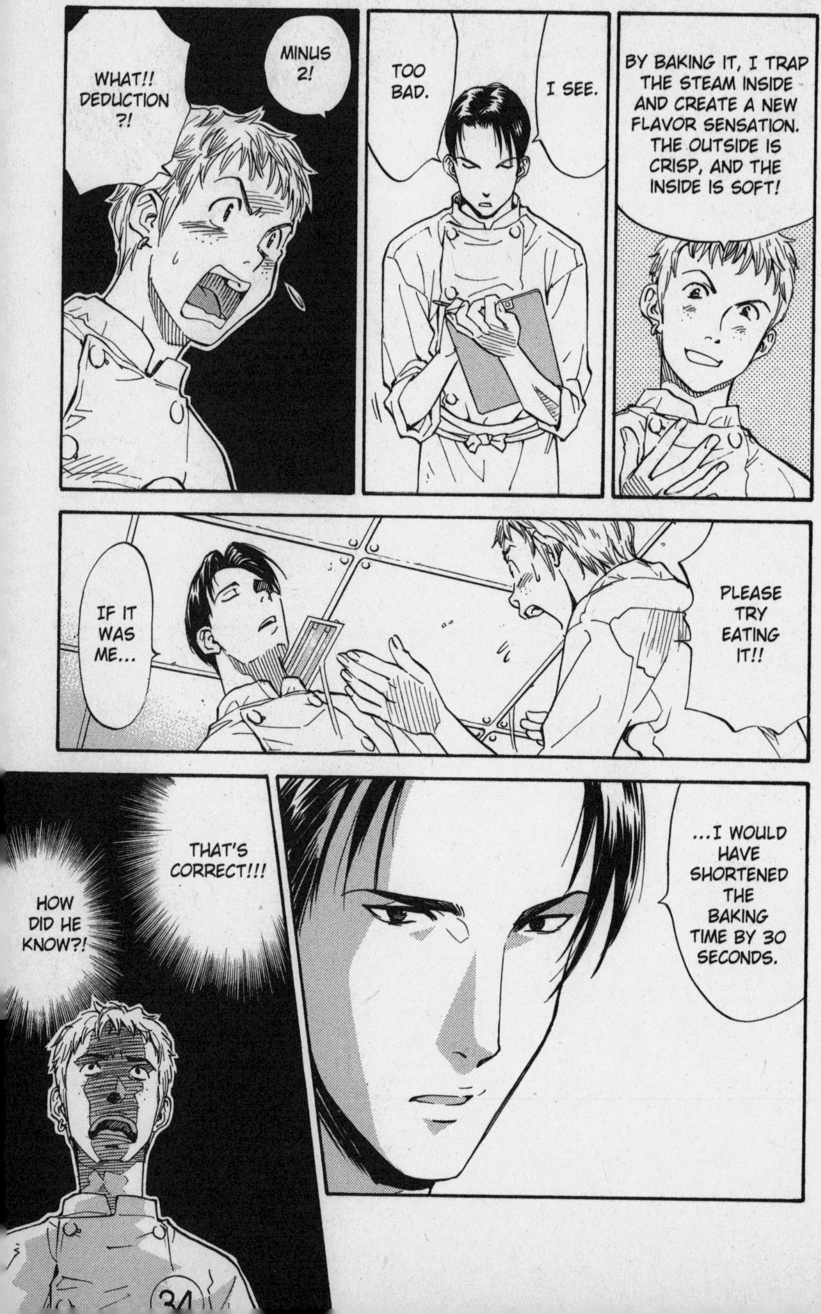
BY BAKING IT, I TRAP THE STEAM INSIDE AND CREATE A NEW FLAVOR SENSATION. THE OUTSIDE IS CRISP, AND THE INSIDE IS SOFT!
I SEE.
TOO BAD.
MINUS 2!
WHAT!! DEDUCTION ?!
PLEASE TRY EATING IT!!
IF IT WAS ME...
...I WOULD HAVE SHORTENED THE BAKING TIME BY 30 SECONDS.
THAT'S CORRECT!!!
HOW DID HE KNOW?!

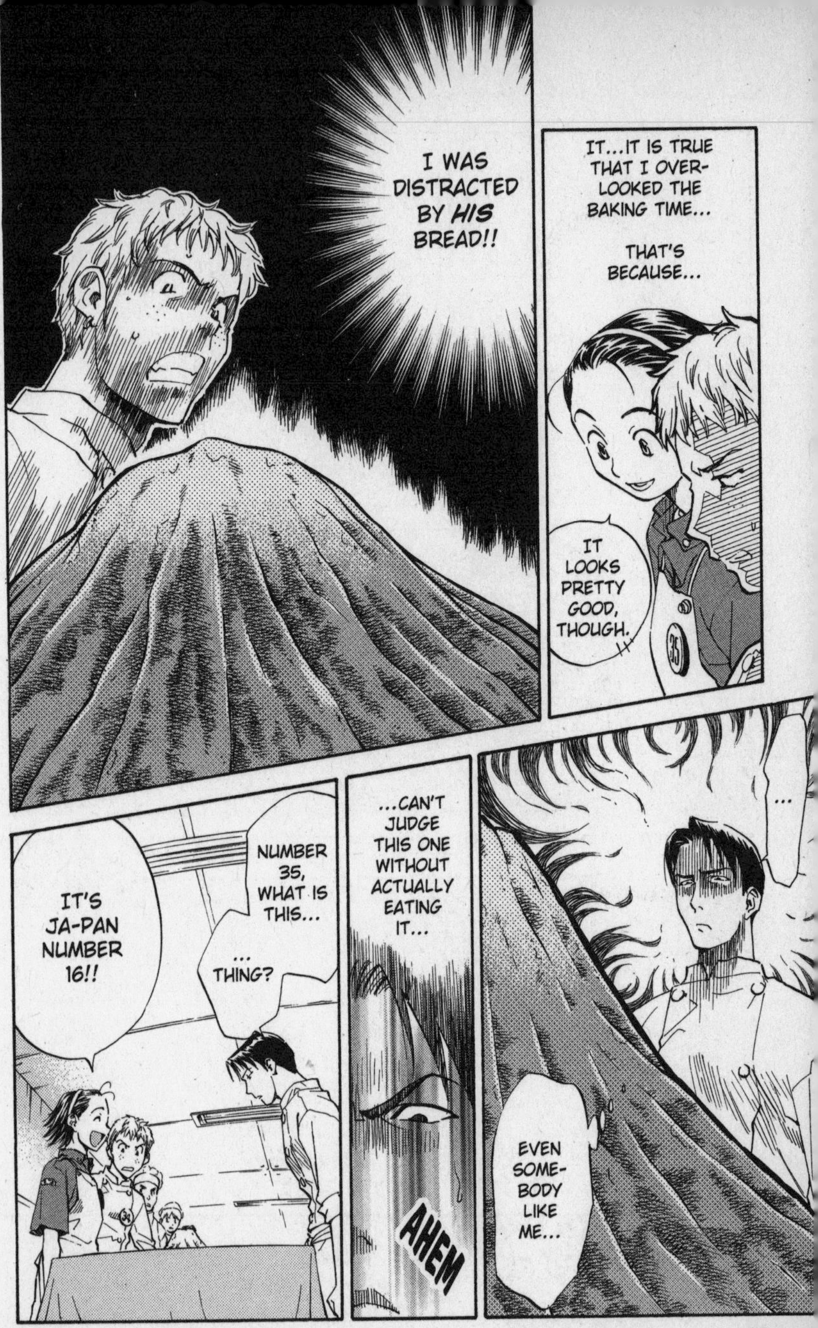
IT...IT IS TRUE THAT I OVER-LOOKED THE BAKING TIME...
THAT'S BECAUSE...
IT LOOKS PRETTY GOOD, THOUGH.
I WAS DISTRACTED BY *HIS* BREAD!!
...
EVEN SOME-BODY LIKE ME...
...CAN'T JUDGE THIS ONE WITHOUT ACTUALLY EATING IT...
AHEM
NUMBER 35, WHAT IS THIS...
... THING?
IT'S JA-PAN NUMBER 16!!

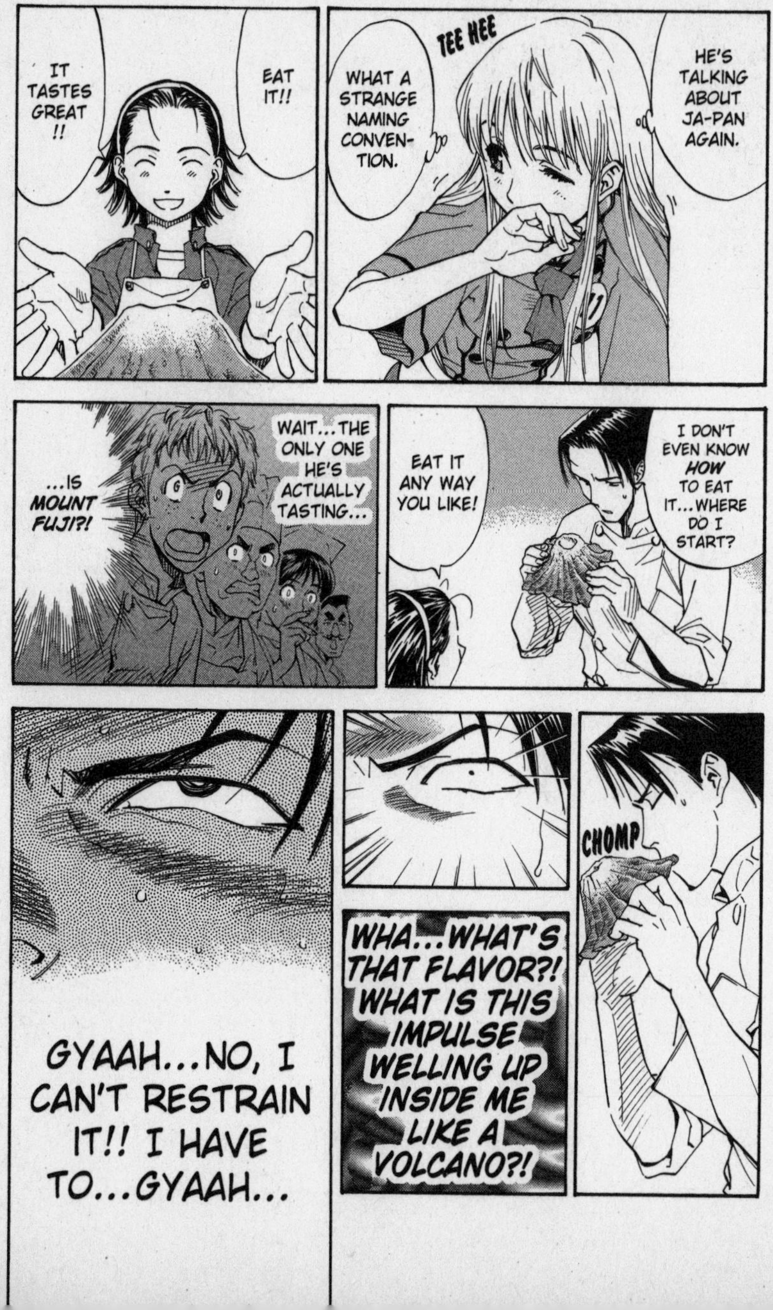
HE'S TALKING ABOUT JA-PAN AGAIN.
TEE HEE
WHAT A STRANGE NAMING CONVEN-TION.
EAT IT!!
IT TASTES GREAT!!
I DON'T EVEN KNOW *HOW* TO EAT IT...WHERE DO I START?
EAT IT ANY WAY YOU LIKE!
WAIT...THE ONLY ONE HE'S ACTUALLY TASTING...
...IS *MOUNT FUJI*?!
CHOMP
WHA...WHAT'S THAT FLAVOR?! WHAT IS THIS IMPULSE WELLING UP INSIDE ME LIKE A VOLCANO?!
GYAAH...NO, I CAN'T RESTRAIN IT!! I HAVE TO...GYAAH...

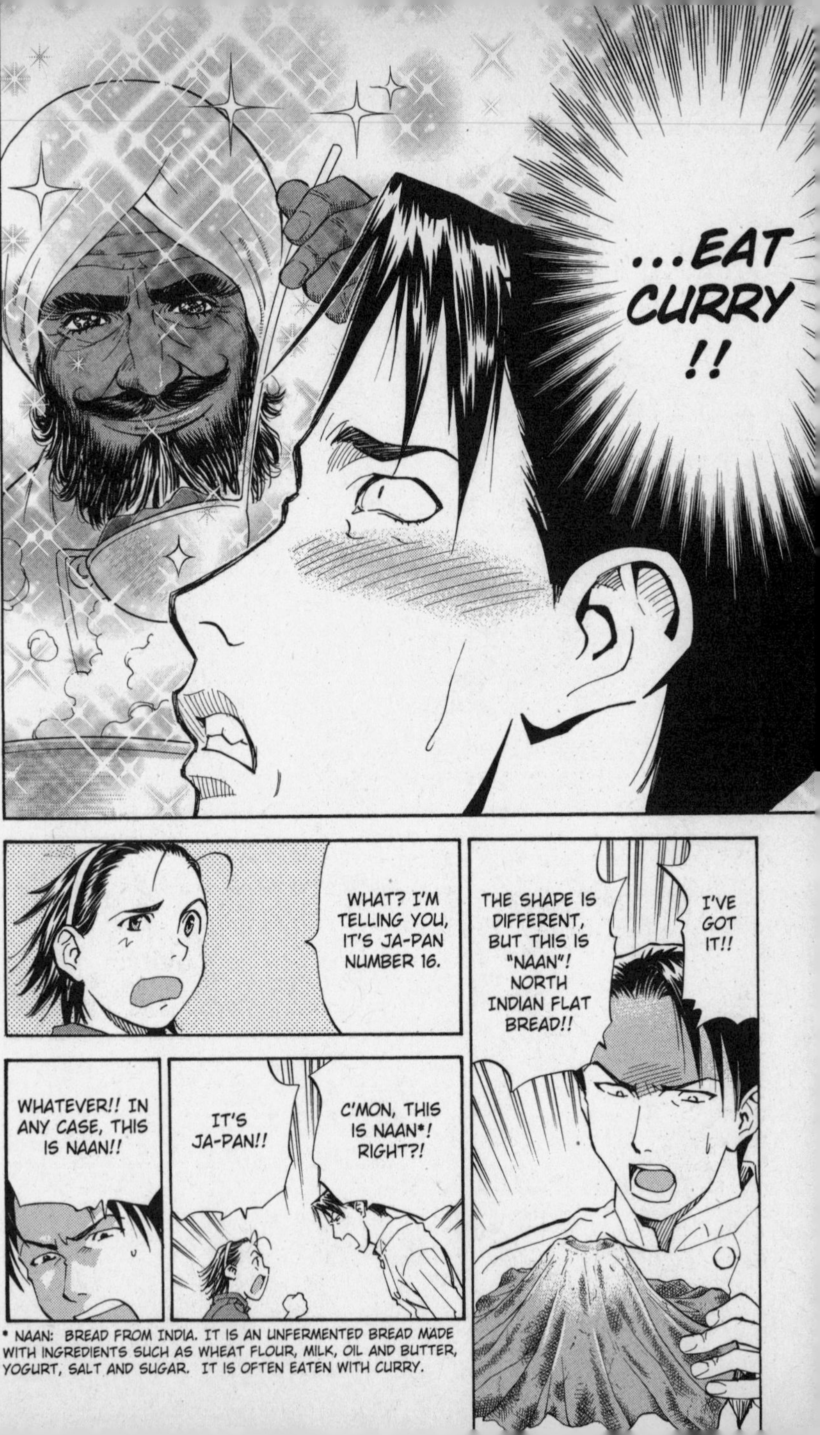
...EAT CURRY!!
I'VE GOT IT!!
THE SHAPE IS DIFFERENT, BUT THIS IS "NAAN"! NORTH INDIAN FLAT BREAD!!
WHAT? I'M TELLING YOU, IT'S JA-PAN NUMBER 16.
C'MON, THIS IS NAAN*! RIGHT?!
IT'S JA-PAN!!
WHATEVER!! IN ANY CASE, THIS IS NAAN!!

* NAAN: BREAD FROM INDIA. IT IS AN UNFERMENTED BREAD MADE WITH INGREDIENTS SUCH AS WHEAT FLOUR, MILK, OIL AND BUTTER, YOGURT, SALT AND SUGAR. IT IS OFTEN EATEN WITH CURRY.

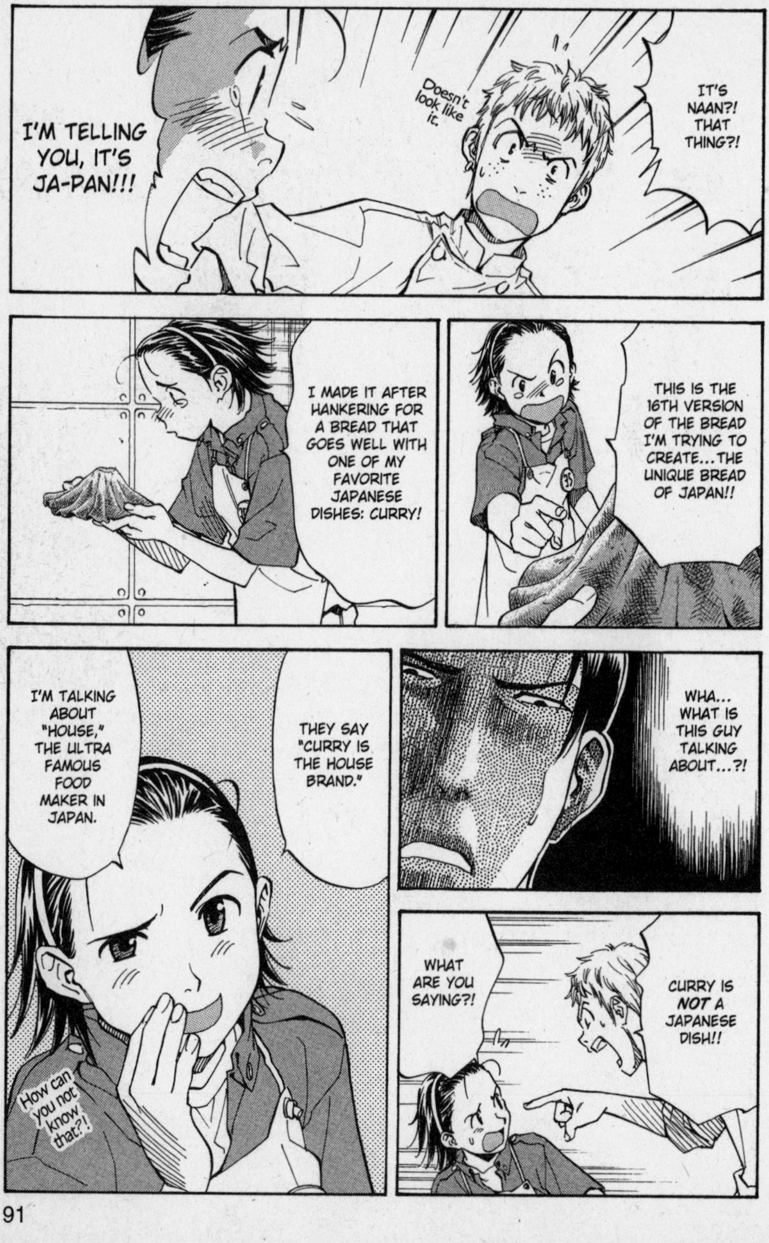
IT'S NAAN?! THAT THING?!
Doesn't look like it.
I'M TELLING YOU, IT'S JA-PAN!!!
THIS IS THE 16TH VERSION OF THE BREAD I'M TRYING TO CREATE...THE UNIQUE BREAD OF JAPAN!!
I MADE IT AFTER HANKERING FOR A BREAD THAT GOES WELL WITH ONE OF MY FAVORITE JAPANESE DISHES: CURRY!
WHA... WHAT IS THIS GUY TALKING ABOUT...?!
CURRY IS *NOT* A JAPANESE DISH!!
WHAT ARE YOU SAYING?!
THEY SAY "CURRY IS THE HOUSE BRAND."
I'M TALKING ABOUT "HOUSE," THE ULTRA FAMOUS FOOD MAKER IN JAPAN.
How can you not know that?!

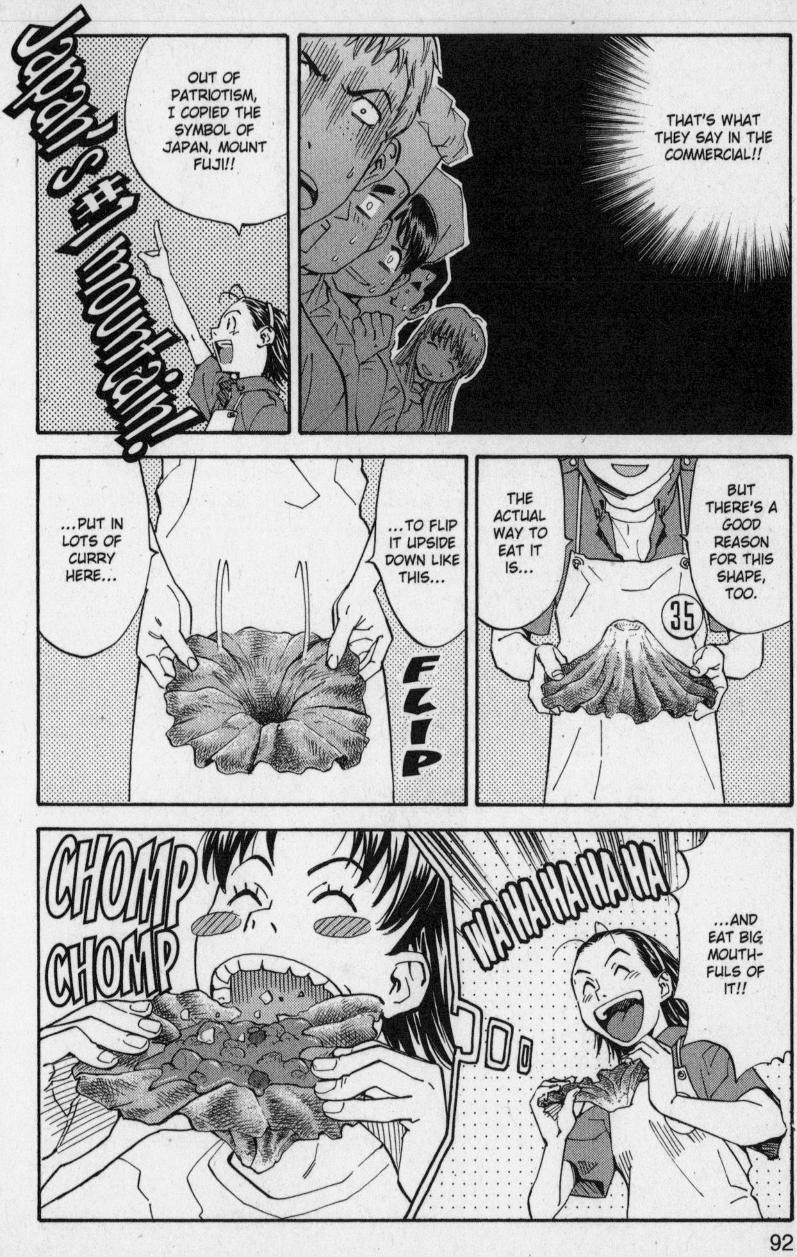
THAT'S WHAT THEY SAY IN THE COMMERCIAL!!
OUT OF PATRIOTISM, I COPIED THE SYMBOL OF JAPAN, MOUNT FUJI!!
Japan's #1 mountain!
BUT THERE'S A GOOD REASON FOR THIS SHAPE, TOO.
THE ACTUAL WAY TO EAT IT IS...
35
...TO FLIP IT UPSIDE DOWN LIKE THIS...
FLIP
...PUT IN LOTS OF CURRY HERE...
...AND EAT BIG MOUTH-FULS OF IT!!
WA HA HA HA HA
CHOMP CHOMP

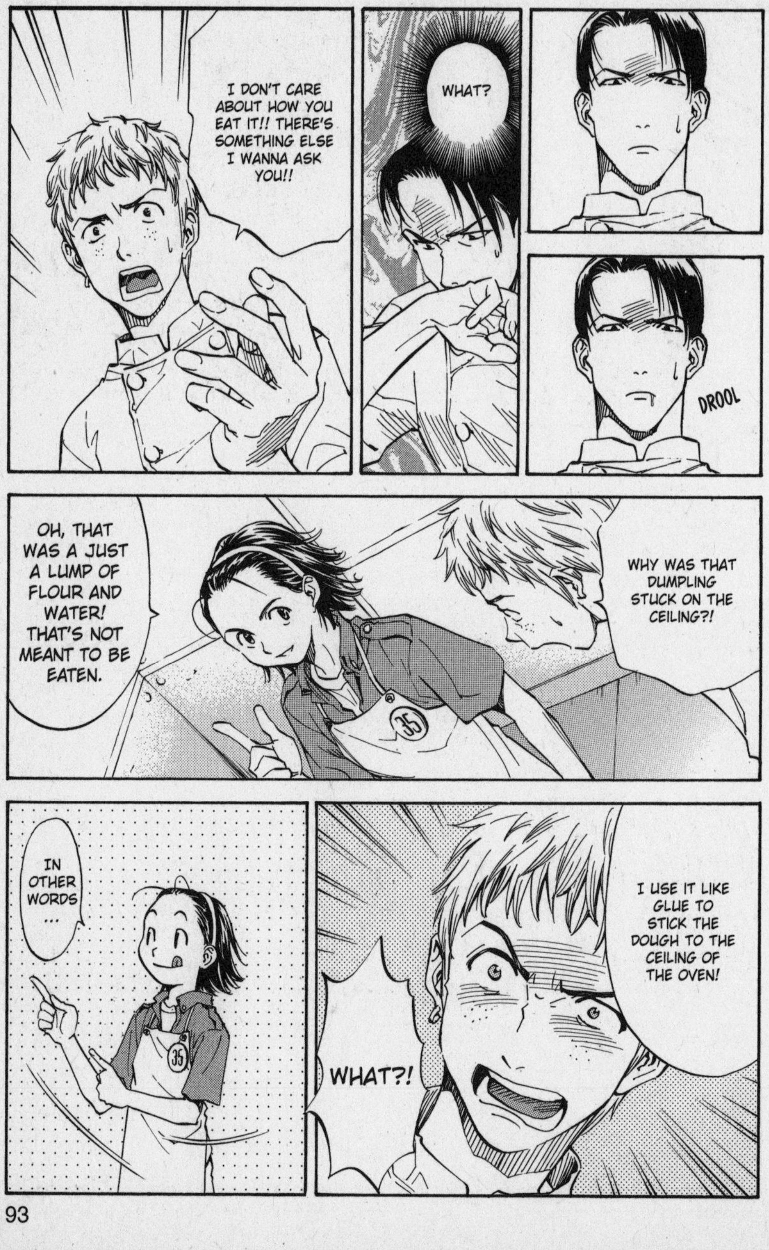
DROOL
WHAT?
I DON'T CARE ABOUT HOW YOU EAT IT!! THERE'S SOMETHING ELSE I WANNA ASK YOU!!
WHY WAS THAT DUMPLING STUCK ON THE CEILING?!
OH, THAT WAS A JUST A LUMP OF FLOUR AND WATER! THAT'S NOT MEANT TO BE EATEN.
I USE IT LIKE GLUE TO STICK THE DOUGH TO THE CEILING OF THE OVEN!
WHAT?!
IN OTHER WORDS ...

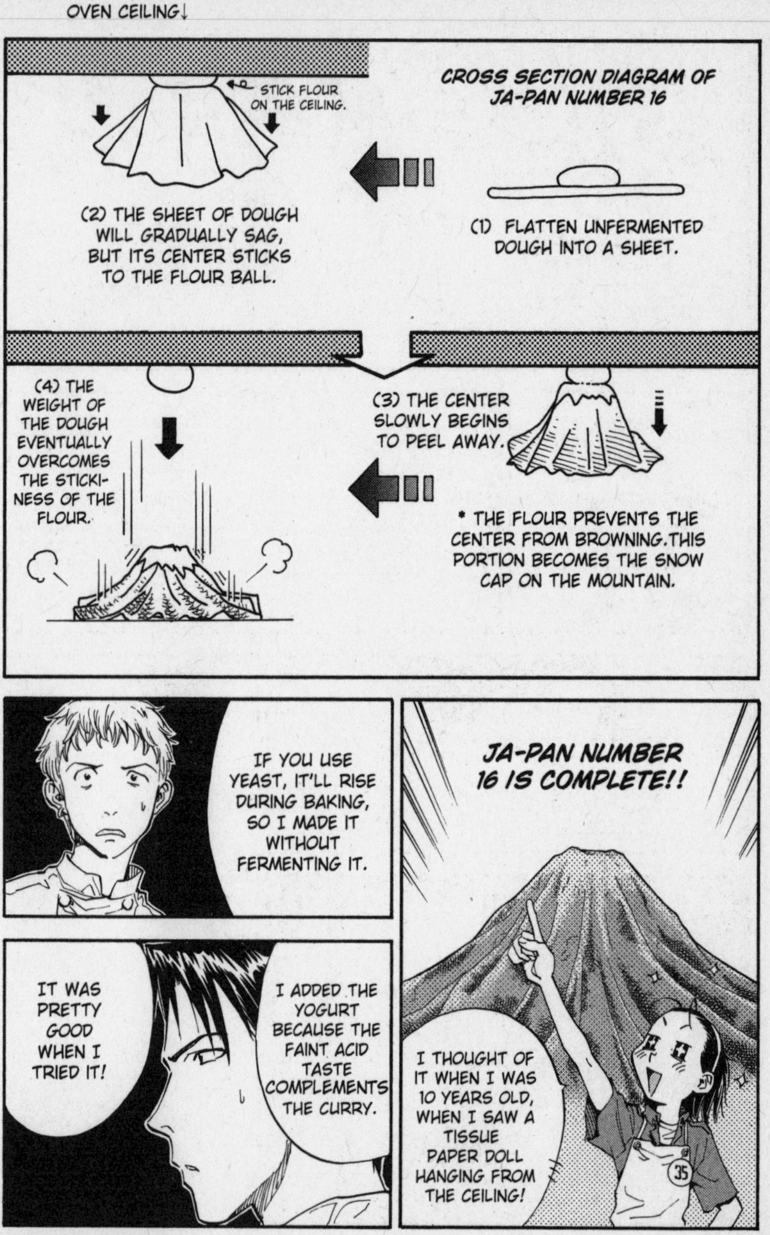
OVEN CEILING↓
CROSS SECTION DIAGRAM OF JA-PAN NUMBER 16
(1) FLATTEN UNFERMENTED DOUGH INTO A SHEET.
STICK FLOUR ON THE CEILING.
(2) THE SHEET OF DOUGH WILL GRADUALLY SAG, BUT ITS CENTER STICKS TO THE FLOUR BALL.
(3) THE CENTER SLOWLY BEGINS TO PEEL AWAY.
* THE FLOUR PREVENTS THE CENTER FROM BROWNING.THIS PORTION BECOMES THE SNOW CAP ON THE MOUNTAIN.
(4) THE WEIGHT OF THE DOUGH EVENTUALLY OVERCOMES THE STICKI-NESS OF THE FLOUR.
JA-PAN NUMBER 16 IS COMPLETE!!
I THOUGHT OF IT WHEN I WAS 10 YEARS OLD, WHEN I SAW A TISSUE PAPER DOLL HANGING FROM THE CEILING!
IF YOU USE YEAST, IT'LL RISE DURING BAKING, SO I MADE IT WITHOUT FERMENTING IT.
I ADDED THE YOGURT BECAUSE THE FAINT ACID TASTE COMPLEMENTS THE CURRY.
IT WAS PRETTY GOOD WHEN I TRIED IT!

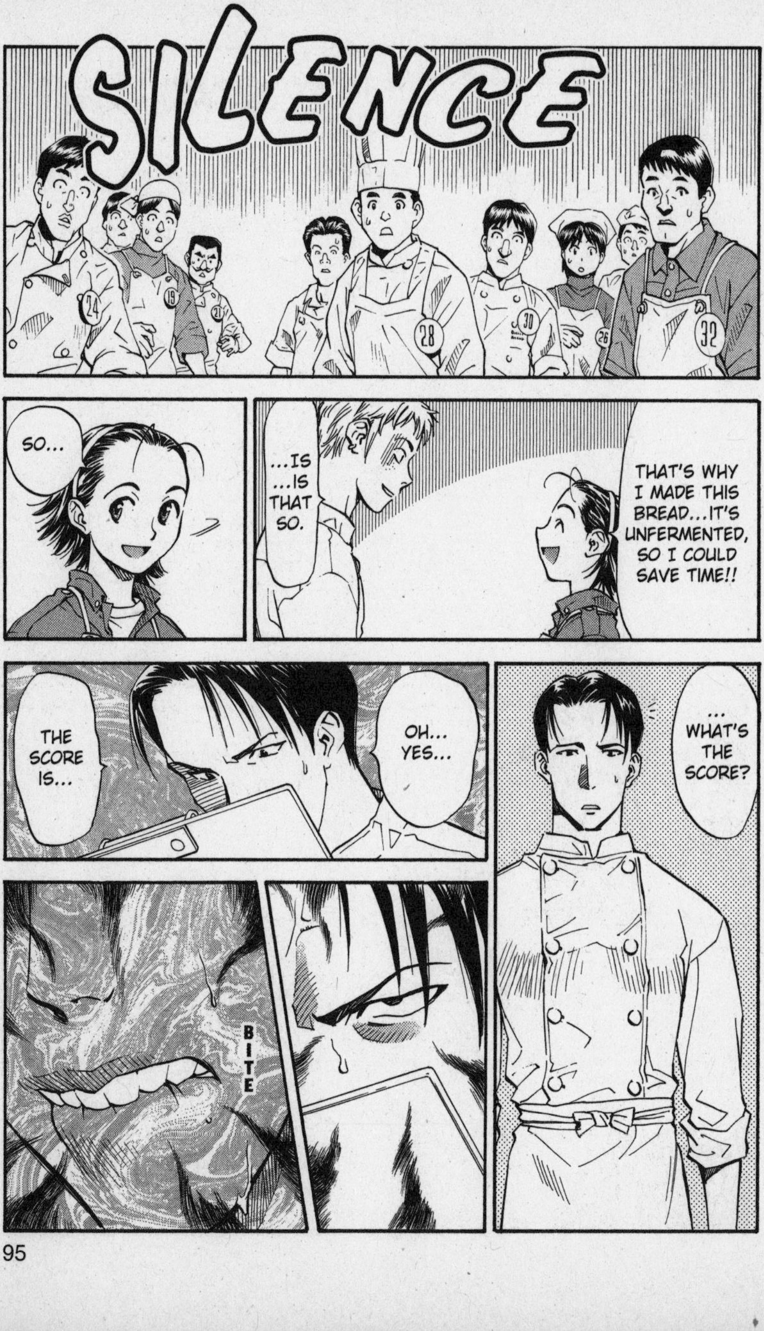
SILENCE
THAT'S WHY I MADE THIS BREAD...IT'S UNFERMENTED, SO I COULD SAVE TIME!!
...IS ...IS THAT SO.
SO...
...WHAT'S THE SCORE?
OH... YES...
THE SCORE IS...
BITE

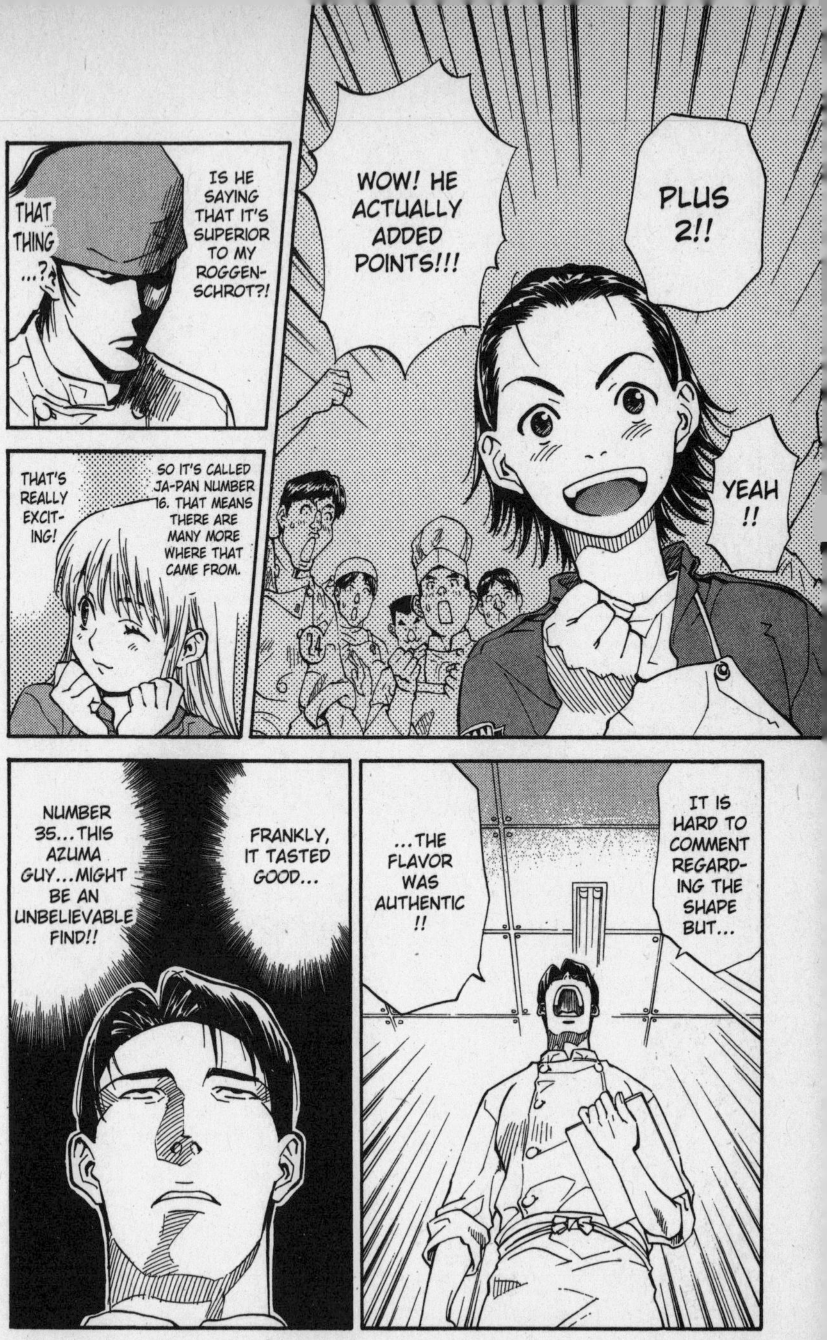
PLUS 2!!
WOW! HE ACTUALLY ADDED POINTS!!!
YEAH !!
IS HE SAYING THAT IT'S SUPERIOR TO MY ROGGEN-SCHROT?!
THAT THING ...?
SO IT'S CALLED JA-PAN NUMBER 16. THAT MEANS THERE ARE MANY MORE WHERE THAT CAME FROM.
THAT'S REALLY EXCIT-ING!
IT IS HARD TO COMMENT REGARD-ING THE SHAPE BUT...
...THE FLAVOR WAS AUTHENTIC !!
FRANKLY, IT TASTED GOOD...
NUMBER 35...THIS AZUMA GUY...MIGHT BE AN UNBELIEVABLE FIND!!

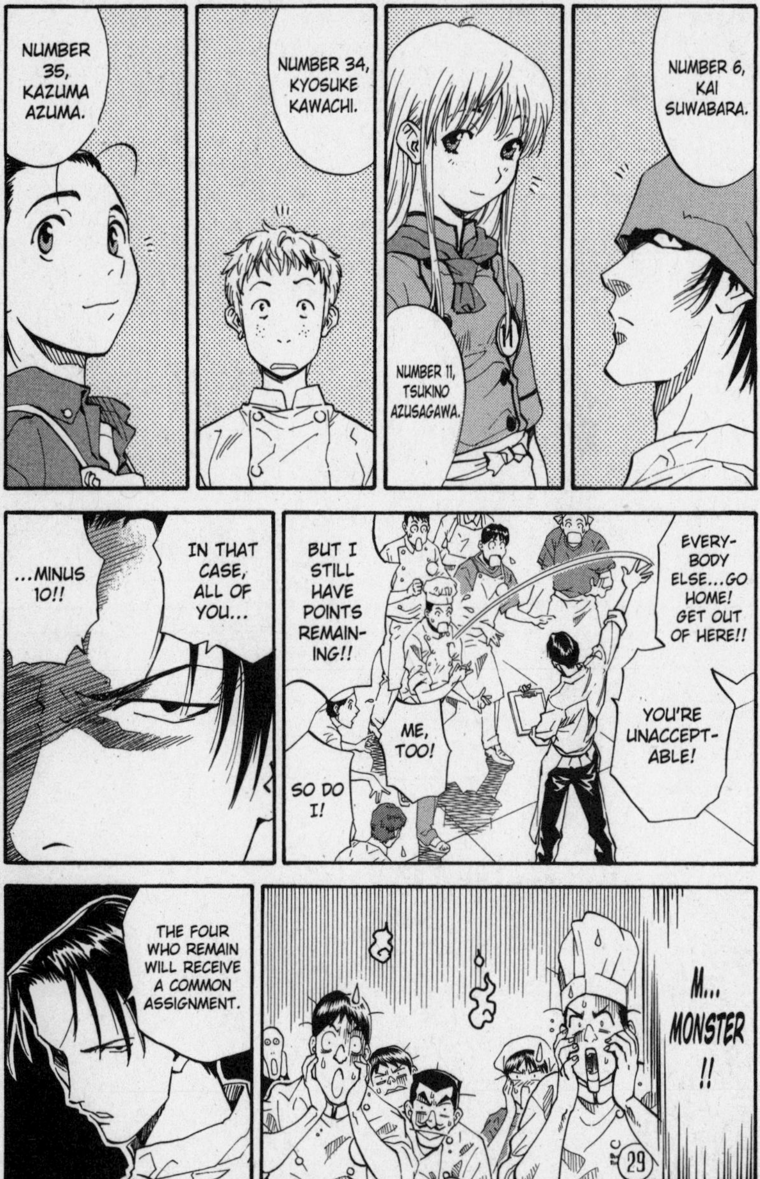
NUMBER 6, KAI SUWABARA.
NUMBER 11, TSUKINO AZUSAGAWA.
NUMBER 34, KYOSUKE KAWACHI.
NUMBER 35, KAZUMA AZUMA.
EVERYBODY ELSE...GO HOME! GET OUT OF HERE!!
YOU'RE UNACCEPTABLE!
BUT I STILL HAVE POINTS REMAINING!!
ME, TOO!
SO DO I!
IN THAT CASE, ALL OF YOU...
...MINUS 10!!
M... MONSTER!!
29
THE FOUR WHO REMAIN WILL RECEIVE A COMMON ASSIGNMENT.

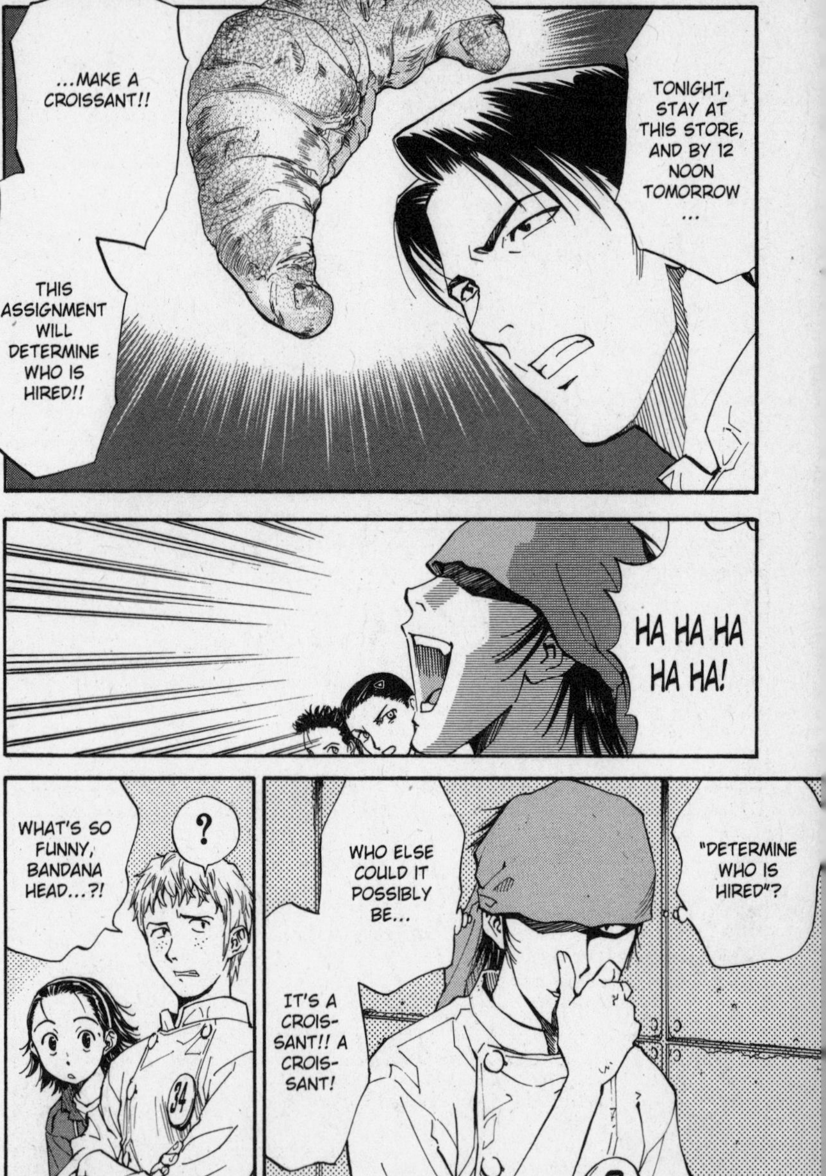
TONIGHT, STAY AT THIS STORE, AND BY 12 NOON TOMORROW ...
...MAKE A CROISSANT!!
THIS ASSIGNMENT WILL DETERMINE WHO IS HIRED!!
HA HA HA HA HA!
"DETERMINE WHO IS HIRED"?
WHO ELSE COULD IT POSSIBLY BE...
IT'S A CROIS-SANT!! A CROIS-SANT!
?
WHAT'S SO FUNNY, BANDANA HEAD...?!

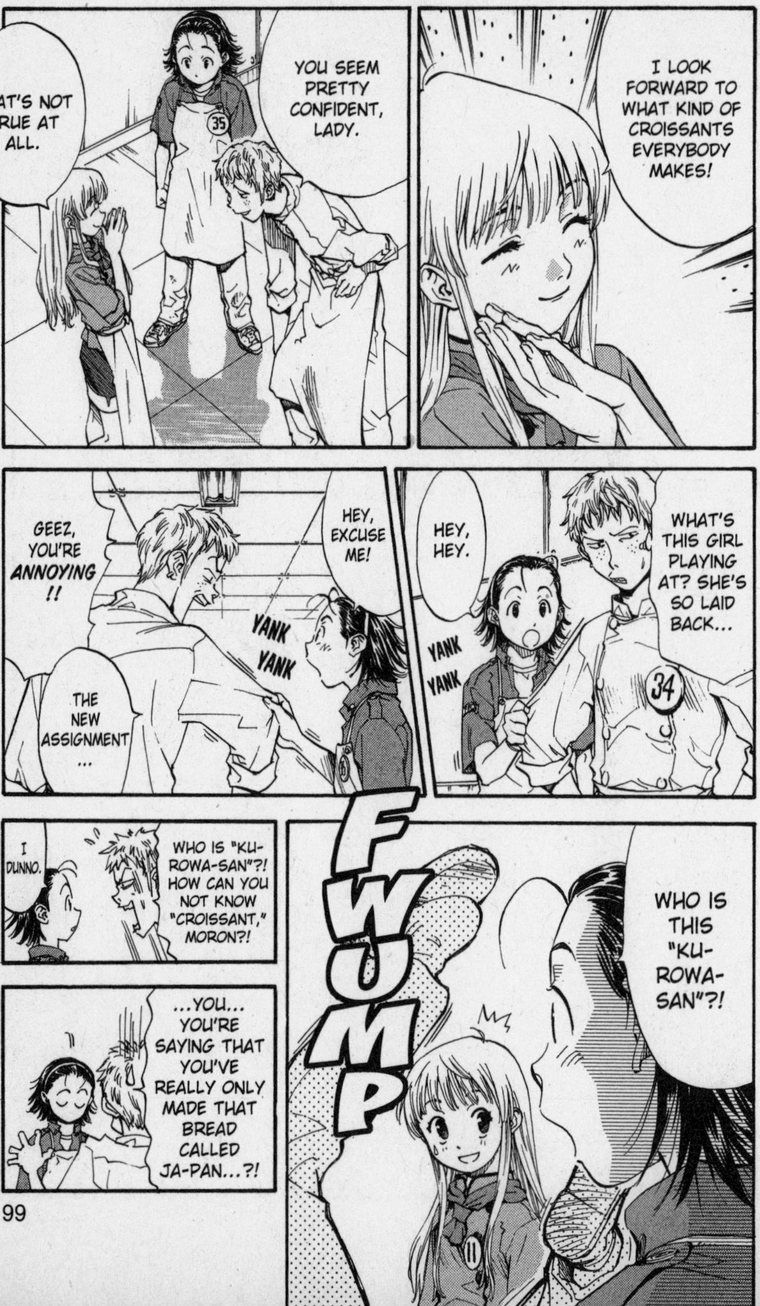
I LOOK FORWARD TO WHAT KIND OF CROISSANTS EVERYBODY MAKES!
YOU SEEM PRETTY CONFIDENT, LADY.
THAT'S NOT TRUE AT ALL.
WHAT'S THIS GIRL PLAYING AT? SHE'S SO LAID BACK...
HEY, HEY.
YANK YANK
HEY, EXCUSE ME!
GEEZ, YOU'RE ANNOYING!!
YANK YANK
THE NEW ASSIGNMENT...
WHO IS THIS "KU-ROWA-SAN"?!
FWUMP
WHO IS "KU-ROWA-SAN"?! HOW CAN YOU NOT KNOW "CROISSANT," MORON?!
I DUNNO.
...YOU... YOU'RE SAYING THAT YOU'VE REALLY ONLY MADE THAT BREAD CALLED JA-PAN...?!

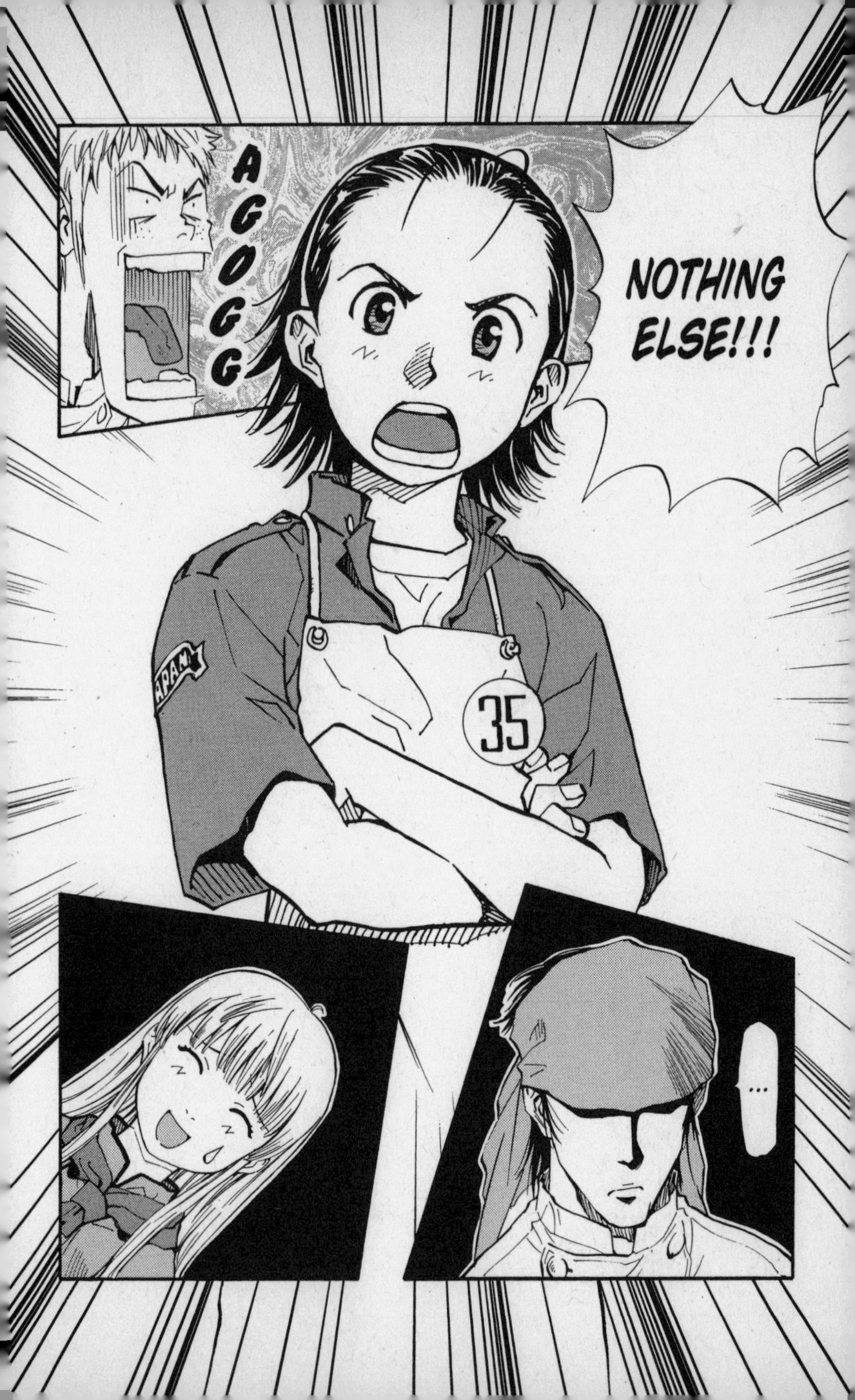
NOTHING ELSE!!!
AGOGG
35
JAPAN
...

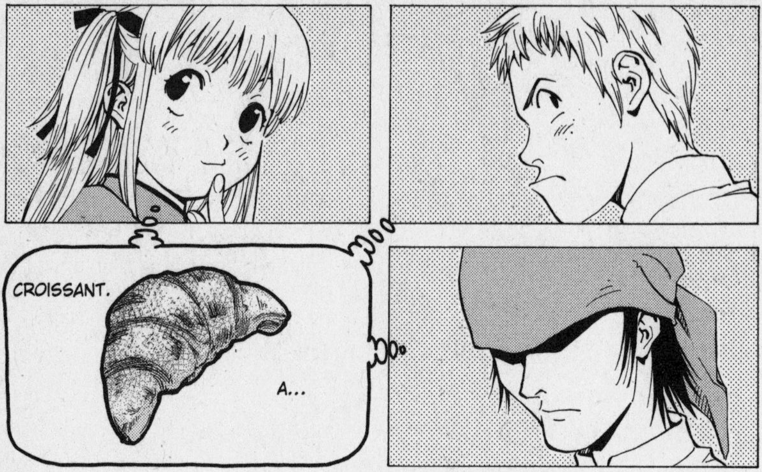
CROISSANT.
A...

Story 4:
324 Layers!

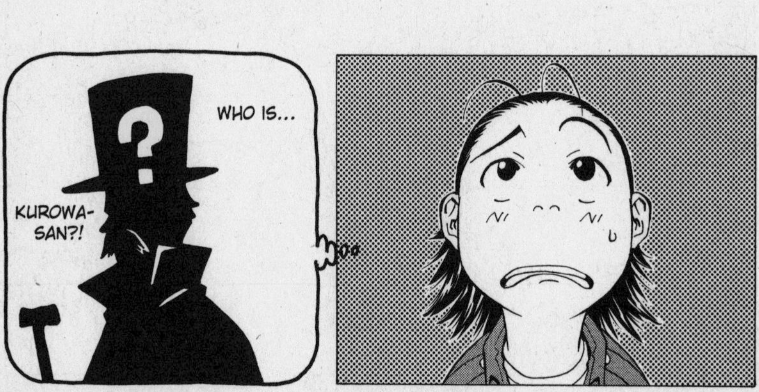
WHO IS...
KUROWA-SAN?!

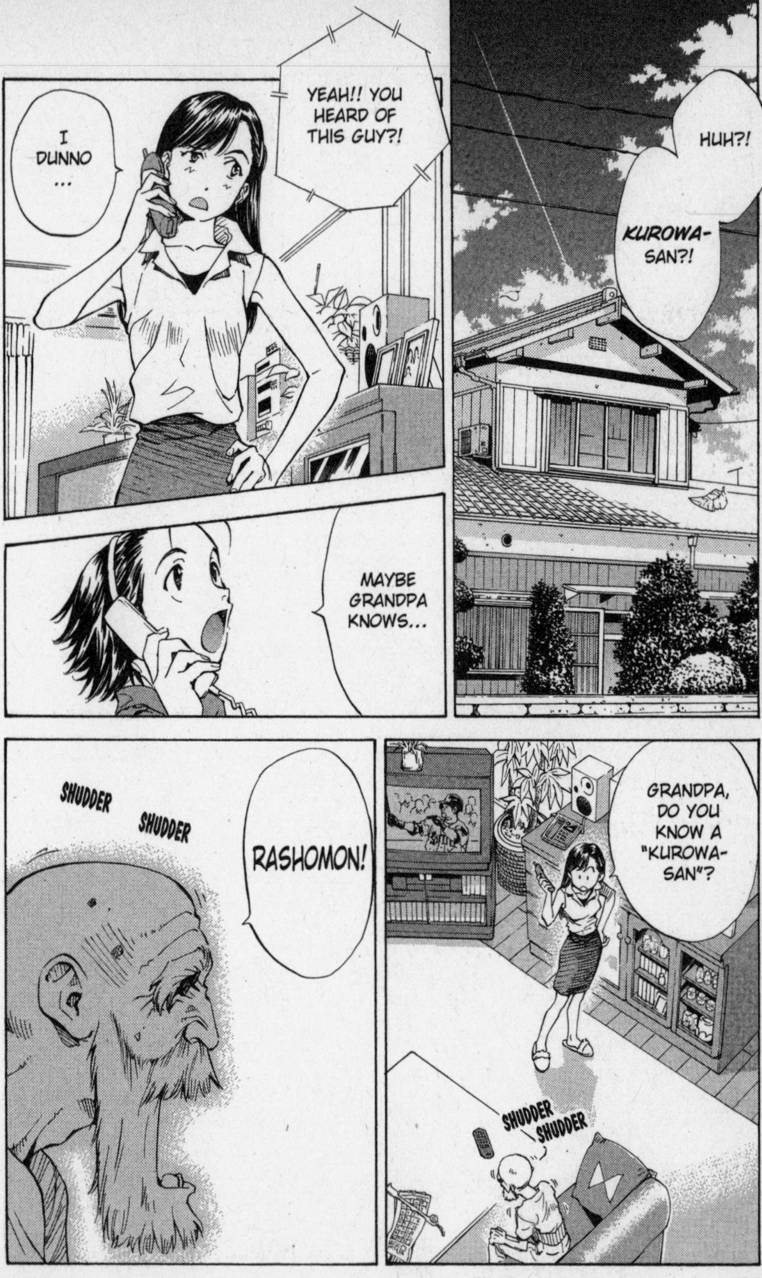
HUH?!
KUROWA-SAN?!
YEAH!! YOU HEARD OF THIS GUY?!
I DUNNO ...
MAYBE GRANDPA KNOWS...
GRANDPA, DO YOU KNOW A "KUROWA-SAN"?
SHUDDER SHUDDER
RASHOMON!
SHUDDER SHUDDER

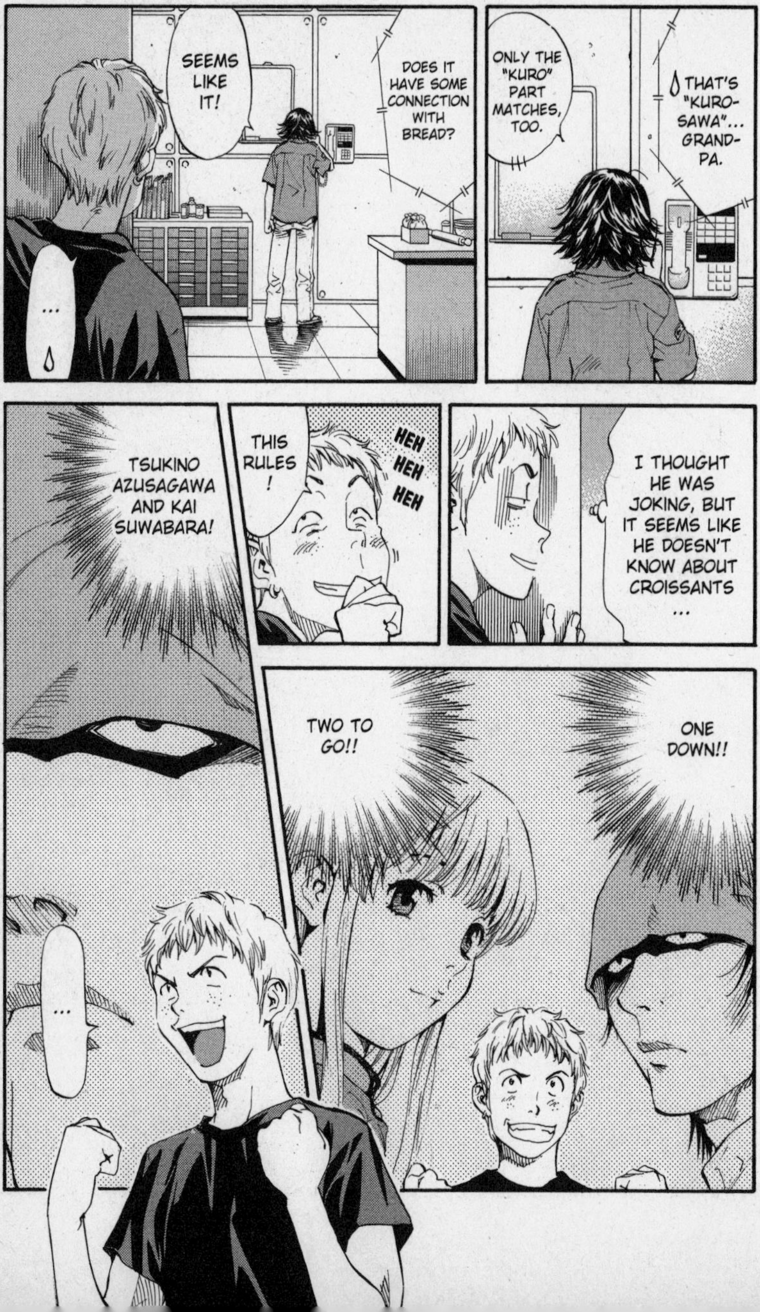
THAT'S "KURO-SAWA"... GRAND-PA.
ONLY THE "KURO" PART MATCHES, TOO.
DOES IT HAVE SOME CONNECTION WITH BREAD?
SEEMS LIKE IT!
...
I THOUGHT HE WAS JOKING, BUT IT SEEMS LIKE HE DOESN'T KNOW ABOUT CROISSANTS...
HEH HEH HEH
THIS RULES!
ONE DOWN!!
TWO TO GO!!
TSUKINO AZUSAGAWA AND KAI SUWABARA!
...

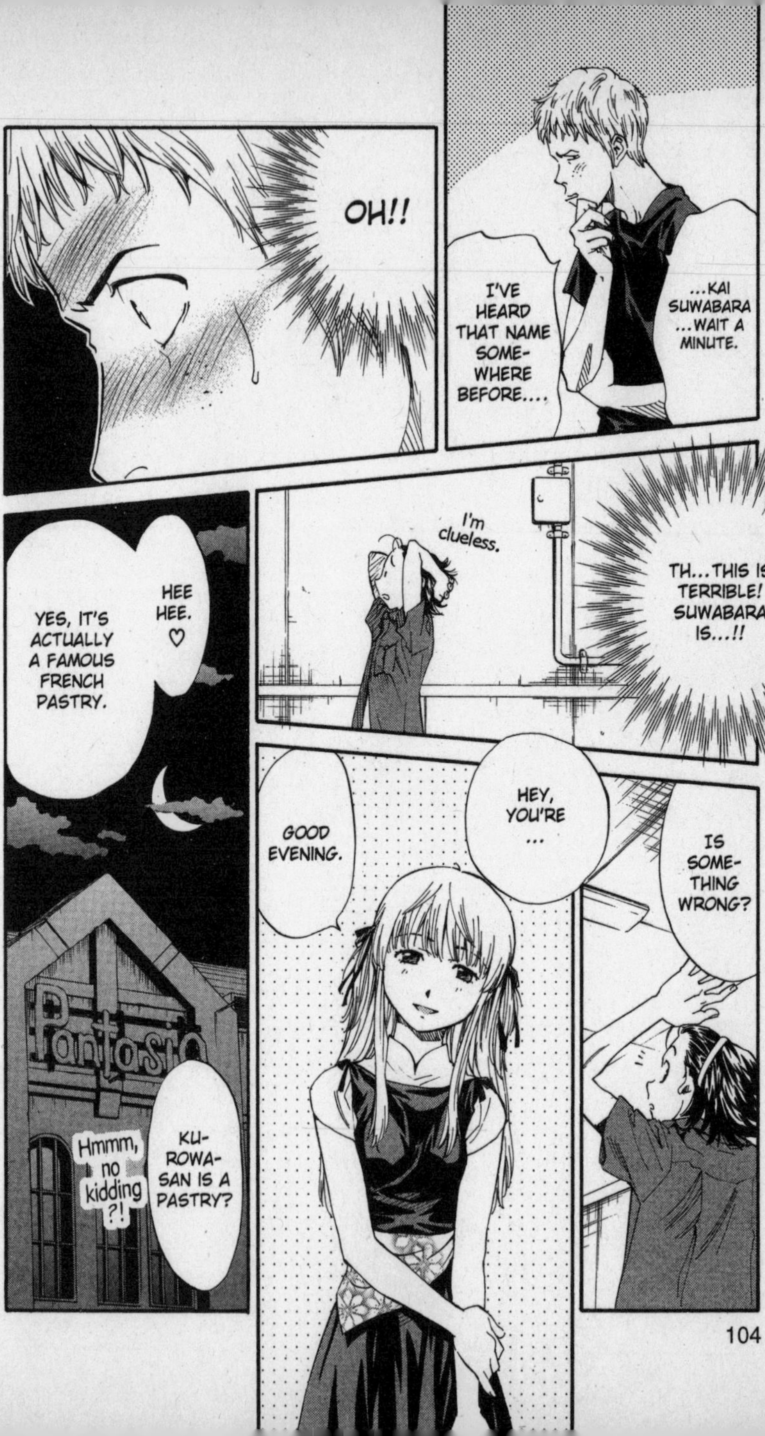
...KAI SUWABARA ...WAIT A MINUTE.
I'VE HEARD THAT NAME SOME-WHERE BEFORE....
OH!!
TH...THIS IS TERRIBLE! SUWABARA IS...!!
I'm clueless.
IS SOME-THING WRONG?
HEY, YOU'RE ...
GOOD EVENING.
YES, IT'S ACTUALLY A FAMOUS FRENCH PASTRY.
HEE HEE. ♡
Pantasia
KU-ROWA-SAN IS A PASTRY?
Hmmm, no kidding ?!

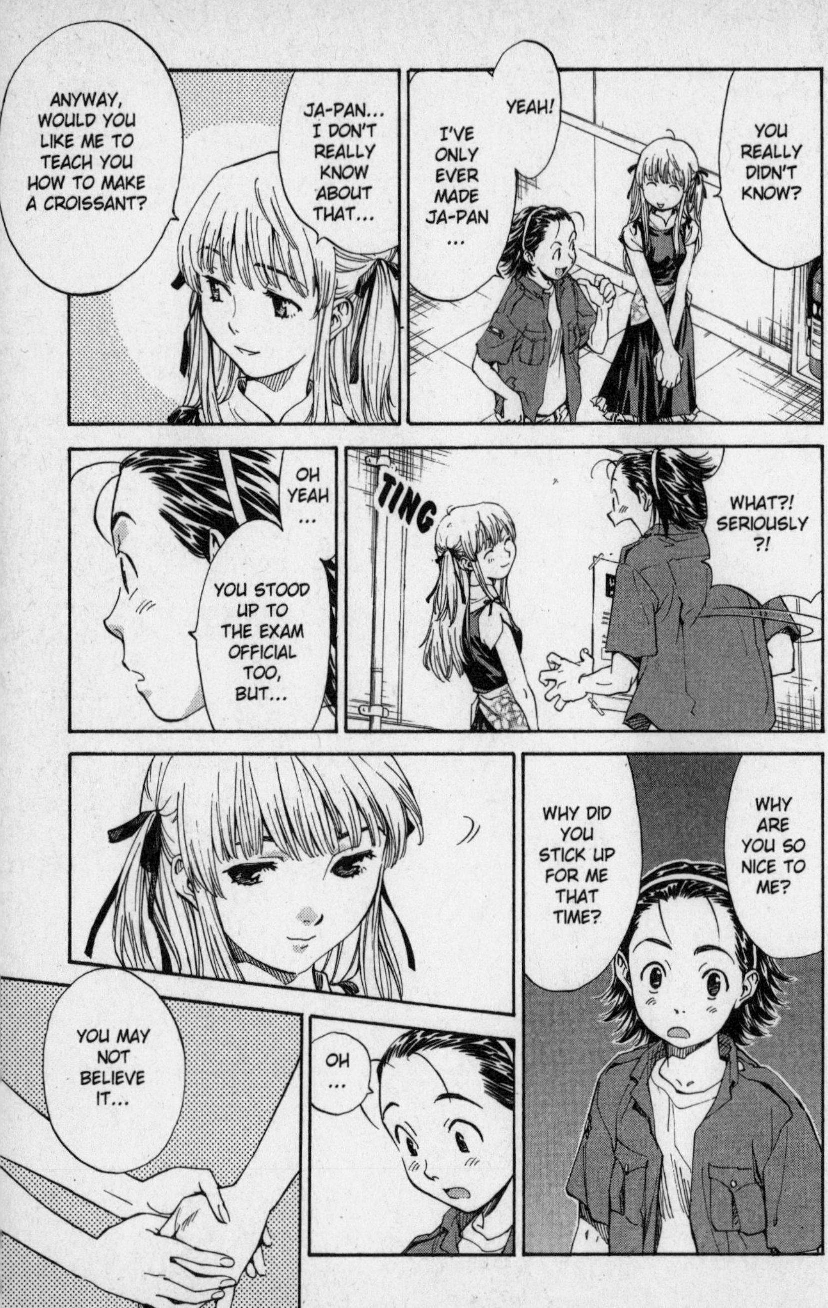
YOU REALLY DIDN'T KNOW?
YEAH!
I'VE ONLY EVER MADE JA-PAN...
JA-PAN... I DON'T REALLY KNOW ABOUT THAT...
ANYWAY, WOULD YOU LIKE ME TO TEACH YOU HOW TO MAKE A CROISSANT?
WHAT?! SERIOUSLY?!
TING
OH YEAH...
YOU STOOD UP TO THE EXAM OFFICIAL TOO, BUT...
WHY ARE YOU SO NICE TO ME?
WHY DID YOU STICK UP FOR ME THAT TIME?
OH...
YOU MAY NOT BELIEVE IT...

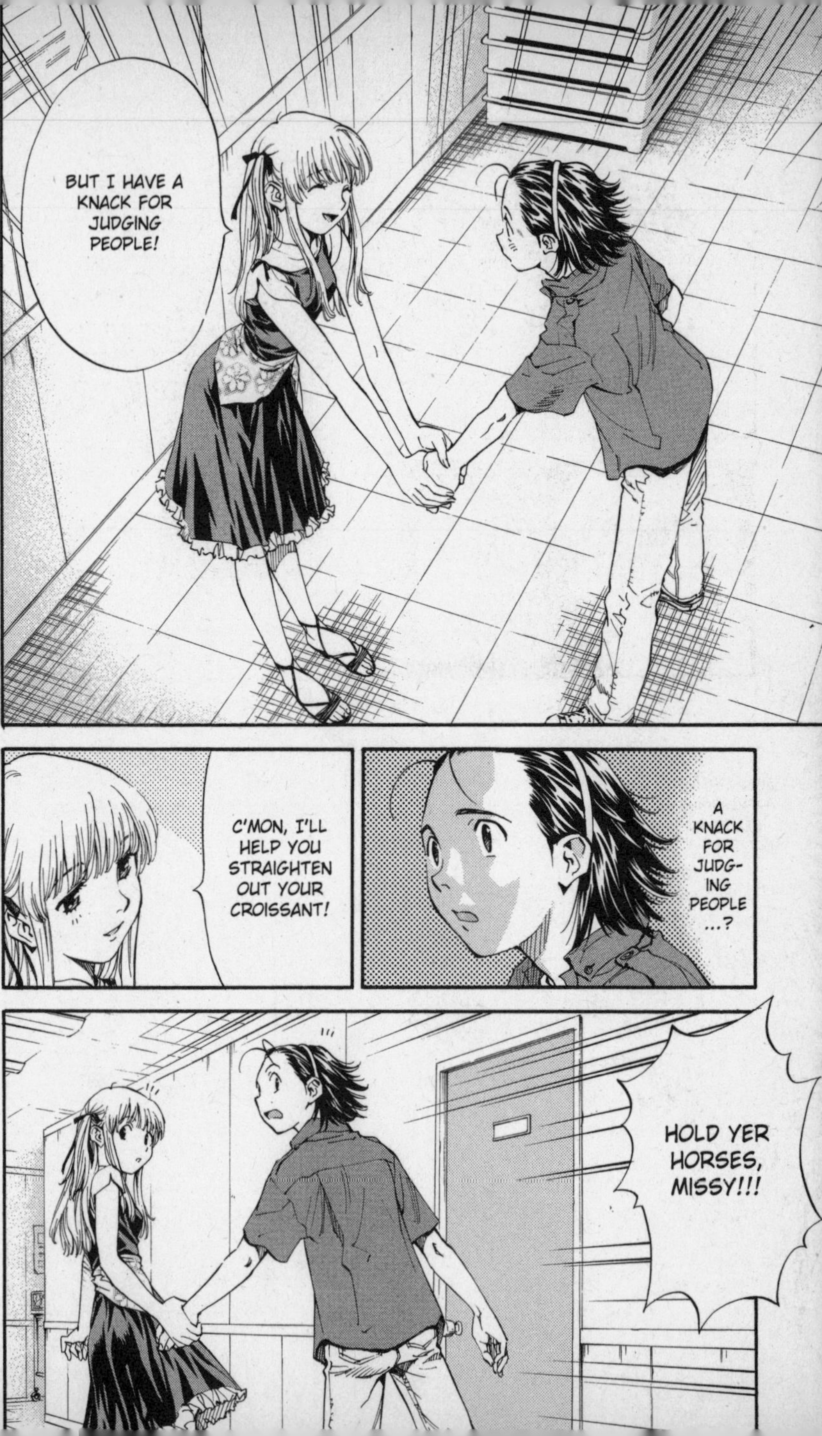
BUT I HAVE A KNACK FOR JUDGING PEOPLE!
A KNACK FOR JUDG-ING PEOPLE ...?
C'MON, I'LL HELP YOU STRAIGHTEN OUT YOUR CROISSANT!
HOLD YER HORSES, MISSY!!!

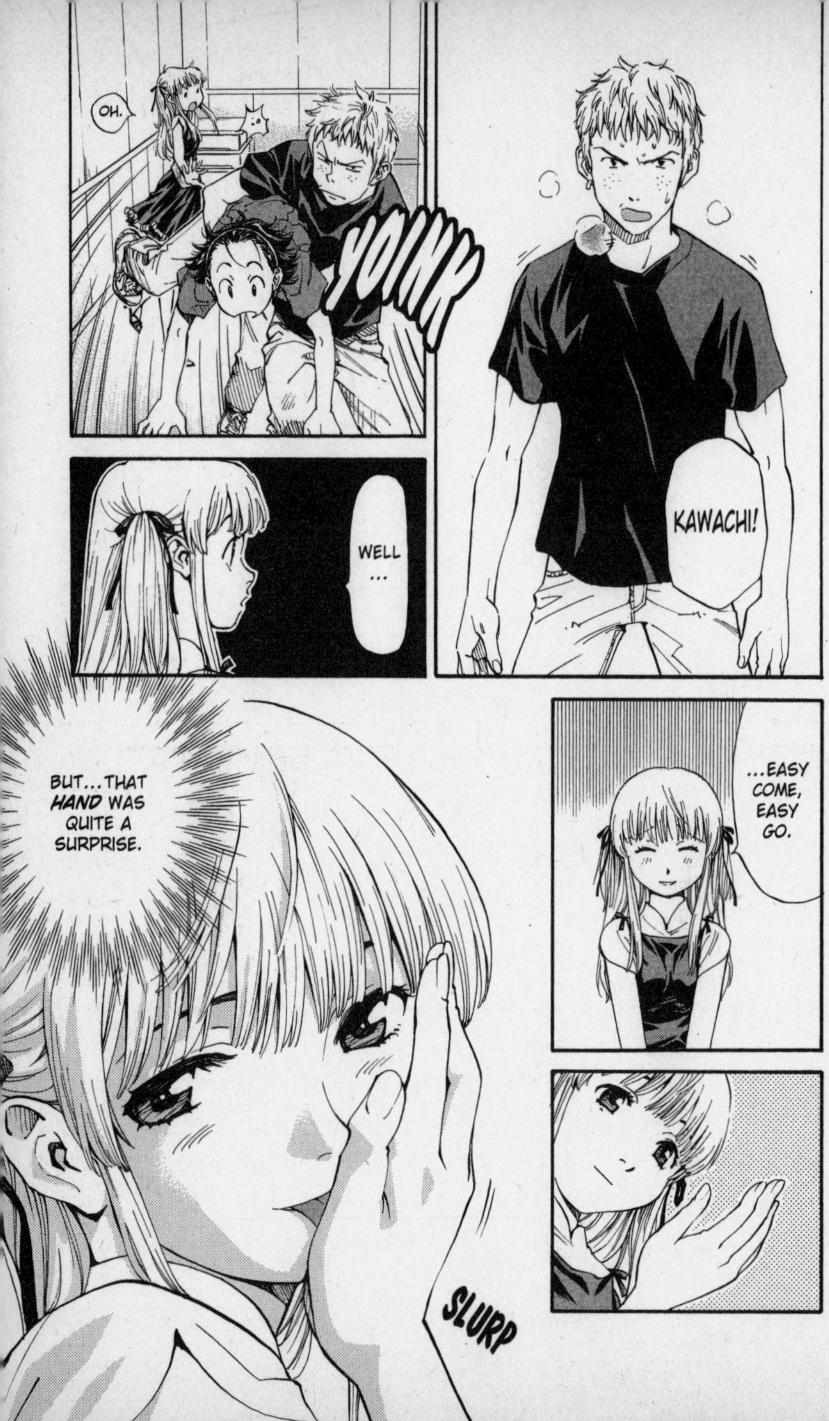
KAWACHI!
YOINK
OH.
WELL ...
...EASY COME, EASY GO.
BUT...THAT HAND WAS QUITE A SURPRISE.
SLURP

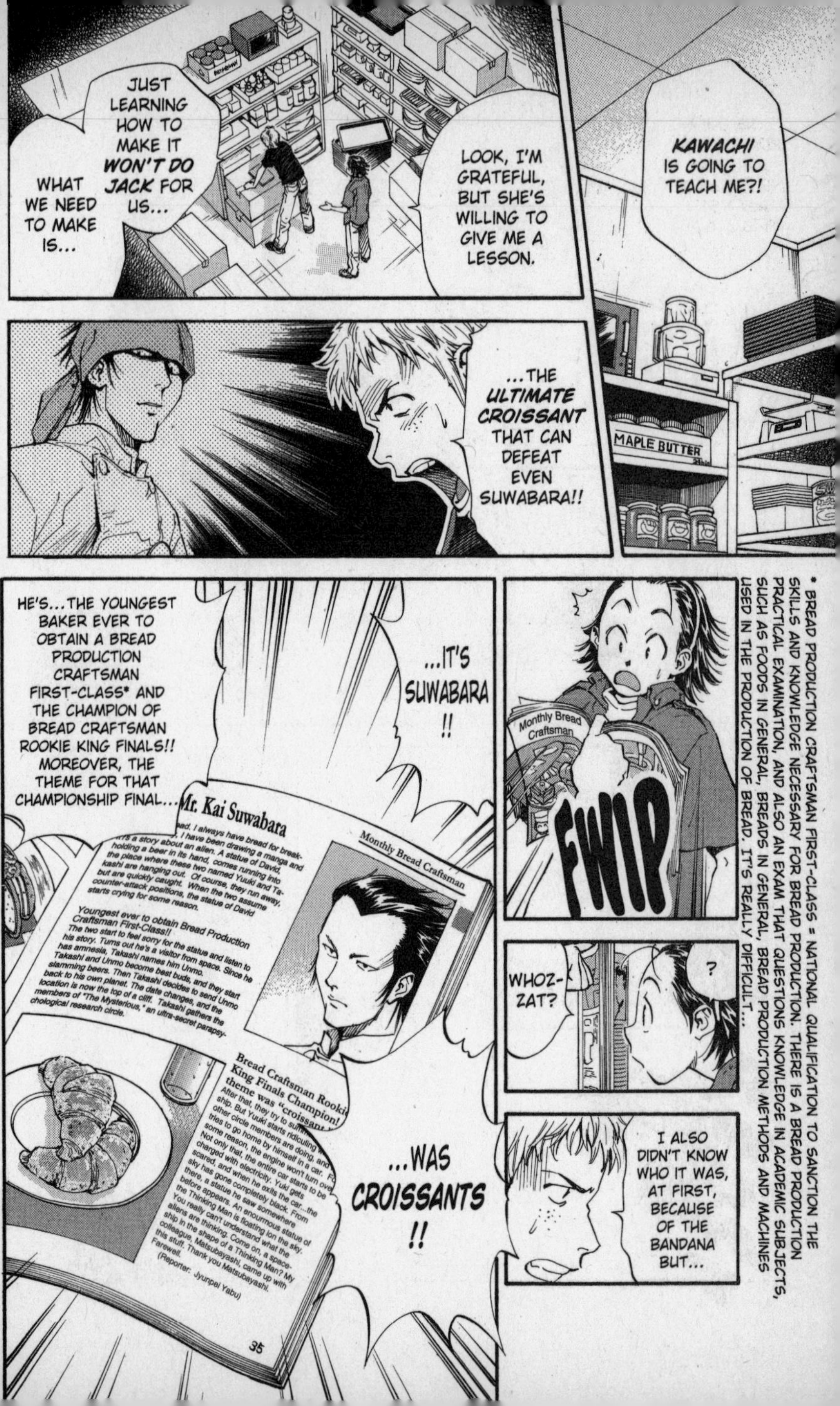
KAWACHI IS GOING TO TEACH ME?!
LOOK, I'M GRATEFUL, BUT SHE'S WILLING TO GIVE ME A LESSON.
JUST LEARNING HOW TO MAKE IT WON'T DO JACK FOR US...
WHAT WE NEED TO MAKE IS...
MAPLE BUTTER
...THE ULTIMATE CROISSANT THAT CAN DEFEAT EVEN SUWABARA!!
Monthly Bread Craftsman
FWIP
?
WHOZ-ZAT?
I ALSO DIDN'T KNOW WHO IT WAS, AT FIRST, BECAUSE OF THE BANDANA BUT...
...IT'S SUWABARA!!
HE'S... THE YOUNGEST BAKER EVER TO OBTAIN A BREAD PRODUCTION CRAFTSMAN FIRST-CLASS* AND THE CHAMPION OF BREAD CRAFTSMAN ROOKIE KING FINALS!! MOREOVER, THE THEME FOR THAT CHAMPIONSHIP FINAL...
Mr. Kai Suwabara
Monthly Bread Craftsman
Youngest ever to obtain Bread Production Craftsman First-Class!!
(Reporter: Jyunpei Yabu)
35
...WAS CROISSANTS!!

* BREAD PRODUCTION CRAFTSMAN FIRST-CLASS = NATIONAL QUALIFICATION TO SANCTION THE SKILLS AND KNOWLEDGE NECESSARY FOR BREAD PRODUCTION. THERE IS A BREAD PRODUCTION PRACTICAL EXAMINATION, AND ALSO AN EXAM THAT QUESTIONS KNOWLEDGE IN ACADEMIC SUBJECTS, SUCH AS FOODS IN GENERAL, BREADS IN GENERAL, BREAD PRODUCTION METHODS AND MACHINES USED IN THE PRODUCTION OF BREAD. IT'S REALLY DIFFICULT...

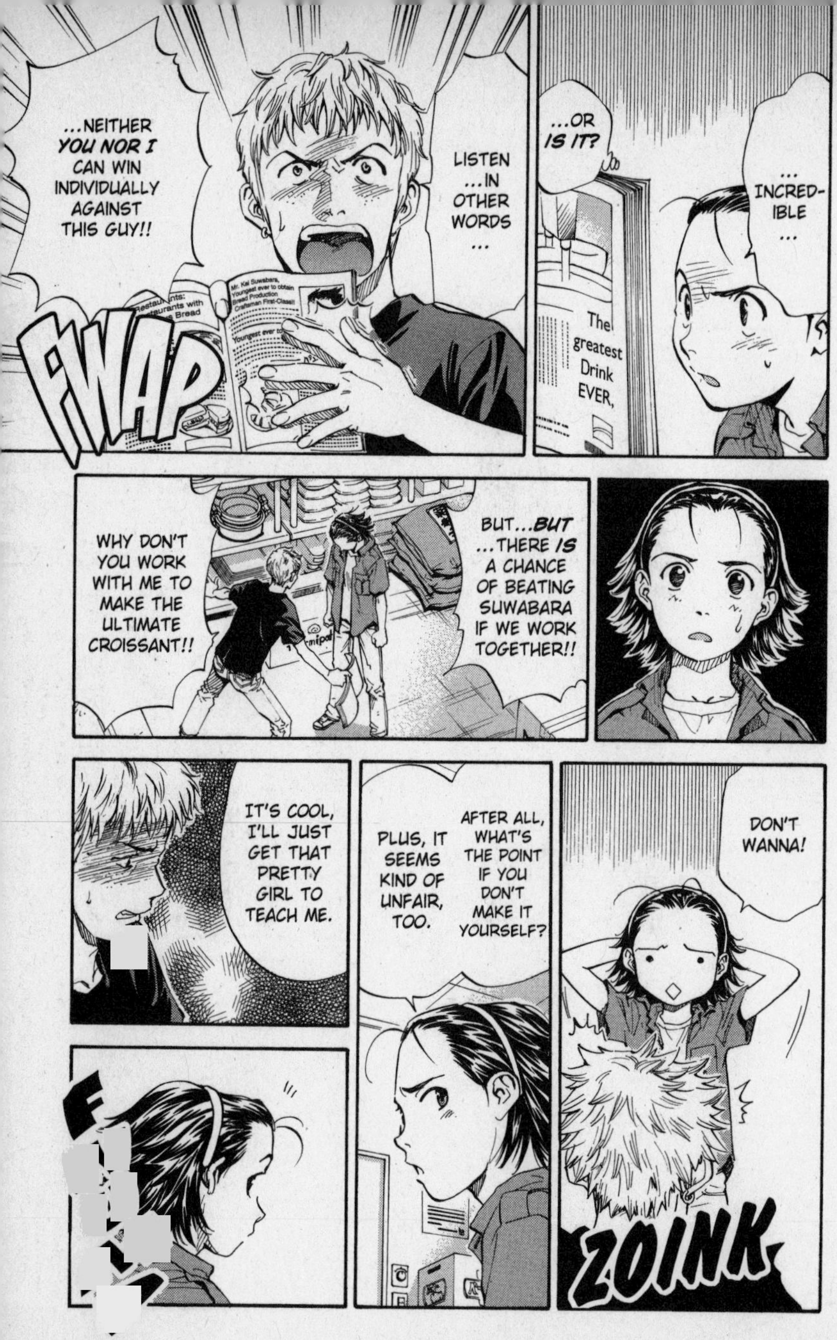
...INCREDIBLE...
...OR IS IT?
The greatest Drink EVER,
LISTEN ...IN OTHER WORDS...
...NEITHER YOU NOR I CAN WIN INDIVIDUALLY AGAINST THIS GUY!!
FWAP
Mr. Kai Suwabara, Youngest ever to obtain Bread Production Craftsman First-Class!!
BUT...BUT ...THERE IS A CHANCE OF BEATING SUWABARA IF WE WORK TOGETHER!!
WHY DON'T YOU WORK WITH ME TO MAKE THE ULTIMATE CROISSANT!!
DON'T WANNA!
ZOINK
AFTER ALL, WHAT'S THE POINT IF YOU DON'T MAKE IT YOURSELF?
PLUS, IT SEEMS KIND OF UNFAIR, TOO.
IT'S COOL, I'LL JUST GET THAT PRETTY GIRL TO TEACH ME.

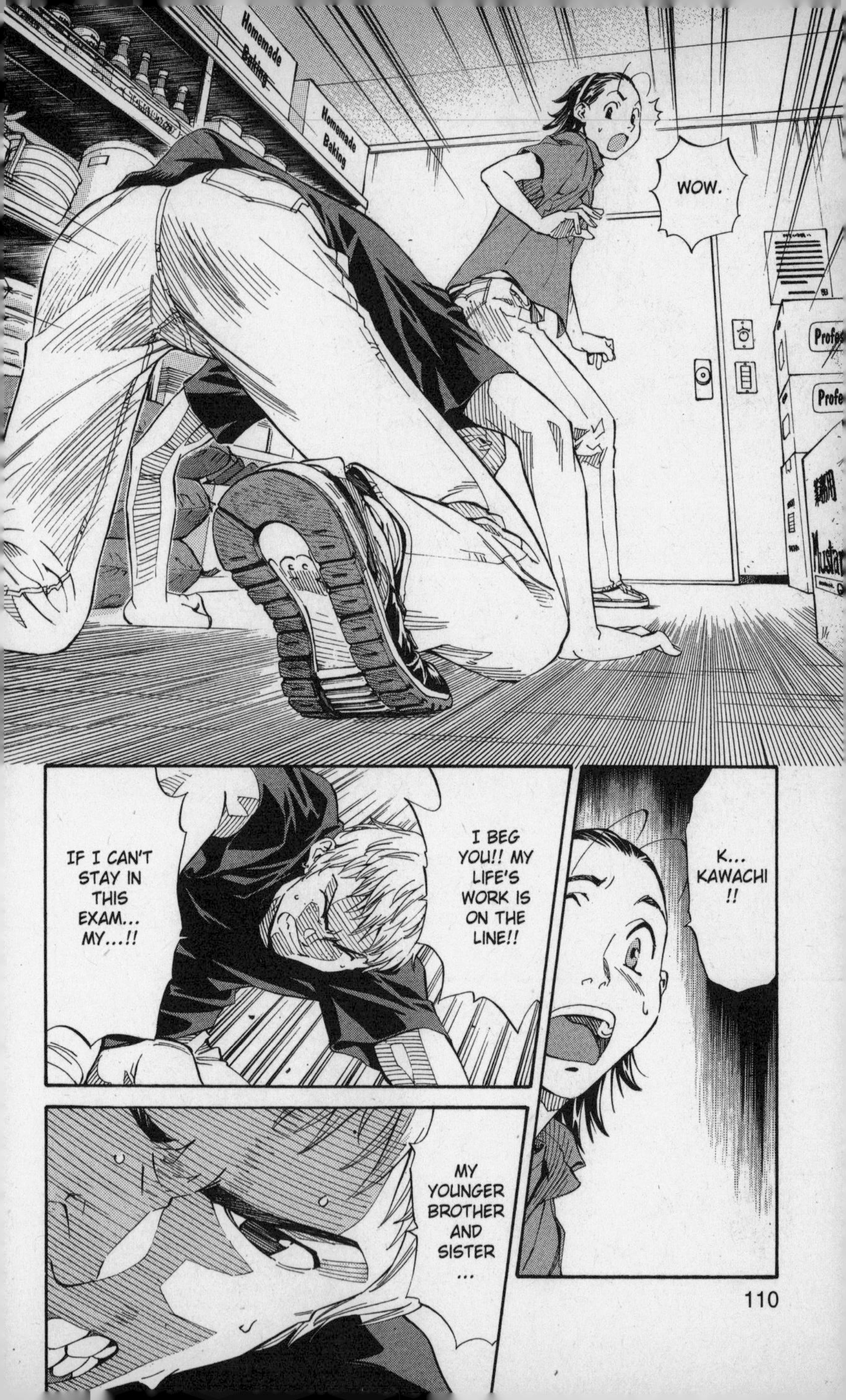
Homemade Baking
Homemade Baking
WOW.
K... KAWACHI !!
I BEG YOU!! MY LIFE'S WORK IS ON THE LINE!!
IF I CAN'T STAY IN THIS EXAM... MY...!!
MY YOUNGER BROTHER AND SISTER ...

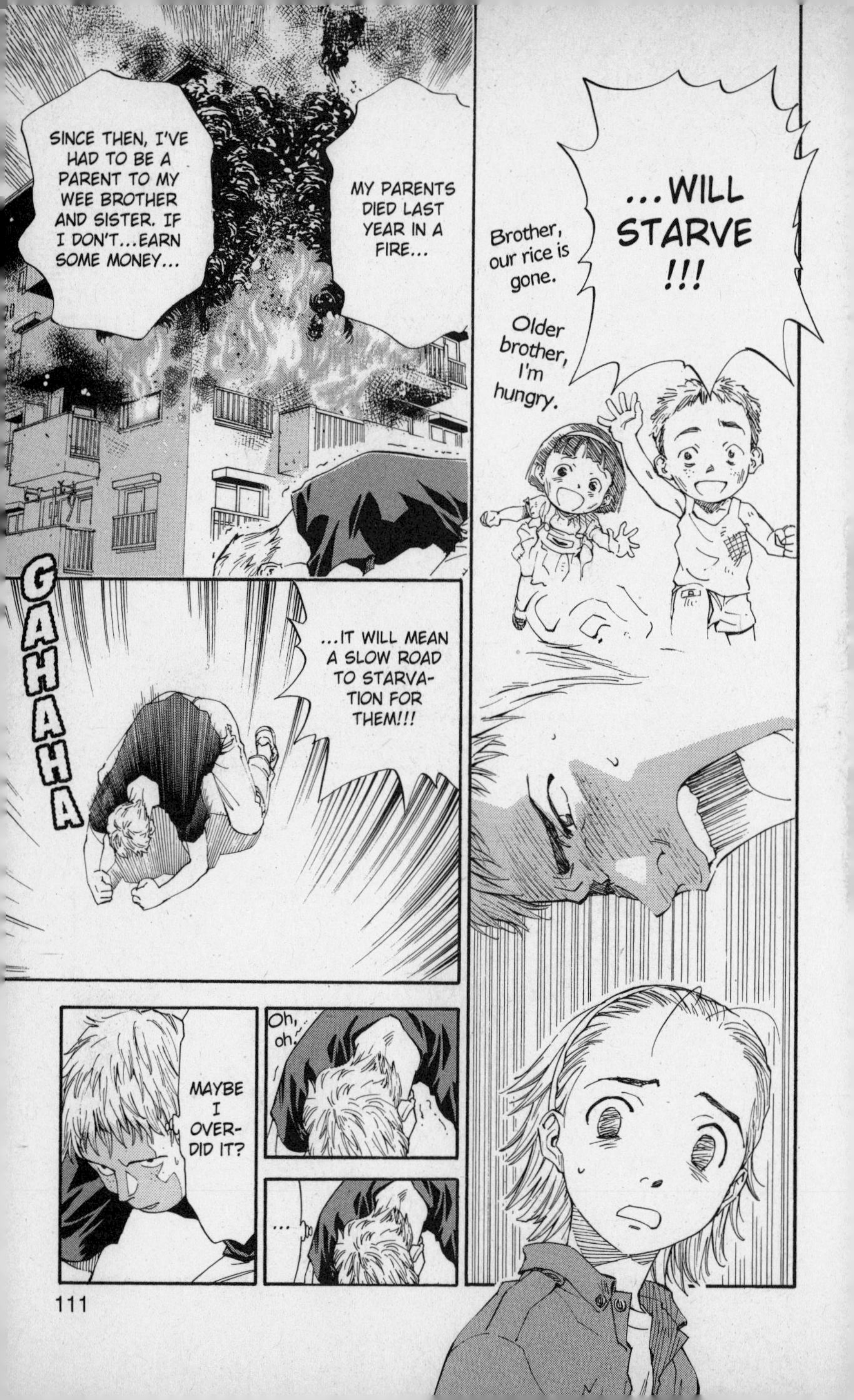
...WILL STARVE !!!
Brother, our rice is gone.
Older brother, I'm hungry.
MY PARENTS DIED LAST YEAR IN A FIRE...
SINCE THEN, I'VE HAD TO BE A PARENT TO MY WEE BROTHER AND SISTER. IF I DON'T...EARN SOME MONEY...
...IT WILL MEAN A SLOW ROAD TO STARVATION FOR THEM!!!
GAHAHA
Oh, oh~
...
MAYBE I OVERDID IT?

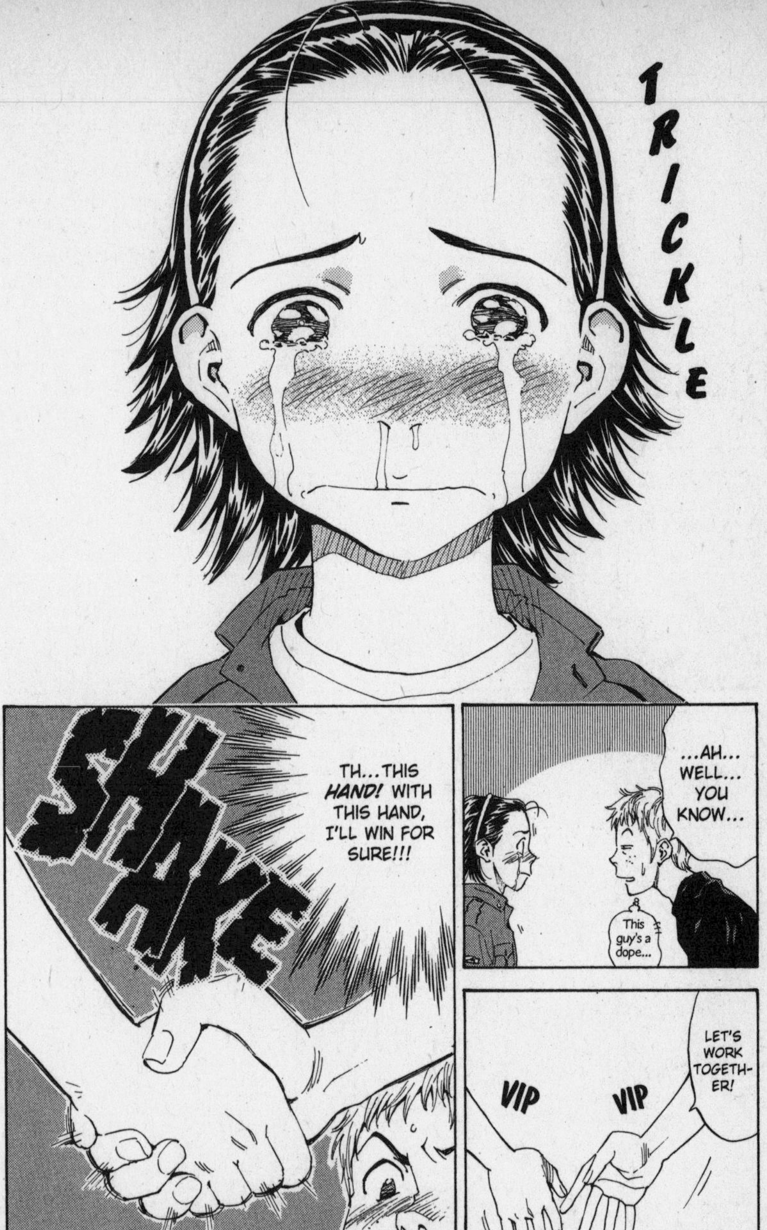
TRICKLE
...AH... WELL... YOU KNOW...
This guy's a dope...
LET'S WORK TOGETHER!
VIP
VIP
SHAKE
TH...THIS HAND! WITH THIS HAND, I'LL WIN FOR SURE!!!

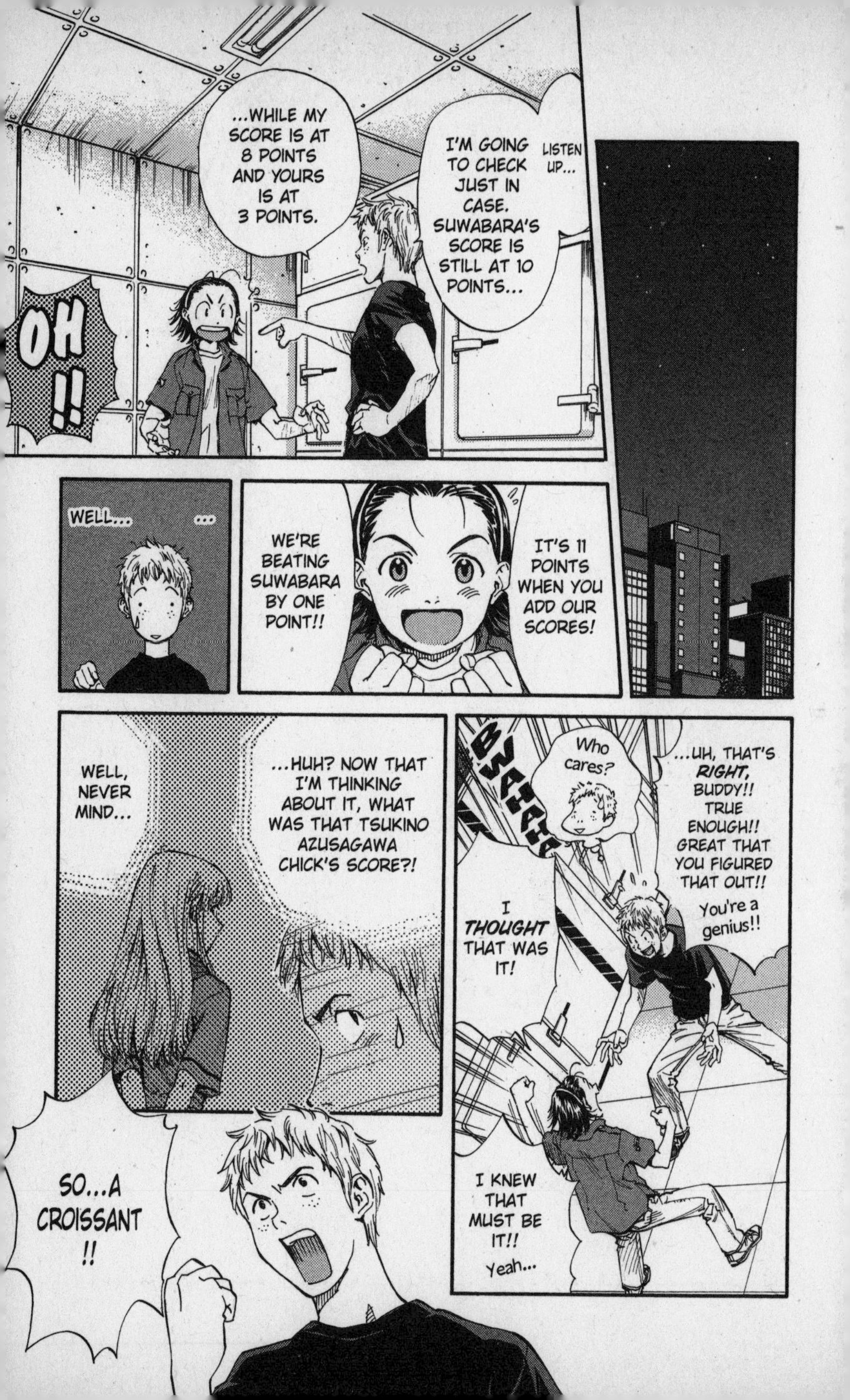
LISTEN UP...
I'M GOING TO CHECK JUST IN CASE. SUWABARA'S SCORE IS STILL AT 10 POINTS...
...WHILE MY SCORE IS AT 8 POINTS AND YOURS IS AT 3 POINTS.
OH!!
IT'S 11 POINTS WHEN YOU ADD OUR SCORES!
WE'RE BEATING SUWABARA BY ONE POINT!!
WELL... ...
...UH, THAT'S *RIGHT,* BUDDY!! TRUE ENOUGH!! GREAT THAT YOU FIGURED THAT OUT!!
You're a genius!!
Who cares?
BWAHA
I *THOUGHT* THAT WAS IT!
I KNEW THAT MUST BE IT!!
Yeah...
...HUH? NOW THAT I'M THINKING ABOUT IT, WHAT WAS THAT TSUKINO AZUSAGAWA CHICK'S SCORE?!
WELL, NEVER MIND...
SO...A CROISSANT!!

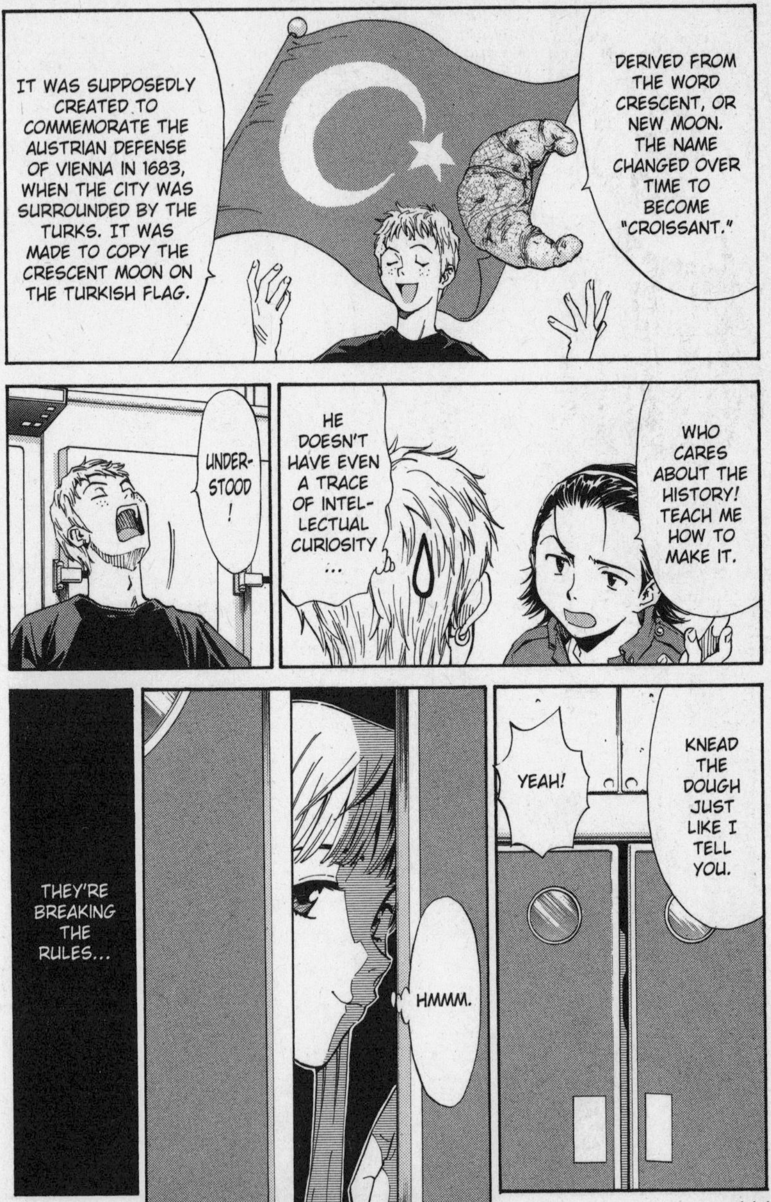
DERIVED FROM THE WORD CRESCENT, OR NEW MOON. THE NAME CHANGED OVER TIME TO BECOME "CROISSANT."
IT WAS SUPPOSEDLY CREATED TO COMMEMORATE THE AUSTRIAN DEFENSE OF VIENNA IN 1683, WHEN THE CITY WAS SURROUNDED BY THE TURKS. IT WAS MADE TO COPY THE CRESCENT MOON ON THE TURKISH FLAG.
WHO CARES ABOUT THE HISTORY! TEACH ME HOW TO MAKE IT.
HE DOESN'T HAVE EVEN A TRACE OF INTEL-LECTUAL CURIOSITY...
UNDER-STOOD!
KNEAD THE DOUGH JUST LIKE I TELL YOU.
YEAH!
HMMM.
THEY'RE BREAKING THE RULES...

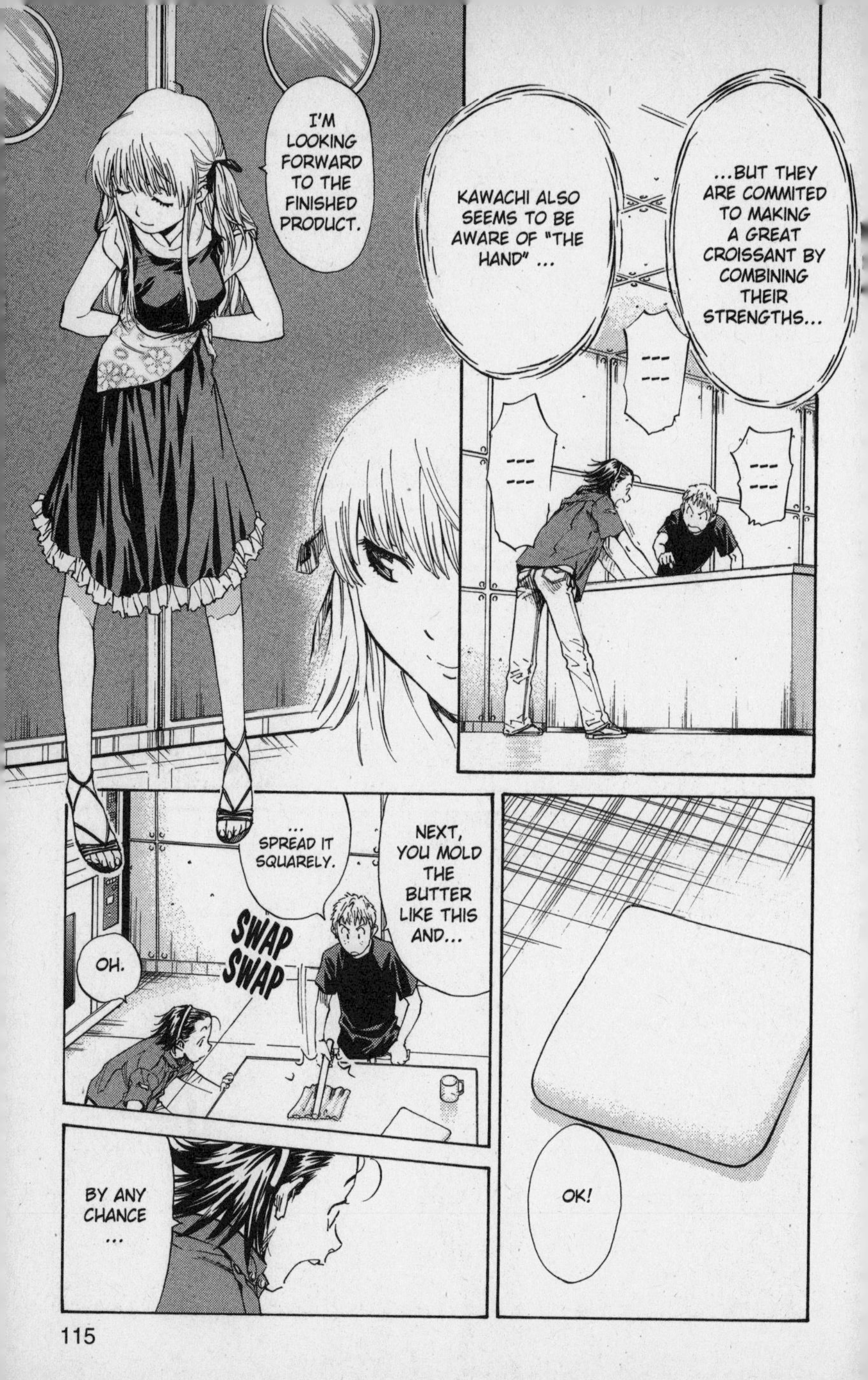
...BUT THEY ARE COMMITED TO MAKING A GREAT CROISSANT BY COMBINING THEIR STRENGTHS...
KAWACHI ALSO SEEMS TO BE AWARE OF "THE HAND" ...
--- ---
--- ---
--- ---
I'M LOOKING FORWARD TO THE FINISHED PRODUCT.
OK!
NEXT, YOU MOLD THE BUTTER LIKE THIS AND...
... SPREAD IT SQUARELY.
SWAP SWAP
OH.
BY ANY CHANCE ...

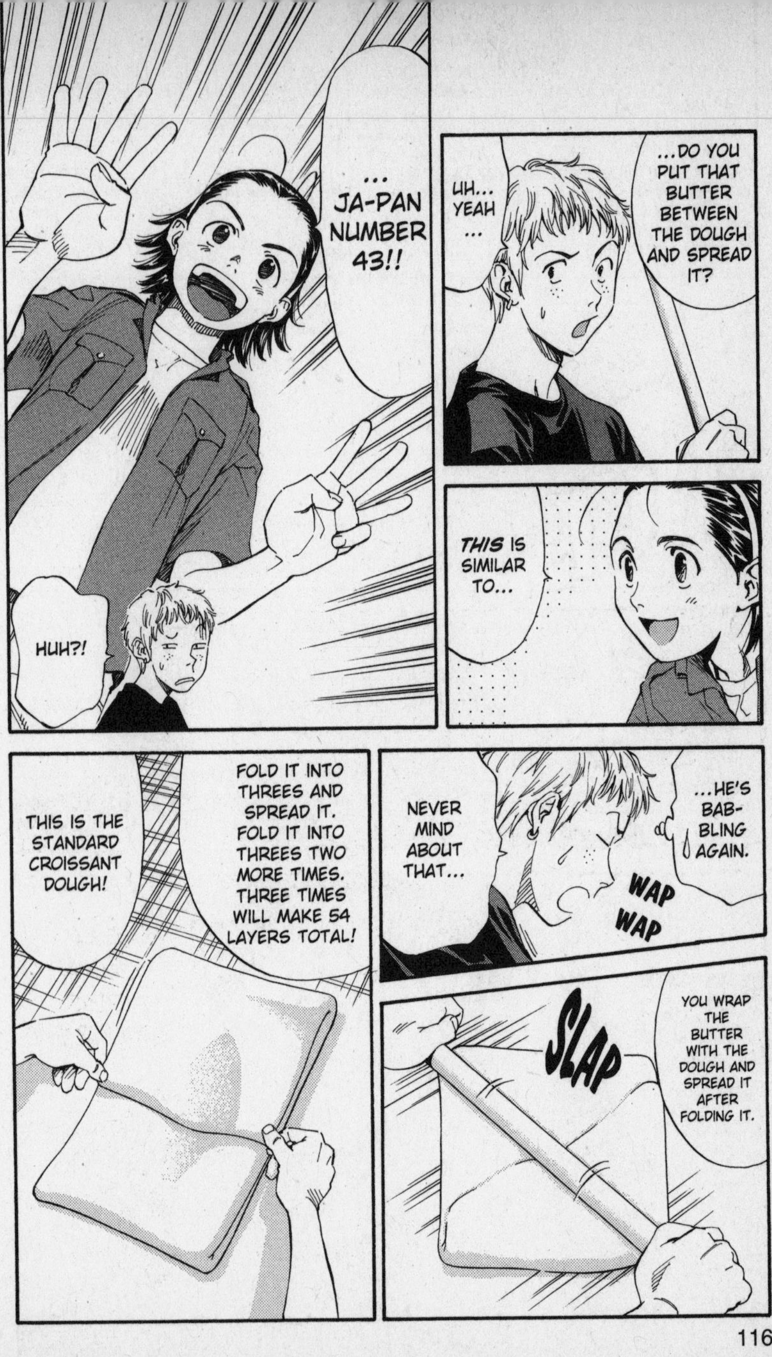
...DO YOU PUT THAT BUTTER BETWEEN THE DOUGH AND SPREAD IT?
UH... YEAH ...
THIS IS SIMILAR TO...
... JA-PAN NUMBER 43!!
HUH?!
...HE'S BAB-BLING AGAIN.
NEVER MIND ABOUT THAT...
WAP WAP
SLAP
YOU WRAP THE BUTTER WITH THE DOUGH AND SPREAD IT AFTER FOLDING IT.
FOLD IT INTO THREES AND SPREAD IT. FOLD IT INTO THREES TWO MORE TIMES. THREE TIMES WILL MAKE 54 LAYERS TOTAL!
THIS IS THE STANDARD CROISSANT DOUGH!

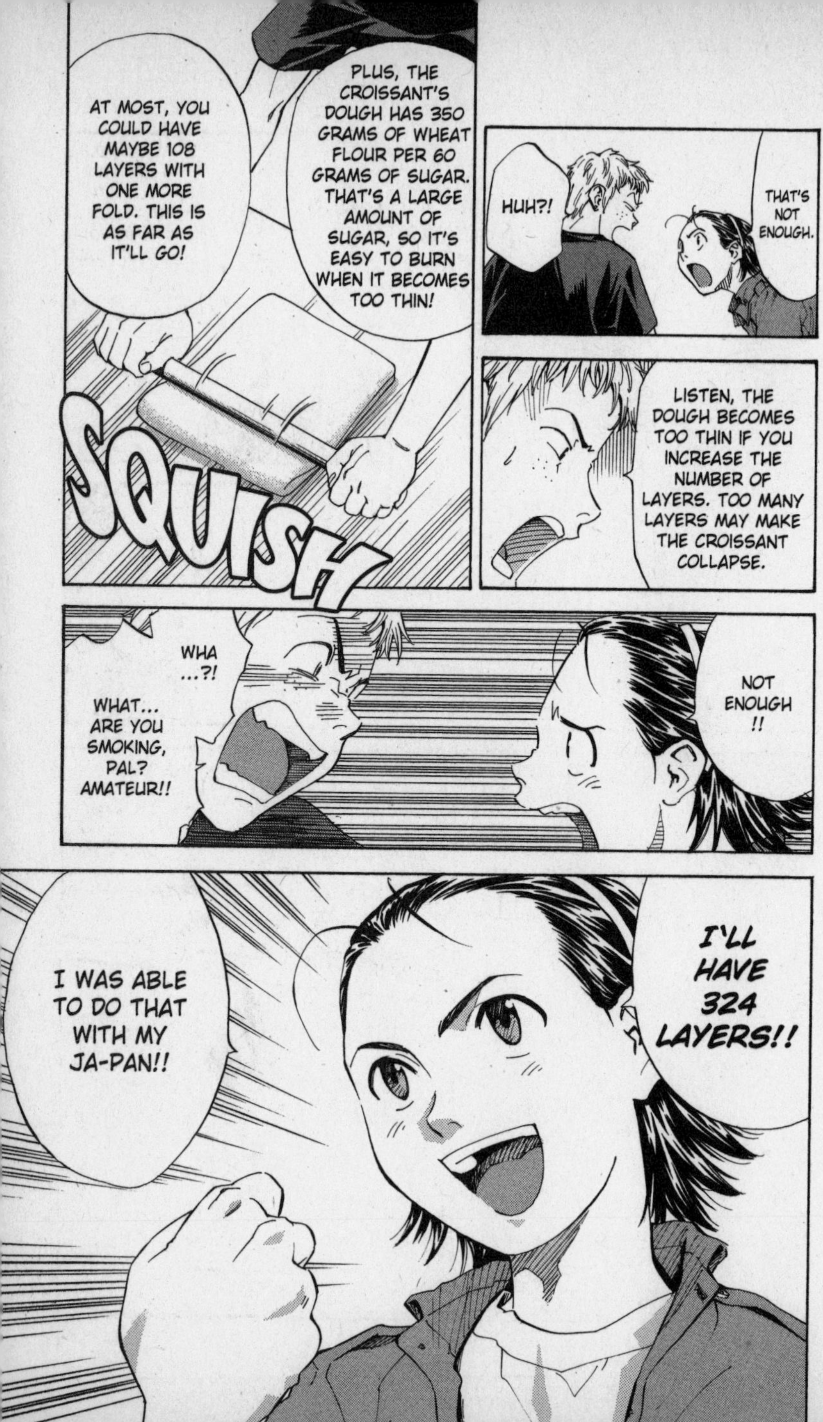
AT MOST, YOU COULD HAVE MAYBE 108 LAYERS WITH ONE MORE FOLD. THIS IS AS FAR AS IT'LL GO!
PLUS, THE CROISSANT'S DOUGH HAS 350 GRAMS OF WHEAT FLOUR PER 60 GRAMS OF SUGAR. THAT'S A LARGE AMOUNT OF SUGAR, SO IT'S EASY TO BURN WHEN IT BECOMES TOO THIN!
SQUISH
THAT'S NOT ENOUGH.
HUH?!
LISTEN, THE DOUGH BECOMES TOO THIN IF YOU INCREASE THE NUMBER OF LAYERS. TOO MANY LAYERS MAY MAKE THE CROISSANT COLLAPSE.
NOT ENOUGH !!
WHA ...?!
WHAT... ARE YOU SMOKING, PAL? AMATEUR!!
I'LL HAVE 324 LAYERS!!
I WAS ABLE TO DO THAT WITH MY JA-PAN!!

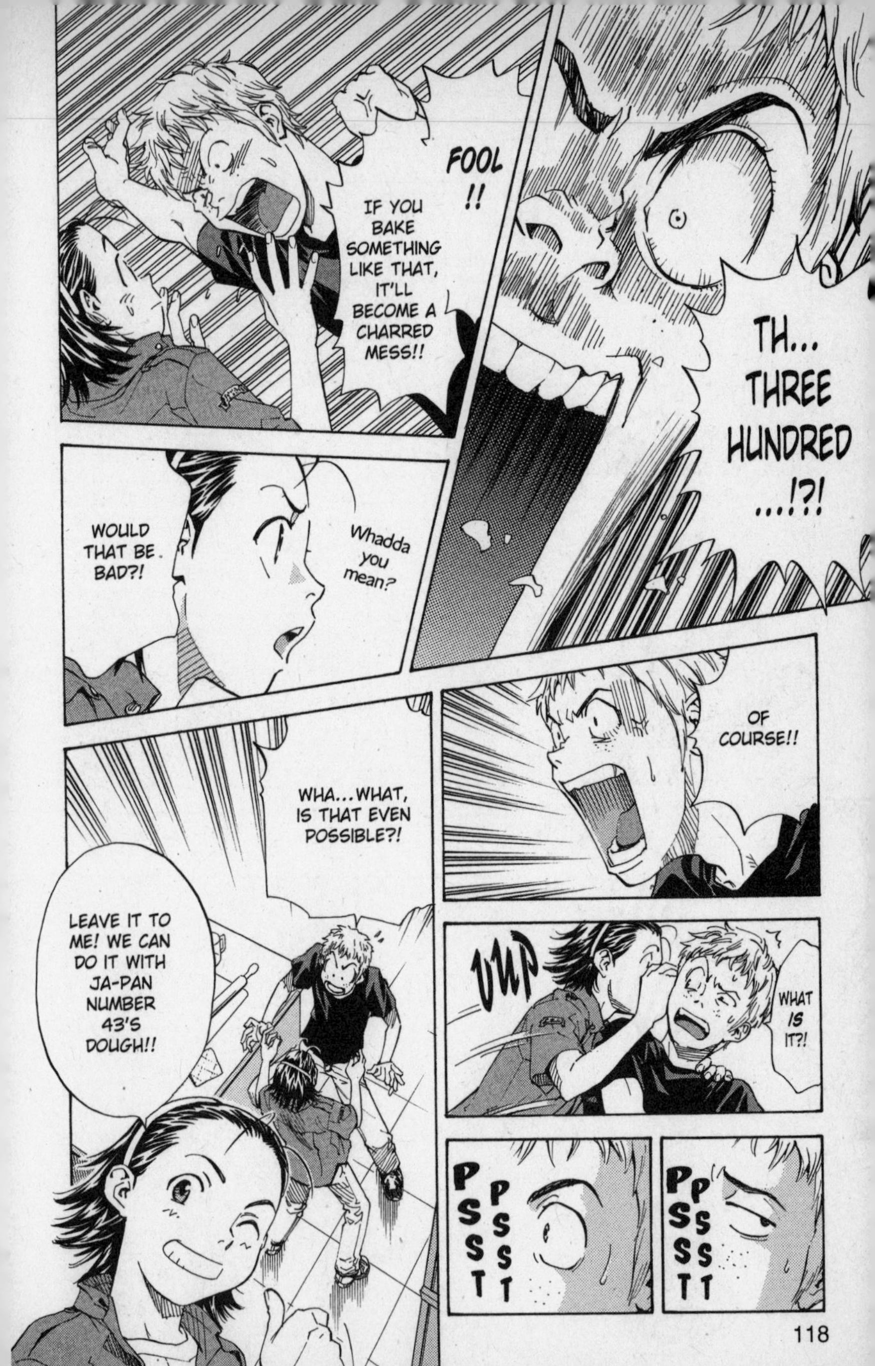
TH... THREE HUNDRED ...!?!
FOOL !!
IF YOU BAKE SOMETHING LIKE THAT, IT'LL BECOME A CHARRED MESS!!
Whadda you mean?
WOULD THAT BE BAD?!
OF COURSE!!
WHA...WHAT, IS THAT EVEN POSSIBLE?!
WHAT IS IT?!
VUP
PSST PSST
PSST PSST
LEAVE IT TO ME! WE CAN DO IT WITH JA-PAN NUMBER 43'S DOUGH!!

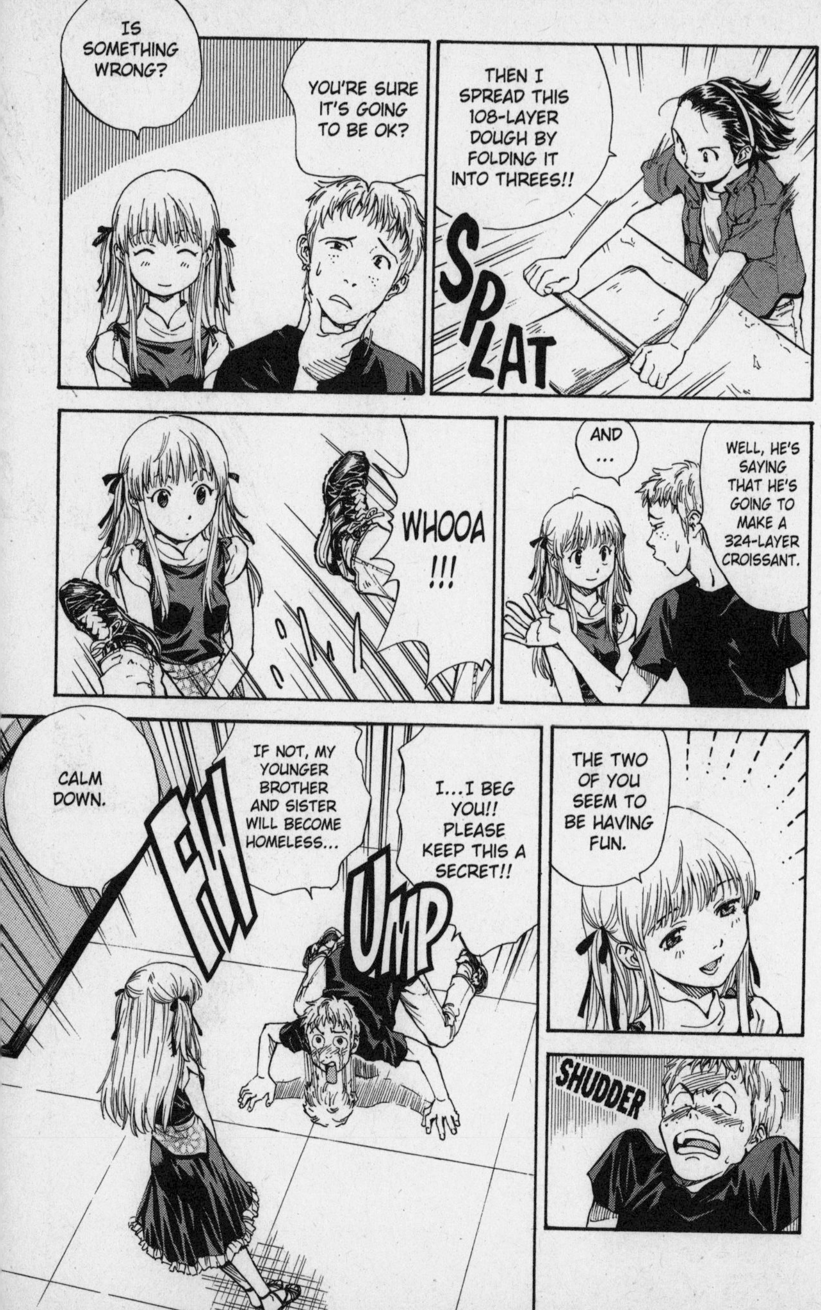
THEN I SPREAD THIS 108-LAYER DOUGH BY FOLDING IT INTO THREES!!
SPLAT
YOU'RE SURE IT'S GOING TO BE OK?
IS SOMETHING WRONG?
WELL, HE'S SAYING THAT HE'S GOING TO MAKE A 324-LAYER CROISSANT.
AND ...
WHOOA !!!
THE TWO OF YOU SEEM TO BE HAVING FUN.
SHUDDER
I...I BEG YOU!! PLEASE KEEP THIS A SECRET!!
UMP
IF NOT, MY YOUNGER BROTHER AND SISTER WILL BECOME HOMELESS...
CALM DOWN.

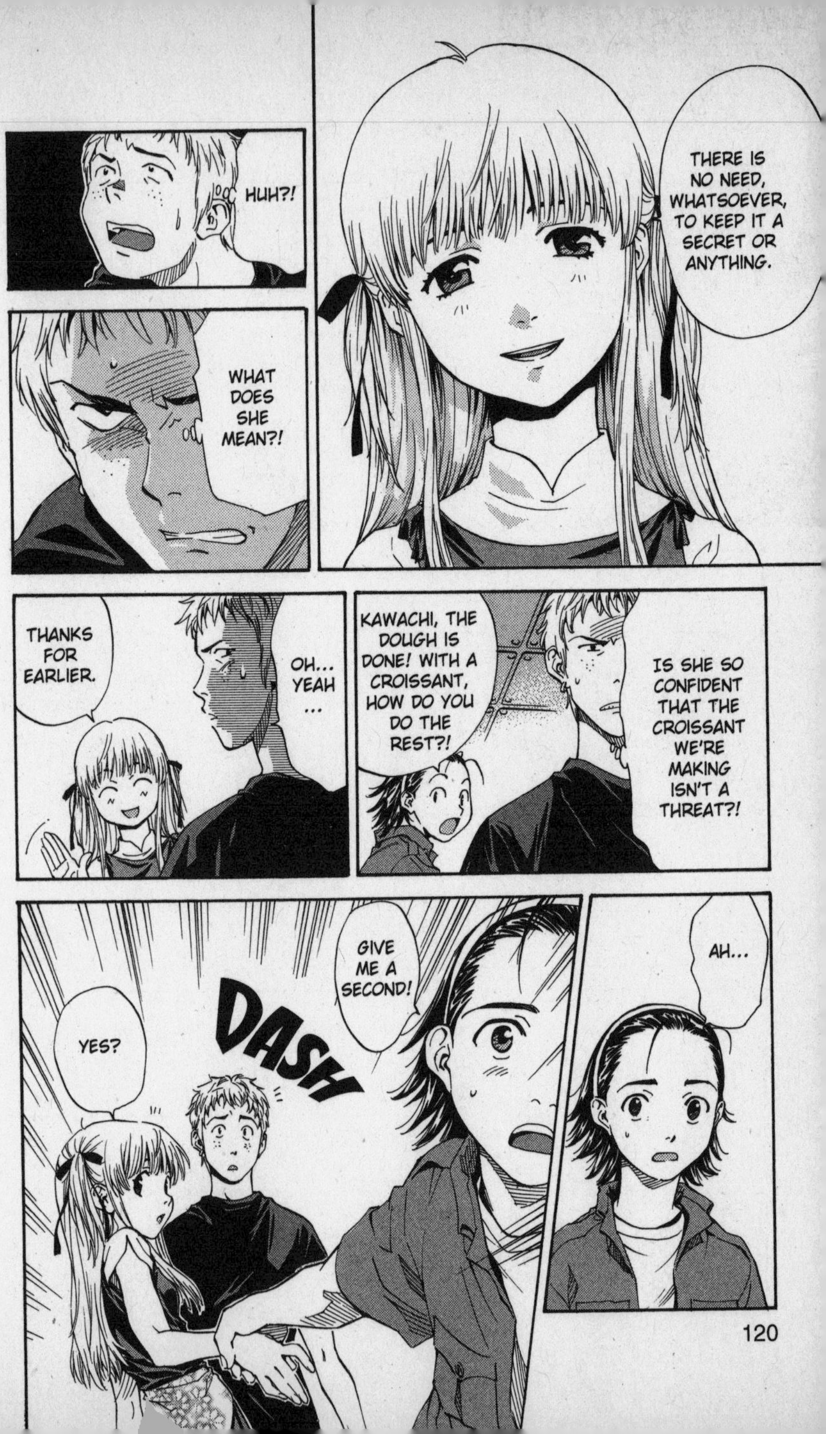
THERE IS NO NEED, WHATSOEVER, TO KEEP IT A SECRET OR ANYTHING.
HUH?!
WHAT DOES SHE MEAN?!
IS SHE SO CONFIDENT THAT THE CROISSANT WE'RE MAKING ISN'T A THREAT?!
KAWACHI, THE DOUGH IS DONE! WITH A CROISSANT, HOW DO YOU DO THE REST?!
THANKS FOR EARLIER.
OH... YEAH ...
AH...
GIVE ME A SECOND!
DASH
YES?

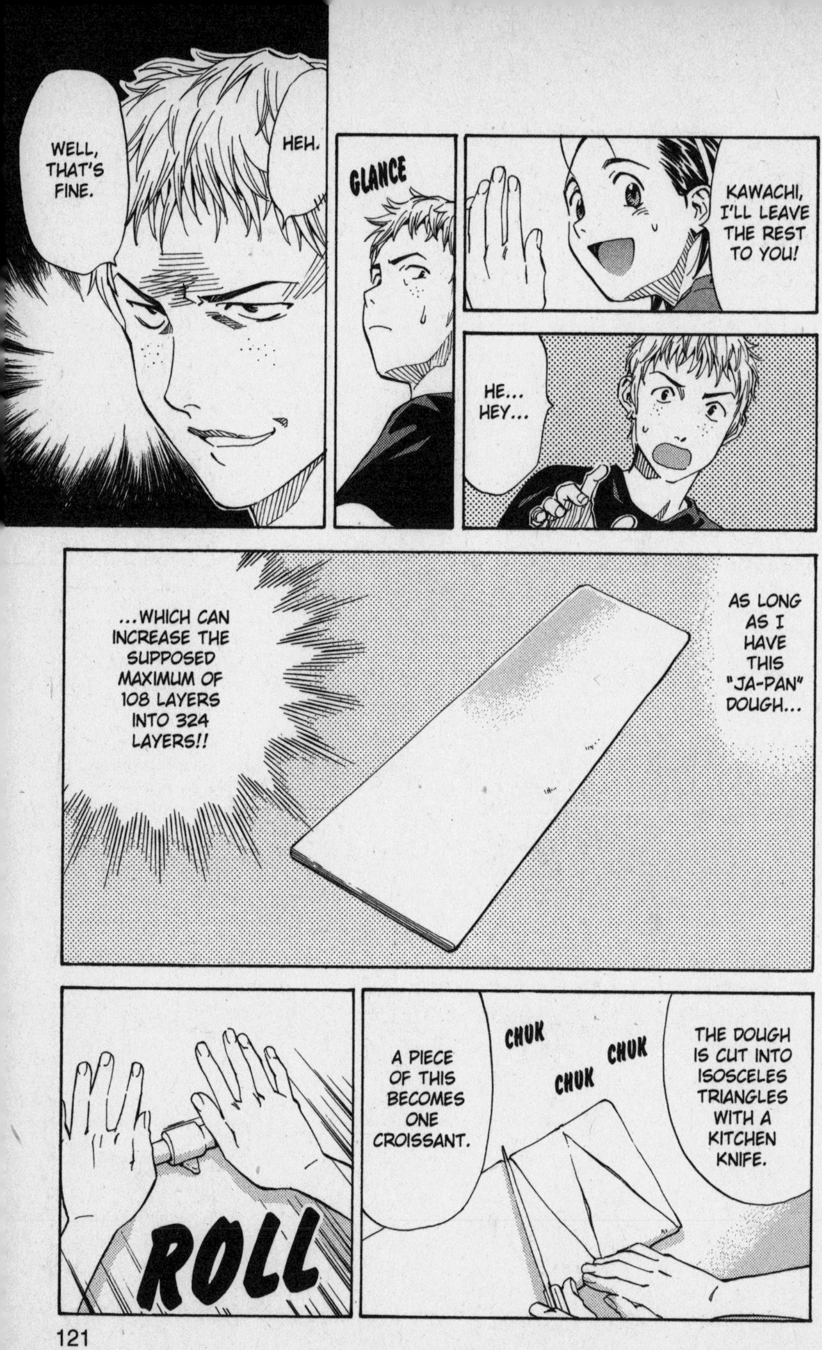
KAWACHI, I'LL LEAVE THE REST TO YOU!
HE... HEY...
GLANCE
HEH.
WELL, THAT'S FINE.
AS LONG AS I HAVE THIS "JA-PAN" DOUGH...
...WHICH CAN INCREASE THE SUPPOSED MAXIMUM OF 108 LAYERS INTO 324 LAYERS!!
THE DOUGH IS CUT INTO ISOSCELES TRIANGLES WITH A KITCHEN KNIFE.
CHUK
CHUK
CHUK
A PIECE OF THIS BECOMES ONE CROISSANT.
ROLL

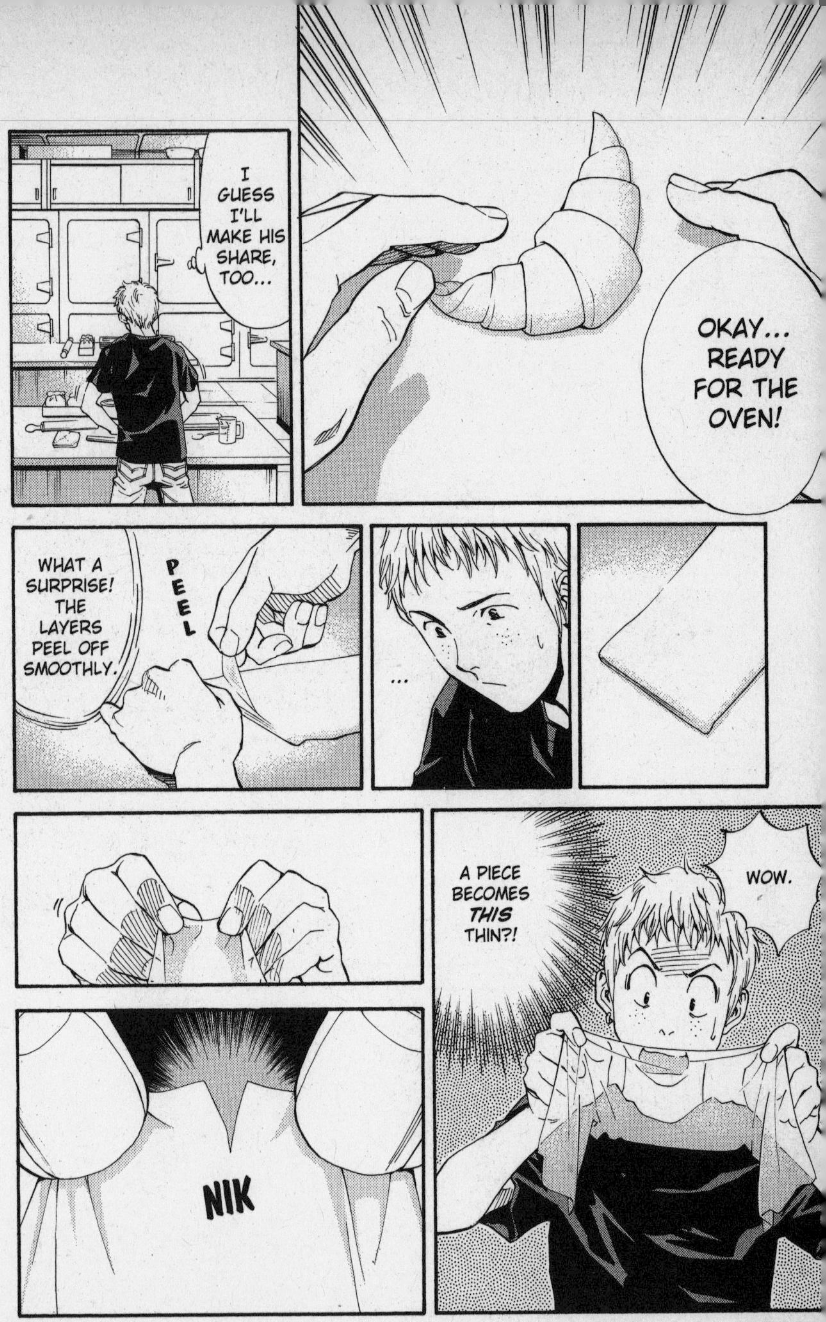
OKAY... READY FOR THE OVEN!
I GUESS I'LL MAKE HIS SHARE, TOO...
...
PEEL
WHAT A SURPRISE! THE LAYERS PEEL OFF SMOOTHLY.
WOW.
A PIECE BECOMES *THIS* THIN?!
NIK

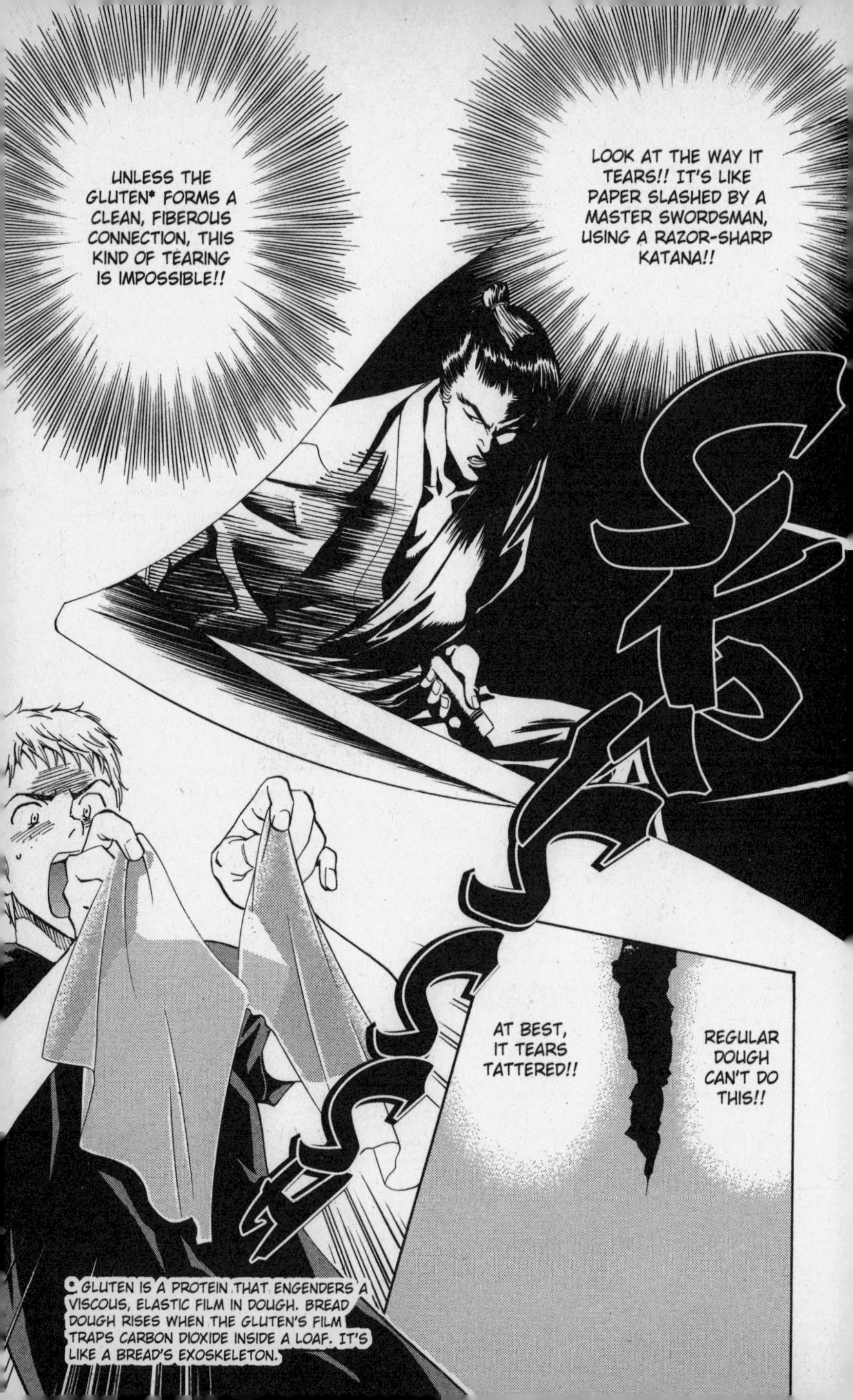

*: GLUTEN IS A PROTEIN THAT ENGENDERS A VISCOUS, ELASTIC FILM IN DOUGH. BREAD DOUGH RISES WHEN THE GLUTEN'S FILM TRAPS CARBON DIOXIDE INSIDE A LOAF. IT'S LIKE A BREAD'S EXOSKELETON.

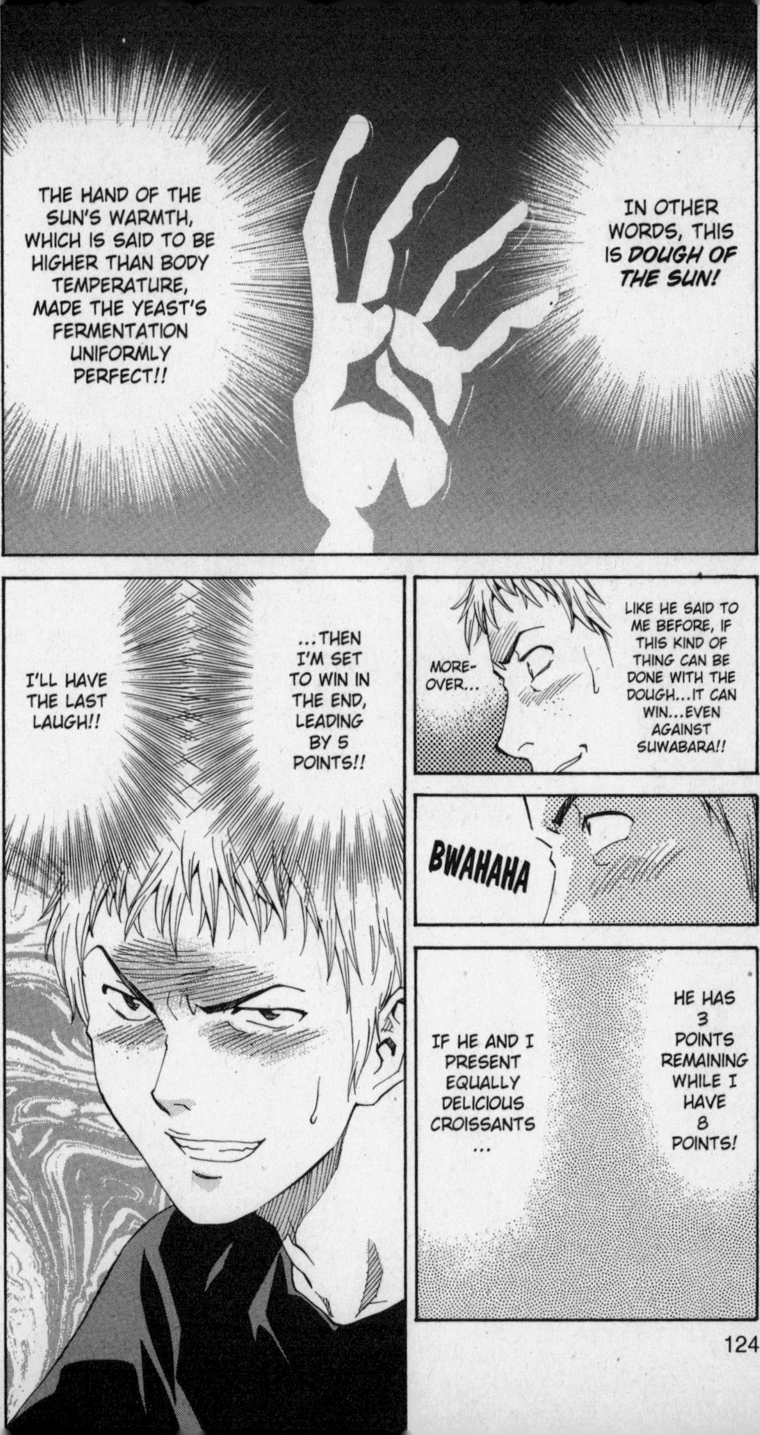
THE HAND OF THE SUN'S WARMTH, WHICH IS SAID TO BE HIGHER THAN BODY TEMPERATURE, MADE THE YEAST'S FERMENTATION UNIFORMLY PERFECT!!
IN OTHER WORDS, THIS IS *DOUGH OF THE SUN!*
LIKE HE SAID TO ME BEFORE, IF THIS KIND OF THING CAN BE DONE WITH THE DOUGH...IT CAN WIN...EVEN AGAINST SUWABARA!!
MORE-OVER...
BWAHAHA
HE HAS 3 POINTS REMAINING WHILE I HAVE 8 POINTS!
IF HE AND I PRESENT EQUALLY DELICIOUS CROISSANTS ...
...THEN I'M SET TO WIN IN THE END, LEADING BY 5 POINTS!!
I'LL HAVE THE LAST LAUGH!!

Story 5: Country Boy

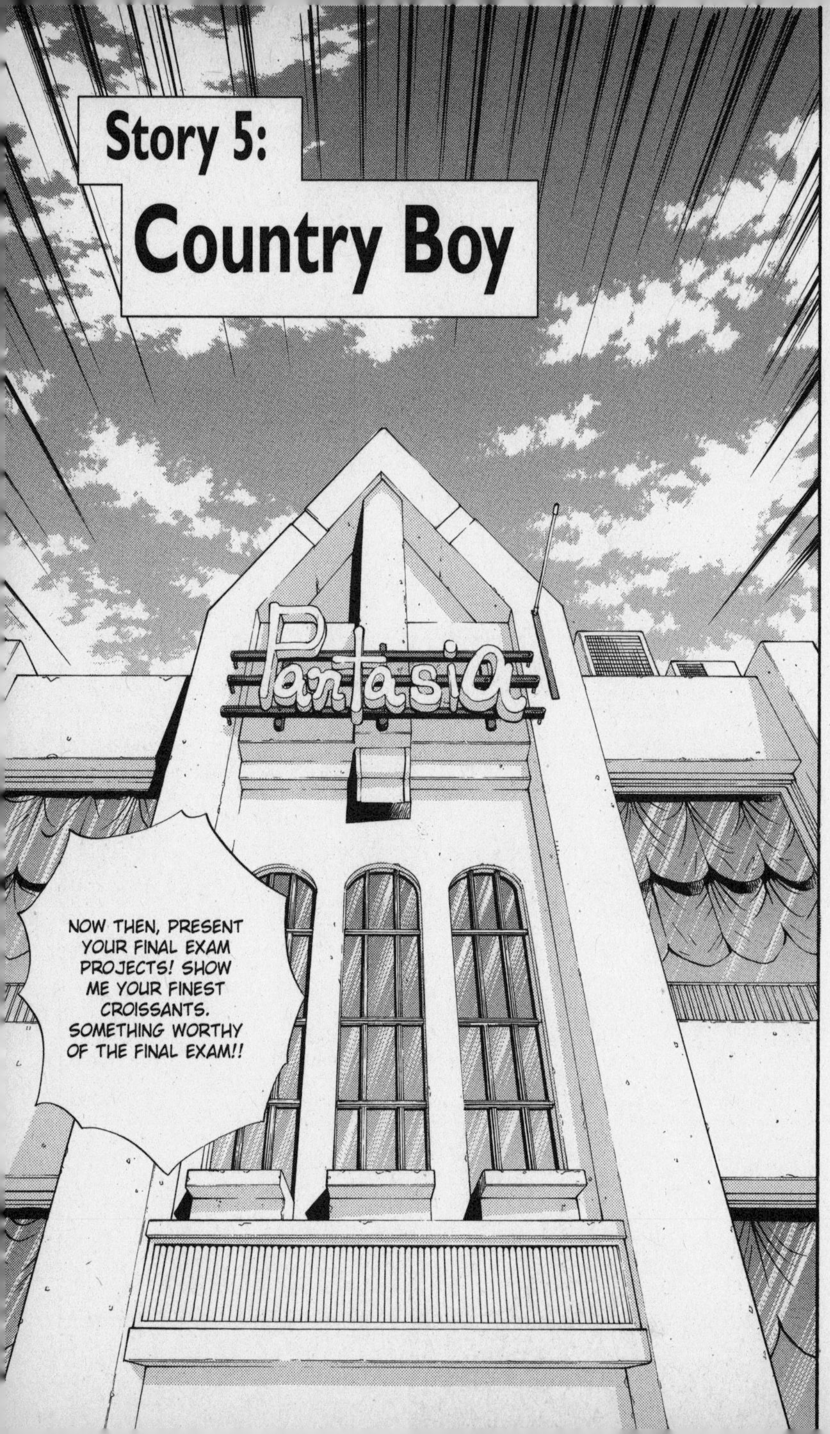
NOW THEN, PRESENT YOUR FINAL EXAM PROJECTS! SHOW ME YOUR FINEST CROISSANTS. SOMETHING WORTHY OF THE FINAL EXAM!!

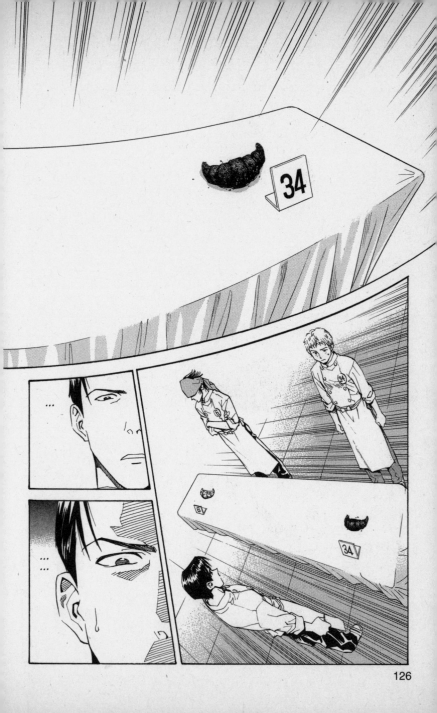

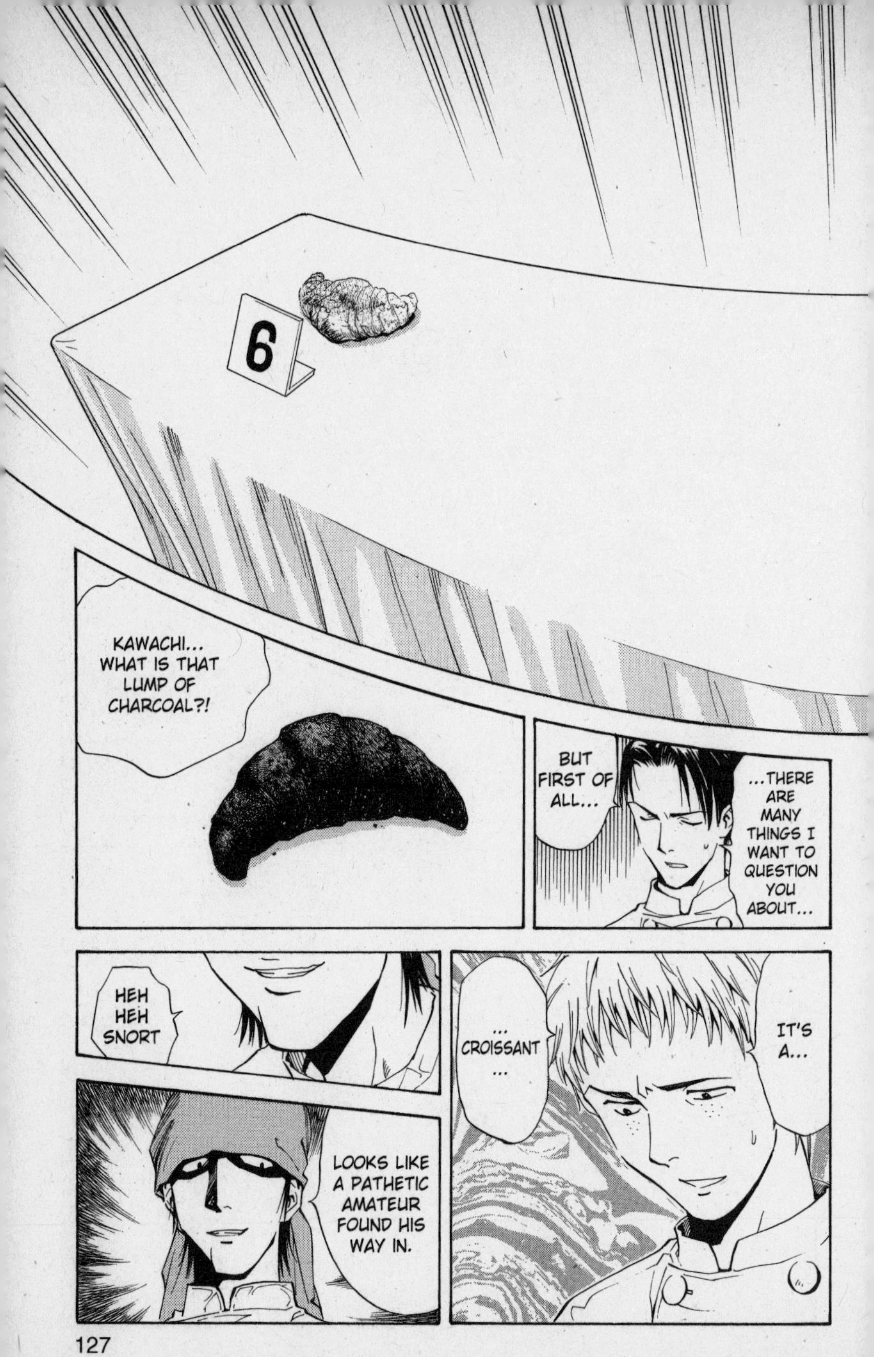
6
BUT FIRST OF ALL...
...THERE ARE MANY THINGS I WANT TO QUESTION YOU ABOUT...
KAWACHI... WHAT IS THAT LUMP OF CHARCOAL?!
IT'S A...
...CROISSANT...
HEH HEH SNORT
LOOKS LIKE A PATHETIC AMATEUR FOUND HIS WAY IN.

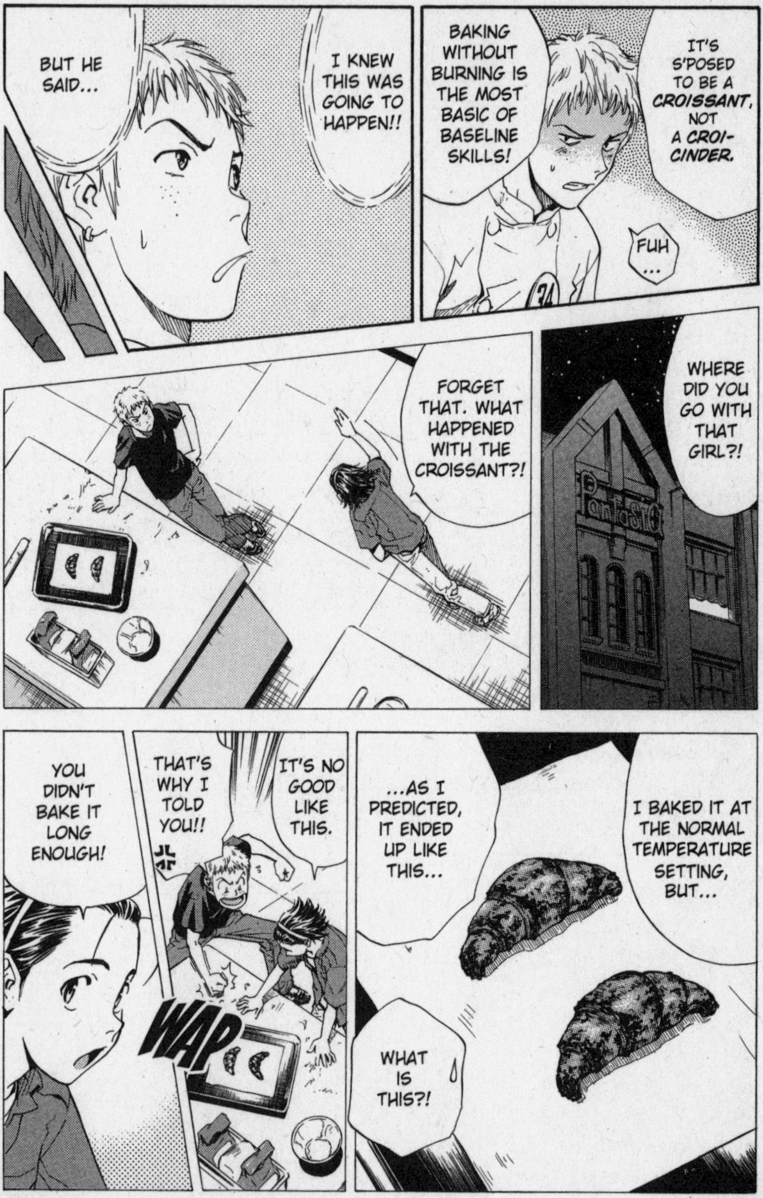
IT'S S'POSED TO BE A *CROISSANT*, NOT A *CROI-CINDER.*
FUH...
BAKING WITHOUT BURNING IS THE MOST BASIC OF BASELINE SKILLS!
I KNEW THIS WAS GOING TO HAPPEN!!
BUT HE SAID...
WHERE DID YOU GO WITH THAT GIRL?!
FORGET THAT. WHAT HAPPENED WITH THE CROISSANT?!
I BAKED IT AT THE NORMAL TEMPERATURE SETTING, BUT...
...AS I PREDICTED, IT ENDED UP LIKE THIS...
WHAT IS THIS?!
IT'S NO GOOD LIKE THIS.
THAT'S WHY I TOLD YOU!!
WAP
YOU DIDN'T BAKE IT LONG ENOUGH!

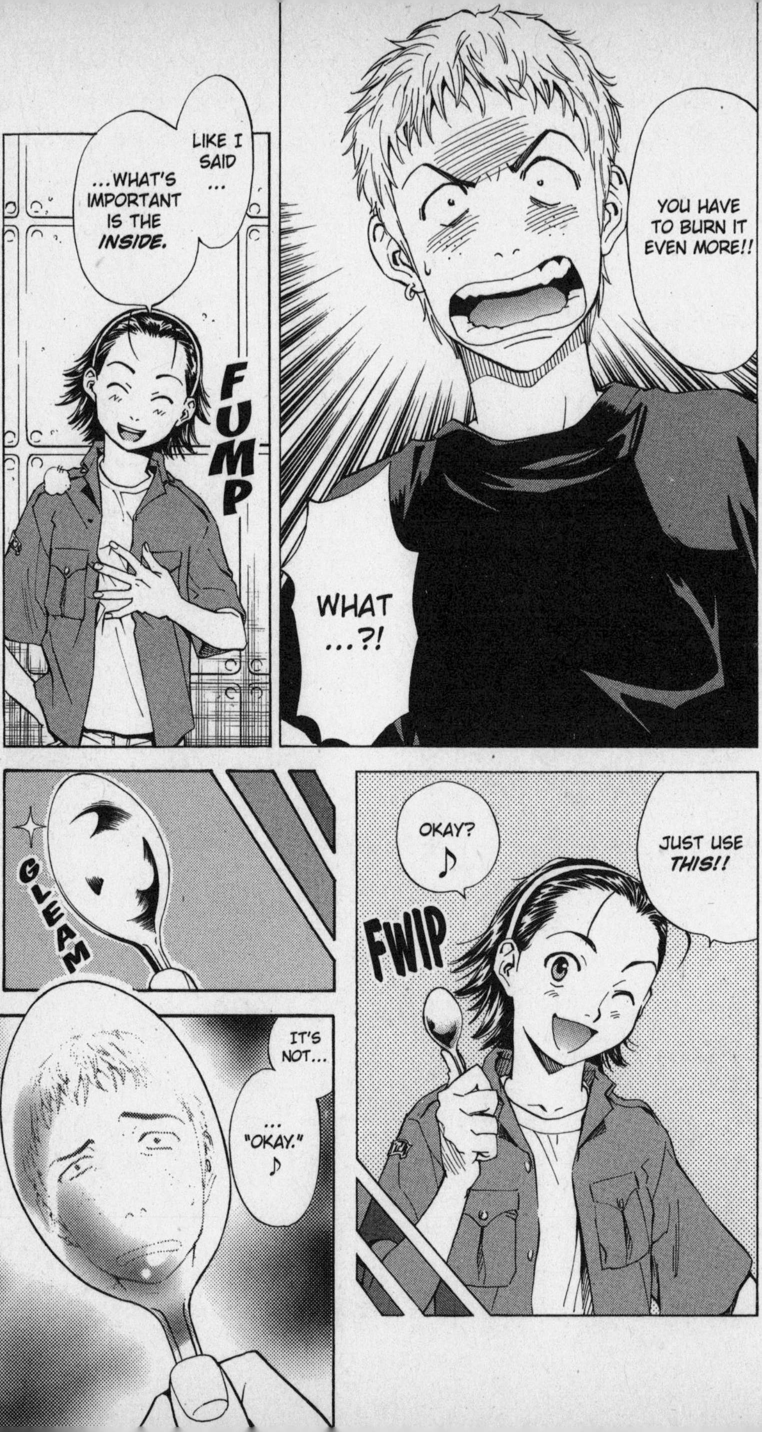
YOU HAVE TO BURN IT EVEN MORE!!
WHAT ...?!
LIKE I SAID ...
...WHAT'S IMPORTANT IS THE *INSIDE.*
FUMP
JUST USE *THIS!!*
OKAY? ♪
FWIP
GLEAM
IT'S NOT...
... "OKAY." ♪

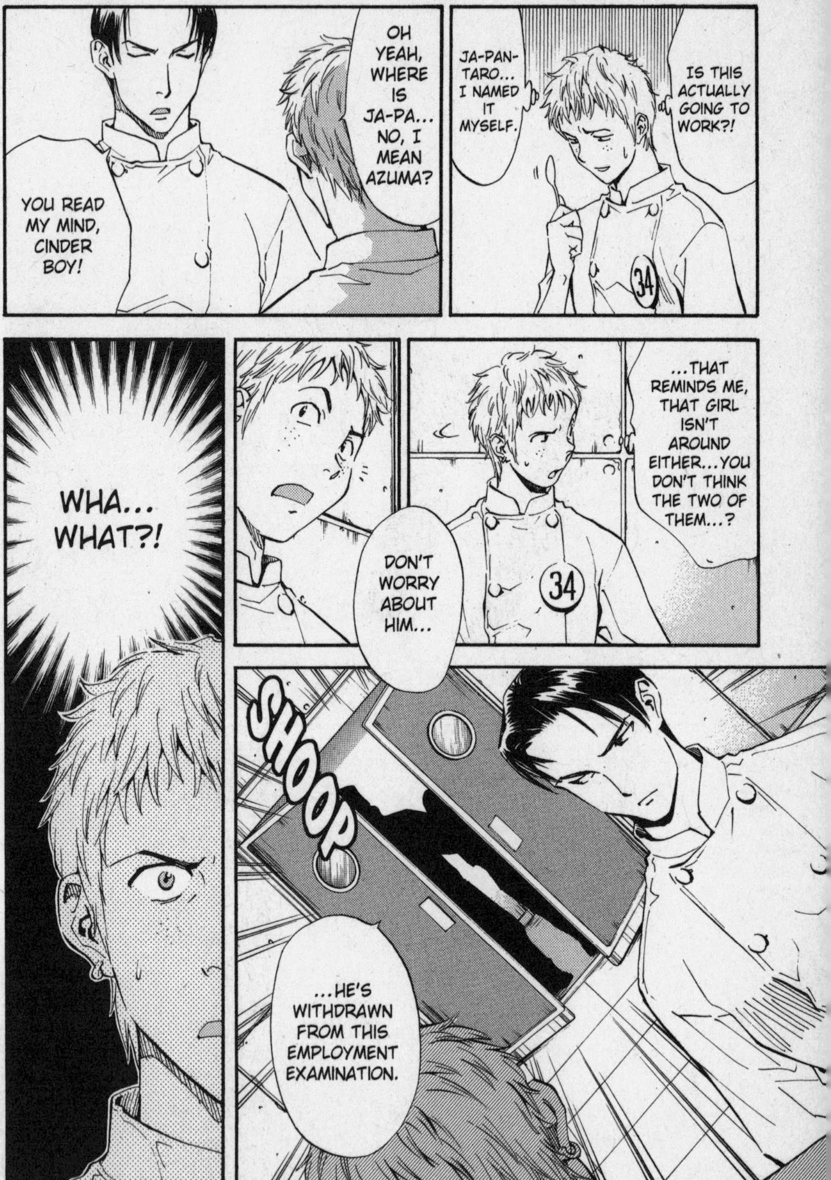
IS THIS ACTUALLY GOING TO WORK?!
JA-PAN-TARO... I NAMED IT MYSELF.
OH YEAH, WHERE IS JA-PA... NO, I MEAN AZUMA?
YOU READ MY MIND, CINDER BOY!
...THAT REMINDS ME, THAT GIRL ISN'T AROUND EITHER...YOU DON'T THINK THE TWO OF THEM...?
DON'T WORRY ABOUT HIM...
SHOOP
...HE'S WITHDRAWN FROM THIS EMPLOYMENT EXAMINATION.
WHA... WHAT?!

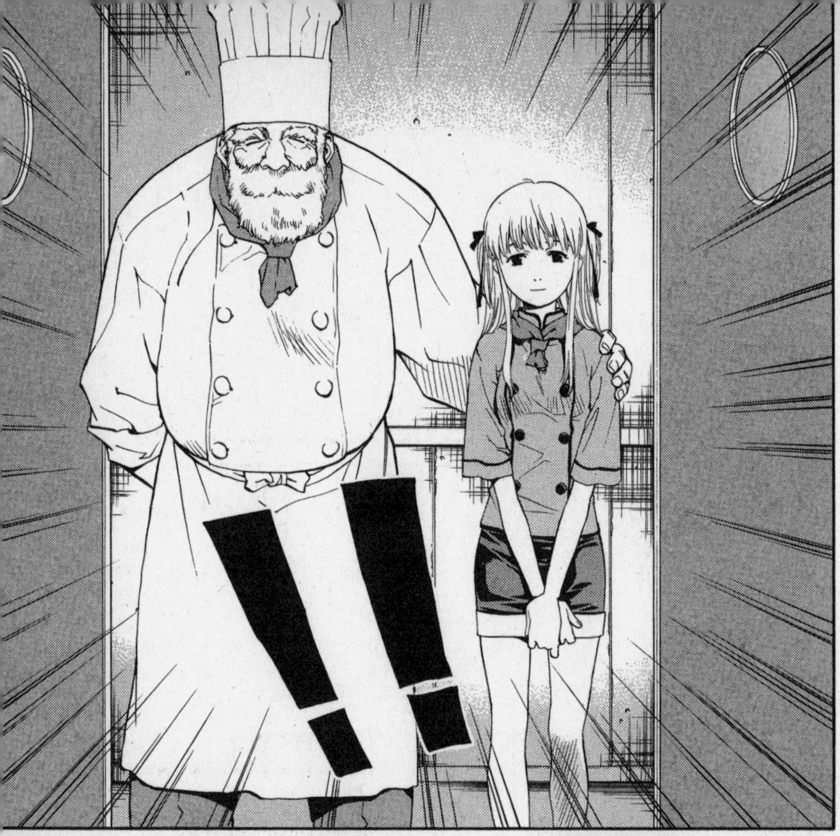
!!

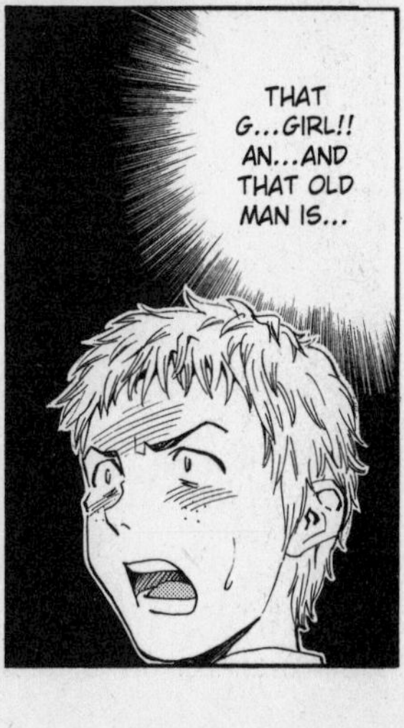
THAT G...GIRL!! AN...AND THAT OLD MAN IS...

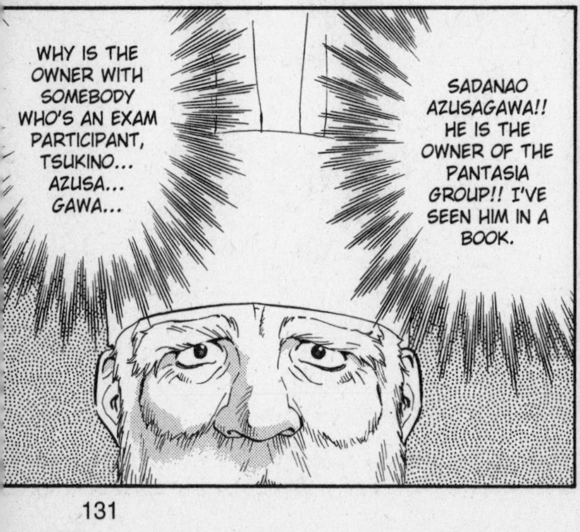
SADANAO AZUSAGAWA!! HE IS THE OWNER OF THE PANTASIA GROUP!! I'VE SEEN HIM IN A BOOK.
WHY IS THE OWNER WITH SOMEBODY WHO'S AN EXAM PARTICIPANT, TSUKINO... AZUSA... GAWA...

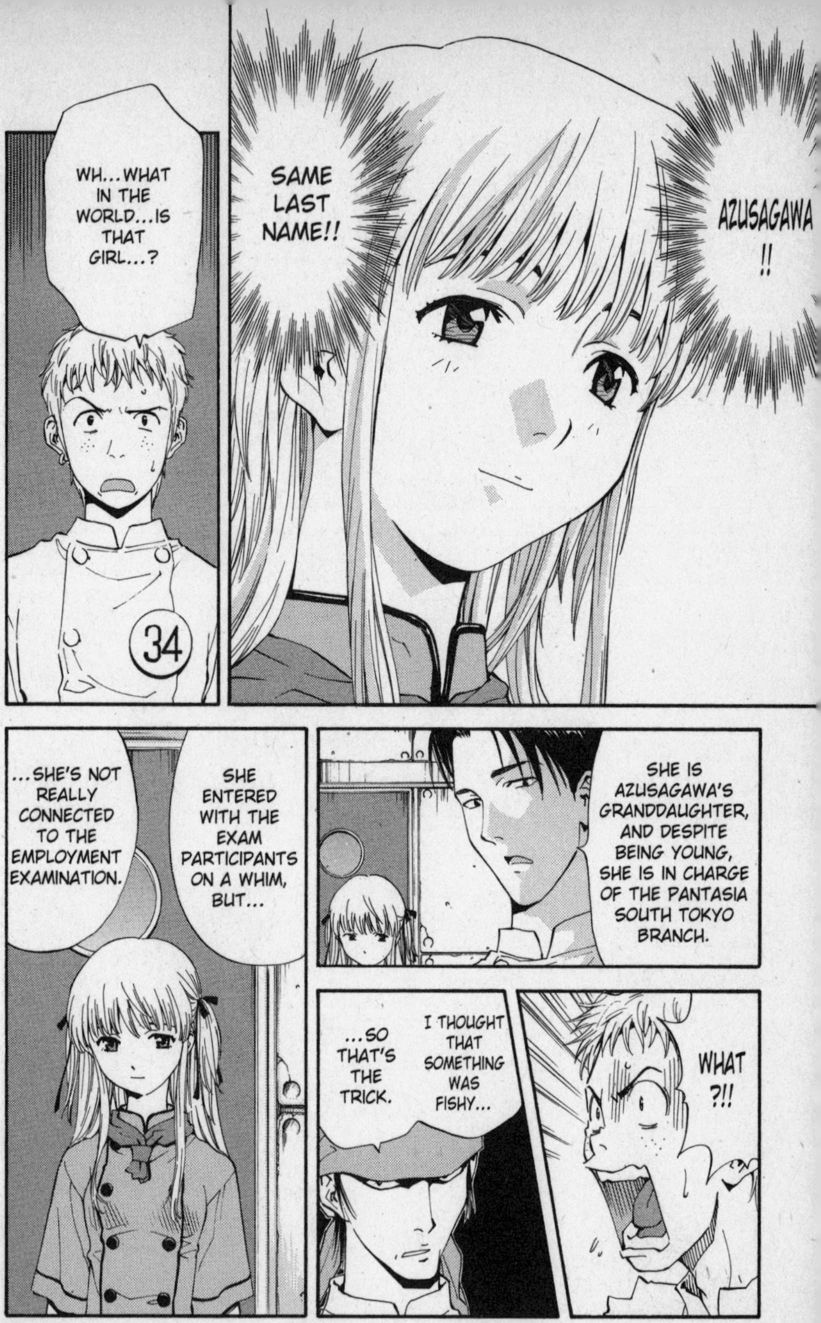
AZUSAGAWA !!
SAME LAST NAME!!
WH...WHAT IN THE WORLD...IS THAT GIRL...?
SHE IS AZUSAGAWA'S GRANDDAUGHTER, AND DESPITE BEING YOUNG, SHE IS IN CHARGE OF THE PANTASIA SOUTH TOKYO BRANCH.
WHAT ?!!
I THOUGHT THAT SOMETHING WAS FISHY...
...SO THAT'S THE TRICK.
SHE ENTERED WITH THE EXAM PARTICIPANTS ON A WHIM, BUT...
...SHE'S NOT REALLY CONNECTED TO THE EMPLOYMENT EXAMINATION.

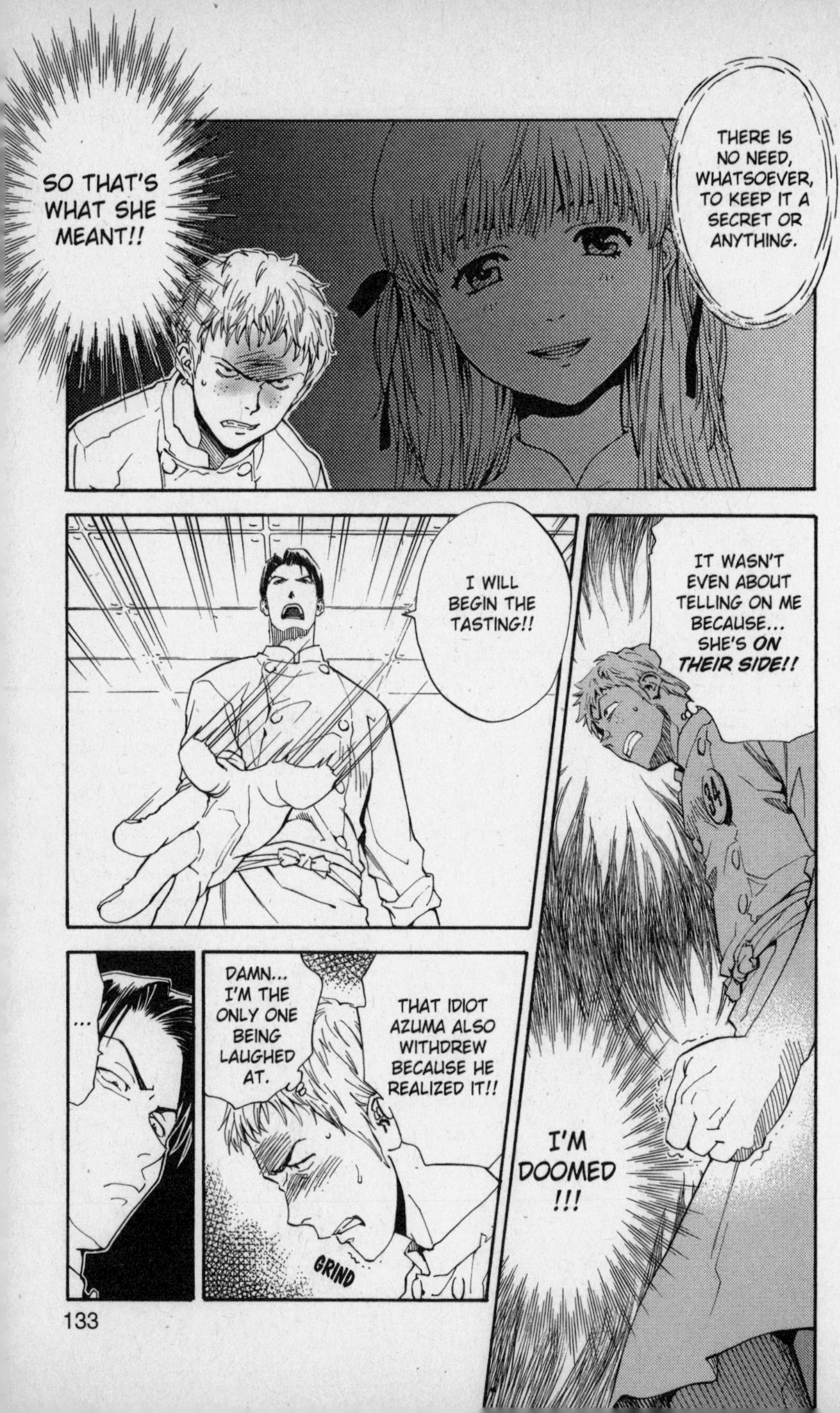
THERE IS NO NEED, WHATSOEVER, TO KEEP IT A SECRET OR ANYTHING.
SO THAT'S WHAT SHE MEANT!!
IT WASN'T EVEN ABOUT TELLING ON ME BECAUSE... SHE'S *ON THEIR SIDE!!*
I'M DOOMED !!!
I WILL BEGIN THE TASTING!!
THAT IDIOT AZUMA ALSO WITHDREW BECAUSE HE REALIZED IT!!
DAMN... I'M THE ONLY ONE BEING LAUGHED AT.
GRIND
...

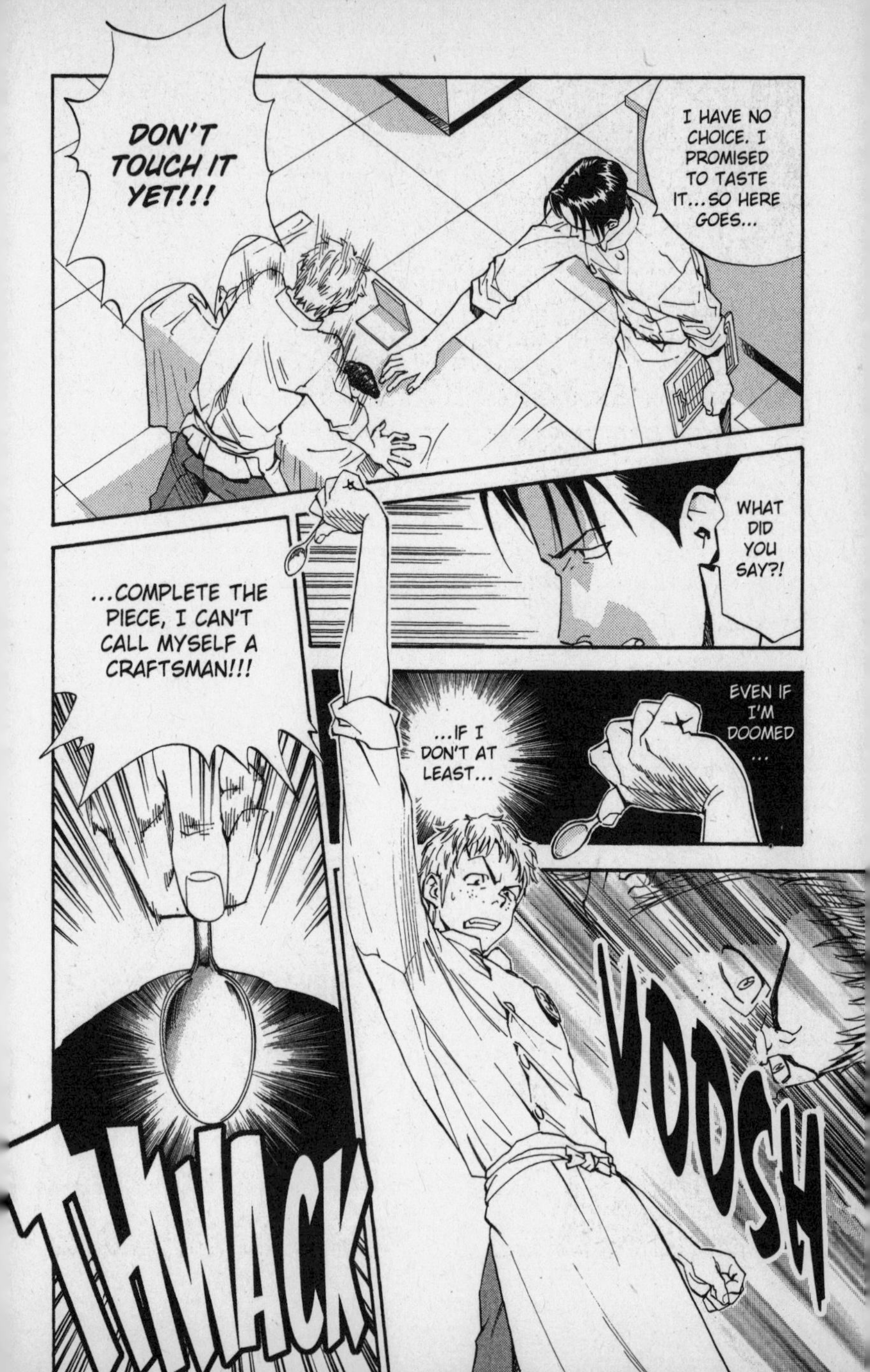
I HAVE NO CHOICE. I PROMISED TO TASTE IT...SO HERE GOES...
DON'T TOUCH IT YET!!!
WHAT DID YOU SAY?!
EVEN IF I'M DOOMED...
...IF I DON'T AT LEAST...
...COMPLETE THE PIECE, I CAN'T CALL MYSELF A CRAFTSMAN!!!
VOOSH
THWACK

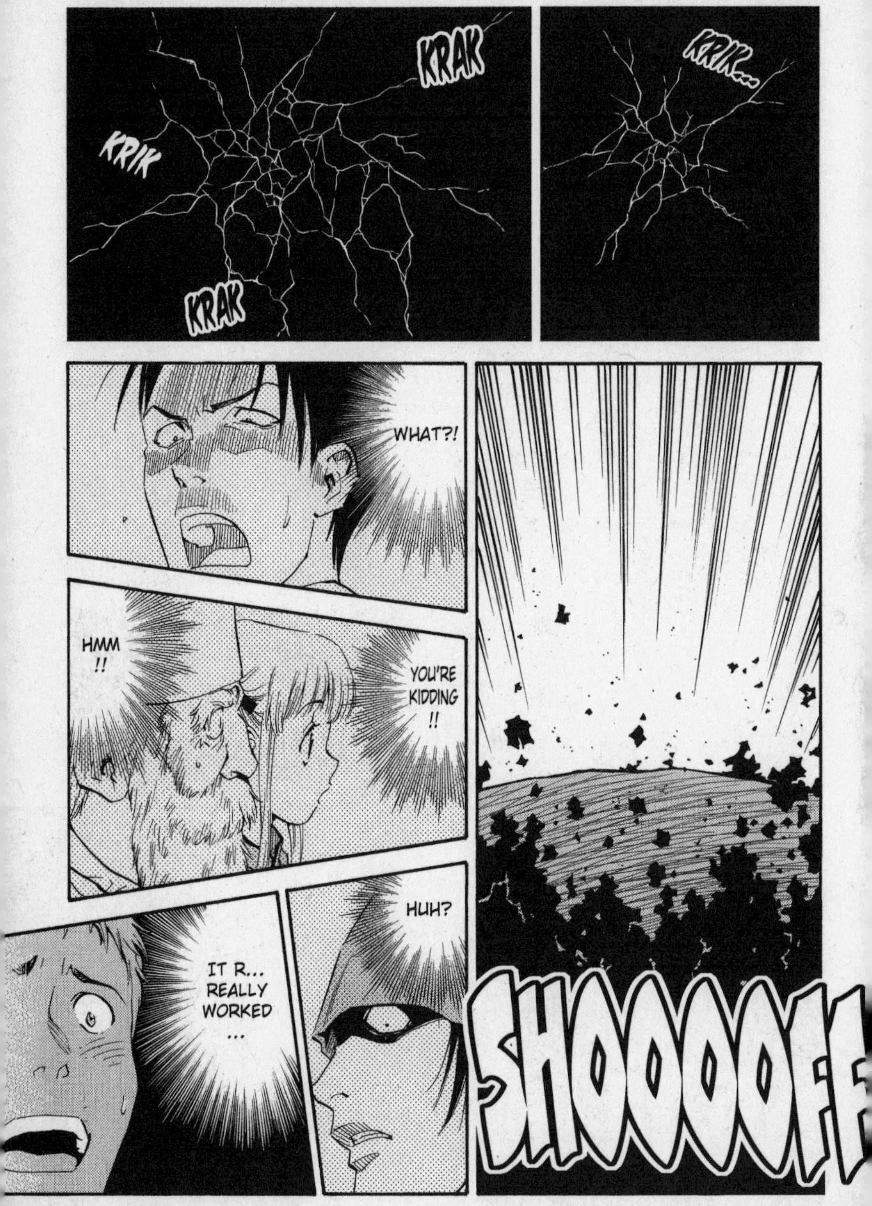
KRIK...
KRAK
KRIK
KRAK
SHOOOOF
WHAT?!
YOU'RE KIDDING !!
HMM !!
HUH?
IT R... REALLY WORKED ...

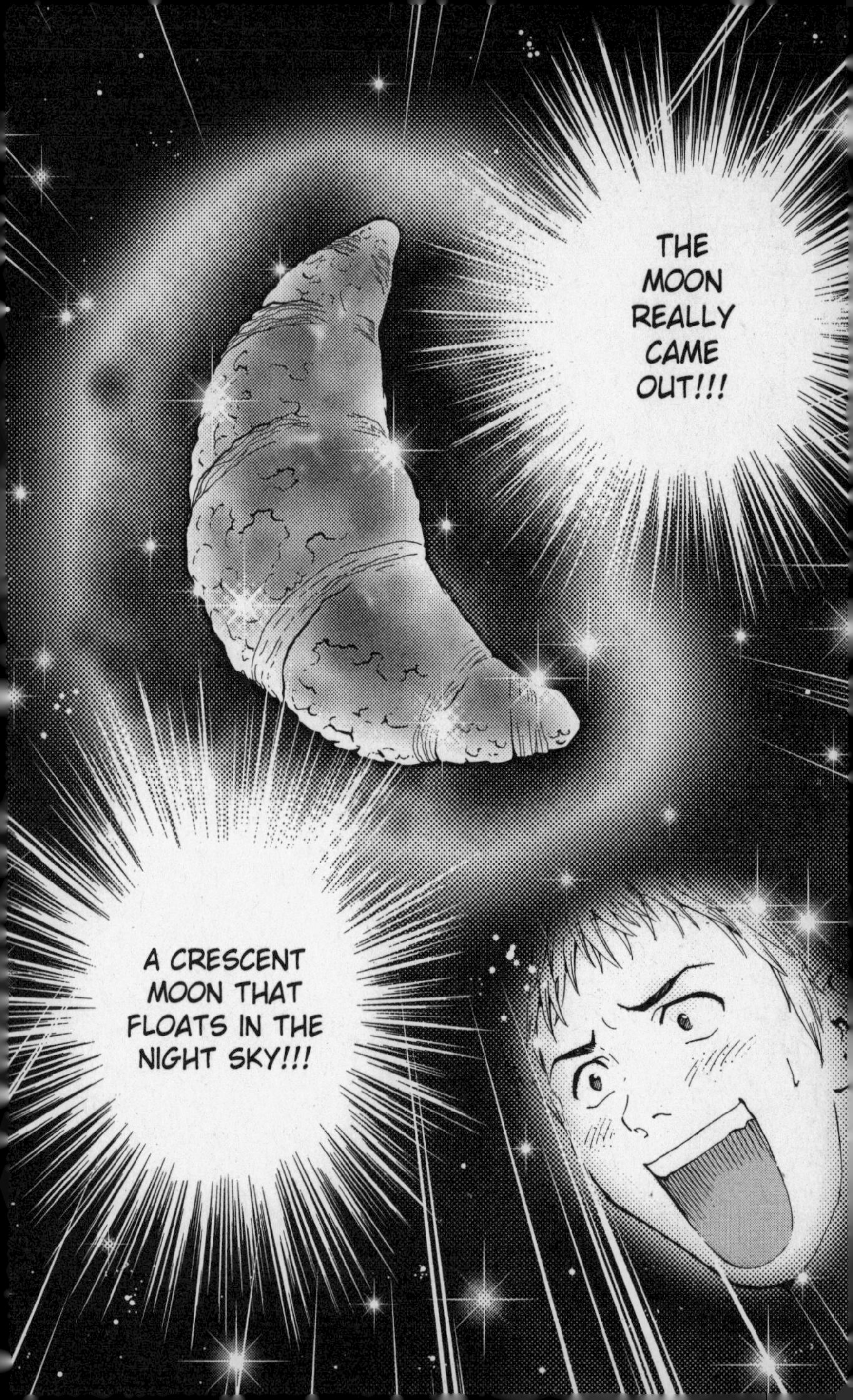
THE MOON REALLY CAME OUT!!!
A CRESCENT MOON THAT FLOATS IN THE NIGHT SKY!!!

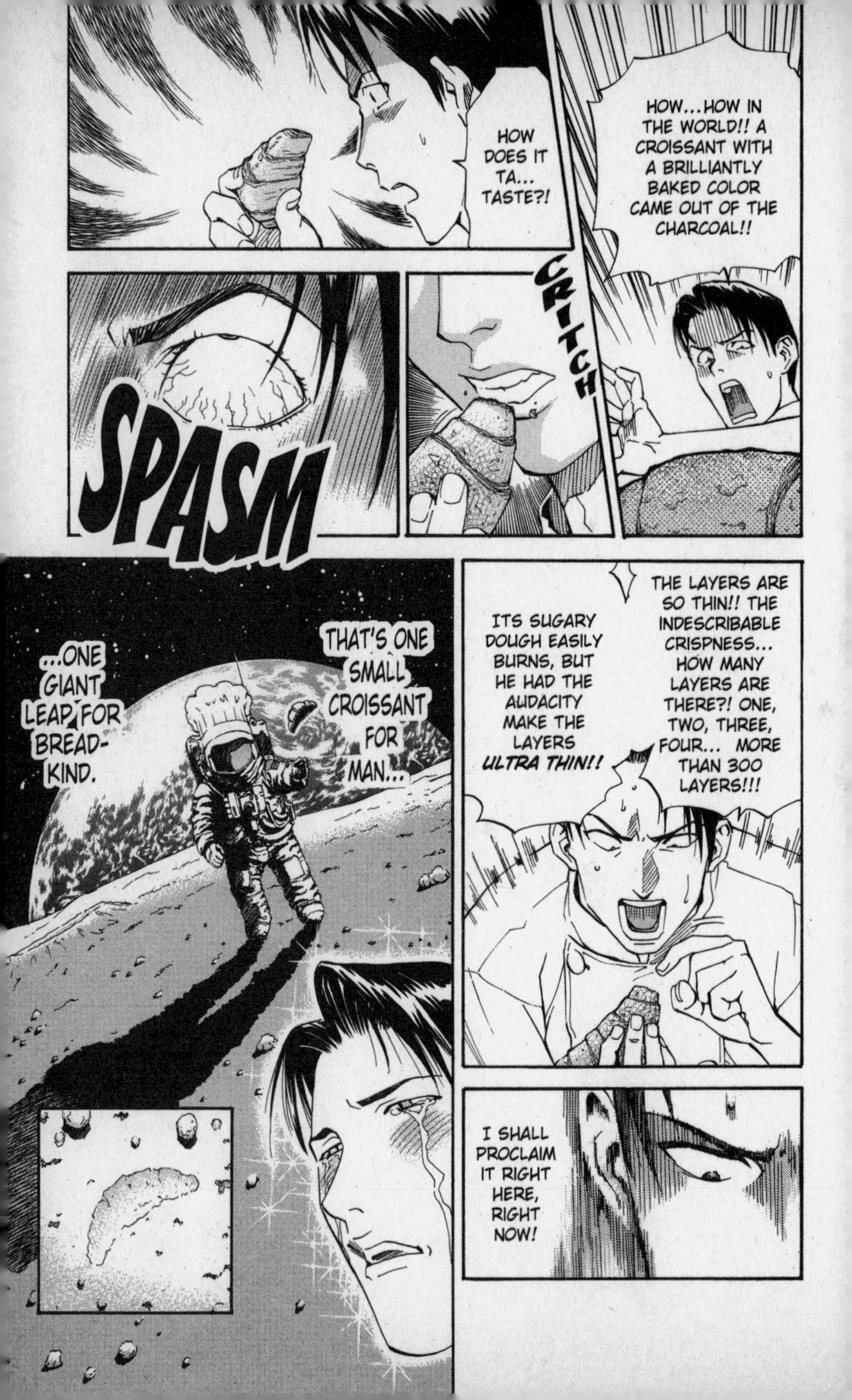
HOW...HOW IN THE WORLD!! A CROISSANT WITH A BRILLIANTLY BAKED COLOR CAME OUT OF THE CHARCOAL!!
HOW DOES IT TA... TASTE?!
CRITCH
SPASM
THE LAYERS ARE SO THIN!! THE INDESCRIBABLE CRISPNESS... HOW MANY LAYERS ARE THERE?! ONE, TWO, THREE, FOUR... MORE THAN 300 LAYERS!!!
ITS SUGARY DOUGH EASILY BURNS, BUT HE HAD THE AUDACITY MAKE THE LAYERS *ULTRA THIN!!*
I SHALL PROCLAIM IT RIGHT HERE, RIGHT NOW!
THAT'S ONE SMALL CROISSANT FOR MAN...
...ONE GIANT LEAP FOR BREAD-KIND.

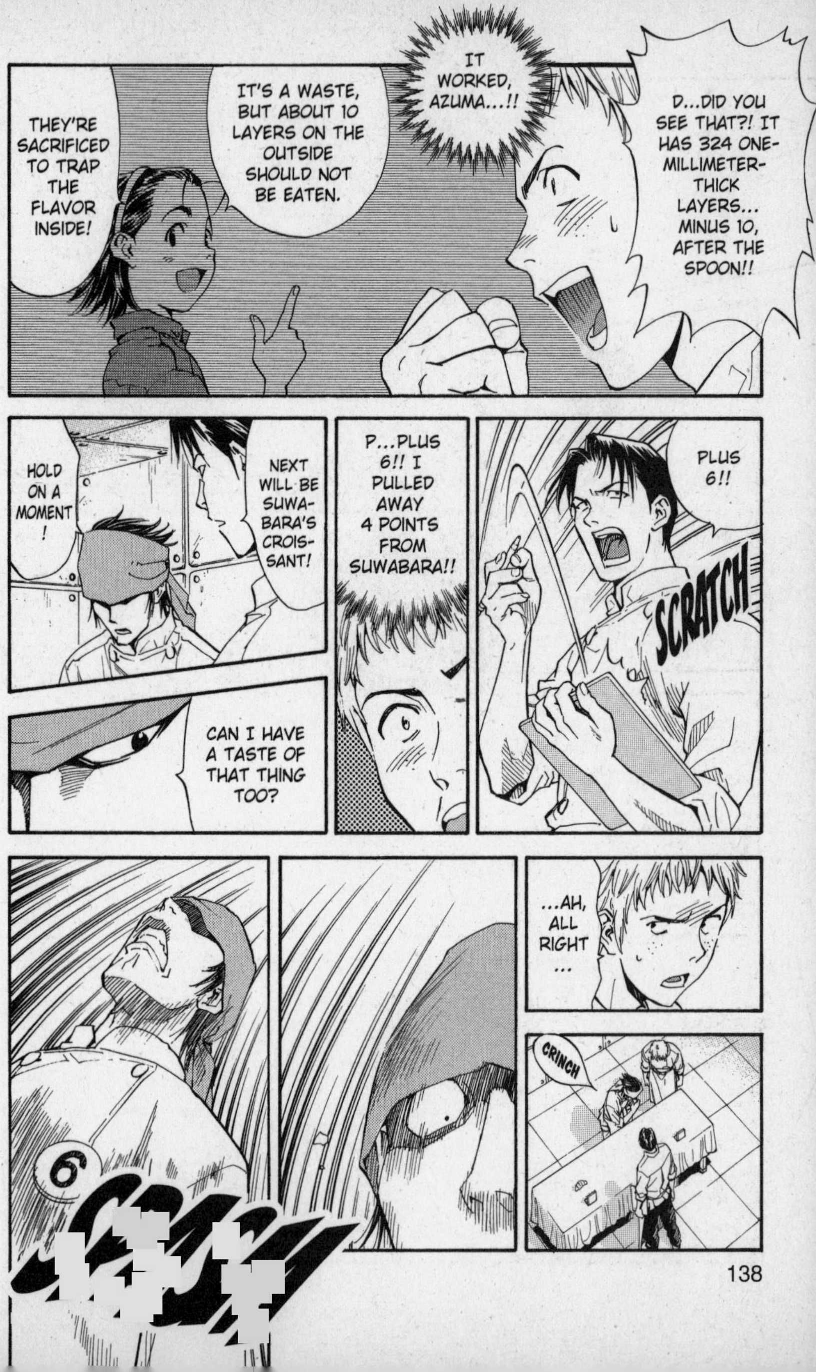
D...DID YOU SEE THAT?! IT HAS 324 ONE-MILLIMETER-THICK LAYERS... MINUS 10, AFTER THE SPOON!!
IT WORKED, AZUMA...!!
IT'S A WASTE, BUT ABOUT 10 LAYERS ON THE OUTSIDE SHOULD NOT BE EATEN.
THEY'RE SACRIFICED TO TRAP THE FLAVOR INSIDE!
PLUS 6!!
SCRATCH
P...PLUS 6!! I PULLED AWAY 4 POINTS FROM SUWABARA!!
NEXT WILL BE SUWABARA'S CROISSANT!
HOLD ON A MOMENT!
CAN I HAVE A TASTE OF THAT THING TOO?
...AH, ALL RIGHT...
CRINCH

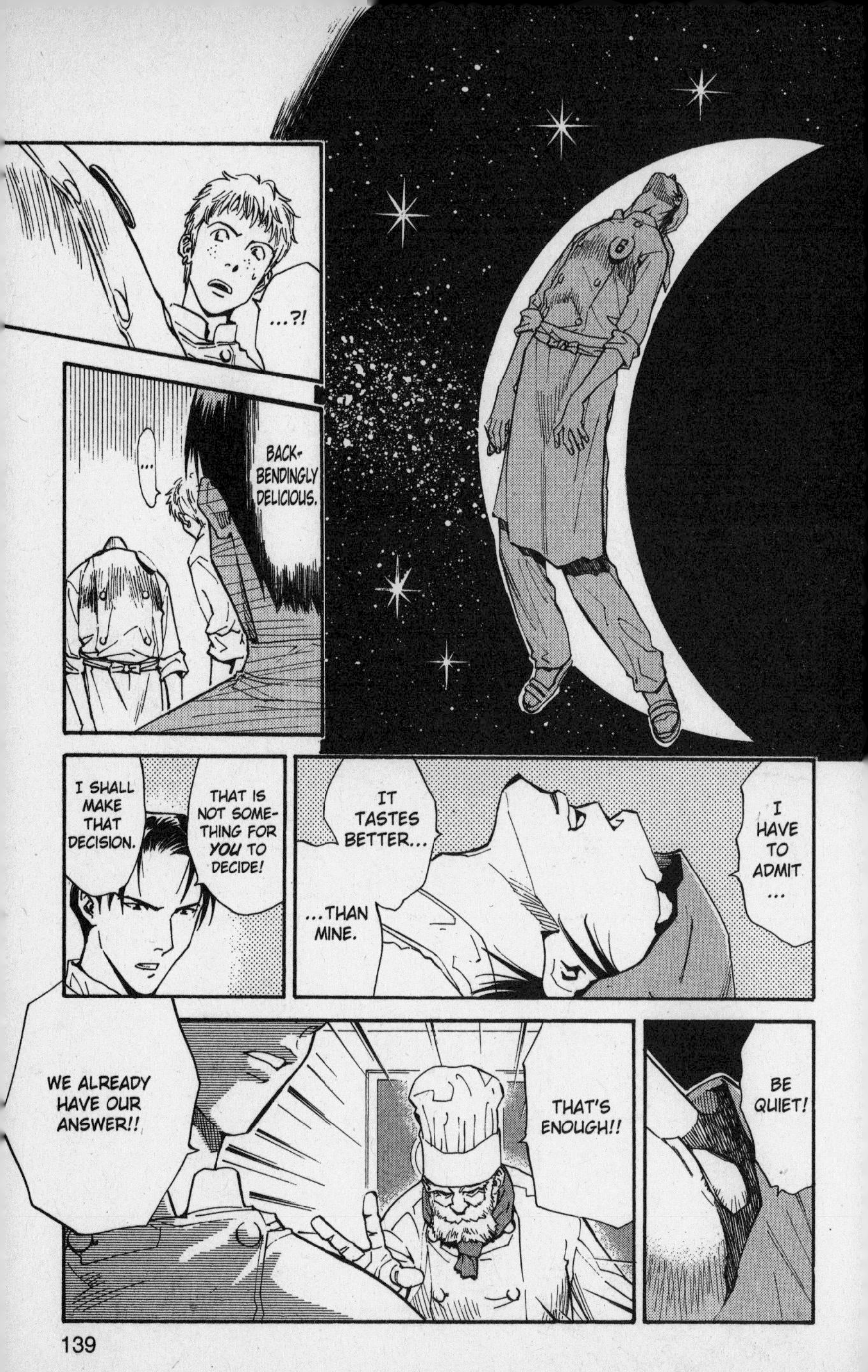
...?!
BACK-BENDINGLY DELICIOUS.
...
I HAVE TO ADMIT...
IT TASTES BETTER...
...THAN MINE.
THAT IS NOT SOMETHING FOR *YOU* TO DECIDE!
I SHALL MAKE THAT DECISION.
BE QUIET!
THAT'S ENOUGH!!
WE ALREADY HAVE OUR ANSWER!!

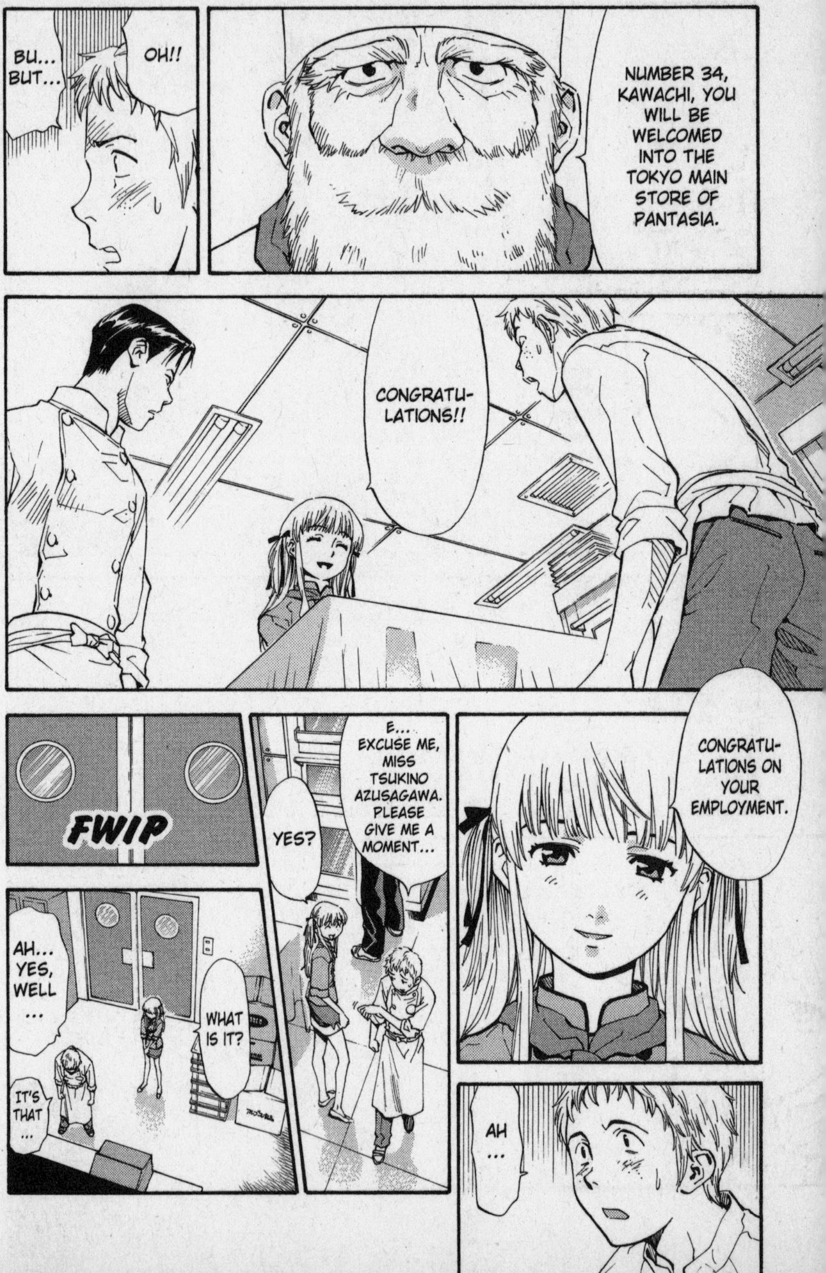
NUMBER 34, KAWACHI, YOU WILL BE WELCOMED INTO THE TOKYO MAIN STORE OF PANTASIA.
OH!!
BU... BUT...
CONGRATU-LATIONS!!
CONGRATU-LATIONS ON YOUR EMPLOYMENT.
AH ...
E... EXCUSE ME, MISS TSUKINO AZUSAGAWA. PLEASE GIVE ME A MOMENT...
YES?
FWIP
WHAT IS IT?
AH... YES, WELL ...
IT'S THAT ...

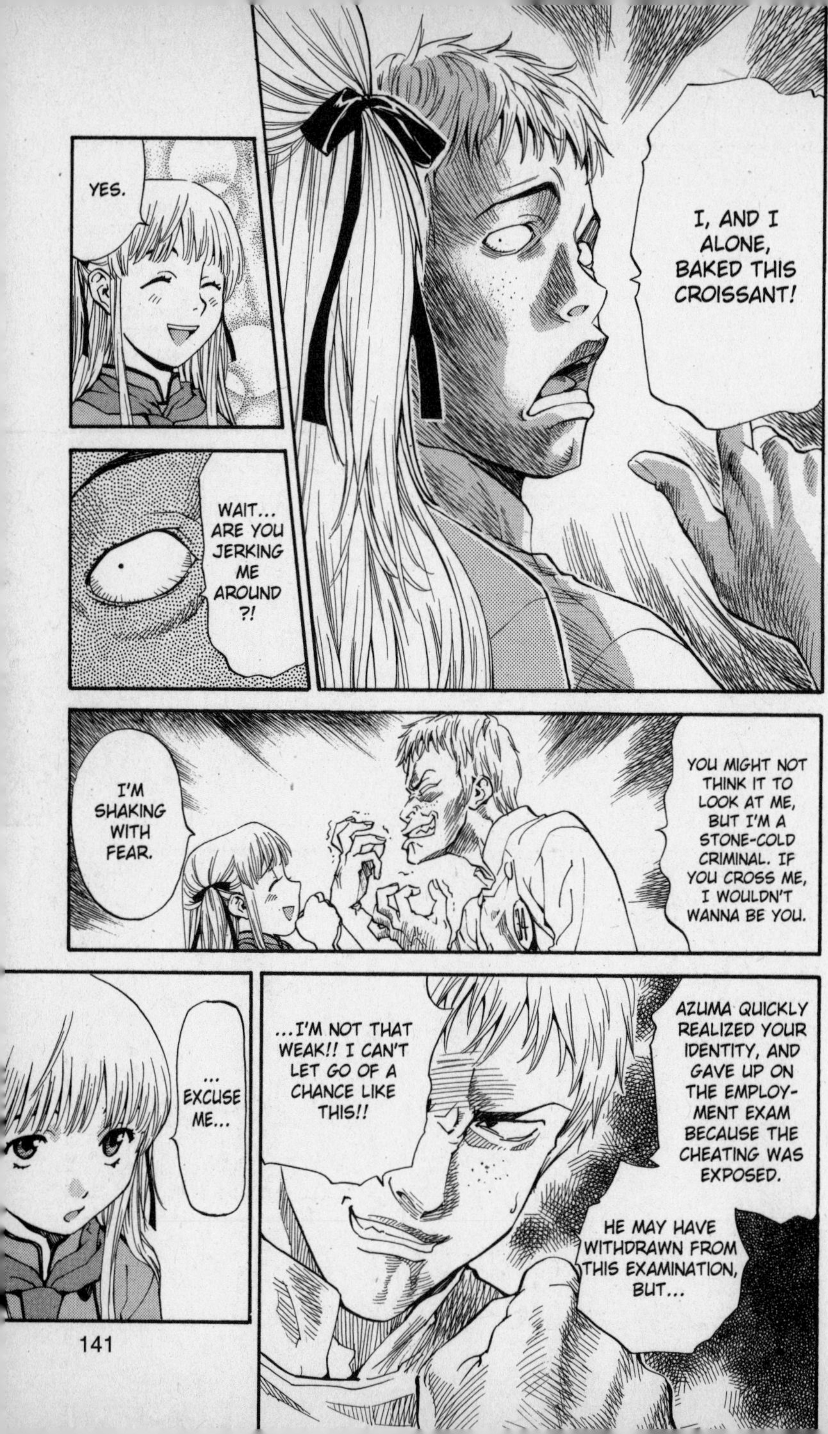
I, AND I ALONE, BAKED THIS CROISSANT!
YES.
WAIT... ARE YOU JERKING ME AROUND ?!
YOU MIGHT NOT THINK IT TO LOOK AT ME, BUT I'M A STONE-COLD CRIMINAL. IF YOU CROSS ME, I WOULDN'T WANNA BE YOU.
I'M SHAKING WITH FEAR.
AZUMA QUICKLY REALIZED YOUR IDENTITY, AND GAVE UP ON THE EMPLOYMENT EXAM BECAUSE THE CHEATING WAS EXPOSED.
HE MAY HAVE WITHDRAWN FROM THIS EXAMINATION, BUT...
...I'M NOT THAT WEAK!! I CAN'T LET GO OF A CHANCE LIKE THIS!!
... EXCUSE ME...

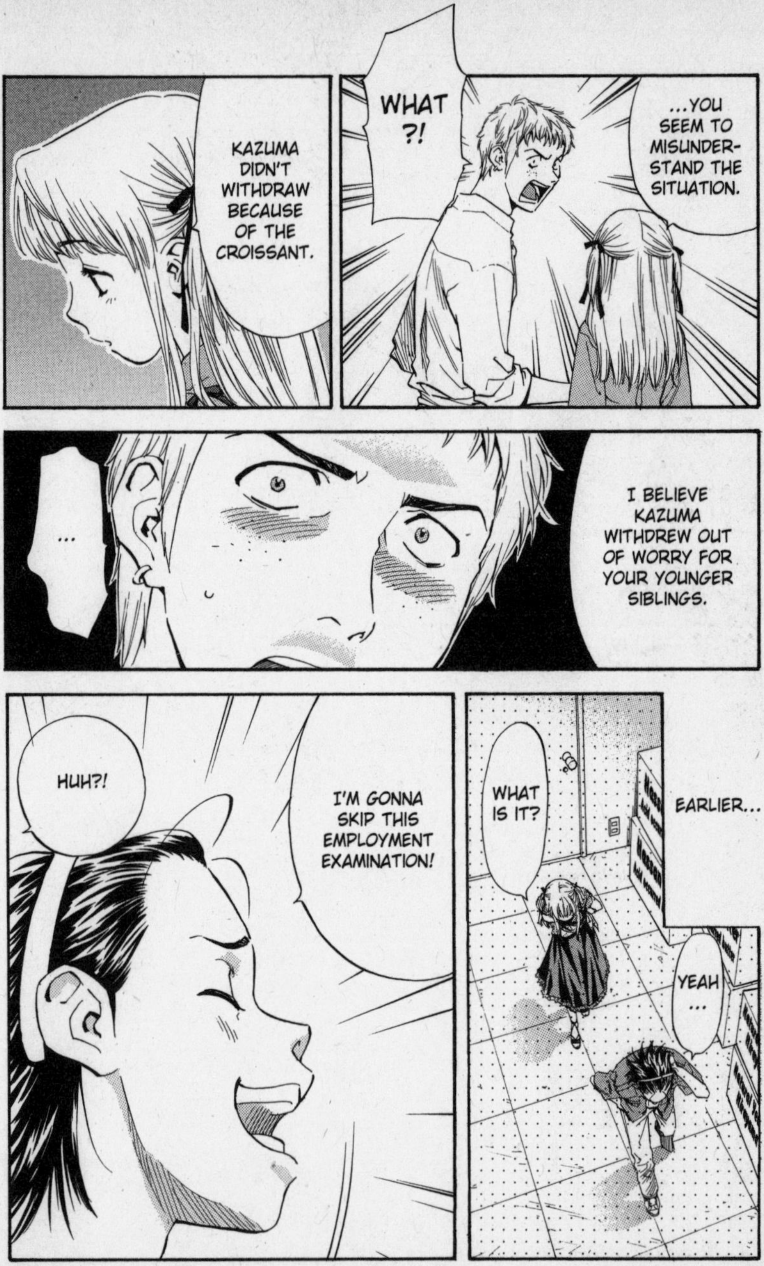
...YOU SEEM TO MISUNDER-STAND THE SITUATION.
WHAT ?!
KAZUMA DIDN'T WITHDRAW BECAUSE OF THE CROISSANT.
I BELIEVE KAZUMA WITHDREW OUT OF WORRY FOR YOUR YOUNGER SIBLINGS.
...
EARLIER...
WHAT IS IT?
YEAH ...
I'M GONNA SKIP THIS EMPLOYMENT EXAMINATION!
HUH?!

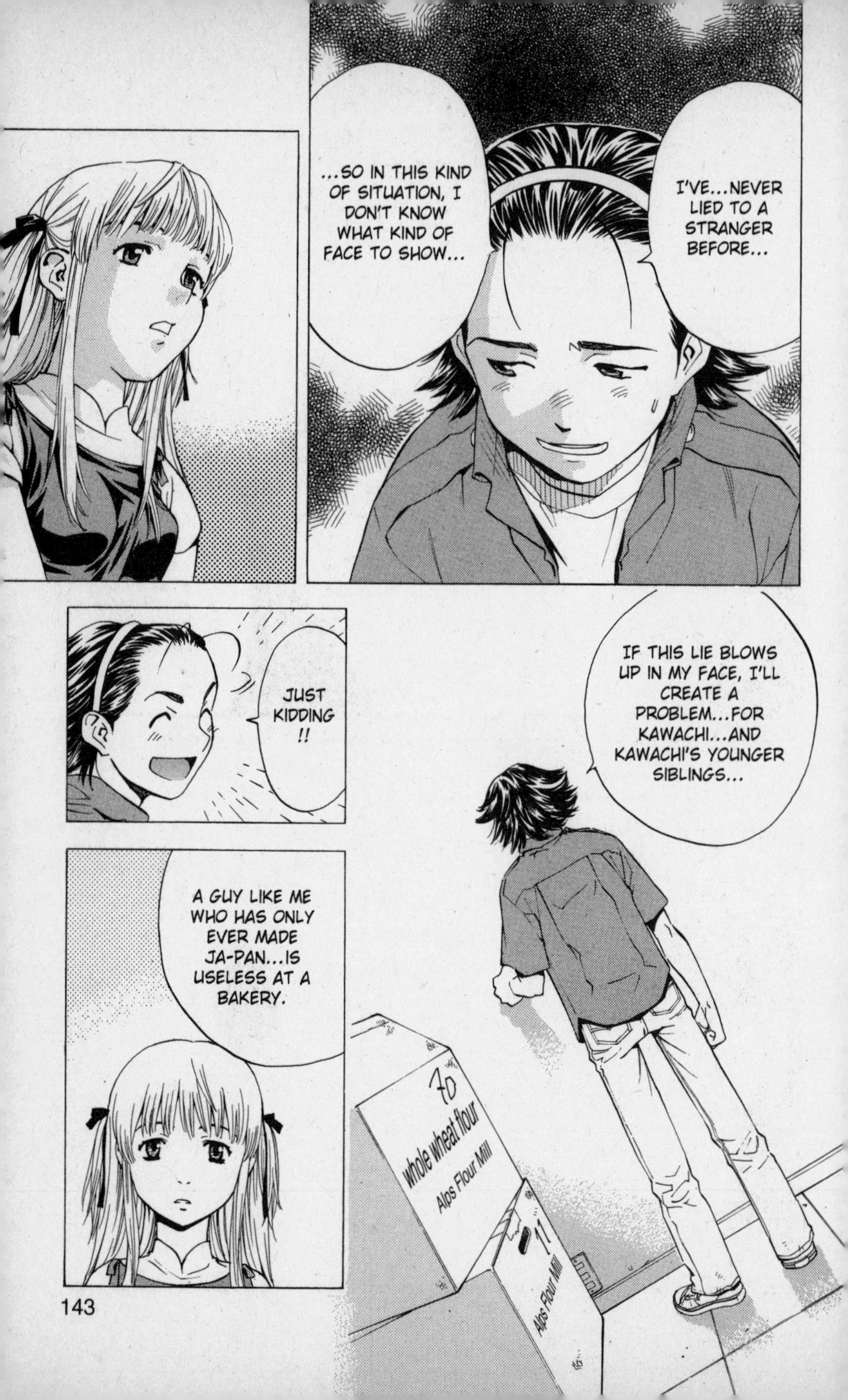
I'VE...NEVER LIED TO A STRANGER BEFORE...
...SO IN THIS KIND OF SITUATION, I DON'T KNOW WHAT KIND OF FACE TO SHOW...
IF THIS LIE BLOWS UP IN MY FACE, I'LL CREATE A PROBLEM...FOR KAWACHI...AND KAWACHI'S YOUNGER SIBLINGS...
70
whole wheat flour
Alps Flour Mill
Alps Flour Mill
JUST KIDDING!!
A GUY LIKE ME WHO HAS ONLY EVER MADE JA-PAN...IS USELESS AT A BAKERY.

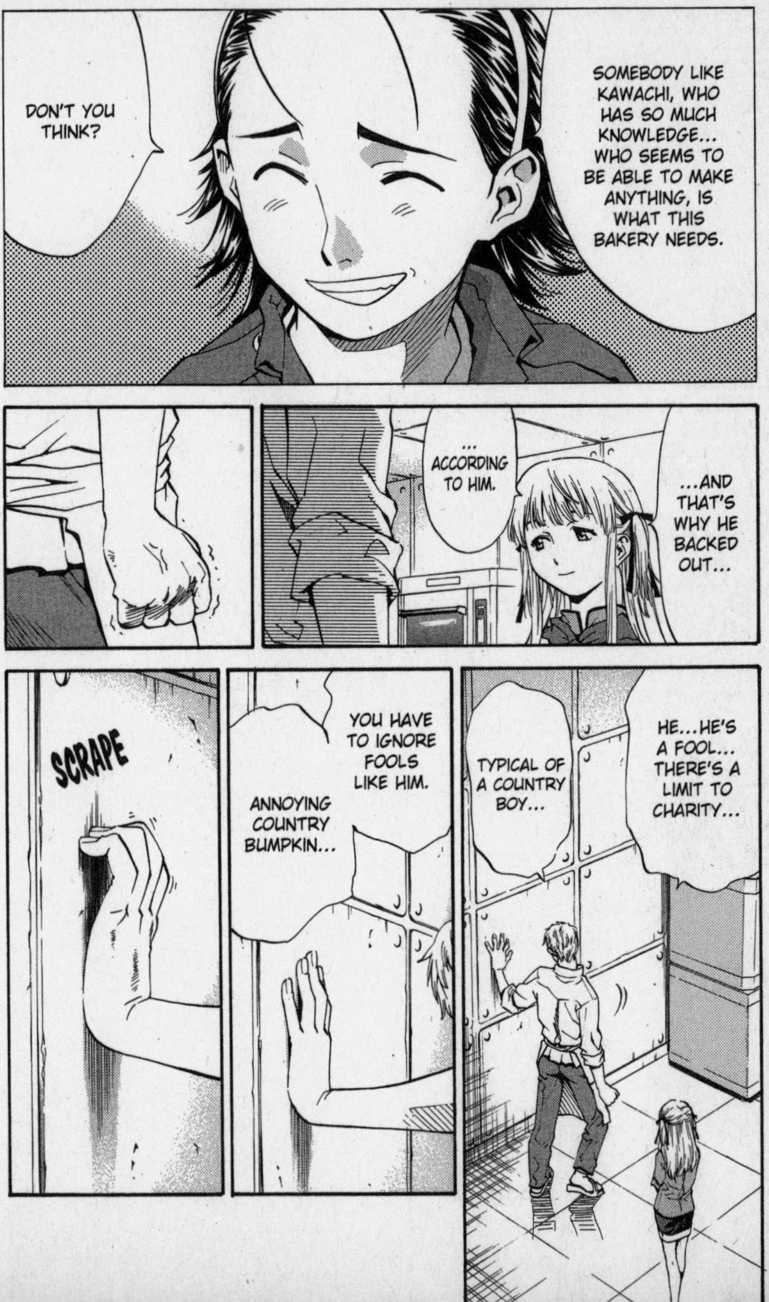
SOMEBODY LIKE KAWACHI, WHO HAS SO MUCH KNOWLEDGE... WHO SEEMS TO BE ABLE TO MAKE ANYTHING, IS WHAT THIS BAKERY NEEDS.
DON'T YOU THINK?
...AND THAT'S WHY HE BACKED OUT...
... ACCORDING TO HIM.
HE...HE'S A FOOL... THERE'S A LIMIT TO CHARITY...
TYPICAL OF A COUNTRY BOY...
YOU HAVE TO IGNORE FOOLS LIKE HIM.
ANNOYING COUNTRY BUMPKIN...
SCRAPE

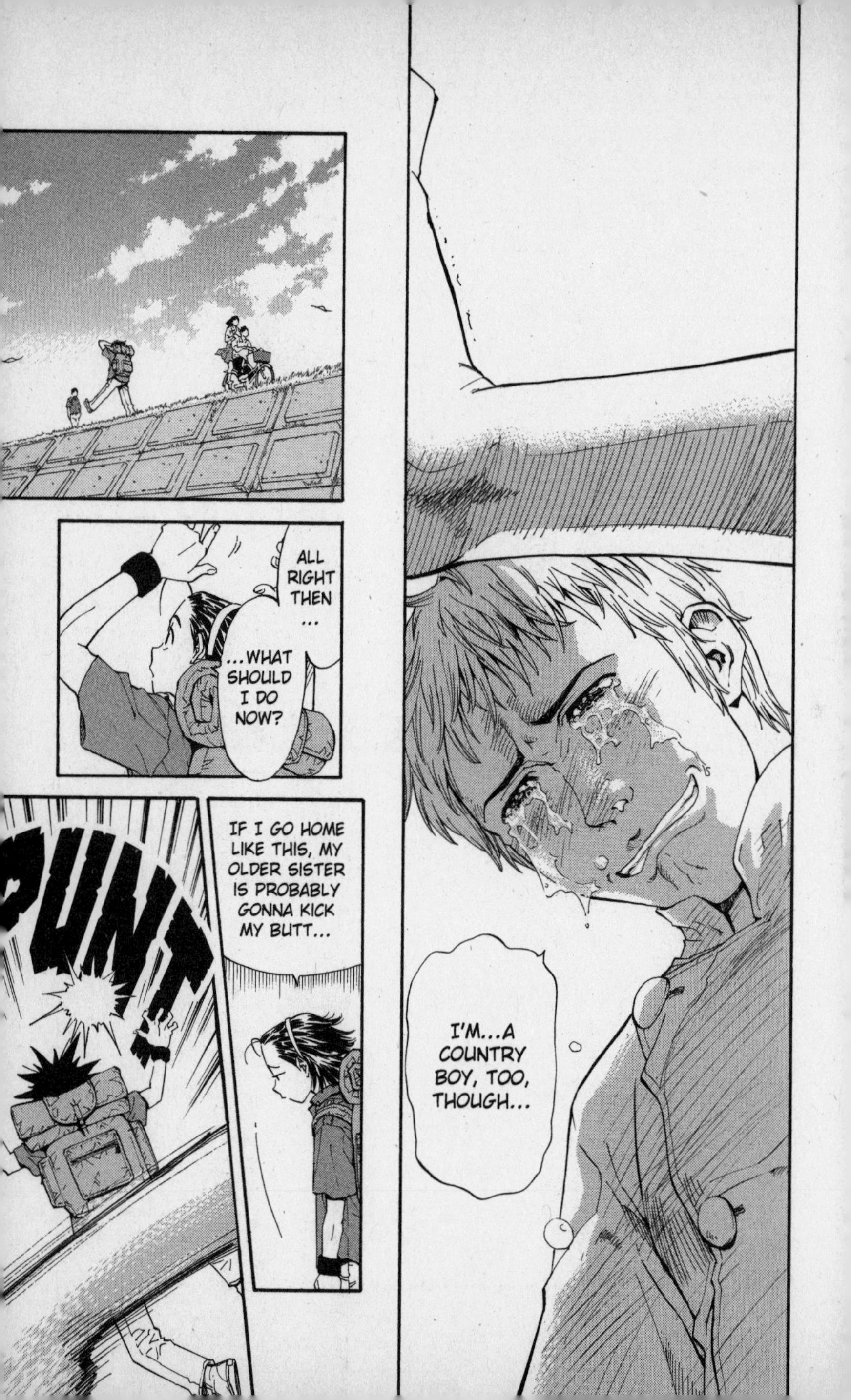
I'M...A COUNTRY BOY, TOO, THOUGH...
ALL RIGHT THEN ...
...WHAT SHOULD I DO NOW?
IF I GO HOME LIKE THIS, MY OLDER SISTER IS PROBABLY GONNA KICK MY BUTT...
PUNT

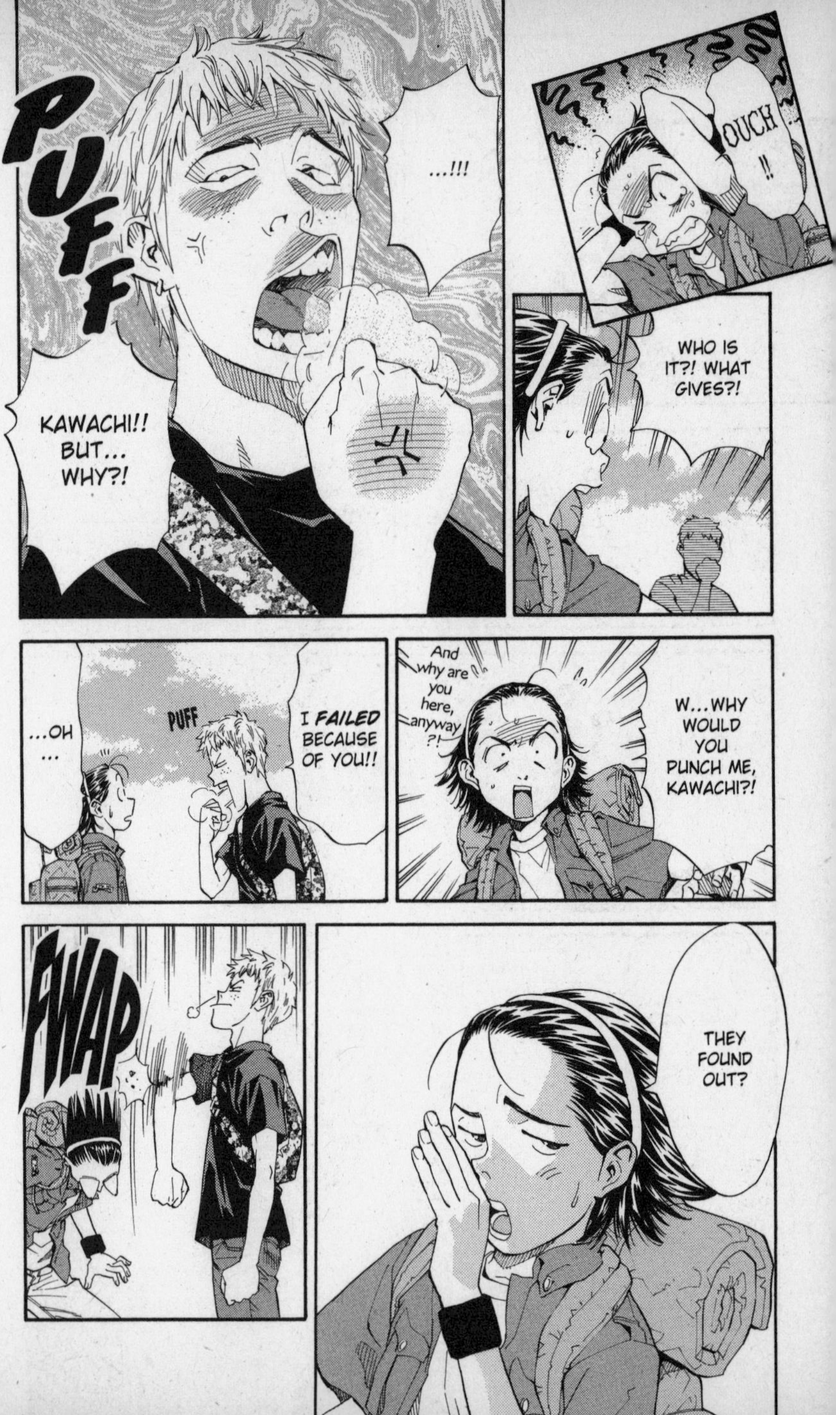
OUCH !!
WHO IS IT?! WHAT GIVES?!
...!!!
PUFF
KAWACHI!! BUT... WHY?!
W...WHY WOULD YOU PUNCH ME, KAWACHI?!
And why are you here, anyway?!
I FAILED BECAUSE OF YOU!!
PUFF
...OH ...
THEY FOUND OUT?
FWAP

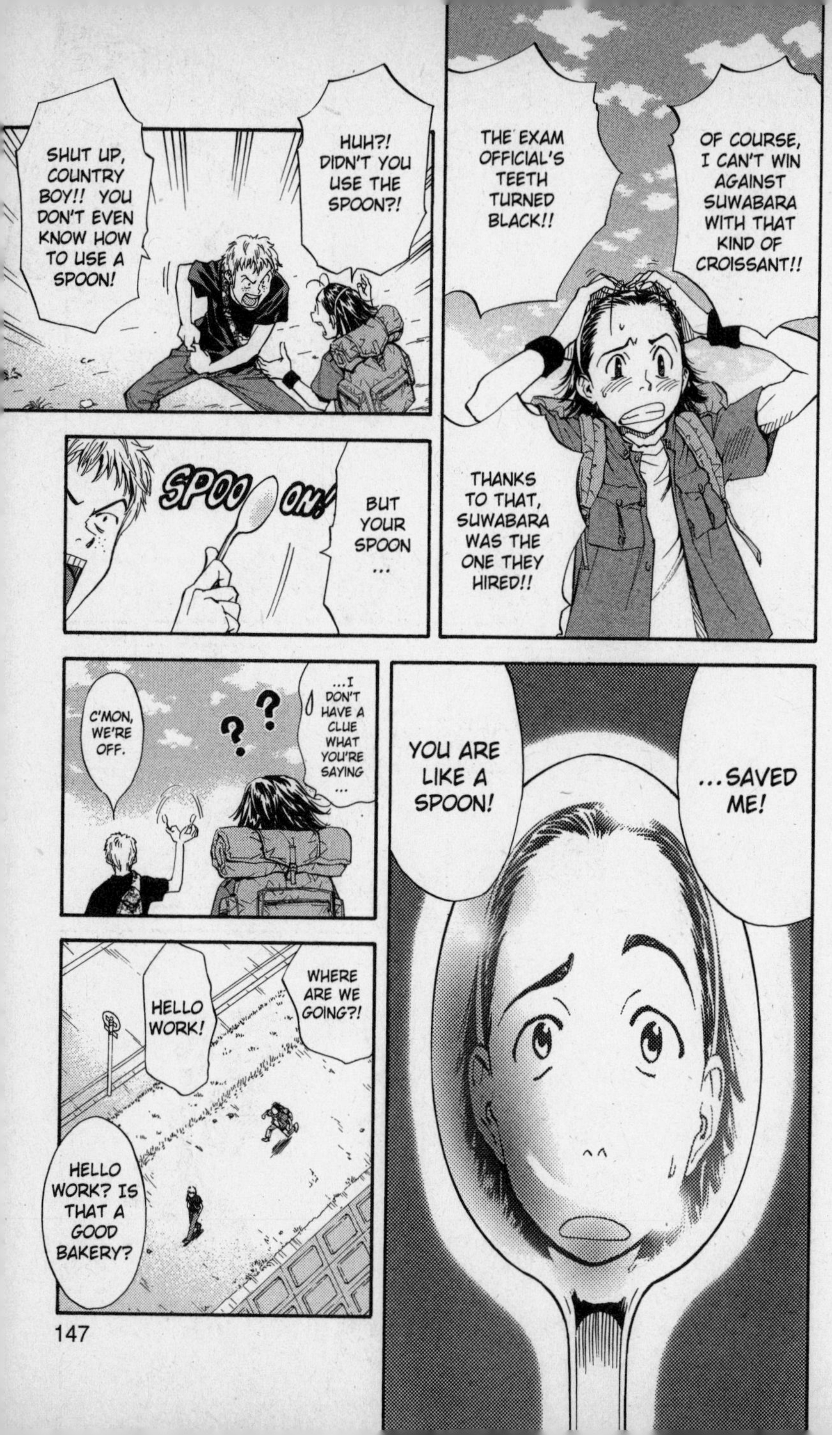
OF COURSE, I CAN'T WIN AGAINST SUWABARA WITH THAT KIND OF CROISSANT!!
THE EXAM OFFICIAL'S TEETH TURNED BLACK!!
THANKS TO THAT, SUWABARA WAS THE ONE THEY HIRED!!
HUH?! DIDN'T YOU USE THE SPOON?!
SHUT UP, COUNTRY BOY!! YOU DON'T EVEN KNOW HOW TO USE A SPOON!
BUT YOUR SPOON ...
SPOOOON!
...SAVED ME!
YOU ARE LIKE A SPOON!
...I DON'T HAVE A CLUE WHAT YOU'RE SAYING ...
C'MON, WE'RE OFF.
WHERE ARE WE GOING?!
HELLO WORK!
HELLO WORK? IS THAT A GOOD BAKERY?

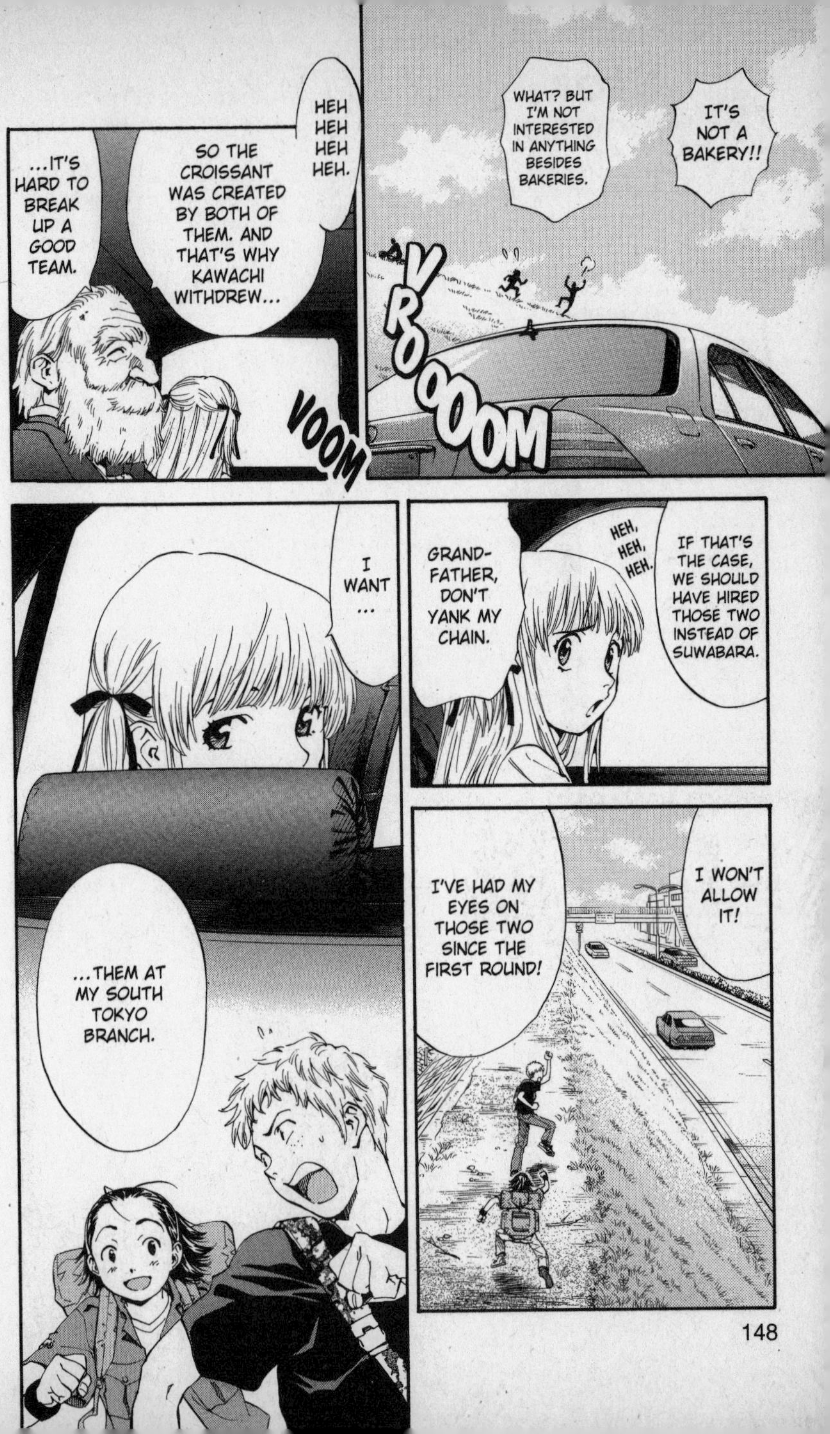
IT'S NOT A BAKERY!!
WHAT? BUT I'M NOT INTERESTED IN ANYTHING BESIDES BAKERIES.
VROOOOOM
HEH HEH HEH HEH.
SO THE CROISSANT WAS CREATED BY BOTH OF THEM. AND THAT'S WHY KAWACHI WITHDREW...
...IT'S HARD TO BREAK UP A GOOD TEAM.
VOOM
IF THAT'S THE CASE, WE SHOULD HAVE HIRED THOSE TWO INSTEAD OF SUWABARA.
HEH, HEH, HEH.
GRANDFATHER, DON'T YANK MY CHAIN.
I WON'T ALLOW IT!
I'VE HAD MY EYES ON THOSE TWO SINCE THE FIRST ROUND!
I WANT ...
...THEM AT MY SOUTH TOKYO BRANCH.

Story 6: The First Job!

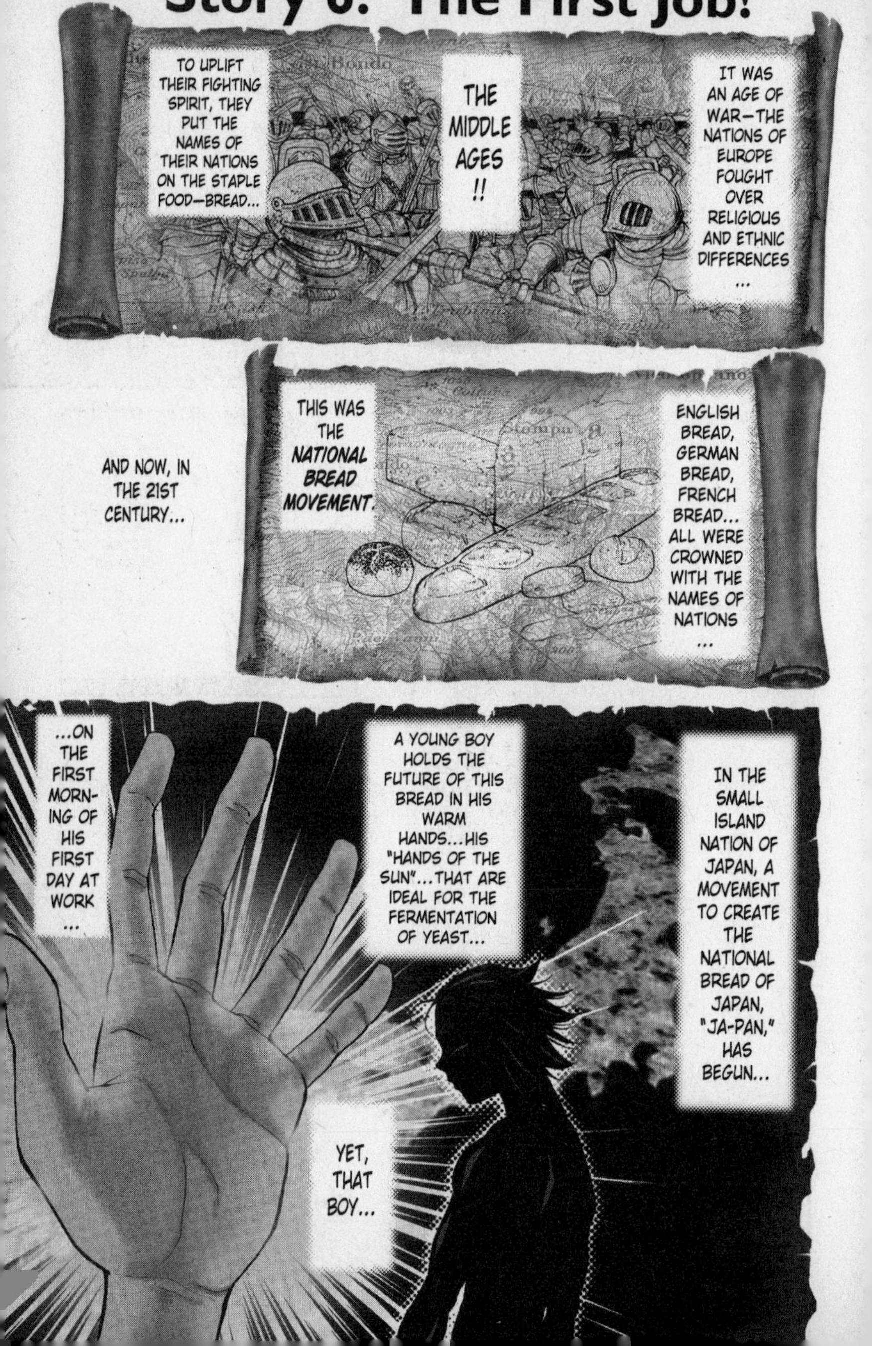
IT WAS AN AGE OF WAR—THE NATIONS OF EUROPE FOUGHT OVER RELIGIOUS AND ETHNIC DIFFERENCES...
THE MIDDLE AGES !!
TO UPLIFT THEIR FIGHTING SPIRIT, THEY PUT THE NAMES OF THEIR NATIONS ON THE STAPLE FOOD—BREAD...
ENGLISH BREAD, GERMAN BREAD, FRENCH BREAD... ALL WERE CROWNED WITH THE NAMES OF NATIONS...
THIS WAS THE NATIONAL BREAD MOVEMENT.
AND NOW, IN THE 21ST CENTURY...
IN THE SMALL ISLAND NATION OF JAPAN, A MOVEMENT TO CREATE THE NATIONAL BREAD OF JAPAN, "JA-PAN," HAS BEGUN...
A YOUNG BOY HOLDS THE FUTURE OF THIS BREAD IN HIS WARM HANDS...HIS "HANDS OF THE SUN"...THAT ARE IDEAL FOR THE FERMENTATION OF YEAST...
...ON THE FIRST MORN-ING OF HIS FIRST DAY AT WORK...
YET, THAT BOY...

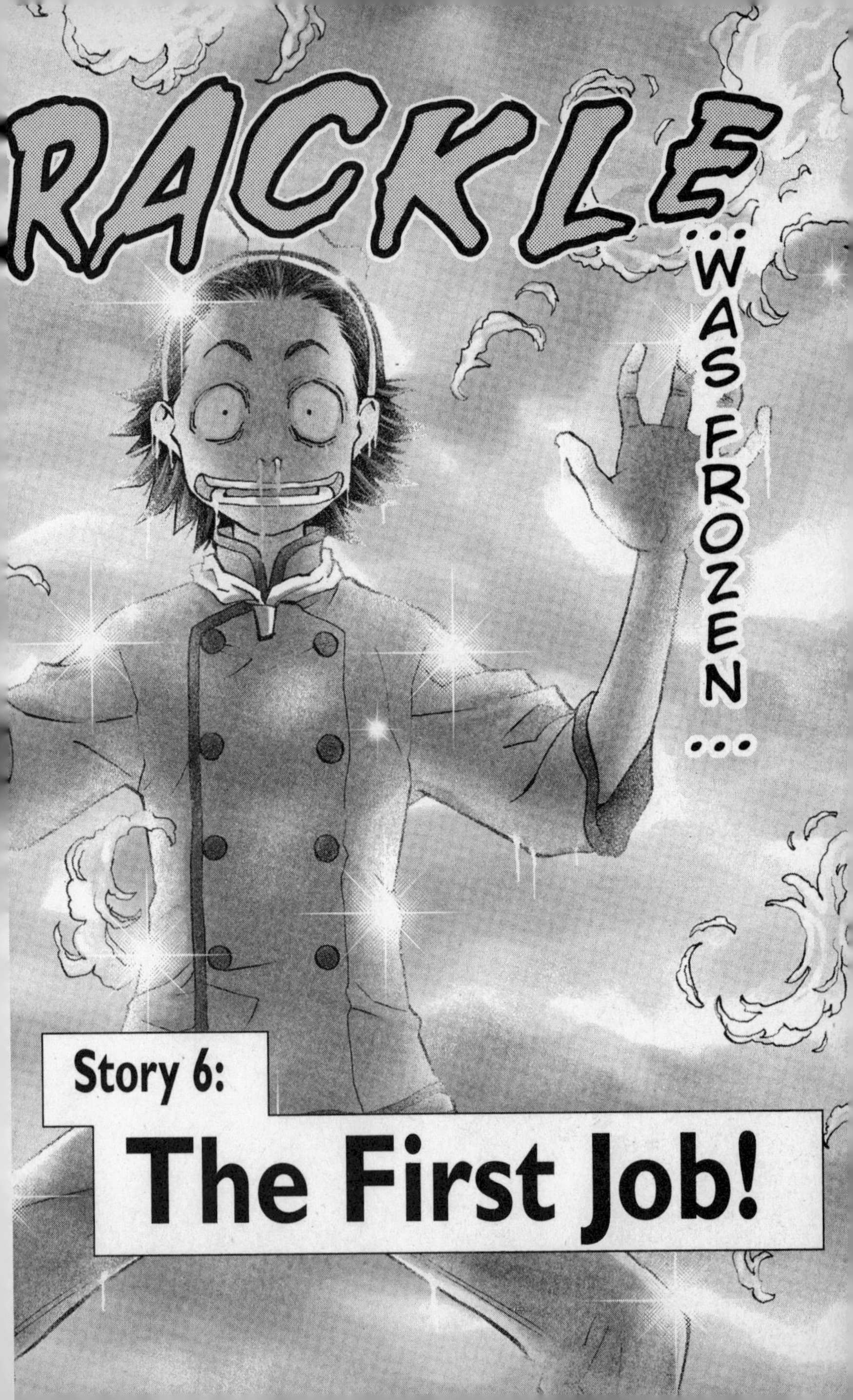

RACKLE
...WAS FROZEN...
Story 6:
The First Job!

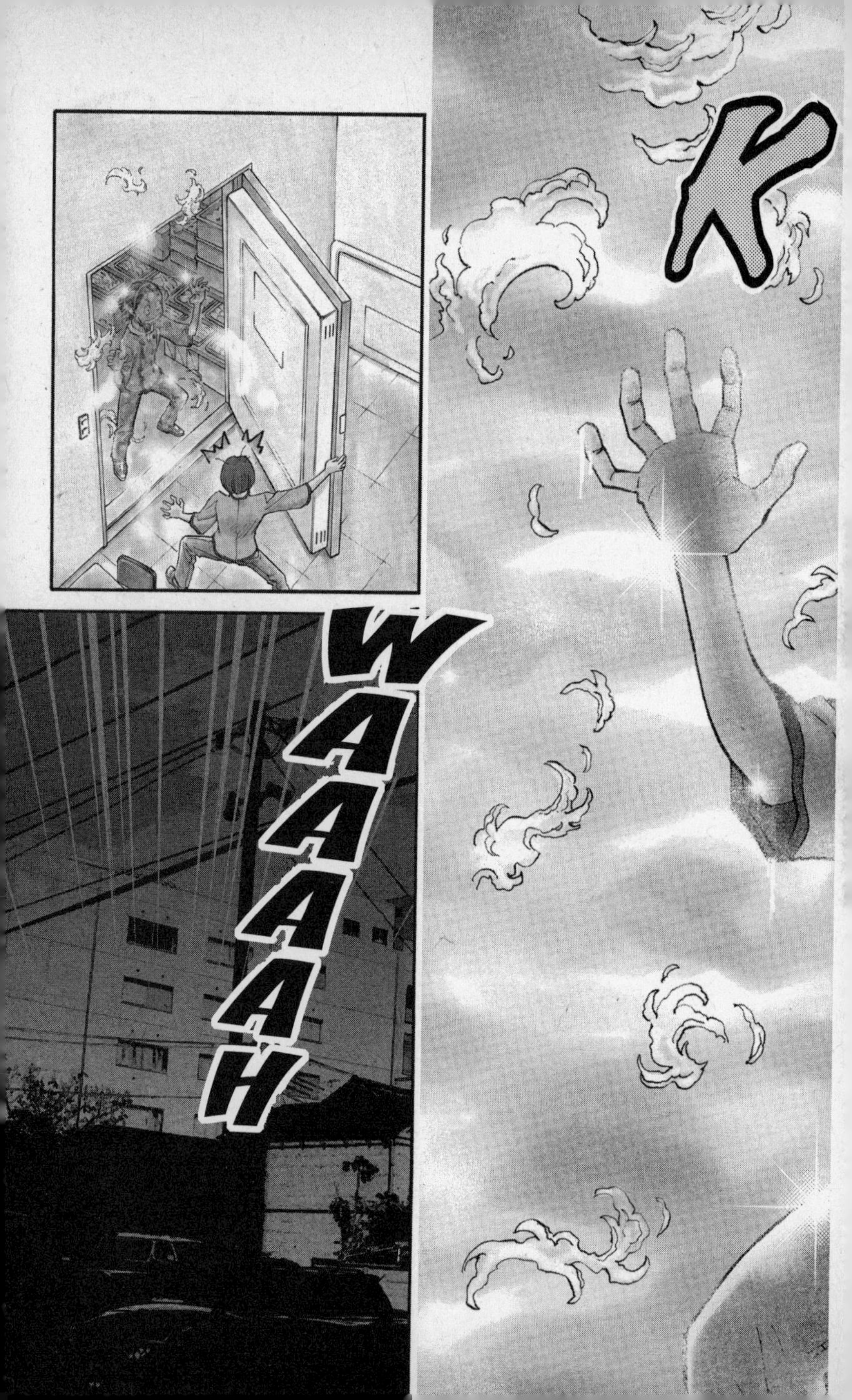
K
WAAAAAH

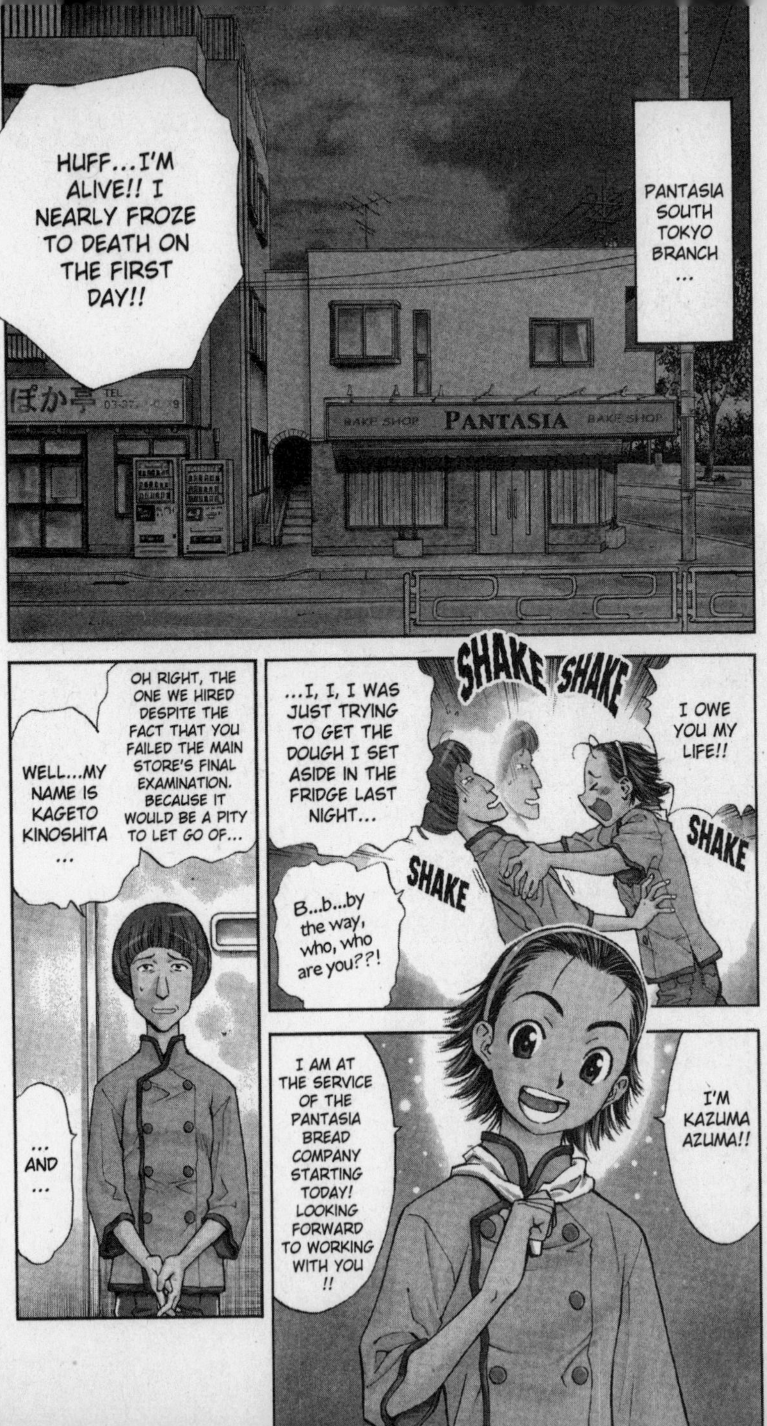
PANTASIA SOUTH TOKYO BRANCH ...
HUFF...I'M ALIVE!! I NEARLY FROZE TO DEATH ON THE FIRST DAY!!
BAKE SHOP PANTASIA BAKE SHOP
I OWE YOU MY LIFE!!
SHAKE SHAKE
...I, I, I WAS JUST TRYING TO GET THE DOUGH I SET ASIDE IN THE FRIDGE LAST NIGHT...
SHAKE
SHAKE
B...b...by the way, who, who are you??!
I'M KAZUMA AZUMA!!
I AM AT THE SERVICE OF THE PANTASIA BREAD COMPANY STARTING TODAY! LOOKING FORWARD TO WORKING WITH YOU !!
OH RIGHT, THE ONE WE HIRED DESPITE THE FACT THAT YOU FAILED THE MAIN STORE'S FINAL EXAMINATION. BECAUSE IT WOULD BE A PITY TO LET GO OF...
WELL...MY NAME IS KAGETO KINOSHITA ...
... AND ...

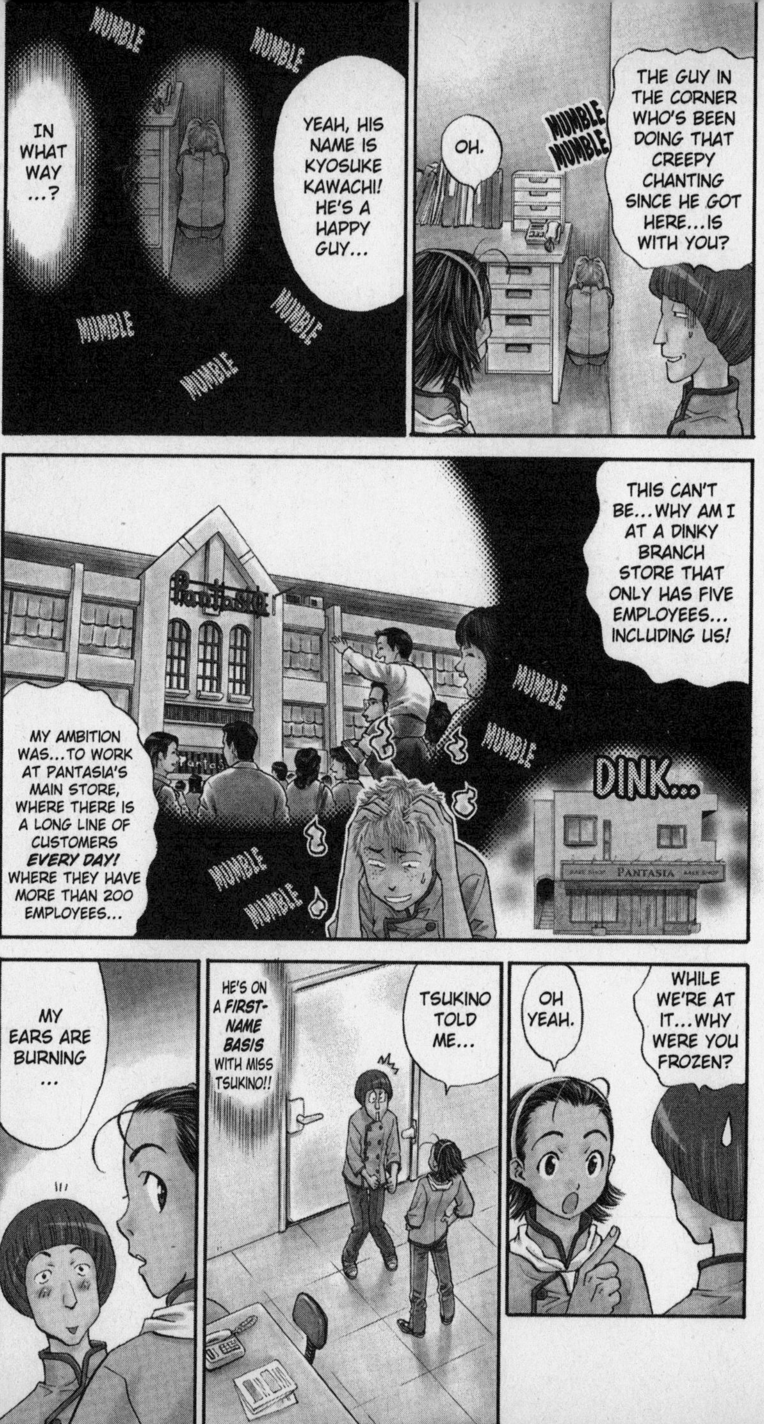
THE GUY IN THE CORNER WHO'S BEEN DOING THAT CREEPY CHANTING SINCE HE GOT HERE...IS WITH YOU?
MUMBLE MUMBLE
OH.
YEAH, HIS NAME IS KYOSUKE KAWACHI! HE'S A HAPPY GUY...
MUMBLE
MUMBLE
IN WHAT WAY ...?
MUMBLE
MUMBLE
MUMBLE
THIS CAN'T BE...WHY AM I AT A DINKY BRANCH STORE THAT ONLY HAS FIVE EMPLOYEES... INCLUDING US!
MUMBLE
MUMBLE
DINK...
PANTASIA
MY AMBITION WAS...TO WORK AT PANTASIA'S MAIN STORE, WHERE THERE IS A LONG LINE OF CUSTOMERS *EVERY DAY!* WHERE THEY HAVE MORE THAN 200 EMPLOYEES...
MUMBLE
MUMBLE
WHILE WE'RE AT IT...WHY WERE YOU FROZEN?
OH YEAH.
TSUKINO TOLD ME...
HE'S ON A *FIRST-NAME BASIS* WITH MISS TSUKINO!!
MY EARS ARE BURNING ...

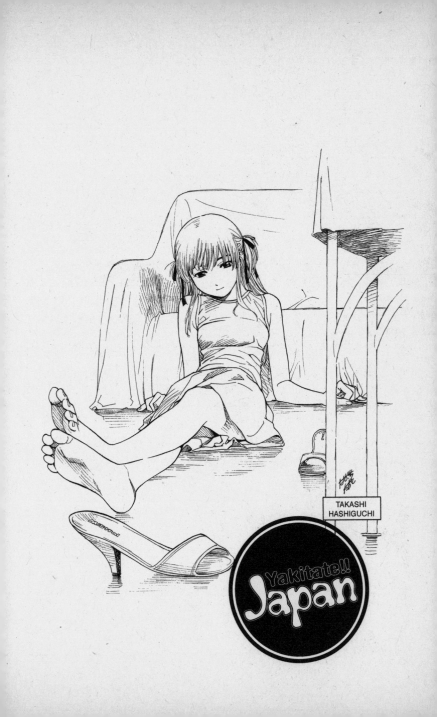

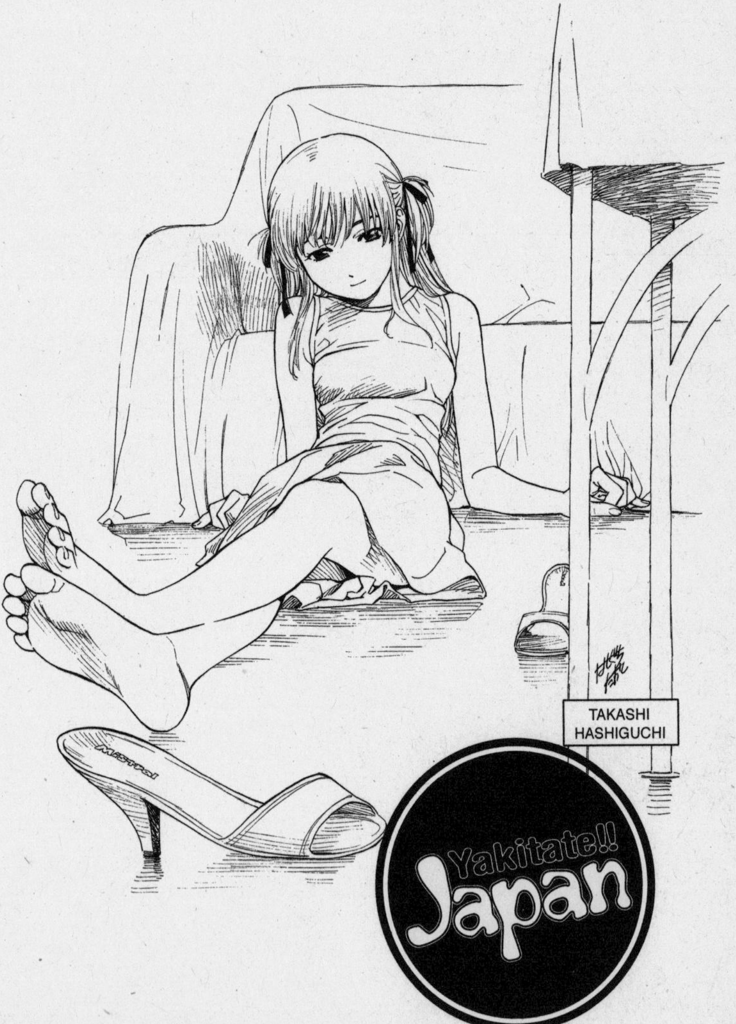
TAKASHI
HASHIGUCHI
Yakitate!!
Japan

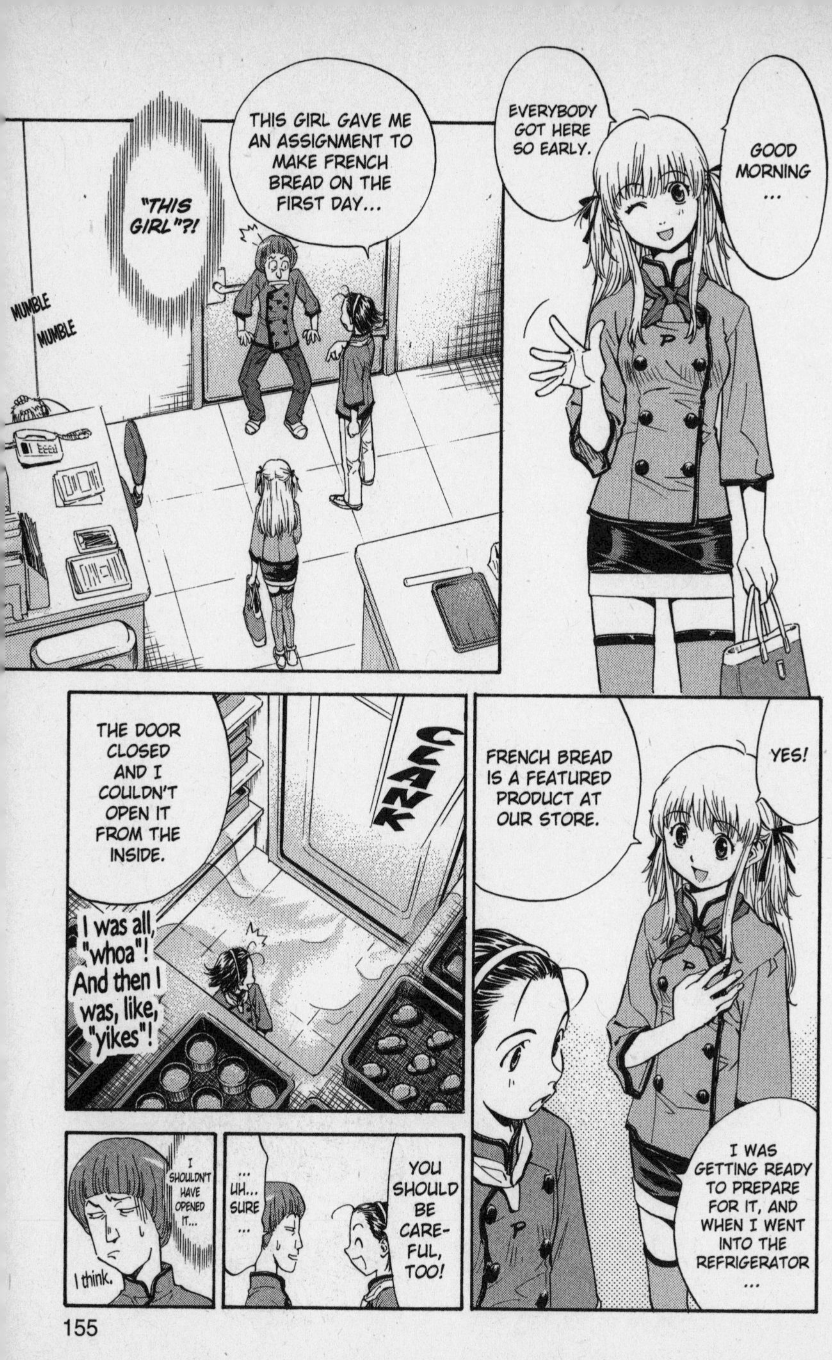
GOOD MORNING ...
EVERYBODY GOT HERE SO EARLY.
THIS GIRL GAVE ME AN ASSIGNMENT TO MAKE FRENCH BREAD ON THE FIRST DAY...
"THIS GIRL"?!
MUMBLE
MUMBLE
YES!
FRENCH BREAD IS A FEATURED PRODUCT AT OUR STORE.
I WAS GETTING READY TO PREPARE FOR IT, AND WHEN I WENT INTO THE REFRIGERATOR ...
CLANK
THE DOOR CLOSED AND I COULDN'T OPEN IT FROM THE INSIDE.
I was all, "whoa"! And then I was, like, "yikes"!
YOU SHOULD BE CARE-FUL, TOO!
... UH... SURE ...
I SHOULDN'T HAVE OPENED IT...
I think.

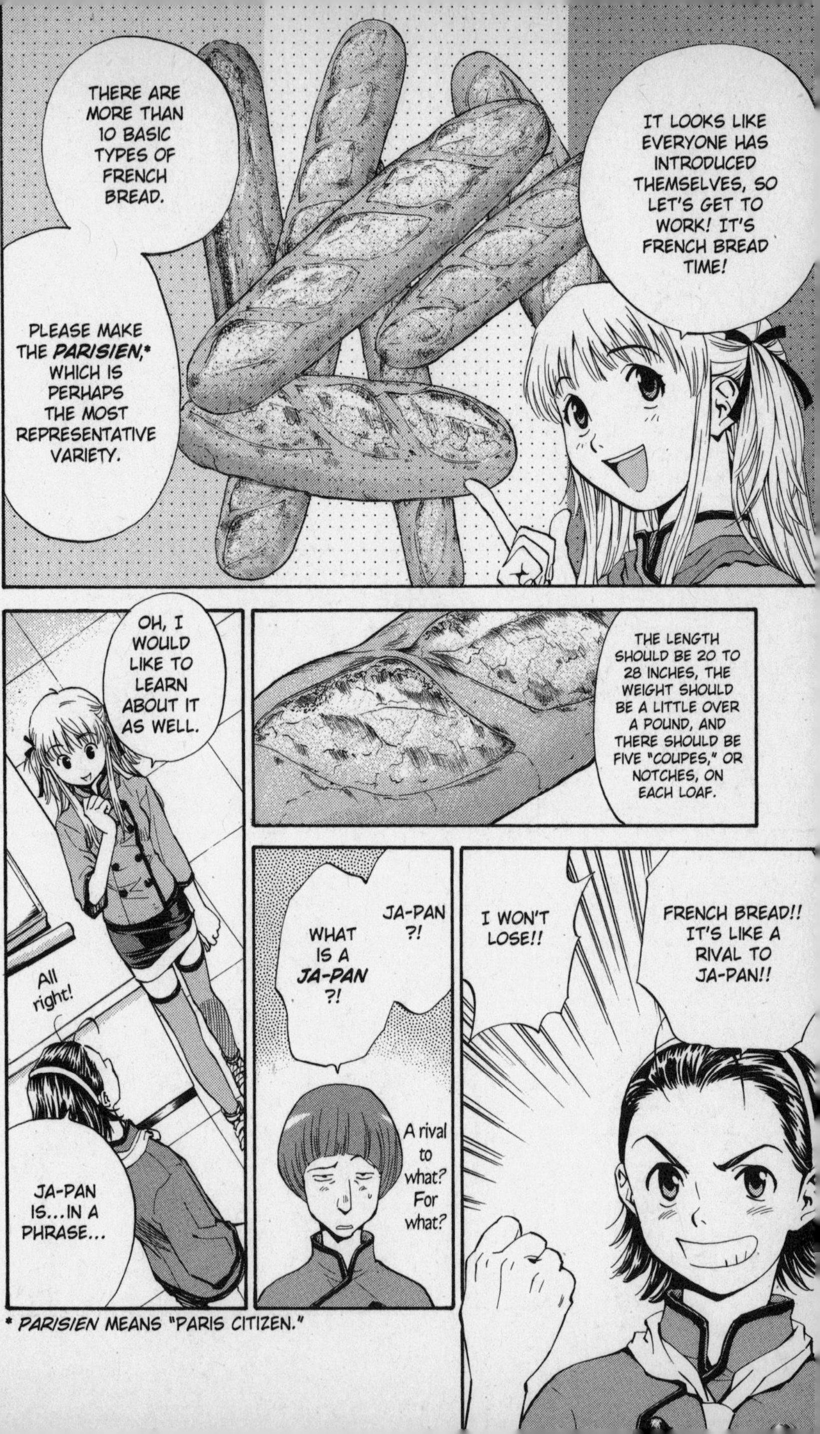

IT LOOKS LIKE EVERYONE HAS INTRODUCED THEMSELVES, SO LET'S GET TO WORK! IT'S FRENCH BREAD TIME!
THERE ARE MORE THAN 10 BASIC TYPES OF FRENCH BREAD.
PLEASE MAKE THE *PARISIEN,** WHICH IS PERHAPS THE MOST REPRESENTATIVE VARIETY.
THE LENGTH SHOULD BE 20 TO 28 INCHES, THE WEIGHT SHOULD BE A LITTLE OVER A POUND, AND THERE SHOULD BE FIVE "COUPES," OR NOTCHES, ON EACH LOAF.
FRENCH BREAD!! IT'S LIKE A RIVAL TO JA-PAN!!
I WON'T LOSE!!
JA-PAN ?!
WHAT IS A *JA-PAN* ?!
A rival to what? For what?
OH, I WOULD LIKE TO LEARN ABOUT IT AS WELL.
All right!
JA-PAN IS...IN A PHRASE...

* *PARISIEN* MEANS "PARIS CITIZEN."

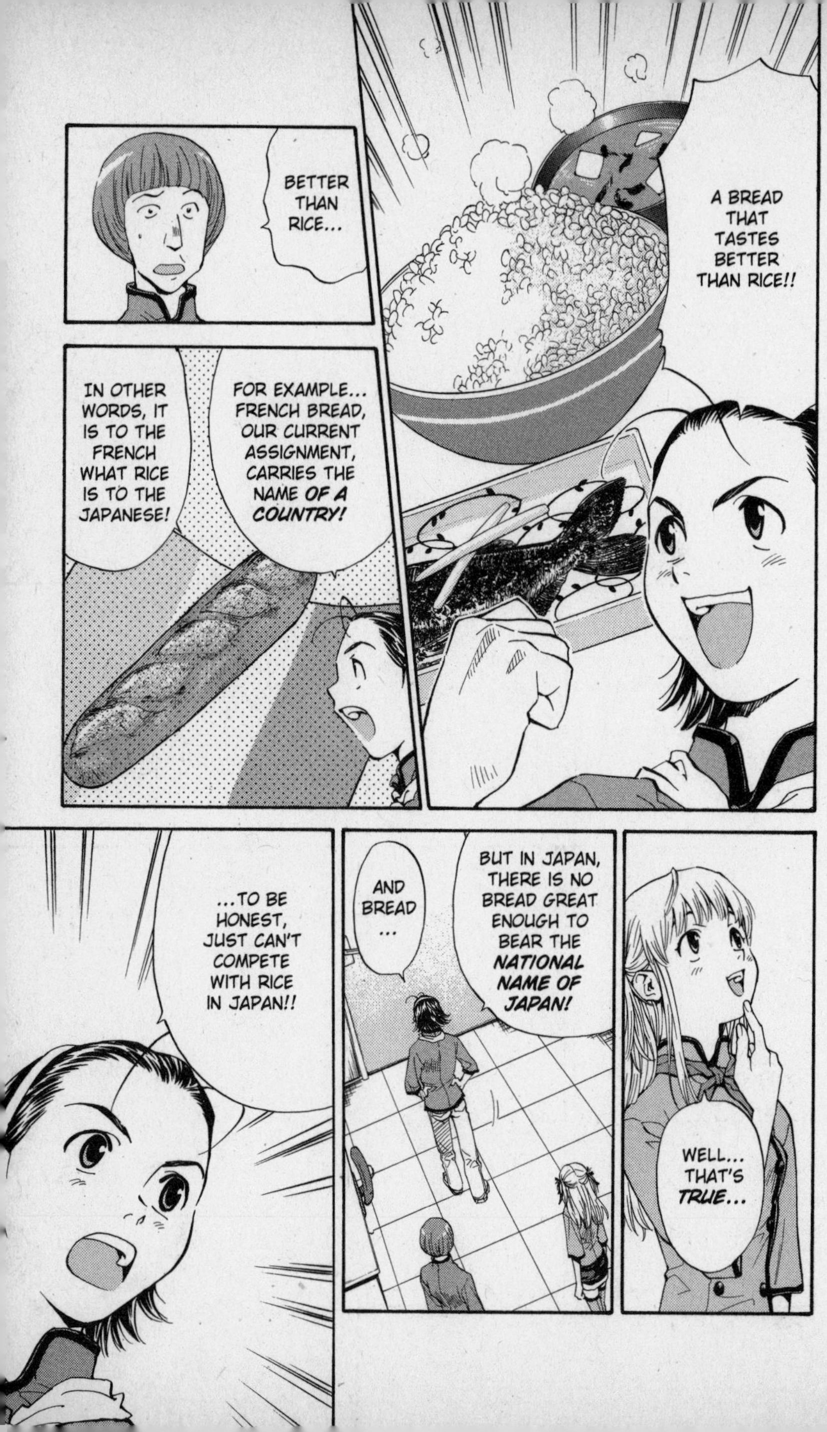

A BREAD THAT TASTES BETTER THAN RICE!!
BETTER THAN RICE...
FOR EXAMPLE... FRENCH BREAD, OUR CURRENT ASSIGNMENT, CARRIES THE NAME *OF A COUNTRY!*
IN OTHER WORDS, IT IS TO THE FRENCH WHAT RICE IS TO THE JAPANESE!
WELL... THAT'S *TRUE...*
BUT IN JAPAN, THERE IS NO BREAD GREAT ENOUGH TO BEAR THE *NATIONAL NAME OF JAPAN!*
AND BREAD...
...TO BE HONEST, JUST CAN'T COMPETE WITH RICE IN JAPAN!!

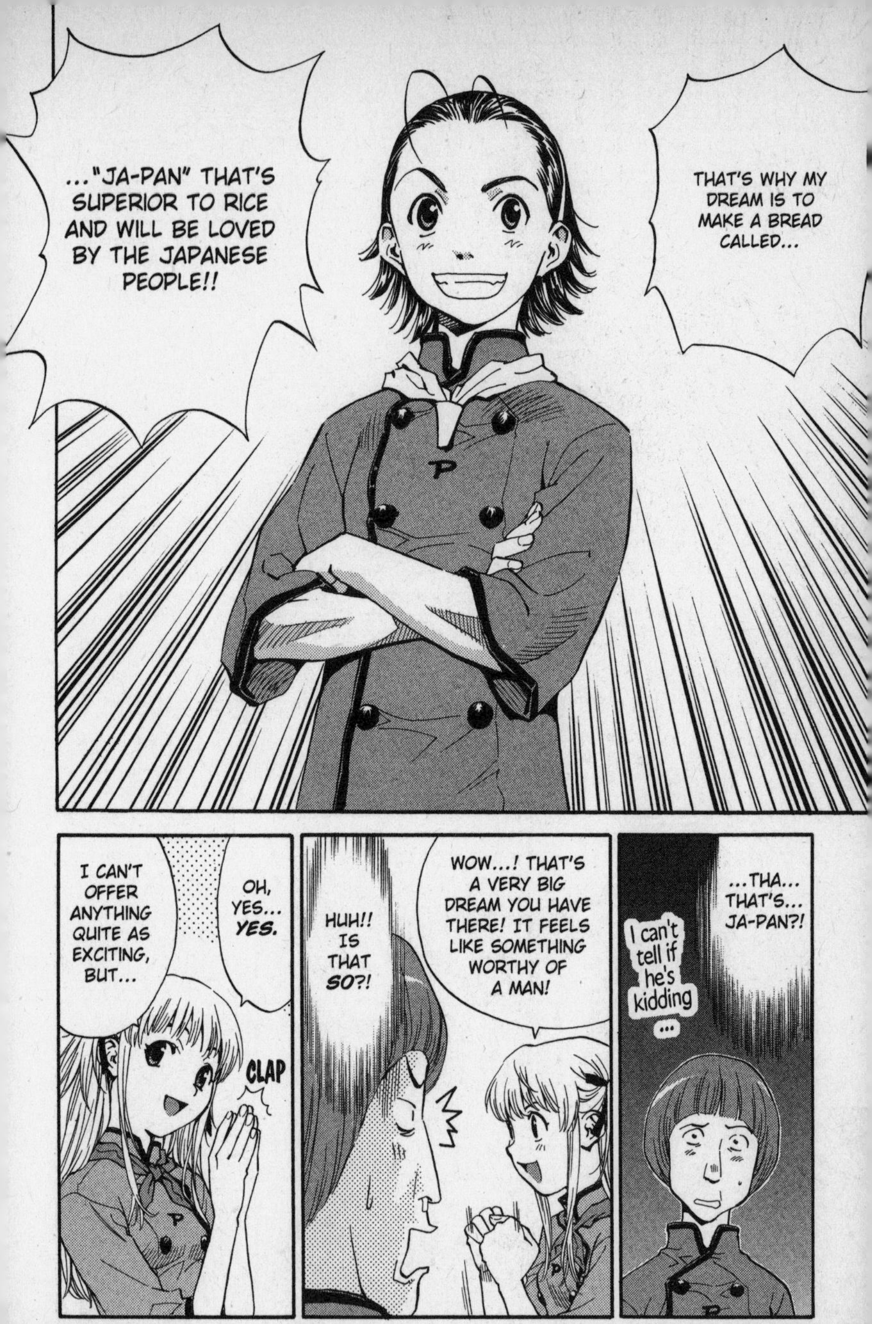

THAT'S WHY MY DREAM IS TO MAKE A BREAD CALLED...
..."JA-PAN" THAT'S SUPERIOR TO RICE AND WILL BE LOVED BY THE JAPANESE PEOPLE!!
...THA... THAT'S... JA-PAN?!
I can't tell if he's kidding...
WOW...! THAT'S A VERY BIG DREAM YOU HAVE THERE! IT FEELS LIKE SOMETHING WORTHY OF A MAN!
HUH!! IS THAT SO?!
OH, YES... YES.
I CAN'T OFFER ANYTHING QUITE AS EXCITING, BUT...
CLAP

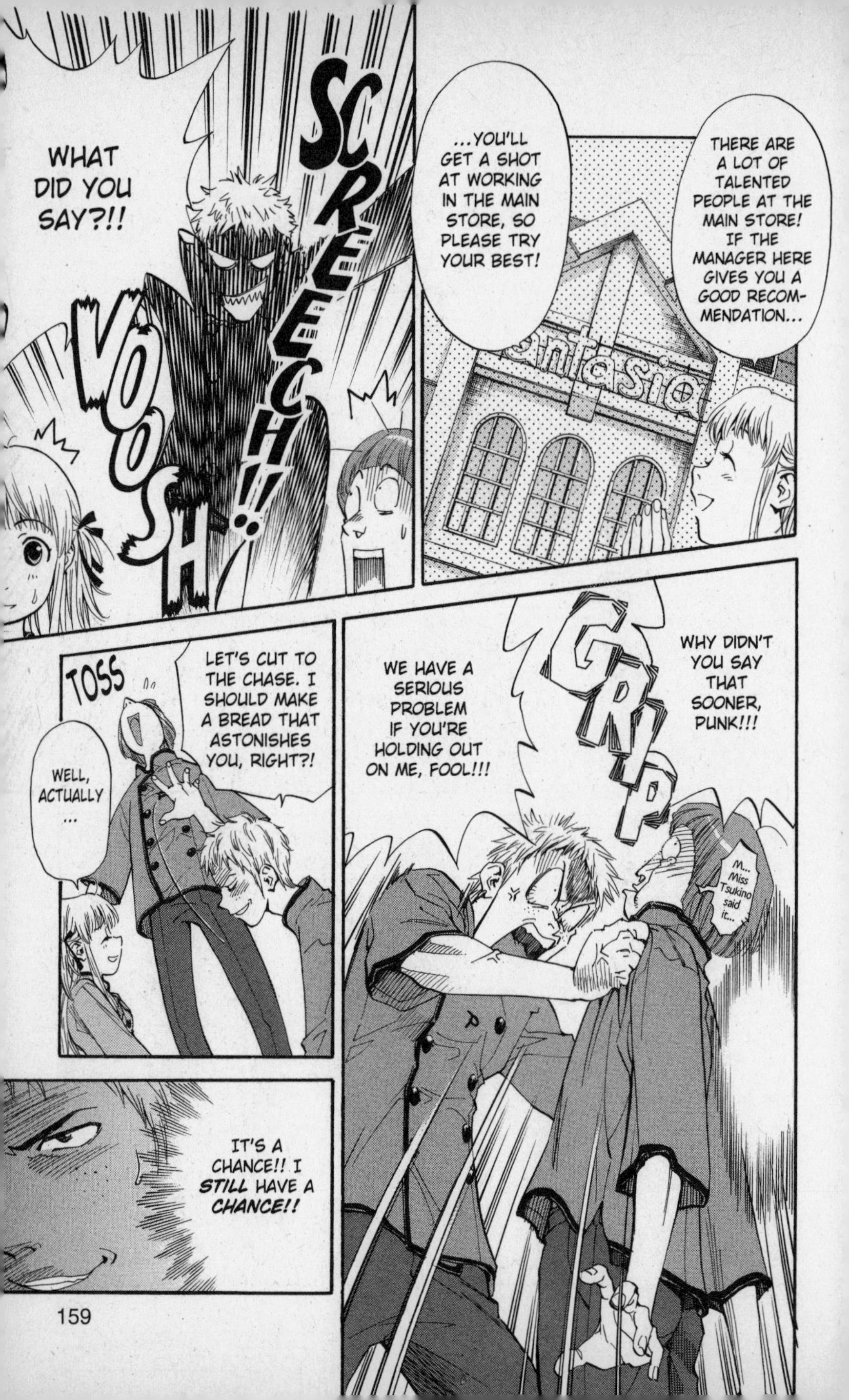
THERE ARE A LOT OF TALENTED PEOPLE AT THE MAIN STORE! IF THE MANAGER HERE GIVES YOU A GOOD RECOMMENDATION...
...YOU'LL GET A SHOT AT WORKING IN THE MAIN STORE, SO PLEASE TRY YOUR BEST!
SCREECH!!
WHAT DID YOU SAY?!!
VOOSH
WHY DIDN'T YOU SAY THAT SOONER, PUNK!!!
GRIP
WE HAVE A SERIOUS PROBLEM IF YOU'RE HOLDING OUT ON ME, FOOL!!!
M... Miss Tsukino said it...
LET'S CUT TO THE CHASE. I SHOULD MAKE A BREAD THAT ASTONISHES YOU, RIGHT?!
TOSS
WELL, ACTUALLY...
IT'S A CHANCE!! I *STILL* HAVE A *CHANCE!!*

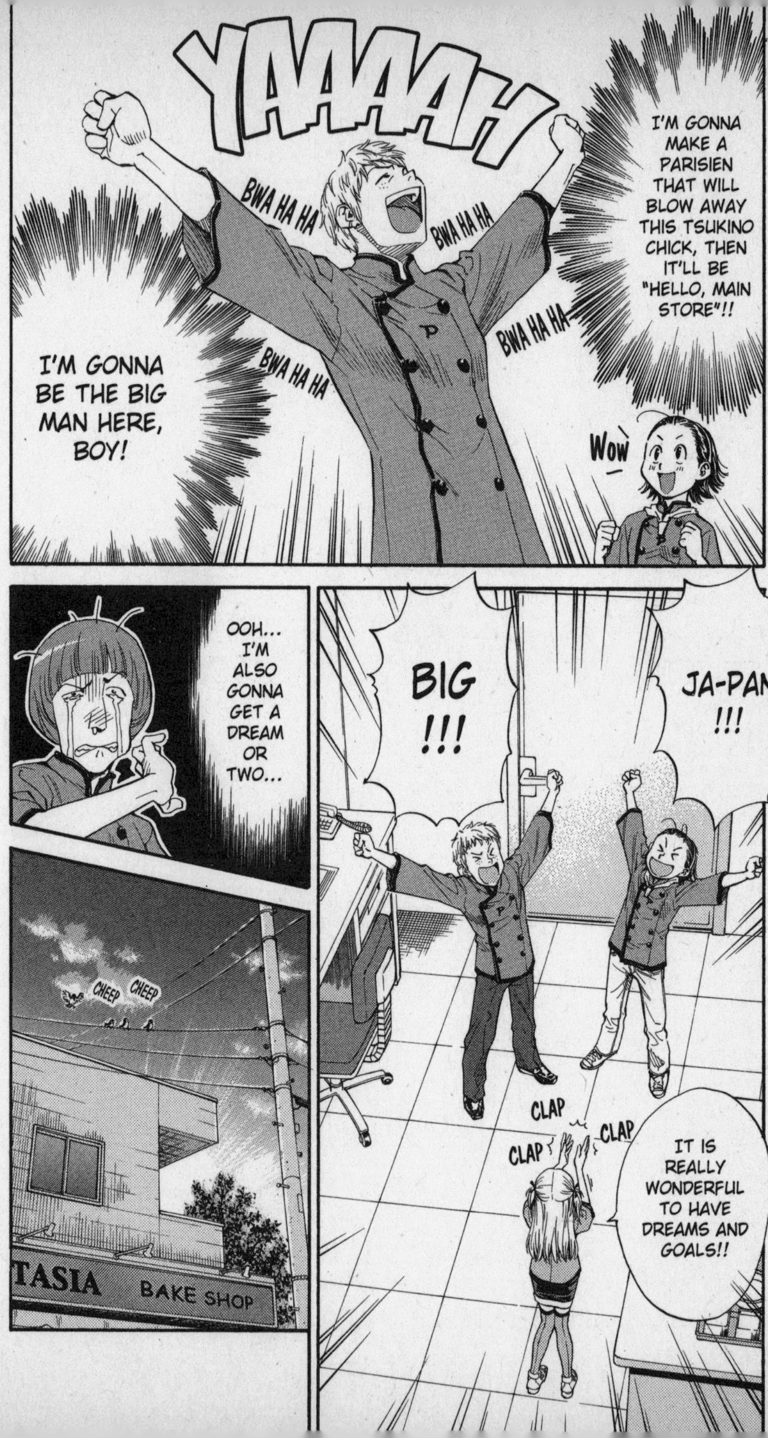
YAAAAH
I'M GONNA MAKE A PARISIEN THAT WILL BLOW AWAY THIS TSUKINO CHICK, THEN IT'LL BE "HELLO, MAIN STORE"!!
BWA HA HA
BWA HA HA
BWA HA HA
BWA HA HA
WOW
I'M GONNA BE THE BIG MAN HERE, BOY!
BIG !!!
JA-PAN !!!
CLAP
CLAP
CLAP
IT IS REALLY WONDERFUL TO HAVE DREAMS AND GOALS!!
OOH... I'M ALSO GONNA GET A DREAM OR TWO...
CHEEP
CHEEP
TASIA BAKE SHOP

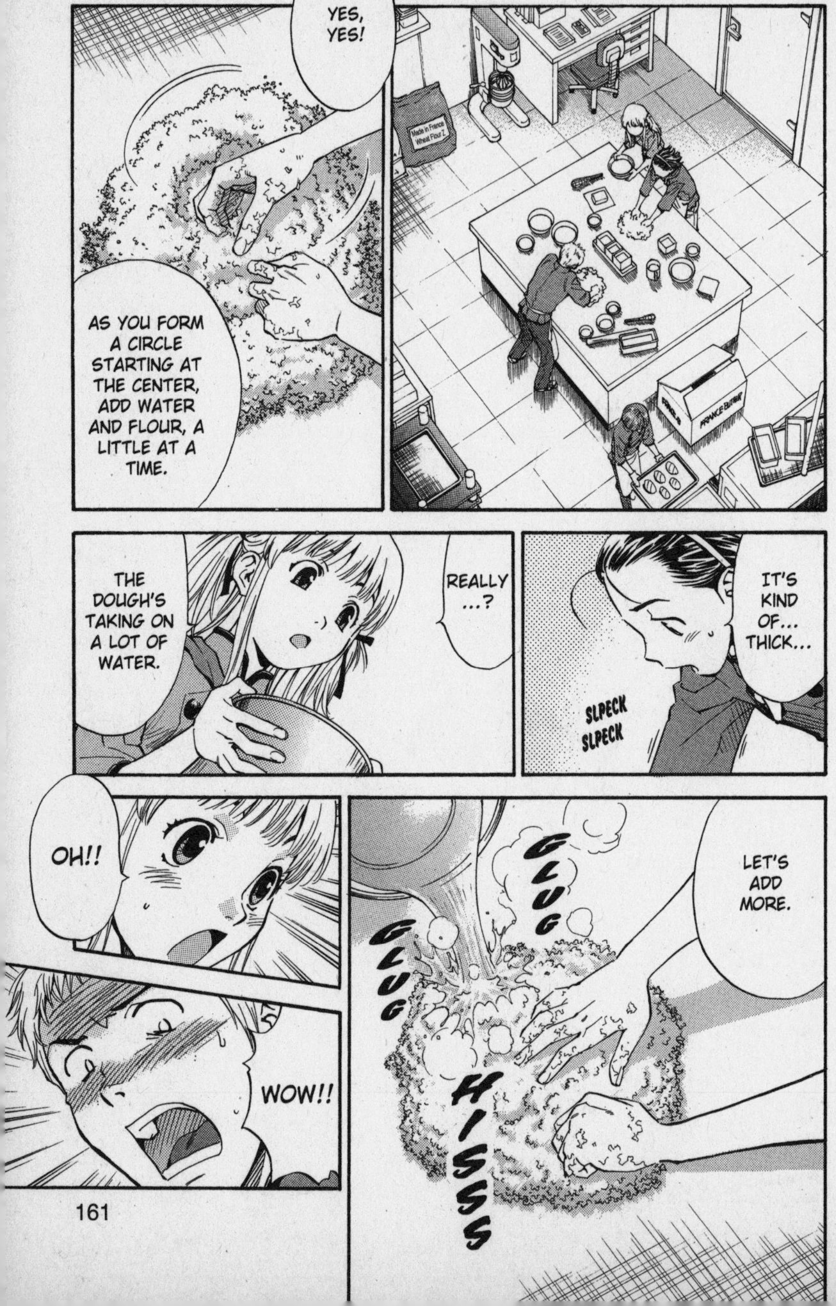
Made in France
Wheat Flour Z
FRANCE BUTTER
YES, YES!
AS YOU FORM A CIRCLE STARTING AT THE CENTER, ADD WATER AND FLOUR, A LITTLE AT A TIME.
IT'S KIND OF... THICK...
SLPECK SLPECK
REALLY ...?
THE DOUGH'S TAKING ON A LOT OF WATER.
LET'S ADD MORE.
GLUG
GLUG
HISSS
OH!!
WOW!!

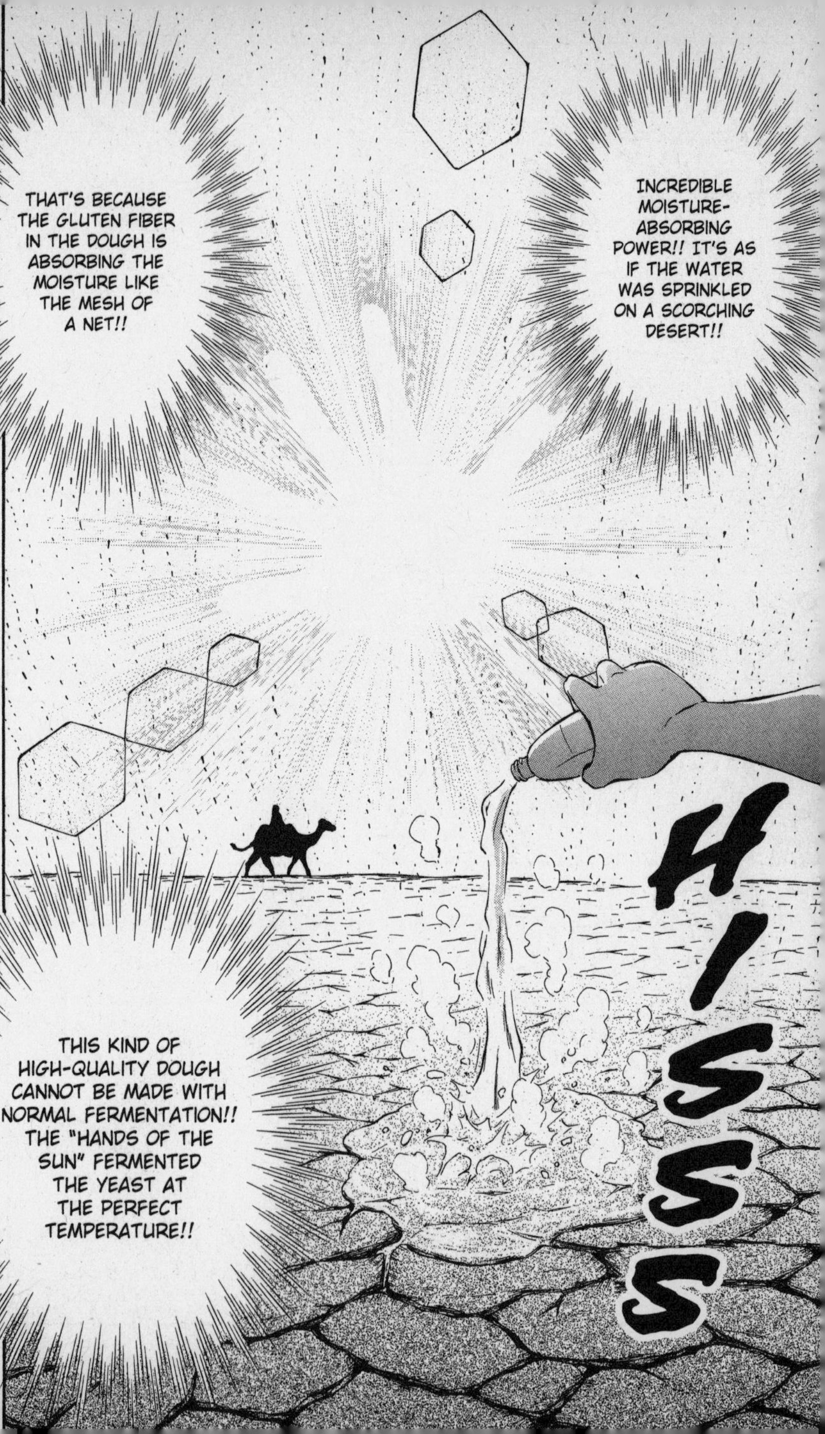
INCREDIBLE MOISTURE-ABSORBING POWER!! IT'S AS IF THE WATER WAS SPRINKLED ON A SCORCHING DESERT!!
THAT'S BECAUSE THE GLUTEN FIBER IN THE DOUGH IS ABSORBING THE MOISTURE LIKE THE MESH OF A NET!!
HISSSS
THIS KIND OF HIGH-QUALITY DOUGH CANNOT BE MADE WITH NORMAL FERMENTATION!! THE "HANDS OF THE SUN" FERMENTED THE YEAST AT THE PERFECT TEMPERATURE!!

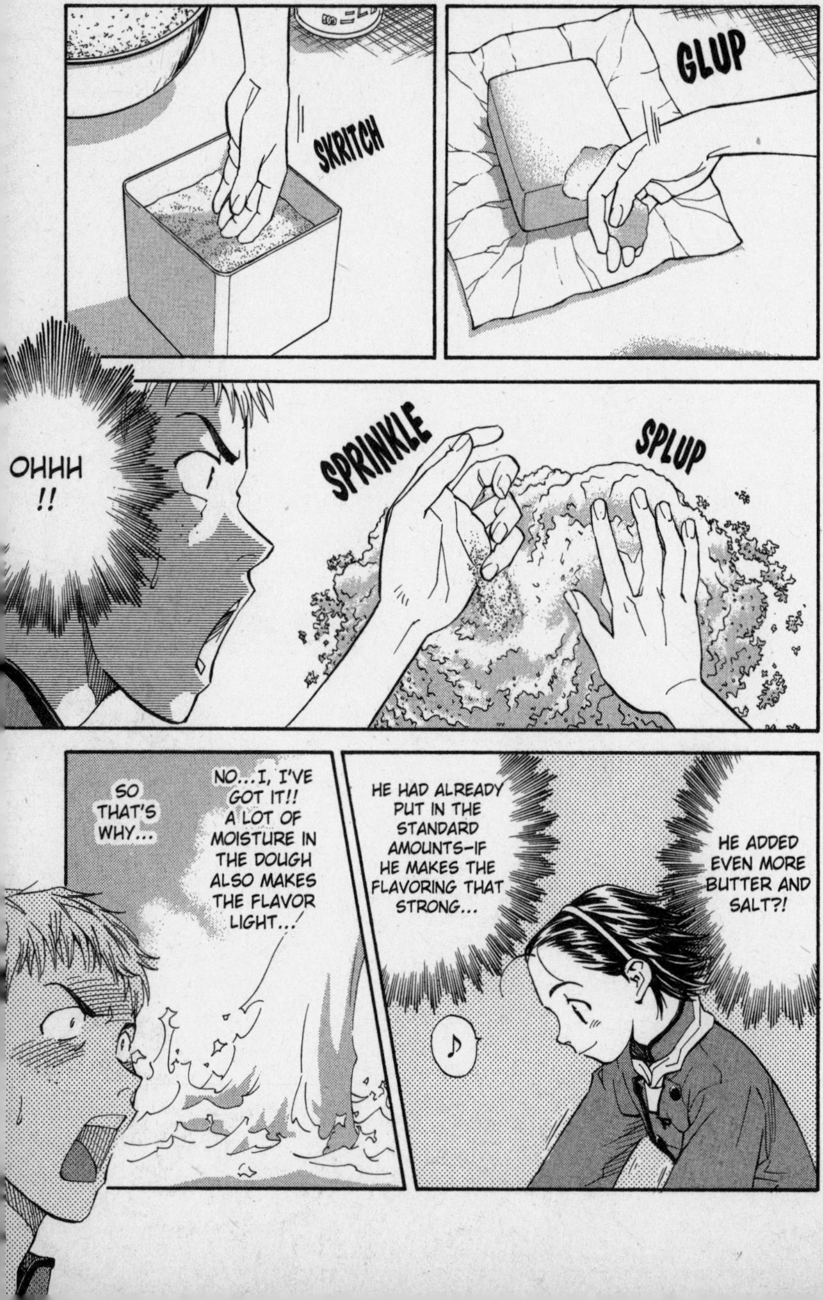
GLUP
SKRITCH
SPLUP
SPRINKLE
OHHH !!
HE ADDED EVEN MORE BUTTER AND SALT?!
HE HAD ALREADY PUT IN THE STANDARD AMOUNTS—IF HE MAKES THE FLAVORING THAT STRONG...
♪
NO...I, I'VE GOT IT!! A LOT OF MOISTURE IN THE DOUGH ALSO MAKES THE FLAVOR LIGHT...!
SO THAT'S WHY...

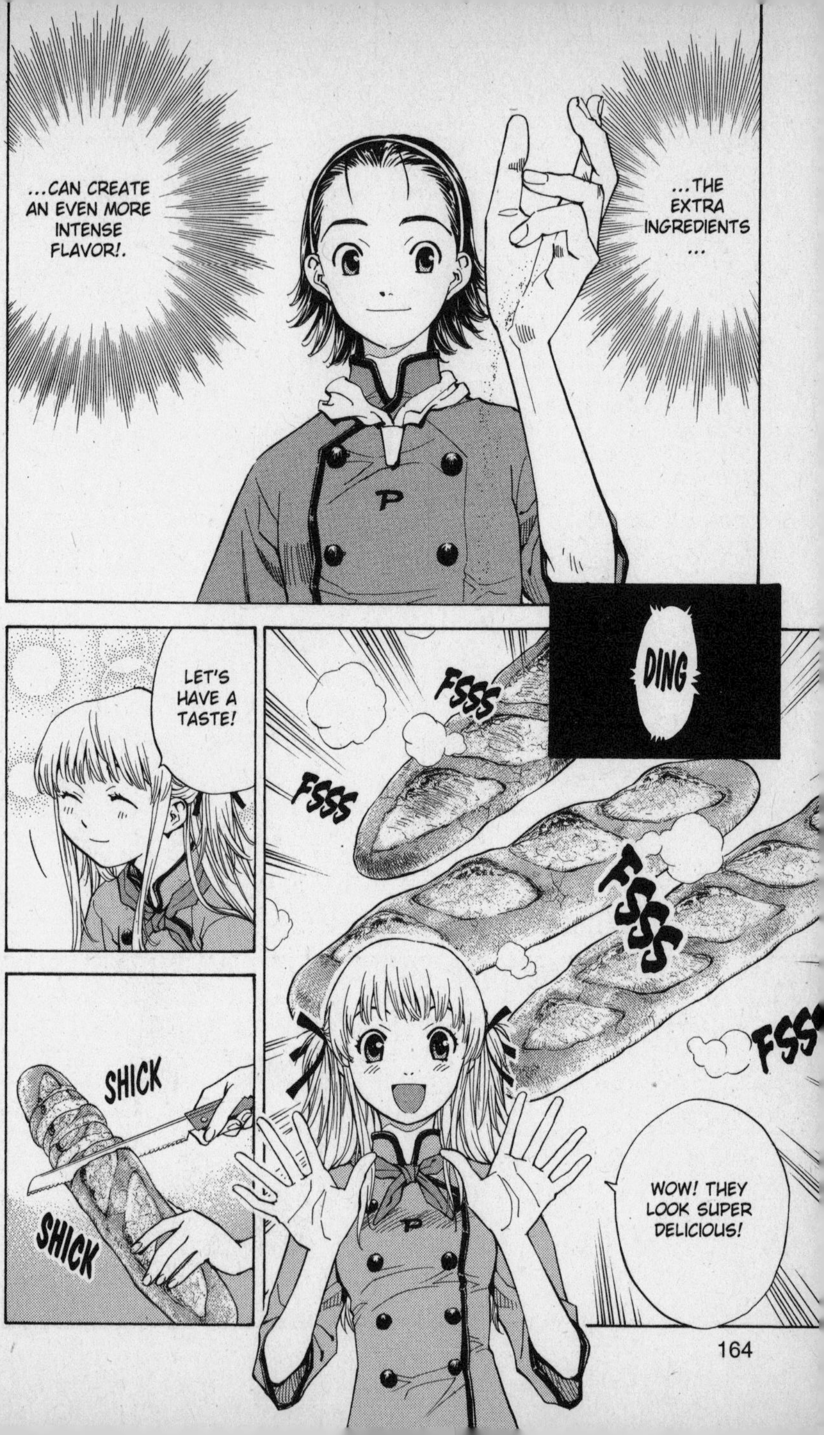
...THE EXTRA INGREDIENTS ...
...CAN CREATE AN EVEN MORE INTENSE FLAVOR!.
DING
FSSS
FSSS
FSSS
FSS
WOW! THEY LOOK SUPER DELICIOUS!
LET'S HAVE A TASTE!
SHICK
SHICK

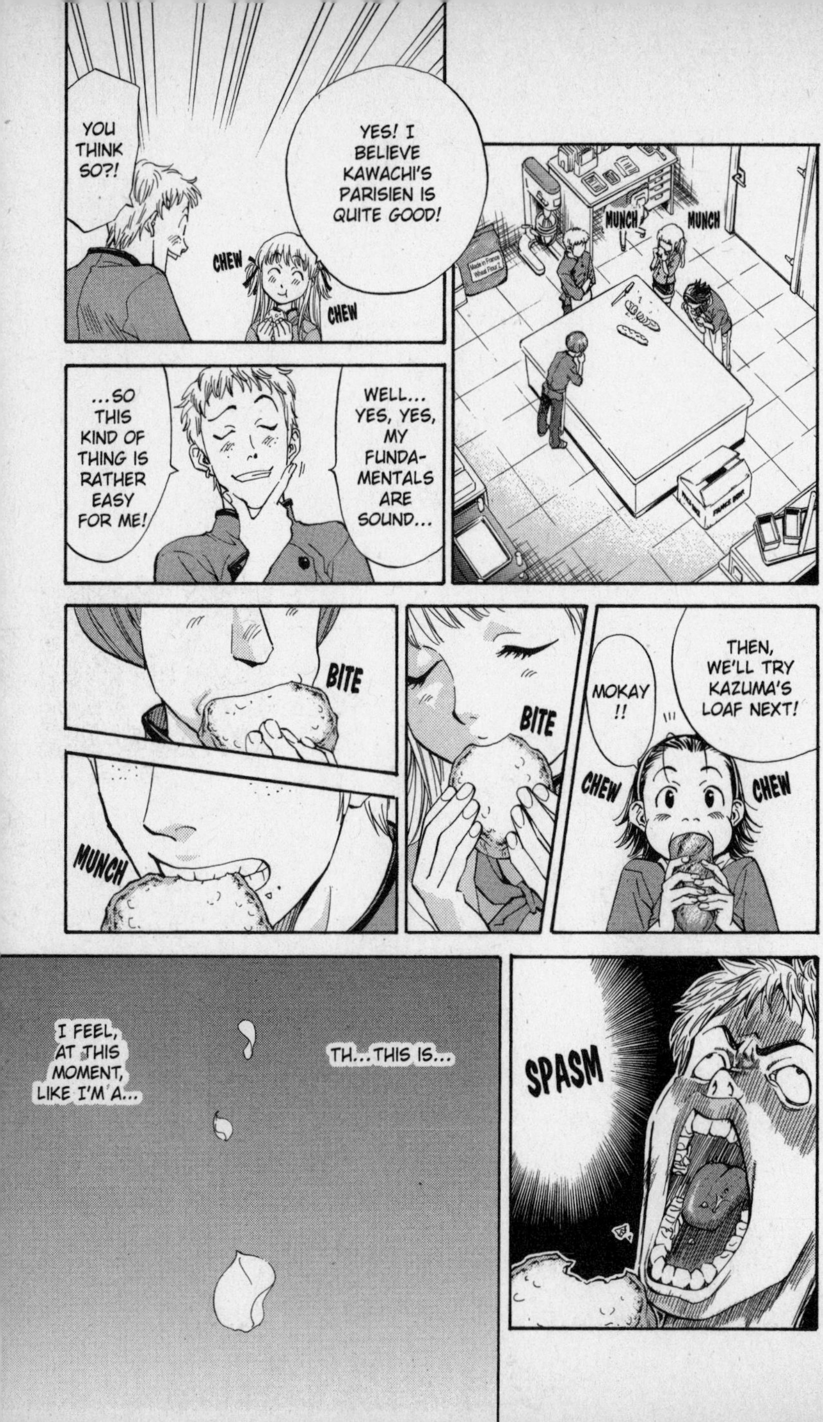
MUNCH
MUNCH
YES! I BELIEVE KAWACHI'S PARISIEN IS QUITE GOOD!
YOU THINK SO?!
CHEW
CHEW
WELL... YES, YES, MY FUNDA-MENTALS ARE SOUND...
...SO THIS KIND OF THING IS RATHER EASY FOR ME!
THEN, WE'LL TRY KAZUMA'S LOAF NEXT!
MOKAY !!
CHEW
CHEW
BITE
BITE
MUNCH
SPASM
TH...THIS IS...
I FEEL, AT THIS MOMENT, LIKE I'M A...

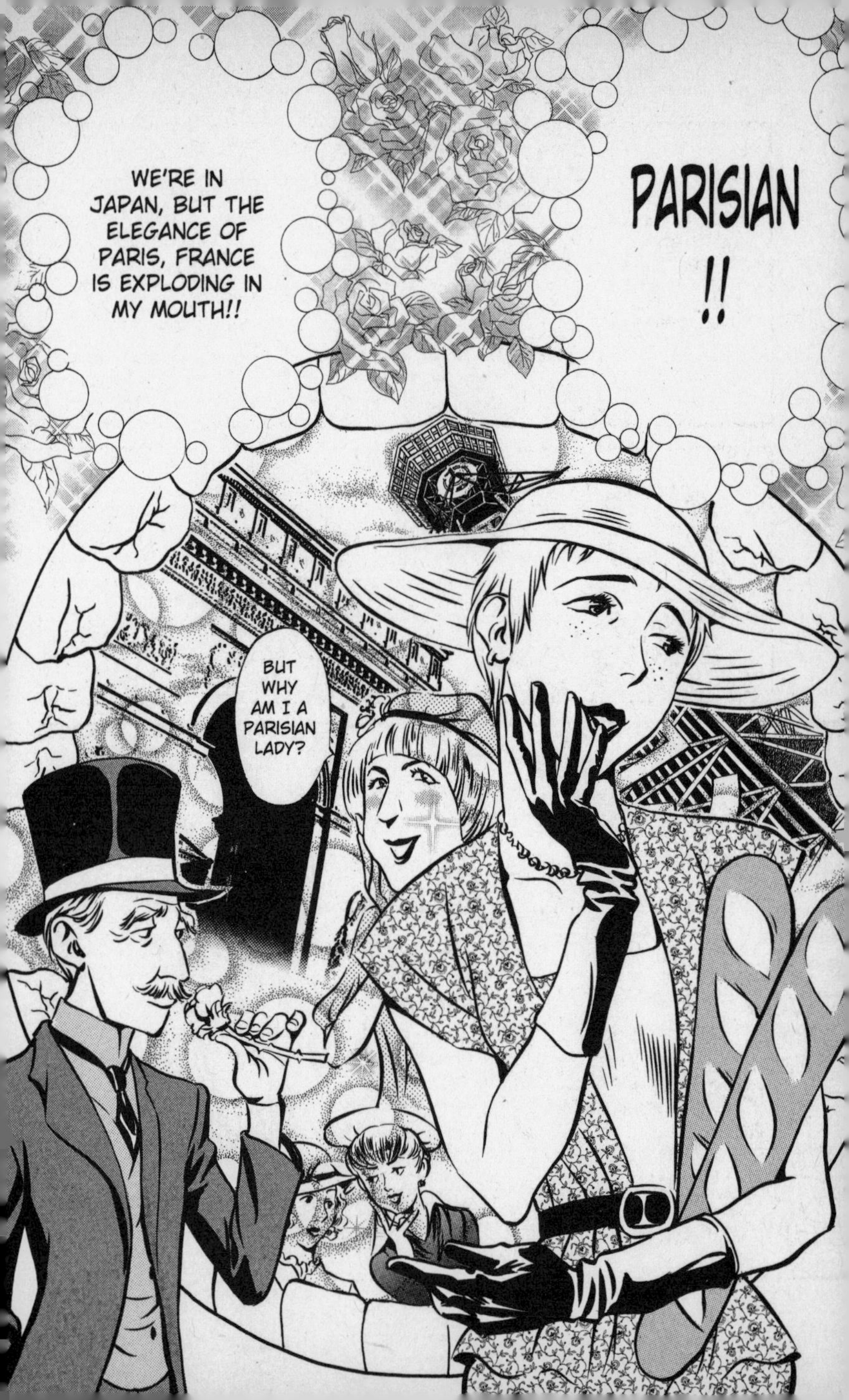
PARISIAN !!
WE'RE IN JAPAN, BUT THE ELEGANCE OF PARIS, FRANCE IS EXPLODING IN MY MOUTH!!
BUT WHY AM I A PARISIAN LADY?

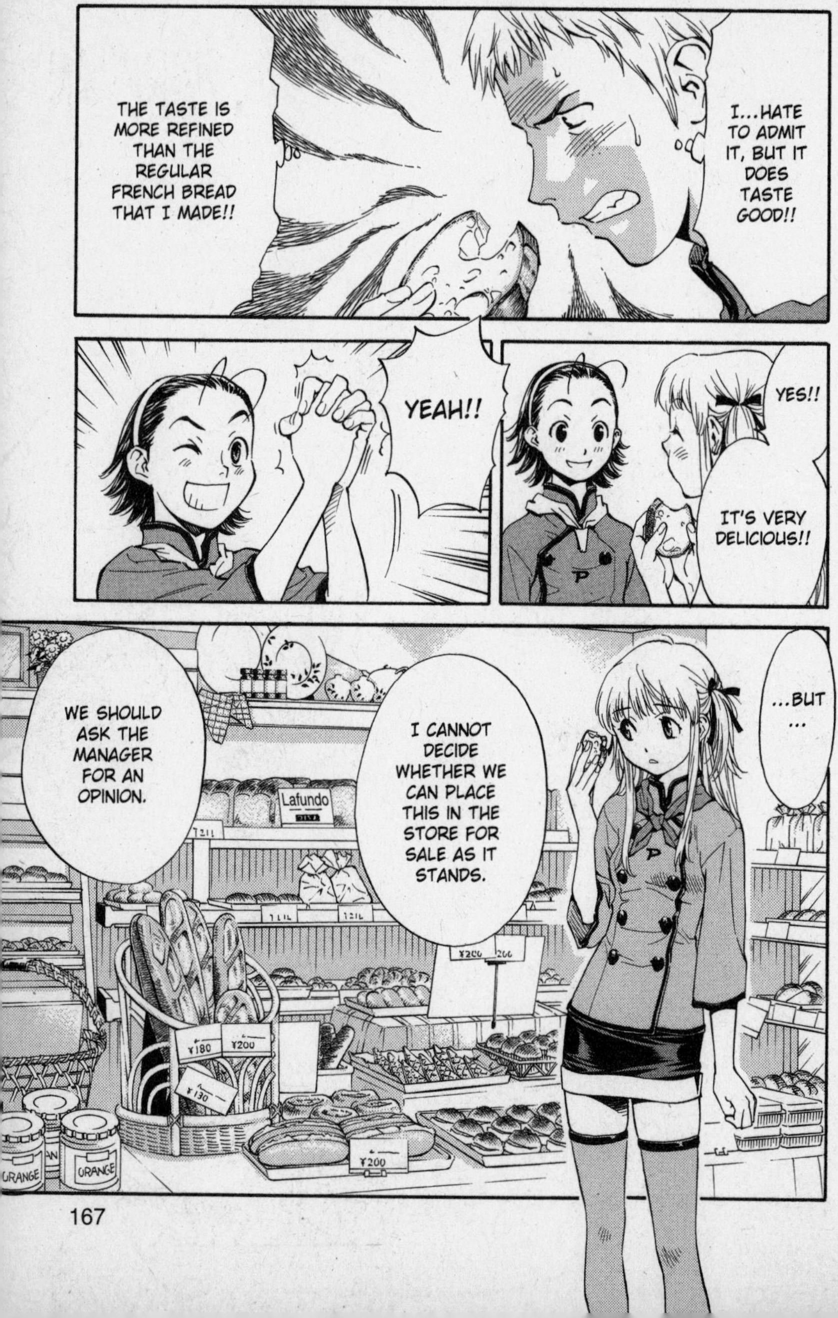
I...HATE TO ADMIT IT, BUT IT DOES TASTE GOOD!!
THE TASTE IS MORE REFINED THAN THE REGULAR FRENCH BREAD THAT I MADE!!
YES!!
IT'S VERY DELICIOUS!!
YEAH!!
...BUT...
I CANNOT DECIDE WHETHER WE CAN PLACE THIS IN THE STORE FOR SALE AS IT STANDS.
WE SHOULD ASK THE MANAGER FOR AN OPINION.
Lafundo
ORANGE
ORANGE

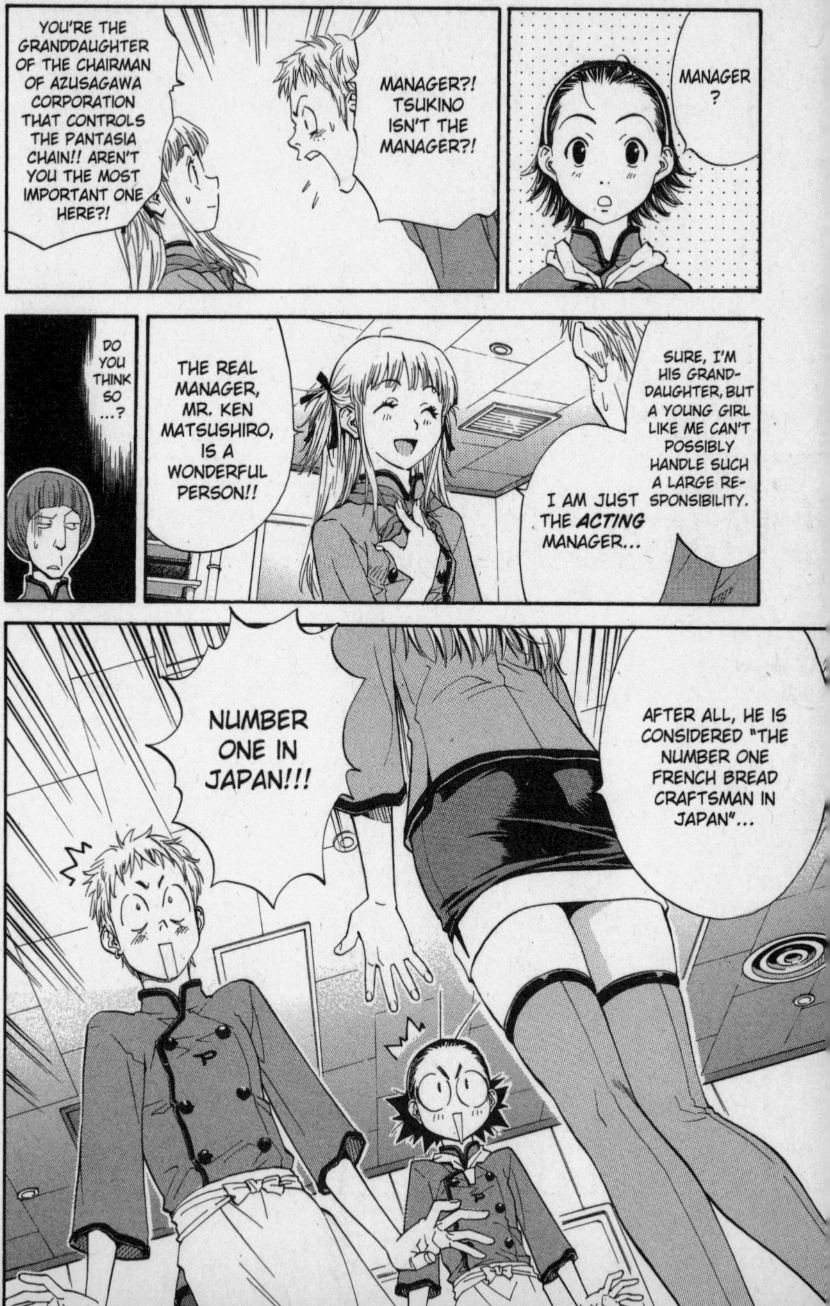
MANAGER ?
MANAGER?! TSUKINO ISN'T THE MANAGER?!
YOU'RE THE GRANDDAUGHTER OF THE CHAIRMAN OF AZUSAGAWA CORPORATION THAT CONTROLS THE PANTASIA CHAIN!! AREN'T YOU THE MOST IMPORTANT ONE HERE?!
SURE, I'M HIS GRAND-DAUGHTER, BUT A YOUNG GIRL LIKE ME CAN'T POSSIBLY HANDLE SUCH A LARGE RE-SPONSIBILITY.
I AM JUST THE *ACTING* MANAGER...
THE REAL MANAGER, MR. KEN MATSUSHIRO, IS A WONDERFUL PERSON!!
DO YOU THINK SO ...?
AFTER ALL, HE IS CONSIDERED "THE NUMBER ONE FRENCH BREAD CRAFTSMAN IN JAPAN"...
NUMBER ONE IN JAPAN!!!

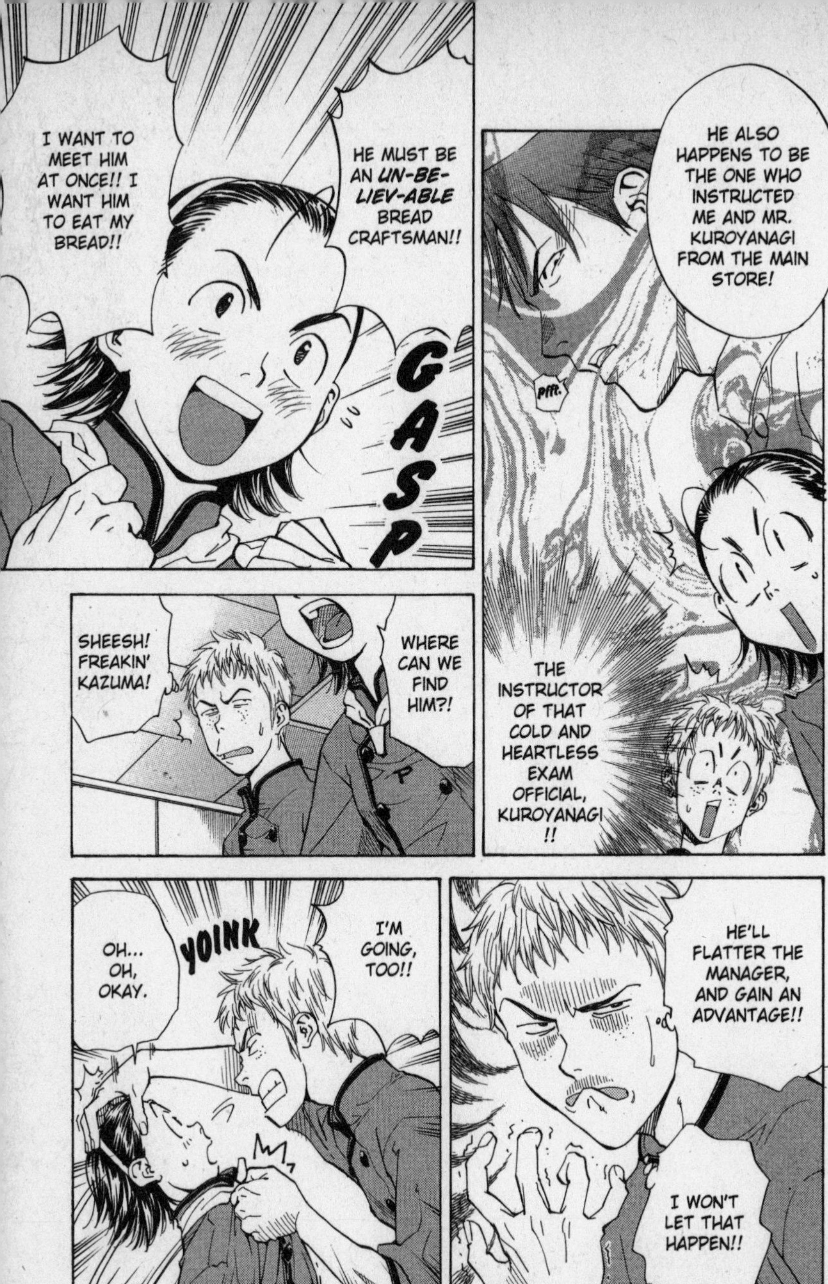
HE MUST BE AN *UN-BE-LIEV-ABLE* BREAD CRAFTSMAN!!
I WANT TO MEET HIM AT ONCE!! I WANT HIM TO EAT MY BREAD!!
GASP
HE ALSO HAPPENS TO BE THE ONE WHO INSTRUCTED ME AND MR. KUROYANAGI FROM THE MAIN STORE!
pfft.
THE INSTRUCTOR OF THAT COLD AND HEARTLESS EXAM OFFICIAL, KUROYANAGI!!
WHERE CAN WE FIND HIM?!
SHEESH! FREAKIN' KAZUMA!
HE'LL FLATTER THE MANAGER, AND GAIN AN ADVANTAGE!!
I WON'T LET THAT HAPPEN!!
I'M GOING, TOO!!
YOINK
OH... OH, OKAY.

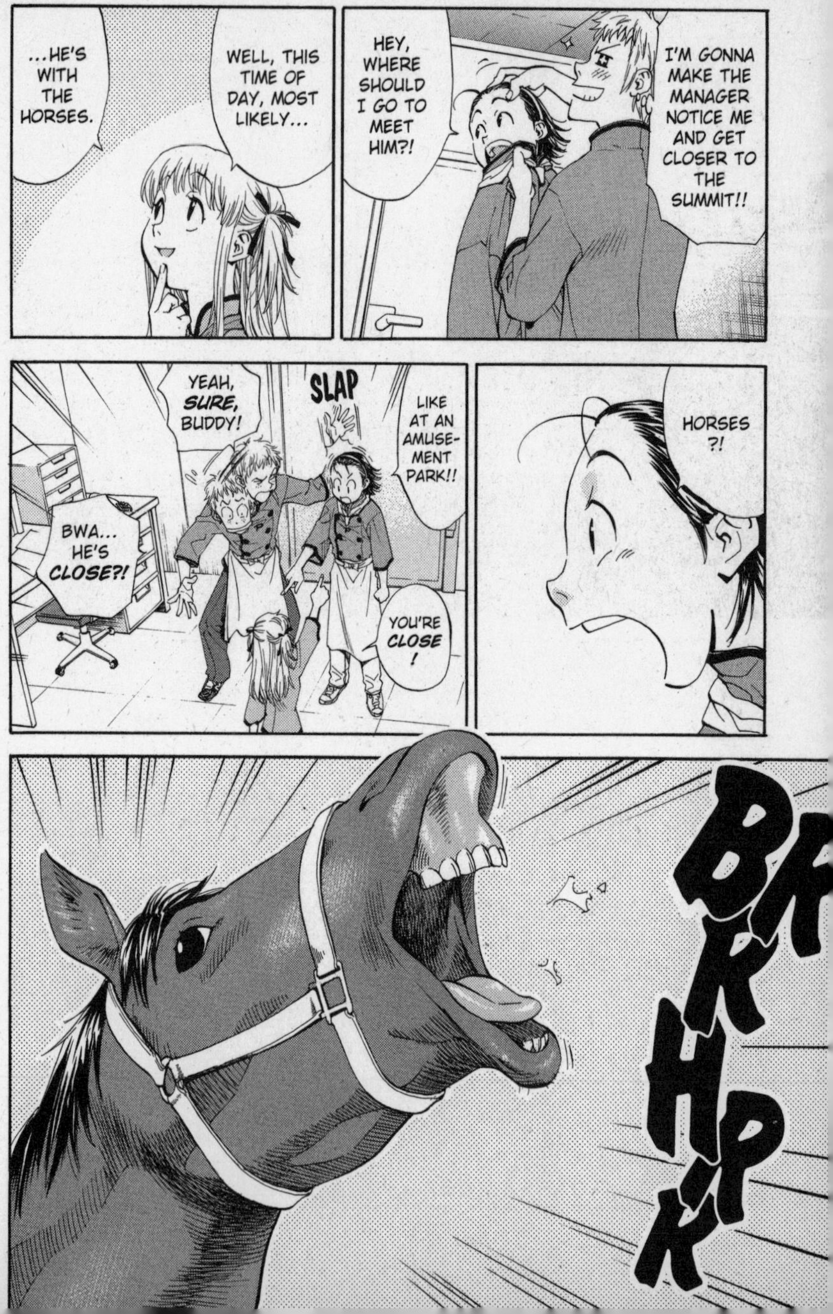
I'M GONNA MAKE THE MANAGER NOTICE ME AND GET CLOSER TO THE SUMMIT!!
HEY, WHERE SHOULD I GO TO MEET HIM?!
WELL, THIS TIME OF DAY, MOST LIKELY...
...HE'S WITH THE HORSES.
HORSES ?!
LIKE AT AN AMUSE-MENT PARK!!
SLAP
YEAH, SURE, BUDDY!
YOU'RE CLOSE !
BWA... HE'S CLOSE?!
BRRHHPPKK

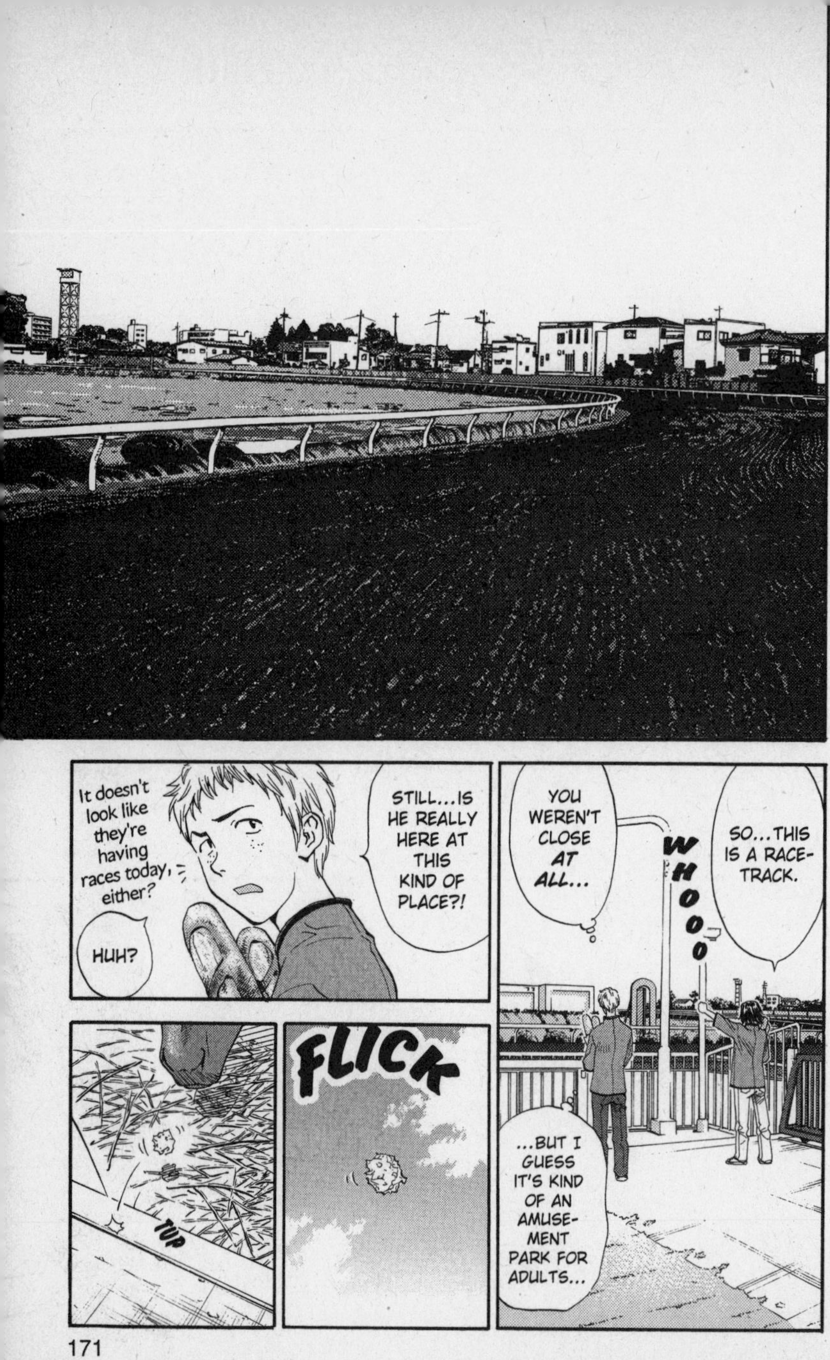
SO...THIS IS A RACE-TRACK.
YOU WEREN'T CLOSE AT ALL...
WHOOO
...BUT I GUESS IT'S KIND OF AN AMUSE-MENT PARK FOR ADULTS...
STILL...IS HE REALLY HERE AT THIS KIND OF PLACE?!
It doesn't look like they're having races today, either?
HUH?
FLICK
TUP

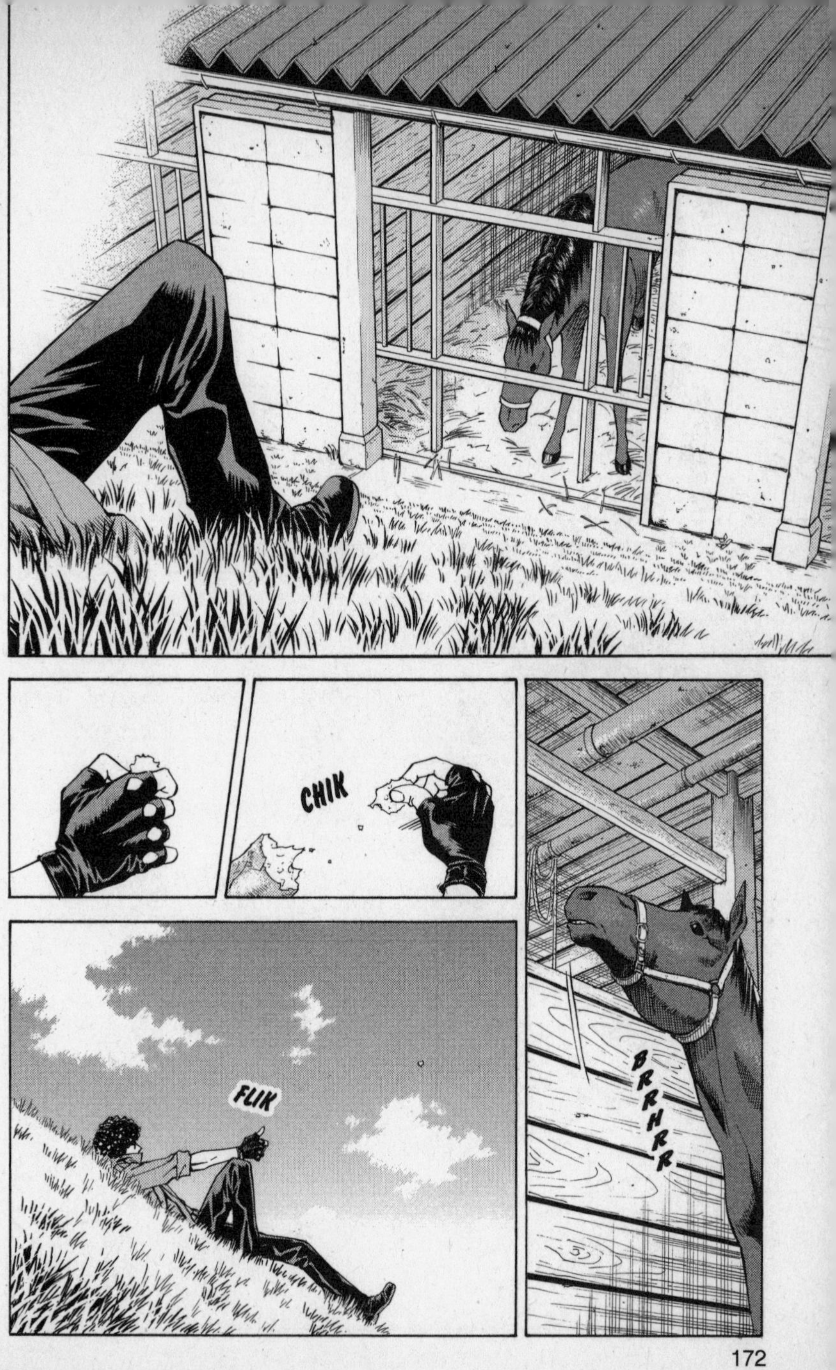
BRRHRR
CHIK
FLIK

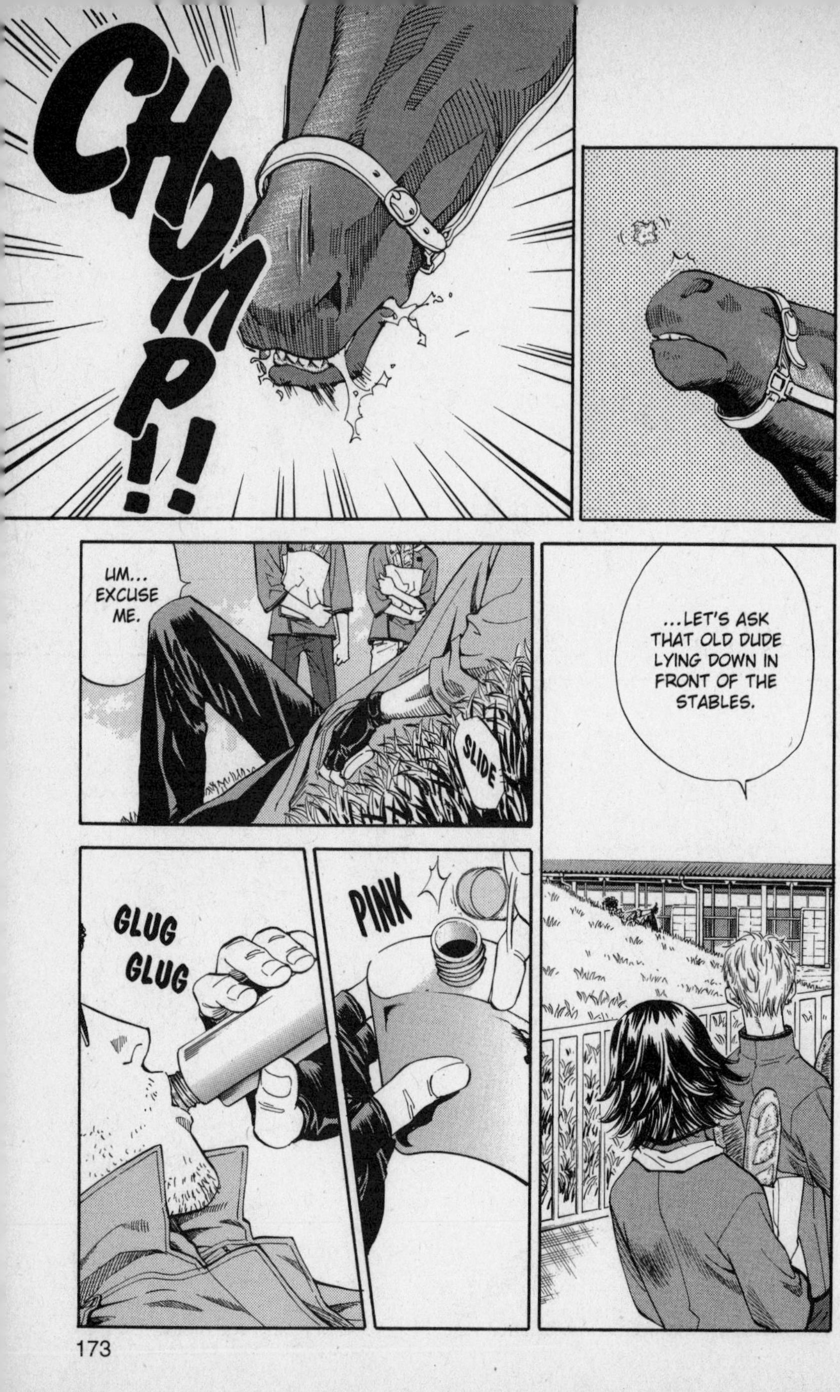
CHOMP!!
...LET'S ASK THAT OLD DUDE LYING DOWN IN FRONT OF THE STABLES.
UM... EXCUSE ME.
SLIDE
PINK
GLUG GLUG

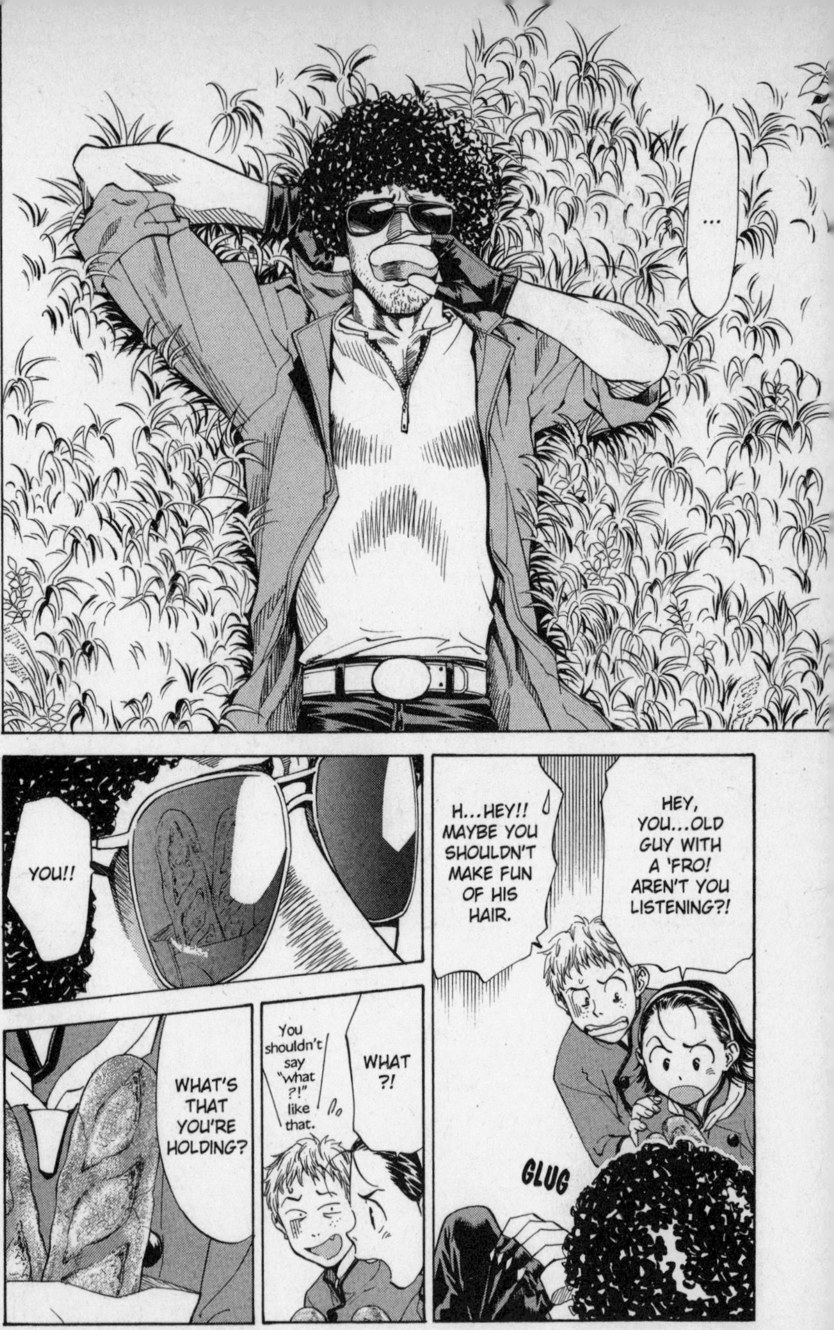
...
HEY, YOU...OLD GUY WITH A 'FRO! AREN'T YOU LISTENING?!
H...HEY!! MAYBE YOU SHOULDN'T MAKE FUN OF HIS HAIR.
GLUG
YOU!!
WHAT?!
You shouldn't say "what?!" like that.
WHAT'S THAT YOU'RE HOLDING?

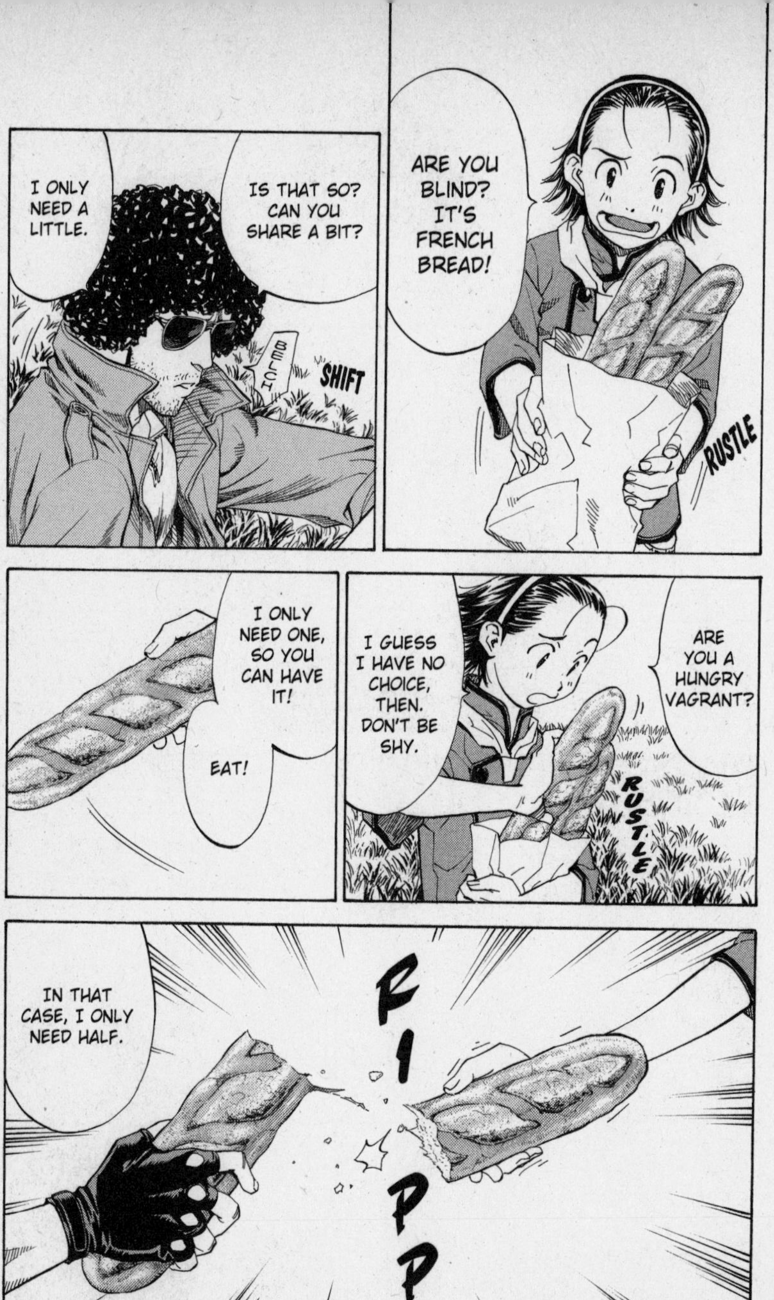
ARE YOU BLIND? IT'S FRENCH BREAD!
RUSTLE
IS THAT SO? CAN YOU SHARE A BIT?
SHIFT
BELCH
I ONLY NEED A LITTLE.
ARE YOU A HUNGRY VAGRANT?
RUSTLE
I GUESS I HAVE NO CHOICE, THEN. DON'T BE SHY.
I ONLY NEED ONE, SO YOU CAN HAVE IT!
EAT!
RIPP
IN THAT CASE, I ONLY NEED HALF.

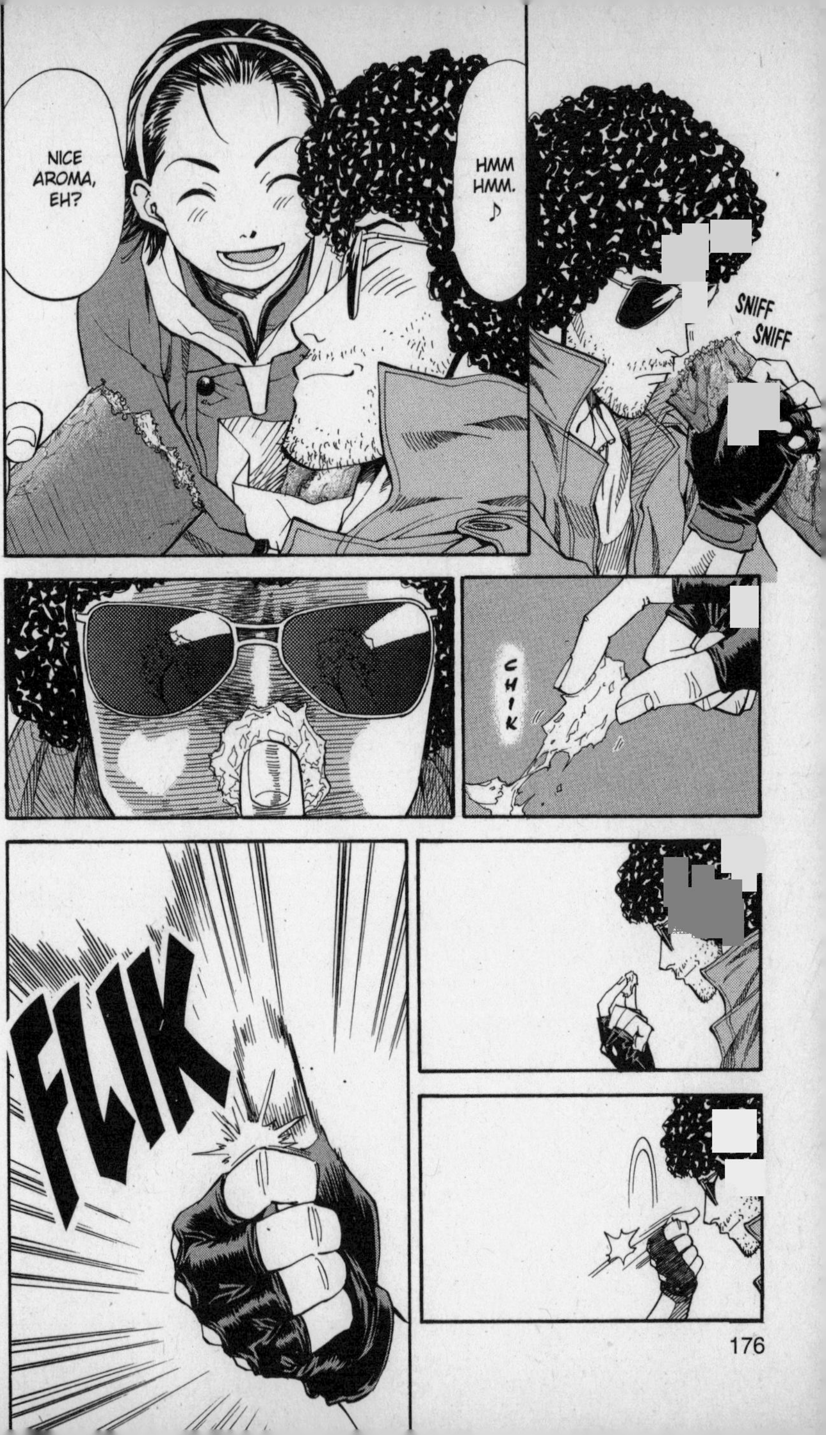
SNIFF SNIFF
HMM HMM. ♪
NICE AROMA, EH?
CHIK
FLIK

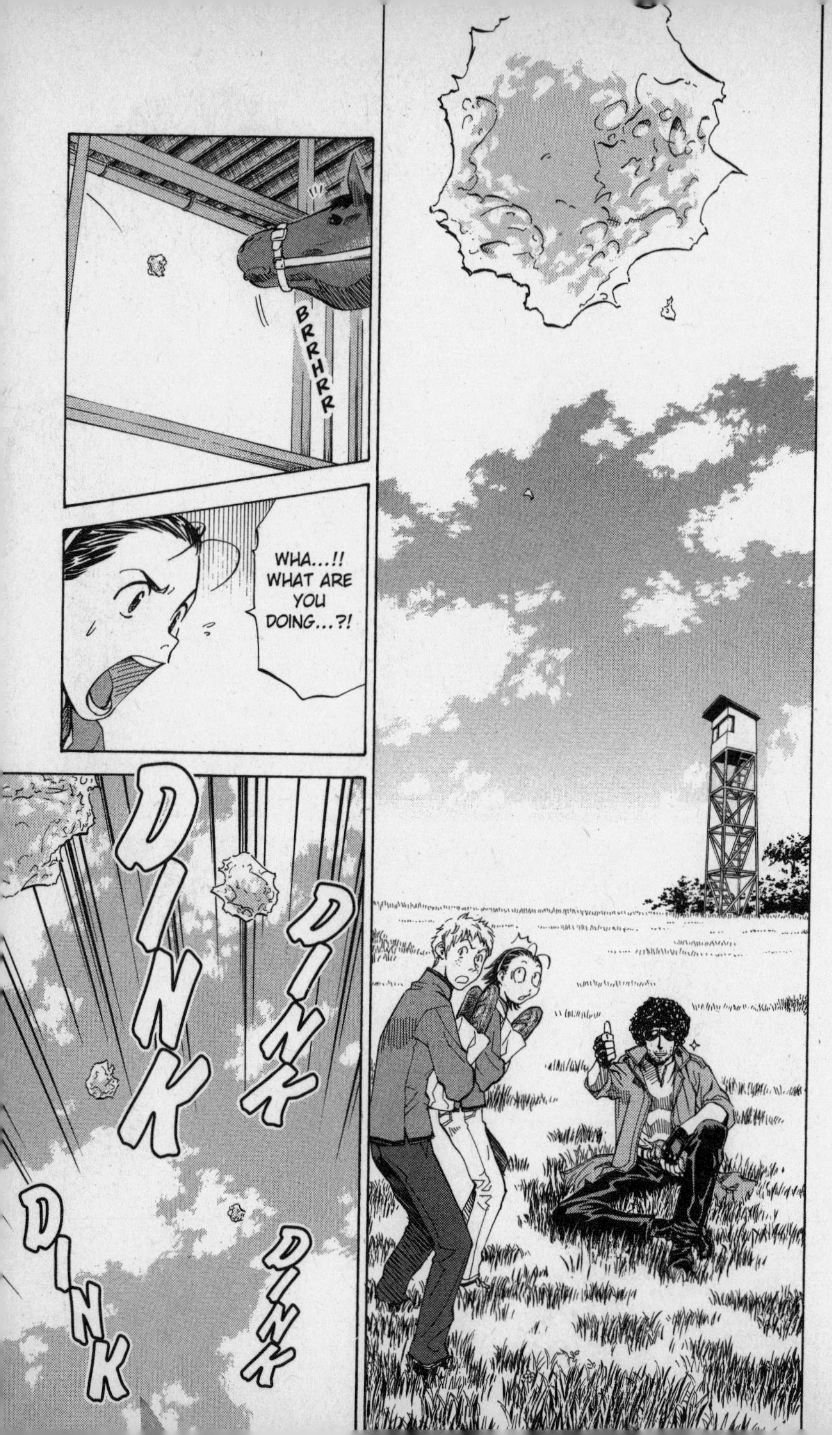
BRRHRR
WHA...!! WHAT ARE YOU DOING...?!
DINK
DINK
DINK
DINK

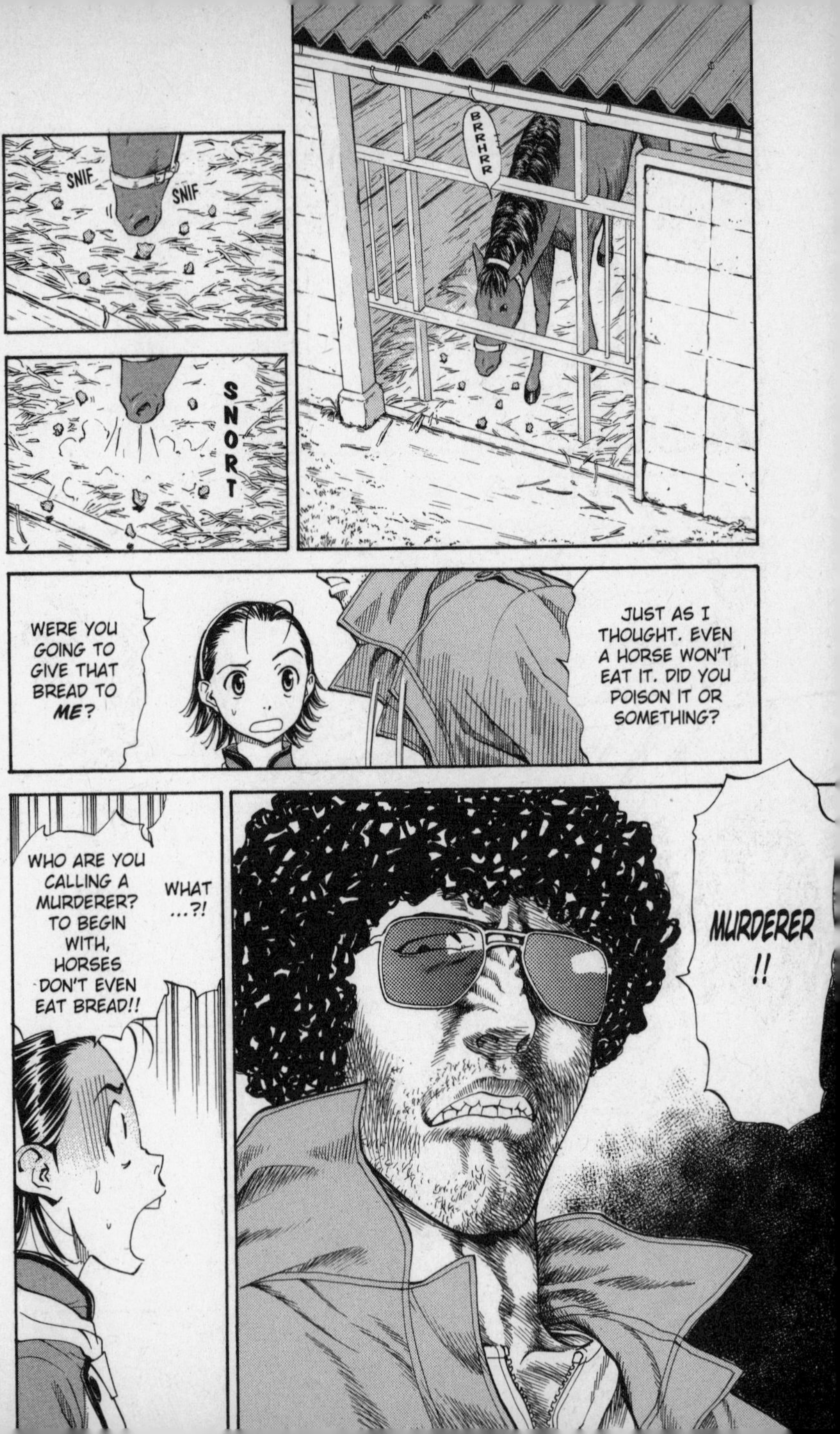
BRRHRR
SNIF
SNIF
SNORT
JUST AS I THOUGHT. EVEN A HORSE WON'T EAT IT. DID YOU POISON IT OR SOMETHING?
WERE YOU GOING TO GIVE THAT BREAD TO *ME*?
MURDERER!!
WHAT...?!
WHO ARE YOU CALLING A MURDERER? TO BEGIN WITH, HORSES DON'T EVEN EAT BREAD!!

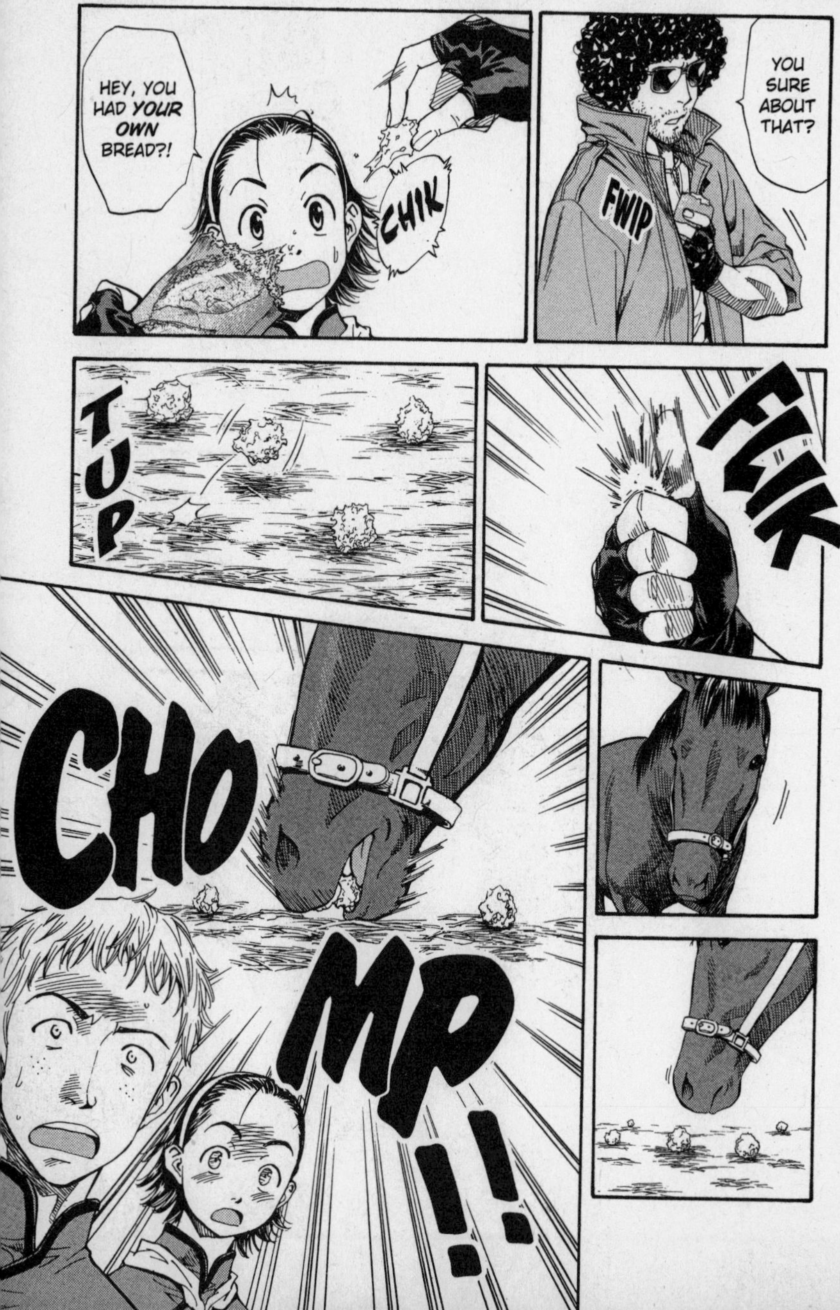

YOU SURE ABOUT THAT?
FWIP
HEY, YOU HAD YOUR OWN BREAD?!
CHIK
FLIK
TUP
CHOMP!!

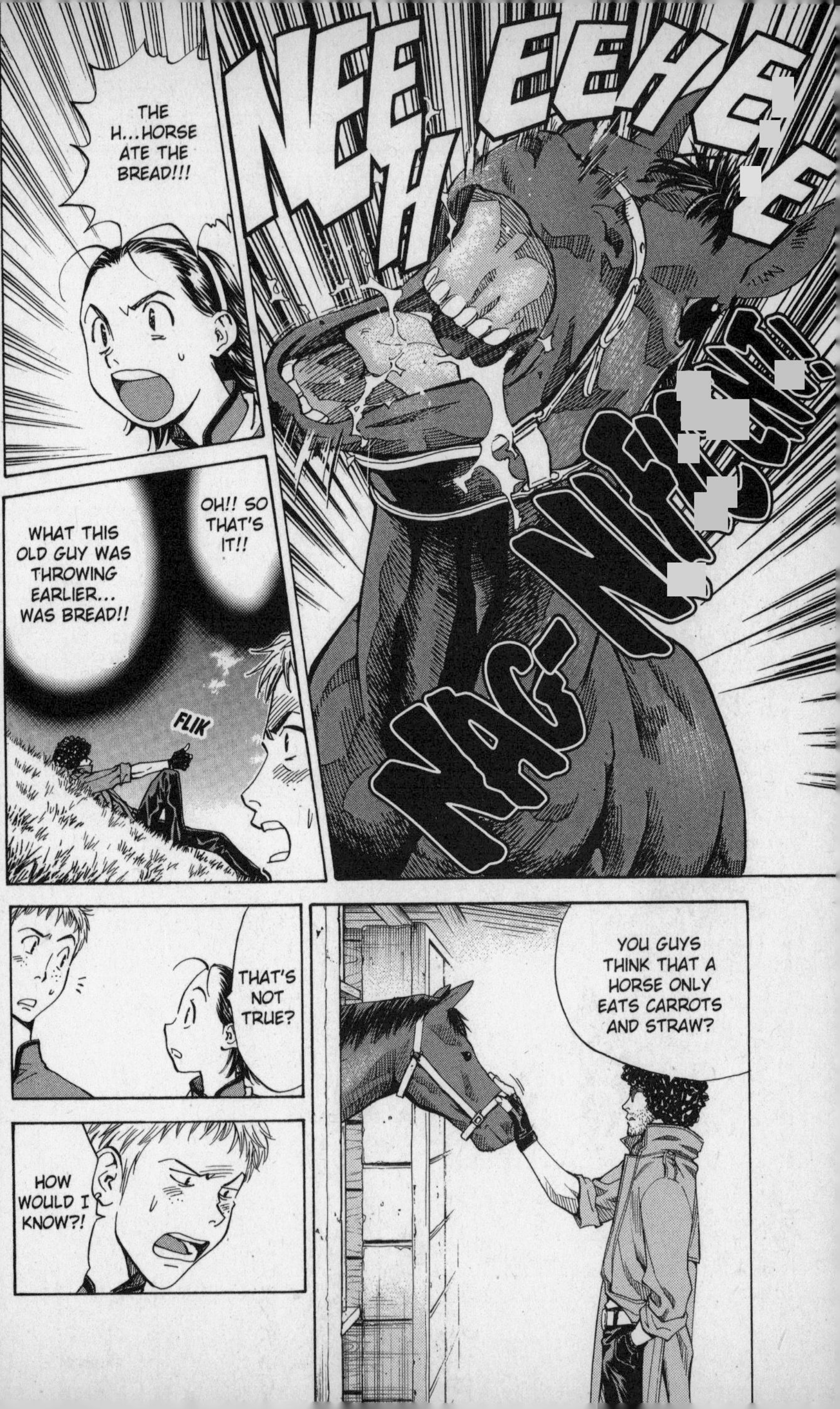
NEEHEEHEE
NAG-NIFICENT!!
THE H...HORSE ATE THE BREAD!!!
OH!! SO THAT'S IT!!
WHAT THIS OLD GUY WAS THROWING EARLIER... WAS BREAD!!
FLIK
YOU GUYS THINK THAT A HORSE ONLY EATS CARROTS AND STRAW?
THAT'S NOT TRUE?
HOW WOULD I KNOW?!

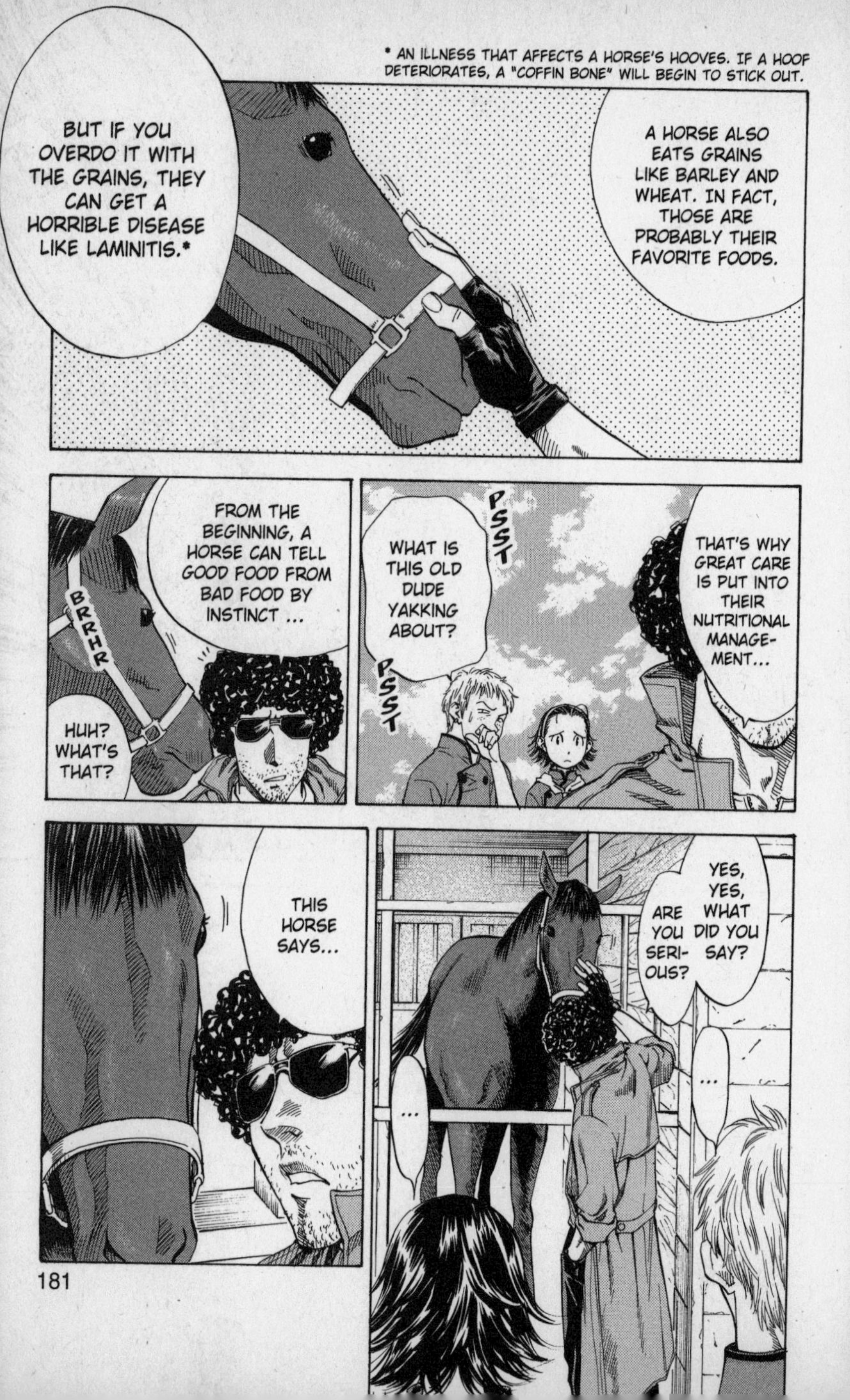
A HORSE ALSO EATS GRAINS LIKE BARLEY AND WHEAT. IN FACT, THOSE ARE PROBABLY THEIR FAVORITE FOODS.
BUT IF YOU OVERDO IT WITH THE GRAINS, THEY CAN GET A HORRIBLE DISEASE LIKE LAMINITIS.*
THAT'S WHY GREAT CARE IS PUT INTO THEIR NUTRITIONAL MANAGE-MENT...
PSST
WHAT IS THIS OLD DUDE YAKKING ABOUT?
PSST
FROM THE BEGINNING, A HORSE CAN TELL GOOD FOOD FROM BAD FOOD BY INSTINCT ...
BRRHR
HUH? WHAT'S THAT?
YES, YES, WHAT DID YOU SAY?
ARE YOU SERI-OUS?
...
...
THIS HORSE SAYS...

* AN ILLNESS THAT AFFECTS A HORSE'S HOOVES. IF A HOOF DETERIORATES, A "COFFIN BONE" WILL BEGIN TO STICK OUT.

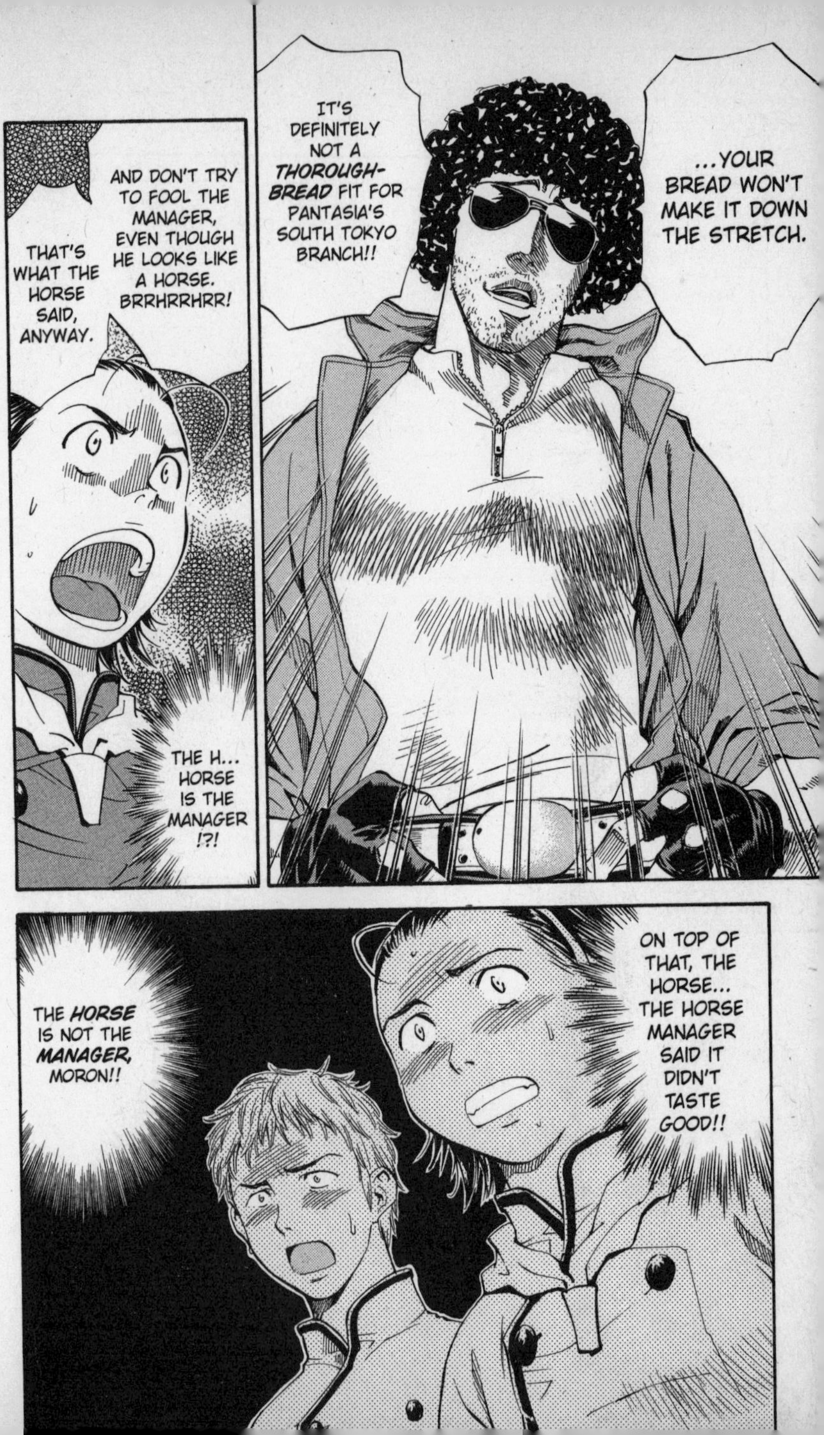
IT'S DEFINITELY NOT A THOROUGHBREAD FIT FOR PANTASIA'S SOUTH TOKYO BRANCH!!
...YOUR BREAD WON'T MAKE IT DOWN THE STRETCH.
AND DON'T TRY TO FOOL THE MANAGER, EVEN THOUGH HE LOOKS LIKE A HORSE. BRRHRRHRR!
THAT'S WHAT THE HORSE SAID, ANYWAY.
THE H... HORSE IS THE MANAGER !?!
ON TOP OF THAT, THE HORSE... THE HORSE MANAGER SAID IT DIDN'T TASTE GOOD!!
THE HORSE IS NOT THE MANAGER, MORON!!

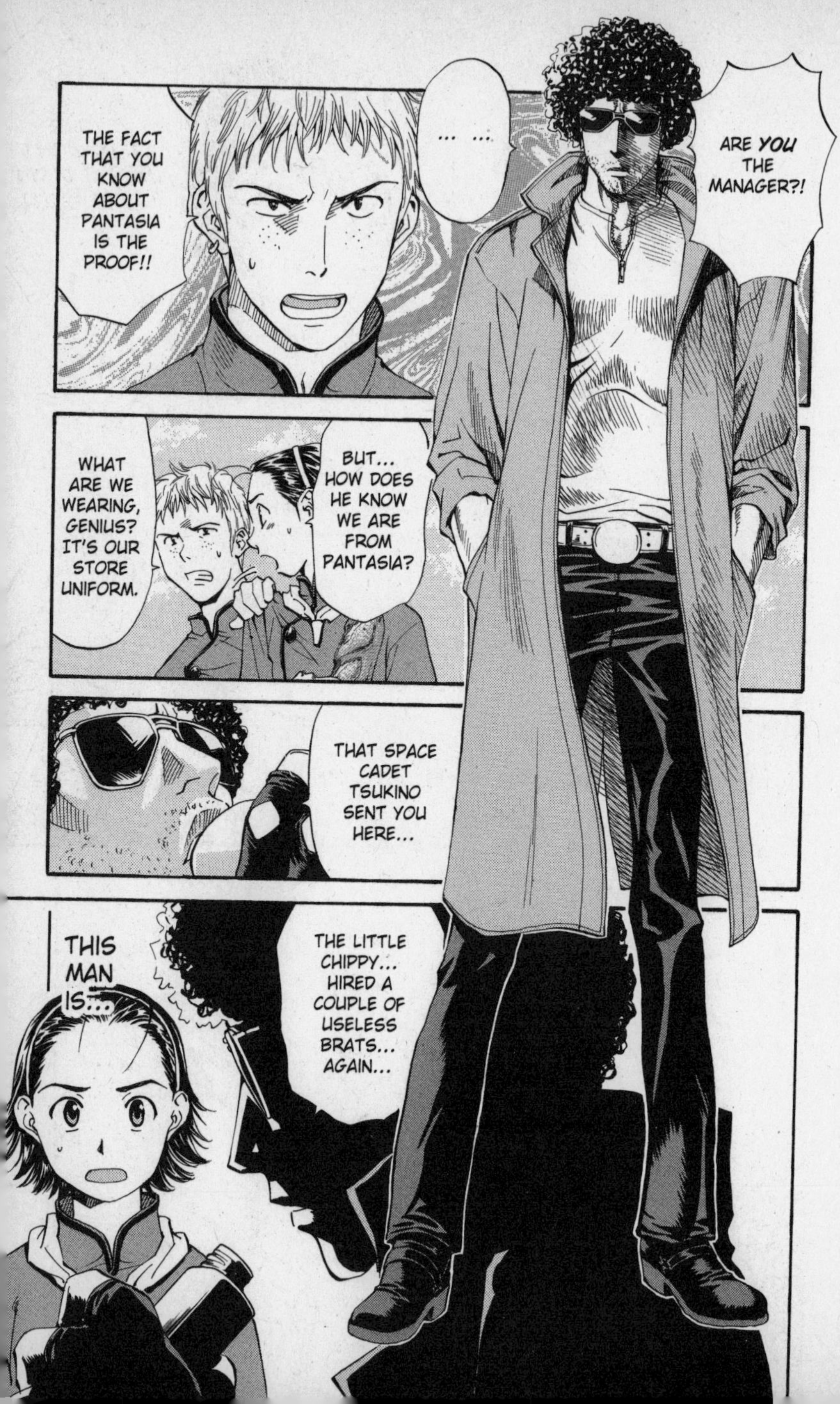
ARE *YOU* THE MANAGER?!
... ...
THE FACT THAT YOU KNOW ABOUT PANTASIA IS THE PROOF!!
BUT... HOW DOES HE KNOW WE ARE FROM PANTASIA?
WHAT ARE WE WEARING, GENIUS? IT'S OUR STORE UNIFORM.
THAT SPACE CADET TSUKINO SENT YOU HERE...
THE LITTLE CHIPPY... HIRED A COUPLE OF USELESS BRATS... AGAIN...
THIS MAN IS...

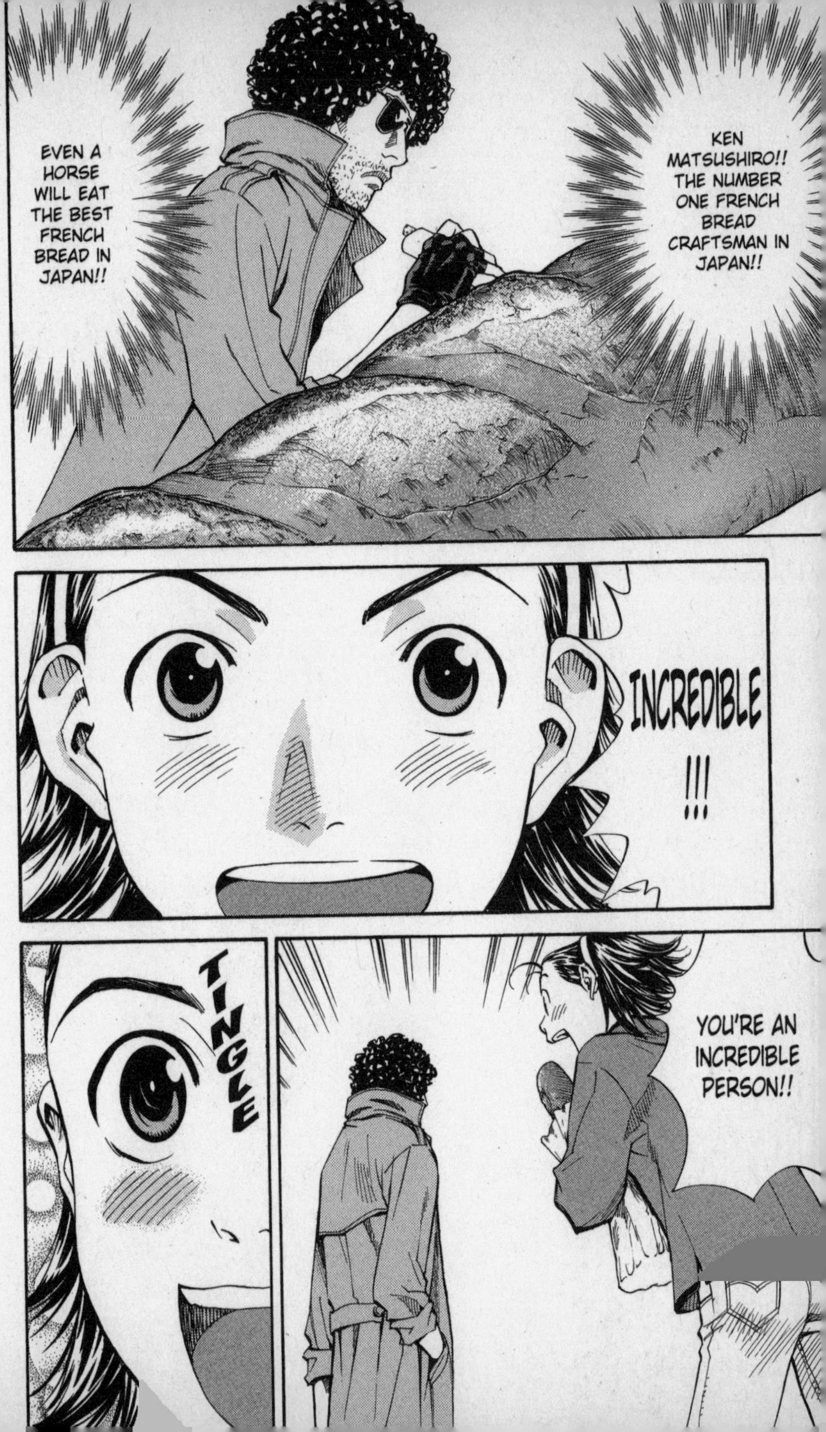
KEN MATSUSHIRO!! THE NUMBER ONE FRENCH BREAD CRAFTSMAN IN JAPAN!!
EVEN A HORSE WILL EAT THE BEST FRENCH BREAD IN JAPAN!!
INCREDIBLE!!!
YOU'RE AN INCREDIBLE PERSON!!
TINGLE

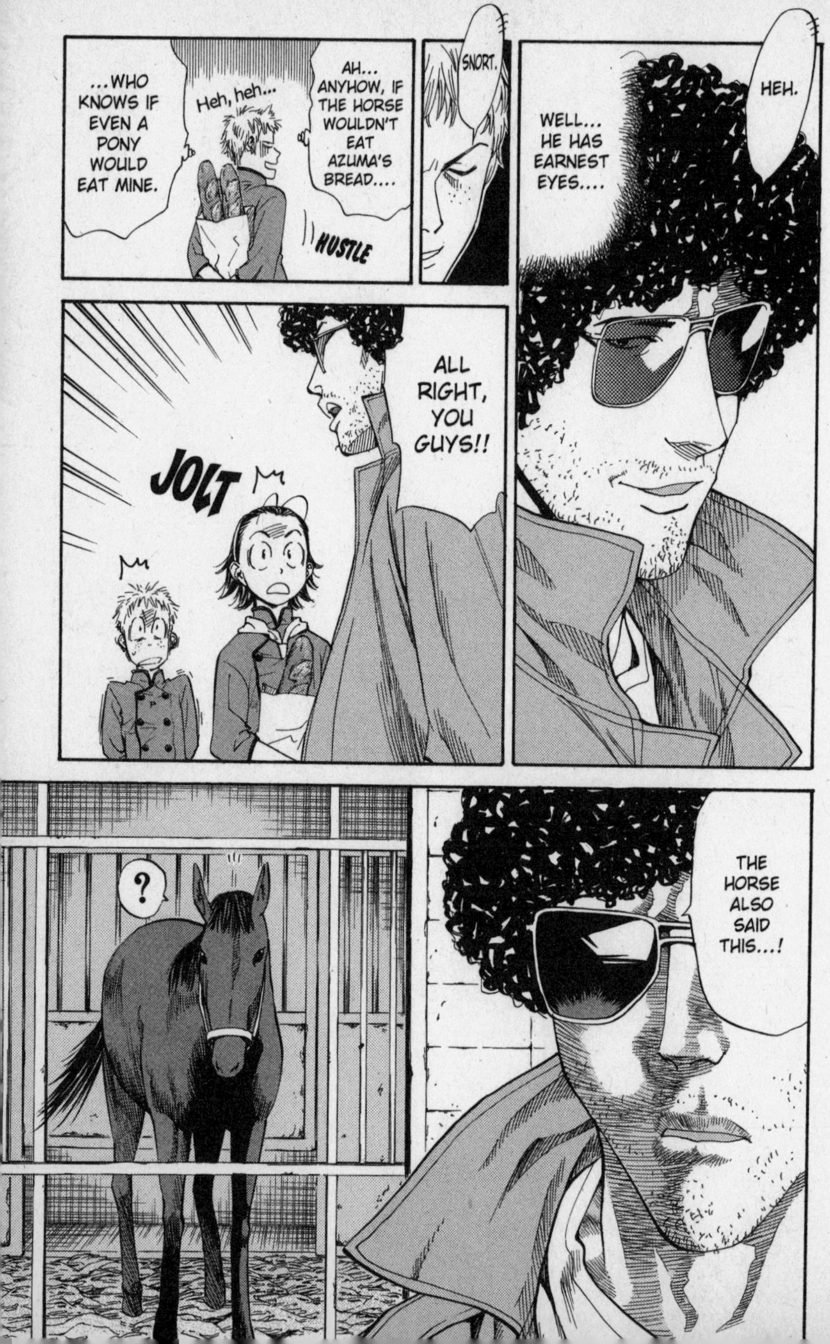
HEH.
WELL... HE HAS EARNEST EYES....
SNORT.
AH... ANYHOW, IF THE HORSE WOULDN'T EAT AZUMA'S BREAD....
Heh, heh...
HUSTLE
...WHO KNOWS IF EVEN A PONY WOULD EAT MINE.
ALL RIGHT, YOU GUYS!!
JOLT
THE HORSE ALSO SAID THIS...!
?

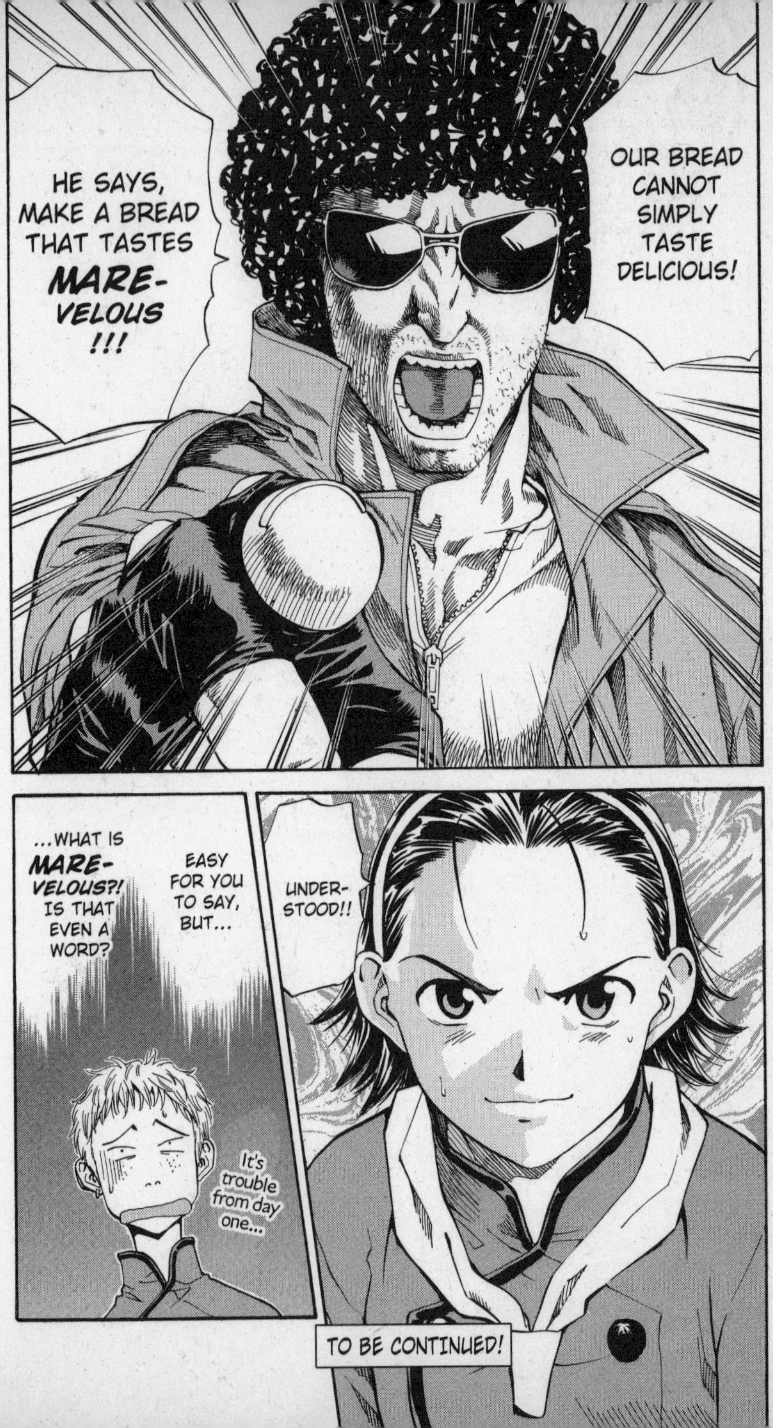
OUR BREAD CANNOT SIMPLY TASTE DELICIOUS!
HE SAYS, MAKE A BREAD THAT TASTES MARE-VELOUS!!!
UNDER-STOOD!!
EASY FOR YOU TO SAY, BUT...
...WHAT IS MARE-VELOUS?! IS THAT EVEN A WORD?
It's trouble from day one...
TO BE CONTINUED!

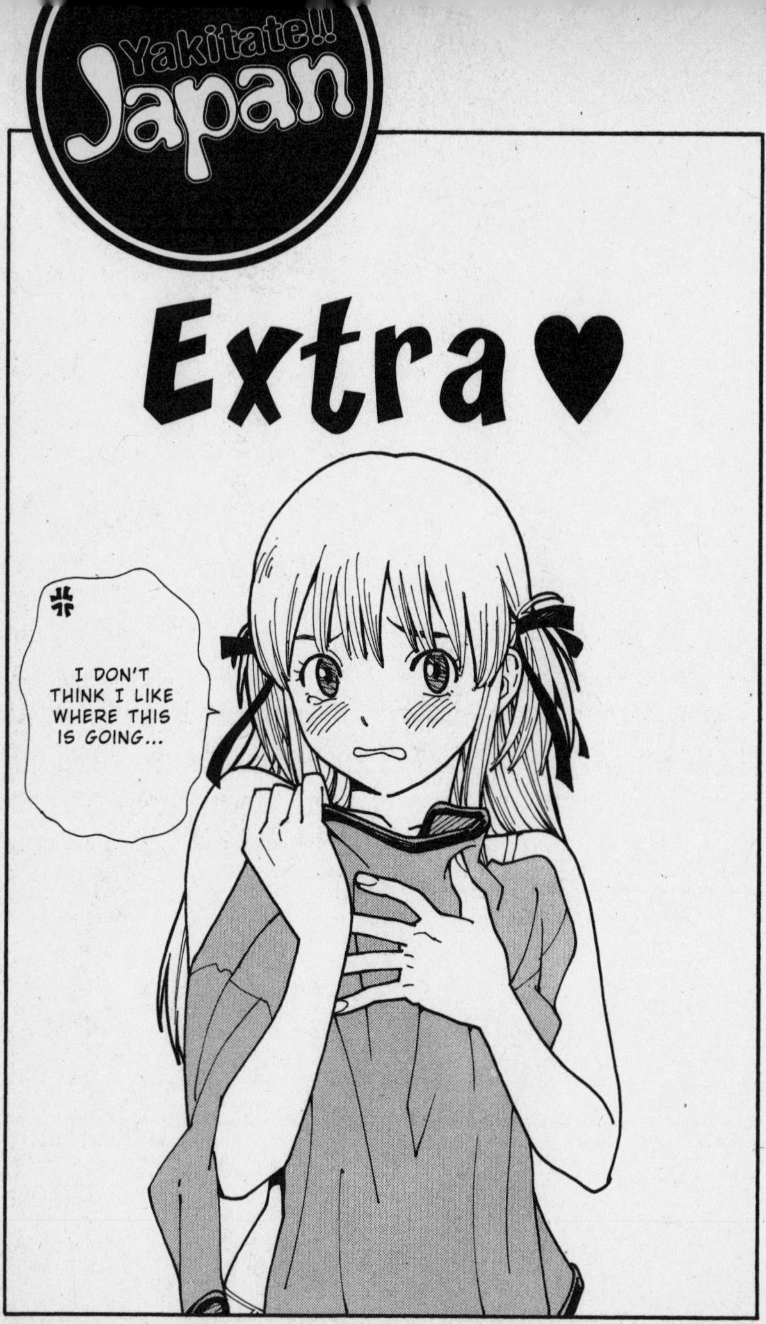
Yakitate!! Japan
Extra♥
I DON'T THINK I LIKE WHERE THIS IS GOING...

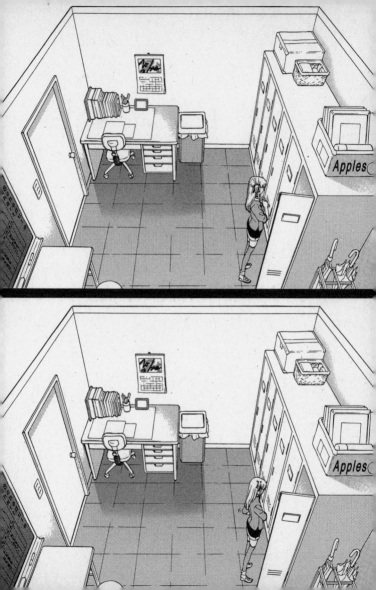

Apples

Apples

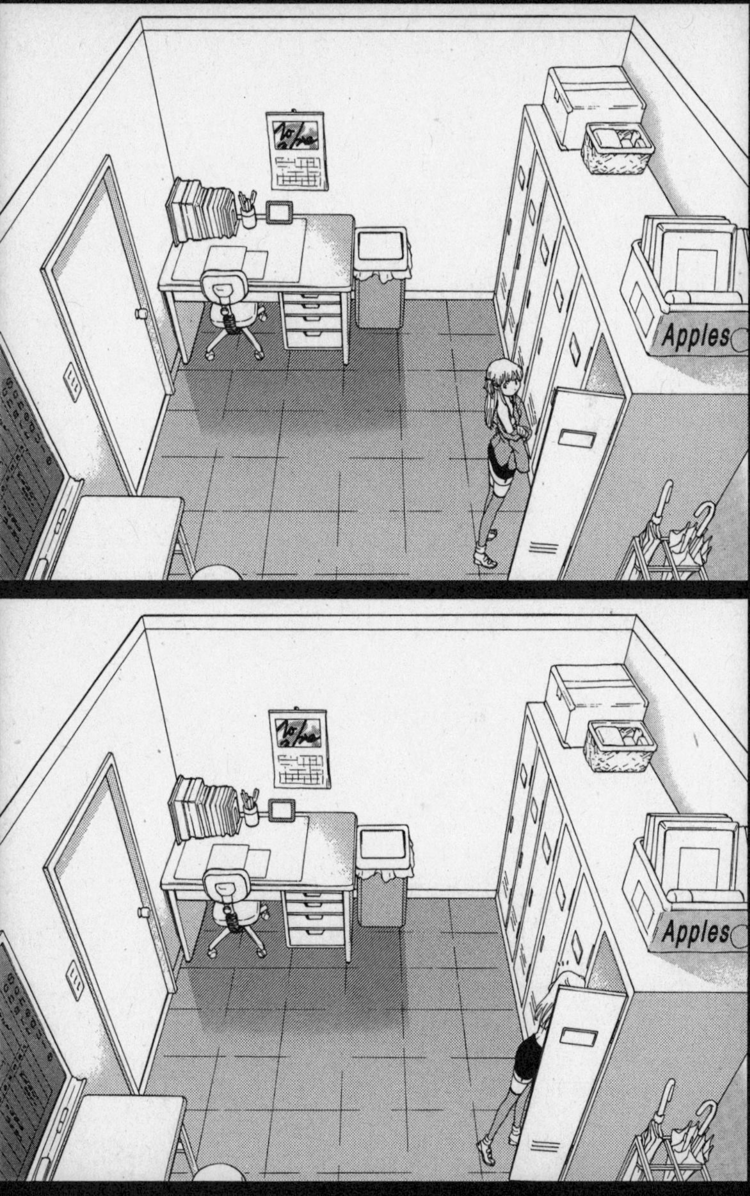
Apples
Apples

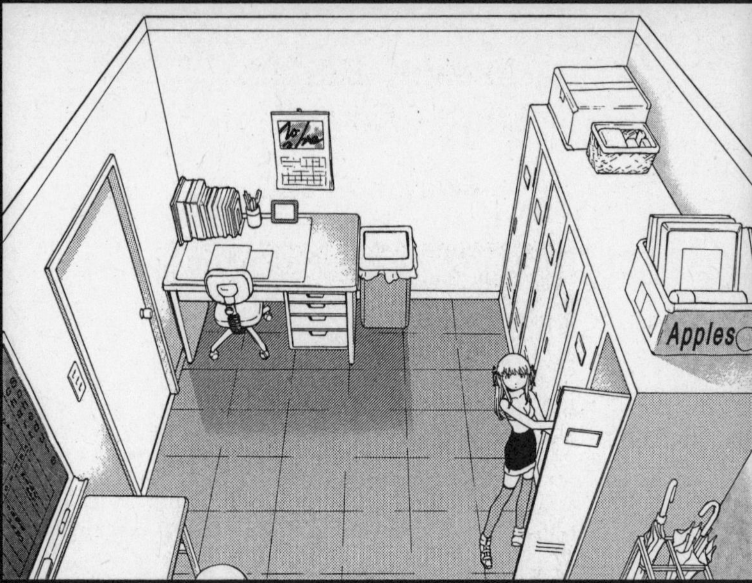
Apples

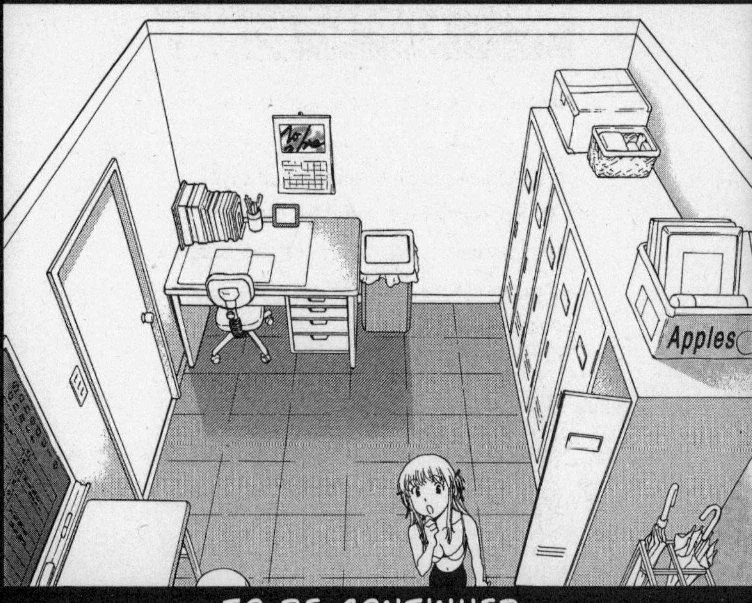
Apples

TO BE CONTINUED...

Freshly Baked!! Mini Information

── French Bread ──

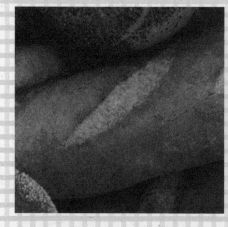

Generally, French bakers do not include butter in their bread dough. In Japan, however, butter is baked into French bread to soften the texture. Different dough better suits the tastes of Japanese consumers, who prefer soft food. So how do they bake it at Pantasia? Find out in future chapters of *Yakitate!! Japan*.

YAKITATE!! JAPAN
VOL. 1

STORY AND ART BY
TAKASHI HASHIGUCHI

English Adaptation/Drew Williams
Translation/Noritaka Minami
Touch-up Art & Lettering/Kelle Han
Cover Design/Yukiko Whitley
Editor/Kit Fox

Managing Editor/Annette Roman
Editorial Director/Elizabeth Kawasaki
Editor in Chief/Alvin Lu
Sr. Director of Acquisitions/Rika Inouye
Senior VP of Marketing/Liza Coppola
Exec. VP of Sales & Marketing/John Easum
Publisher/Hyoe Narita

Printed in the U.S.A.

Published by VIZ Media, LLC
P.O. Box 77010
San Francisco, CA 94107

10 9 8 7 6 5 4 3 2 1
First printing, September 2006

viz
media
www.viz.com

store.viz.com

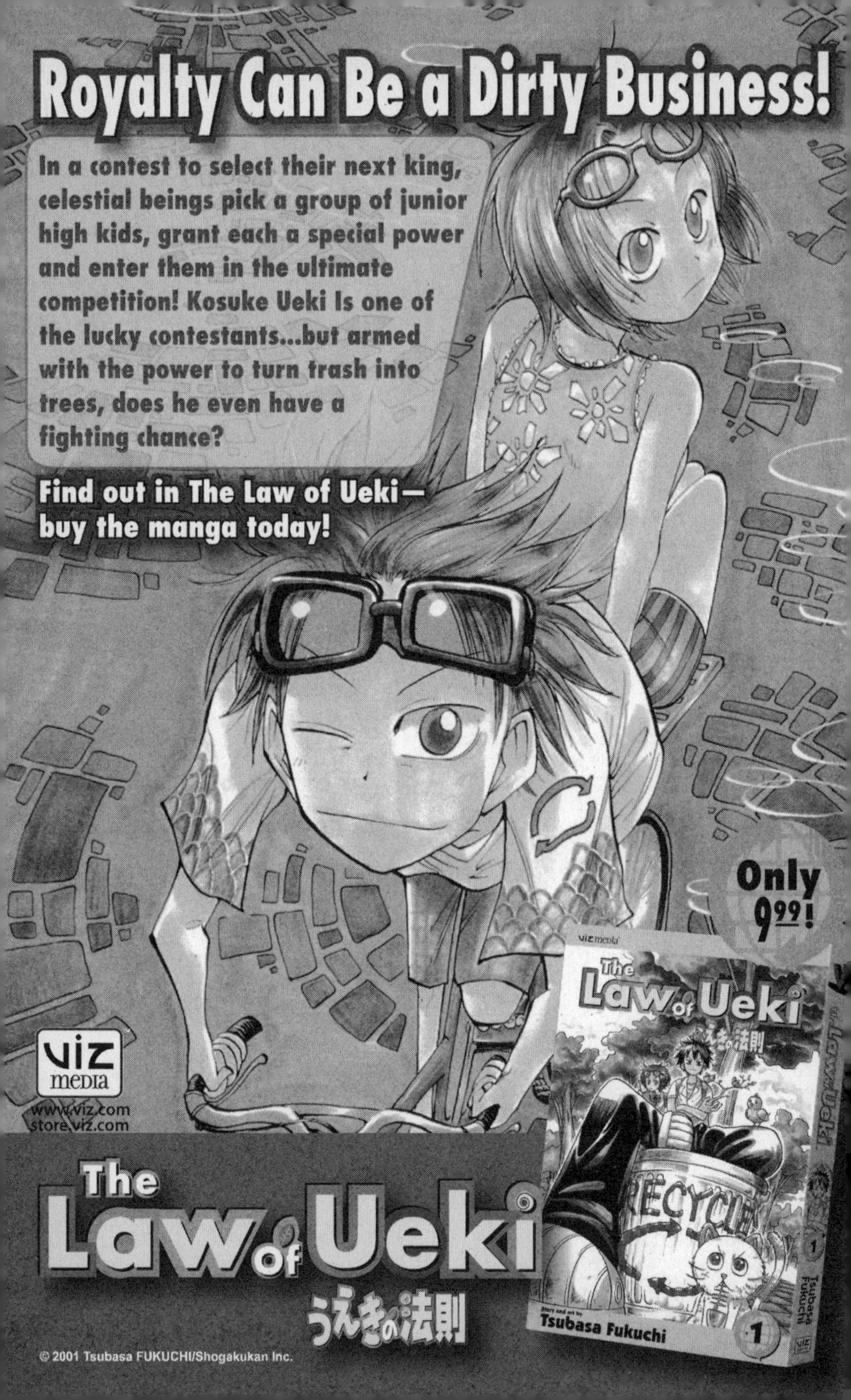
Royalty Can Be a Dirty Business!
In a contest to select their next king, celestial beings pick a group of junior high kids, grant each a special power and enter them in the ultimate competition! Kosuke Ueki Is one of the lucky contestants...but armed with the power to turn trash into trees, does he even have a fighting chance?
Find out in The Law of Ueki—buy the manga today!
Only 9.99!
viz media
www.viz.com
store.viz.com
The Law of Ueki
うえきの法則
viz media
The Law of Ueki
うえきの法則
RECYCLE
Story and art by
Tsubasa Fukuchi
1
© 2001 Tsubasa FUKUCHI/Shogakukan Inc.

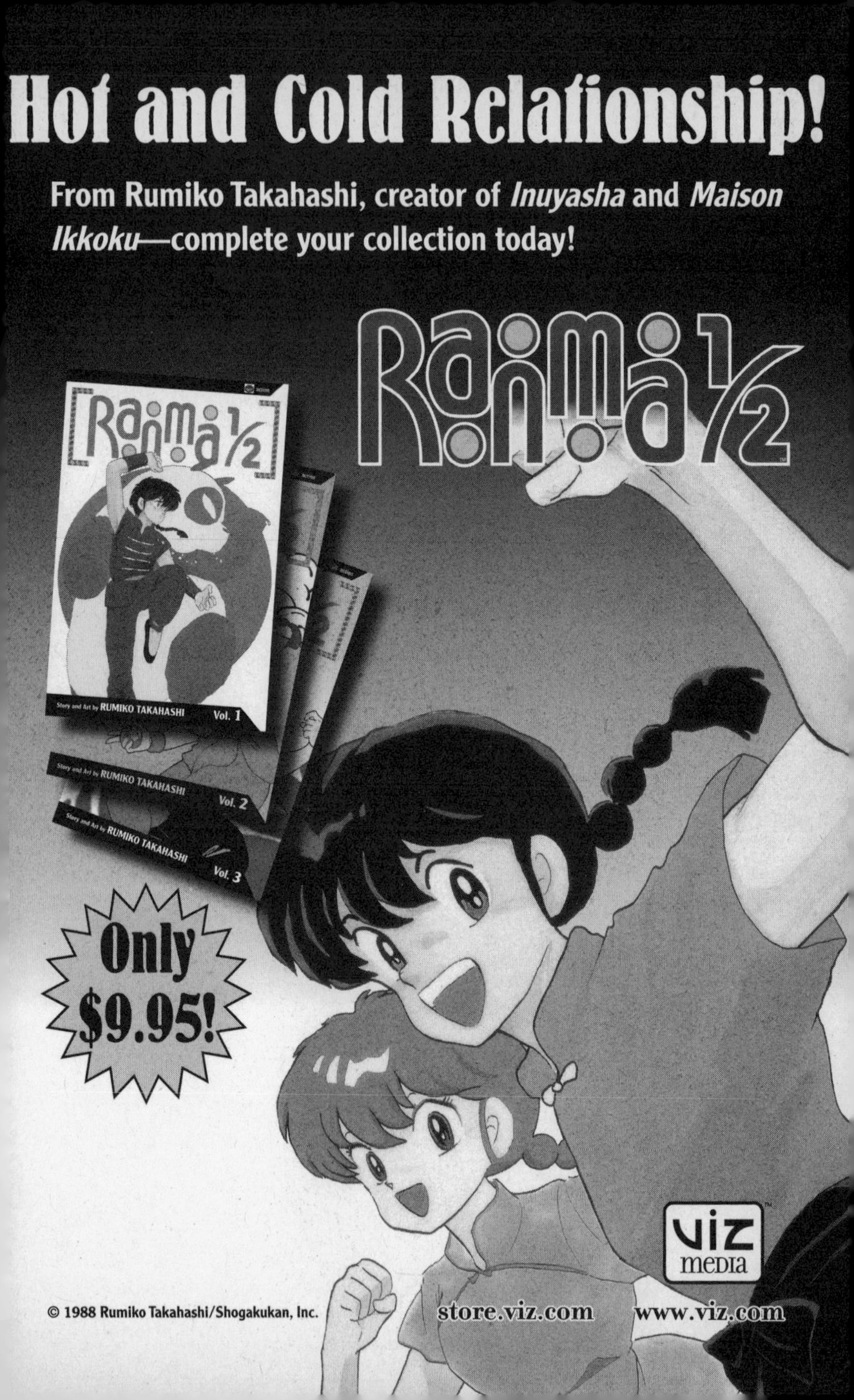
Hot and Cold Relationship!
From Rumiko Takahashi, creator of Inuyasha and Maison Ikkoku—complete your collection today!
Ranma 1/2
Ranma 1/2
Story and Art by RUMIKO TAKAHASHI Vol. 1
Story and Art by RUMIKO TAKAHASHI Vol. 2
Story and Art by RUMIKO TAKAHASHI Vol. 3
Only $9.95!
viz media
© 1988 Rumiko Takahashi/Shogakukan, Inc.
store.viz.com
www.viz.com

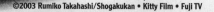

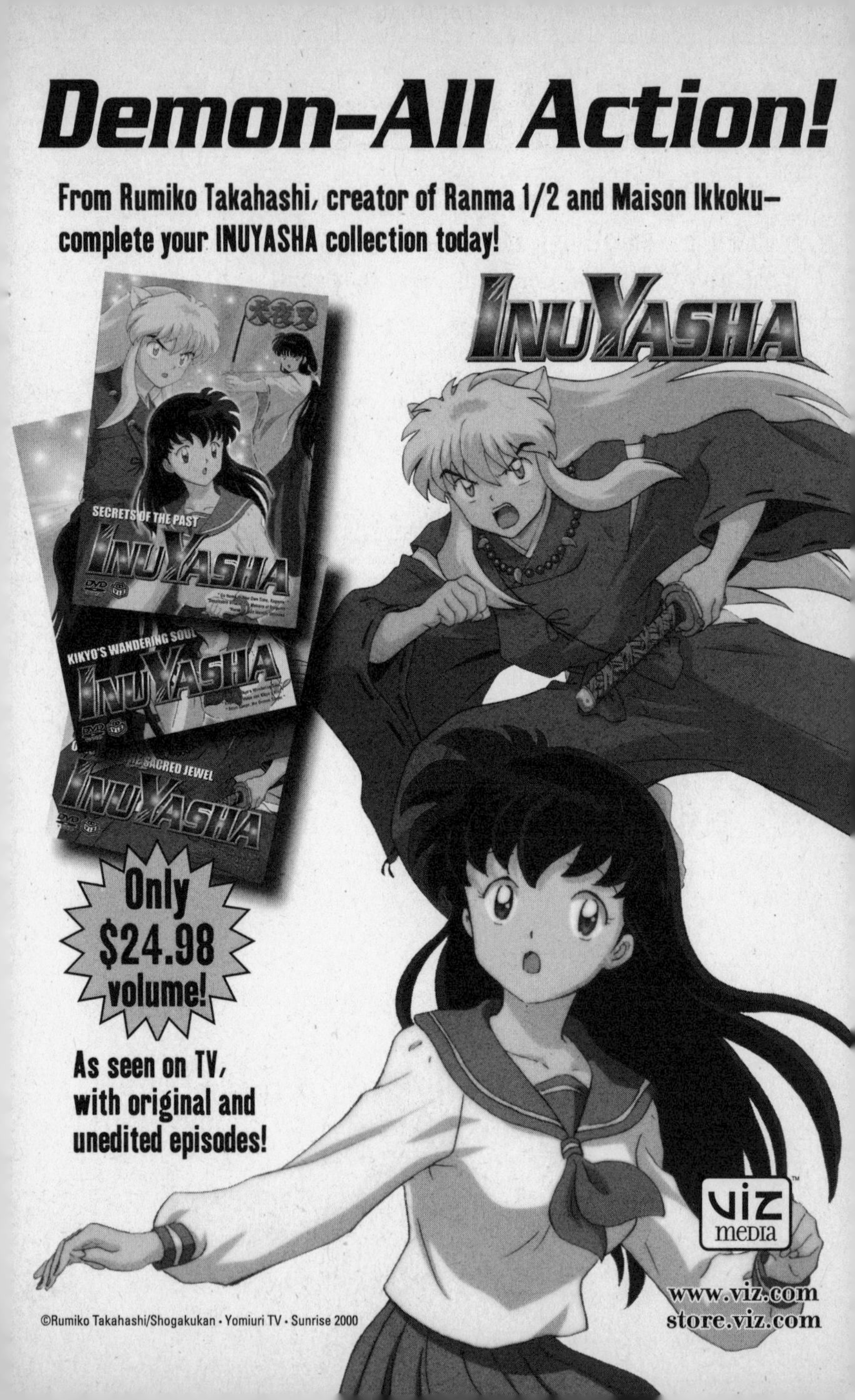

Demon-All Action!
From Rumiko Takahashi, creator of Ranma 1/2 and Maison Ikkoku–
complete your INUYASHA collection today!
INUYASHA
SECRETS OF THE PAST
INUYASHA
KIKYO'S WANDERING SOUL
INUYASHA
INUYASHA
Only
$24.98
volume!
As seen on TV,
with original and
unedited episodes!
VIZ
MEDIA
www.viz.com
store.viz.com
©Rumiko Takahashi/Shogakukan • Yomiuri TV • Sunrise 2000

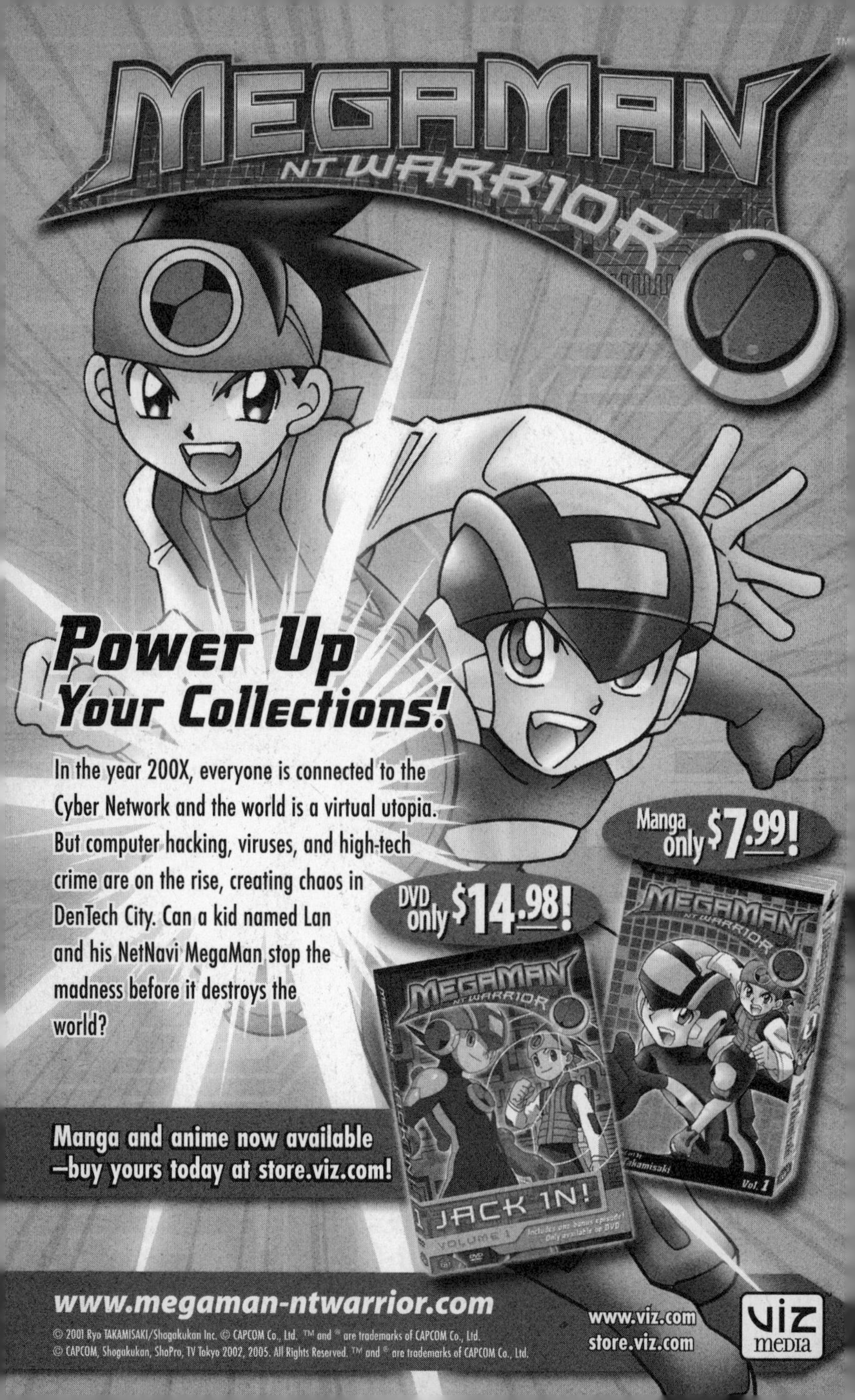
MEGAMAN
NT WARRIOR
Power Up Your Collections!
In the year 200X, everyone is connected to the Cyber Network and the world is a virtual utopia. But computer hacking, viruses, and high-tech crime are on the rise, creating chaos in DenTech City. Can a kid named Lan and his NetNavi MegaMan stop the madness before it destroys the world?
Manga only $7.99!
DVD only $14.98!
MEGAMAN
NT WARRIOR
JACK IN!
VOLUME 1
MEGAMAN
NT WARRIOR
Vol. 1
Manga and anime now available —buy yours today at store.viz.com!
www.megaman-ntwarrior.com
© 2001 Ryo TAKAMISAKI/Shogakukan Inc. © CAPCOM Co., Ltd. ™ and ® are trademarks of CAPCOM Co., Ltd.
© CAPCOM, Shogakukan, ShoPro, TV Tokyo 2002, 2005. All Rights Reserved. ™ and ® are trademarks of CAPCOM Co., Ltd.
www.viz.com
store.viz.com
viz media

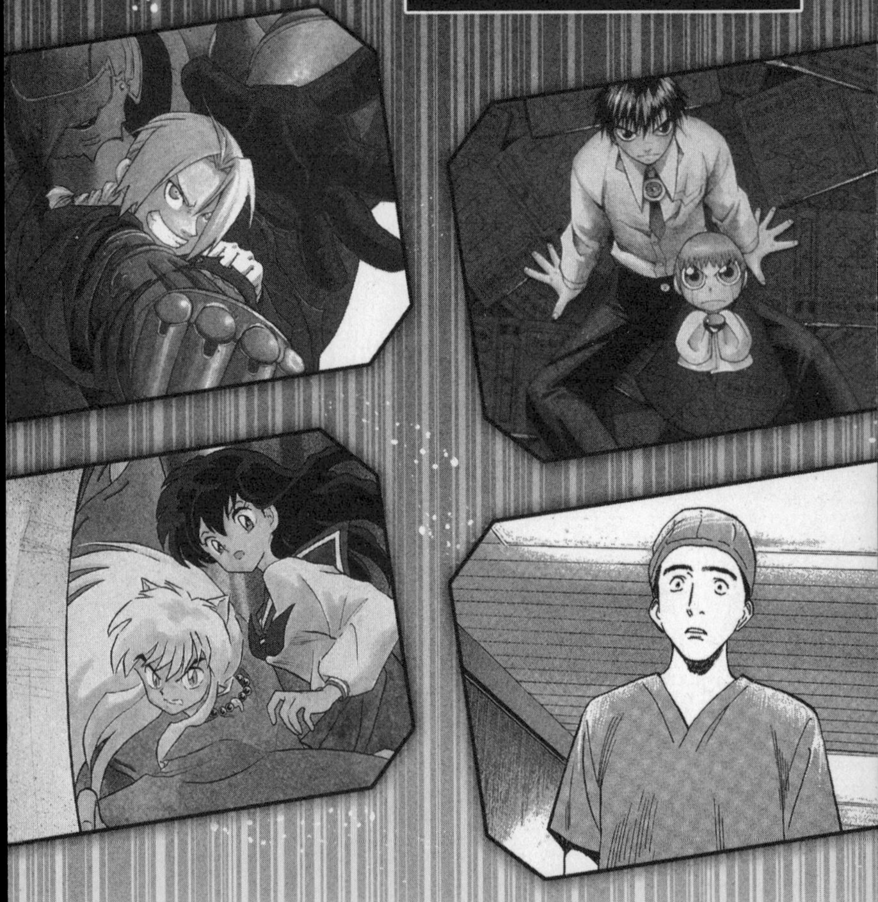